Religious Legal Traditions, International Human Rights Law and Muslim States

Studies in Religion, Secular Beliefs and Human Rights

VOLUME 7

Religious Legal Traditions, International Human Rights Law and Muslim States

By

Kamran Hashemi

MARTINUS NIJHOFF PUBLISHERS

LEIDEN • BOSTON
2008

This book is printed on acid-free paper.

Library of Congress Cataloging-in-Publication Data

Hashemi, Kamran.
Religious legal traditions, international human rights law and Muslim states / by Kamran Hashemi.
p. cm. — (Studies in religion, secular beliefs, and human rights ; v. 7)
Includes bibliographical references and index.
ISBN 978-90-04-16555-7 (hardback : alk. paper) 1. Discrimination—Law and legislation—Islamic countries. 2. Human rights—Islamic countries. 3. Human rights (Islamic law) 4. Dhimmis—Legal status, laws, etc.—Islamic countries. I. Title.

K3242.H37 2008
341.4'8091767—dc22

2008023353

ISSN 1871-7829
ISBN 978 90 04 16555 7

PRINTED IN THE NETHERLANDS

To my family,
Soheyla, Mohammad and Yasmin,
With all my love and gratitude
for their patience and company

CONTENTS

PART B PROTECTION OF RELIGIOUS MINORITIES (*DHIMMAH*)

FOREWORD

I am pleased to endorse this scholarly contribution by Kamran Hashemi to the promotion and protection of human rights from an Islamic perspective, but should first clarify the terms of the intersection of human rights and religious legal traditions. Assumptions about the relationship between these two paradigms, whether seen as positive or negative, can be misleading and counterproductive for both sides of the issue. To place the contribution of this book in context, it may therefore be helpful to attempt a brief exploration of why and in what sense is the study of religious legal traditions and human rights important for scholars and policy makers on both sides of this relationship.

The idea that all human beings are entitled to the same fundamental rights without any distinction on such grounds as race, sex or religion, is as challenging to all human societies today as it was when first proclaimed in the Universal Declaration of Human Rights of 1948. This idea tends to contradict the common human tendency to either discriminate among people in terms of attributes like sex and religion, or to expect them to conform to our own ethnocentric and uniform notion of a universal human being. Moreover, universal values, like those affirmed by human rights norms, do not exist in the abstract to be discovered or proclaimed through declarations and treaties because we all tend to perceive such values through the relativity of our own cultural and contextual world view and experience.

It is also relevant to note here that the Universal Declaration avoided identifying religious justifications in an effort to find common grounds among believers and non-believers. But this does not mean that human rights can only be founded on secular justifications, because that does not address the question of how to make human rights equally valid and legitimate from the perspectives of the wide variety of believers, as well as non-believers, around the world. The underlying rationale of the human rights doctrine itself would entitle believers to seek to found their commitment to these norms on their own religious beliefs, in the same way that others may seek to affirm the same on their secular philosophy. All sides are entitled to require equal commitment to the human rights doctrine by others, but cannot prescribe the grounds on which that commitment is founded.

In relation to the subject of this book in particular, it is difficult to determine a particular causal relationship between Islamic legal traditions and the status of human rights in any country or society. Many factors influence the level of protection of or respect for human rights in each situation, including sociological, political and economic relations and institutions which apparently have little to do with religious considerations as such. The level of compliance with human rights norms are more likely to be associated with conditions of political instability and economic and social under-development in post-colonial Islamic societies, than determined by Islam as such. Moreover, to the extent that Islam is a factor, its role cannot be understood in isolation from other factors that influence how Muslims interpret and attempt to comply with their religious tradition. In other words, one cannot predict or explain the degree or quality of human rights compliance by Islamic societies as the logical consequence of the relationship between Islam and human rights in an abstract theoretical sense.

Nevertheless, this relationship is important enough for most Muslims that their motivation to uphold human rights norms will probably diminish if they perceive those norms to be inconsistent with Islamic principles. This is not to suggest that the Islamic tradition at large is inherently or permanently inconsistent with all human rights norms because that is simply not true. But certain specifics aspects of that historical tradition are clearly problematic from a human rights point of view, like issues of freedom of religion and protection of religious minorities examined by the author of this book. The importance of religion for the moral and political choices and behavior of believers calls for well-informed and thoughtful consideration of the relationship of religious principles and human rights.

Debate about this relationship have serious practical implications, and should not be dismissed as simply a pretext to justify human rights violations or excuse for avoiding these international obligations. The widest possible acceptance of the universality of human rights is essential for generating the political will to implement or enforce these rights at home, and for engaging in their enforcement abroad. On the first count, a government is unlikely to allocate the necessary resources for the implementation of human rights, or ensure the accountability of its officials for violating these rights, without political pressure from within the country. Even if a government is somehow committed to upholding human rights norms which limits its own powers, it is unlikely to insist on enforcing these rights against the wishes of its own population. By the same token, a government is unlikely to risk its national economic, security or other interest in pressuring other governments to respect the human rights of the population of those countries without either internal political pressure to do so, or at least a willingness among its own population to accept the consequences. It is clear that local populations are unlikely to pressure their own government to protect their own human rights, include the protection of these rights in the country's foreign policy, or accept the material or other costs of doing so, unless they accept the universal validity of human rights.

In light of the preceding remarks, it is clear that the universality of human rights is a product of a process, and cannot mean the assertion of the relativist values of one society or group of societies over the rest of humanity. Since our perception of human rights is necessarily relative to our own cultural/religious traditions, it is necessary to actively promote consensus on human rights norms over time, instead of simply proclaiming or taking them for granted. As I have argued elsewhere,[1] this process of promoting consensus over the universality of human rights should occur through an internal discourse within different cultures, and dialogue among them. The question is therefore how to create conductive conditions for an effective internal discourse within cultures and dialogue among them to promote consensus and cooperation on the protection of human rights.

This book by Kamran Hashemi is a valuable contribution to these debates not only for clearly and honestly examining three specific problematic themes in Islamic legal traditions (apostasy, protection of religious minorities and rights of the child) but also for exploring possibilities of their resolution. The author's central argument is that it is possible to distinguish core principles of Islam from the corpus of rules and precepts that constitute Muslim legal traditions which can be adapted to different contexts and challenges. From this perspective, there is much greater convergence possible between the international law of human rights which is binding on many Muslim majority countries and Islam. Whether one agrees with this approach or not, it is important to consider it seriously in formulating our respective positions on the issues.

Professor Abdullahi Ahmed An-Na'im, Ph.D.
Emory University School of Law
Atlanta, GA, USA

1 See, for example, "Introduction," in Abdullahi Ahmed An-Na'im (ed.) *Human Rights in Cross-Cultural Perspectives: Quest for Consensus* (University of Pennsylvania Press, 1992).

ACKNOWLEDGMENTS

First and foremost I would like to thank my PhD thesis supervisor, Professor William Schabas, Director of the Irish Centre of Human Rights (National University of Ireland, Galway), for his invaluable academic guidance and all the support and encouragement throughout the years spent on this study. I am also indebted to all the staff at the Centre, particularly Professor Ray Murphy for having shared their time, enthusiasm, knowledge and friendship.

I am very much grateful to Professor Djamchid Momtaz and Professor Javad Zarif, my teachers at Tehran University, as well as Dr. Behrouz Moradi, for their encouragement and support in starting my PhD programme.

Also I am very much thankful to some dear friends who provided great help in editing my English while working on the thesis. Special words of gratitude go to Mrs. Mohraz, the first who read and edited the initial draft of each part of the work. I also benefited from the invaluable comments of Dr. David Keane and Dr. Edel Hughes.

Along with my parents, Tahereh Jalali and Ehsanollah Hashemi, whom for all my life, I have relied on their love and prayers, my lovely relatives have always supported and encouraged my education in every way. My special gratitude goes to my aunt Turan Jalali and my mother in law, Parvaneh Azimirad, for all their prayers, courage and support throughout my study and beyond.

In some parts of this book I have developed upon some ideas on the subject, which were first published elsewhere. Sections of part B of the book contain material from my previous article: 'The Right of Minorities to Identity and the Challenge of Non-discrimination: Study on the Effects of Traditional Muslims' *Dhimmah* on Current States Practices' 13 *Journal of Minorities and Group Rights* 1 (2006). Also the main part of chapter 8 of this book was first published in my previous article: 'Religious Legal Traditions, Muslim States and the Convention on the Rights of the Child: An Essay on the Relevant UN Documentation', 29 *Human Rights Quarterly* 1 (2007).The latter article is reprinted with the permission of the Johns Hopkins University Press. I thank the respective journals for permission to reuse the relevant passages.

My final words of appreciation go to my wife Soheyla and my children Mohammad and Yasmin, whose love and company have been central in my life and during the long-distance loneliness working on the PhD thesis.

"Eternal Traveler"

And in each station
I see off
With regret

The sight of a friendly and kind eye
That I used to sink into its depth
For a while
Or swim in its blue

The train is passing so fast
One station comes after another
And I have just a few seconds
To know a new eye
With eagerness

Being an eternal traveler
I can just keep the secret of each eye
In my heart
For the rest of my journey

And the destination?
'Traveling'

Kamran Hashemi
15 September 2003

INTRODUCTION

Developing an approach to a religious interpretation that can integrate legal traditions with universal human rights principles is a priority for the international community. This research undertakes a comparative study of the legislation and legal practices of Muslim states, in order to discern ways that the official application of specific areas of Muslim legal traditions may relate to the particular norms articulated in the Universal Declaration of Human Rights (UDHR),[1] and in subsequent human rights instruments.

Islam, with an age of fourteen centuries, and with more than one billion followers throughout the world, is, like all of the great religions, a diverse body of essential principles, moral values and worship, with spiritual, agnostic, ethical, theological and philosophical aspects running parallel to human elements, including history, civilization, culture, politics, law and related customs and traditions of different communities. Among the many different components of Islam, this study addresses only some specific parts of Muslim legal traditions relating to the three specific areas of apostasy (*irtidad*), protection of religious minorities (*Dhimmah*), and rights of the child.

Many theoretical visions of Islam and human rights presume both sides are rigid and fixed entities. This study, by contrast, provides a practical perspective on the flexibility of both, wherein Muslim legal traditions have been subject to different practices and modifications, while on the other side, "perspectives on human rights likewise change over times".[2]

This approach is more readily subject to localization of universal human rights principles within Muslim communities. It explores the elements presented historically in religious principles and traditions for the enrichment of human rights standards; as Lindholm states: "When the two normative systems,

---

1 Universal Declaration of Human Rights (UDHR), G.A. res. 217A (III), U.N.Doc.A/810 at 71 (1948).

2 Anne Elizabeth Mayer, 'The Islam and Human Rights Nexus: Shifting Dimensions', paper presented at the conference: *Reframing Islam: Politics into Law*: 10–11 Sept. 2005 at Irish Centre for Human Rights, National University of Ireland, Galway, available at: <http://www.nuigalway.ie/human_rights/reframing_Islam/Docs/Papers/Martinez.pdf>. She adds, "One has only to compare the 1948 Universal Declaration of Human Rights with the panoply of subsequently developed rights instruments for evidence of this evolution." *Ibid.*

traditional *Shariah* and internationally codified human rights, do address the same subject matters we find significant areas of agreement."[3]

For the purpose of this study, Muslim legal traditions are divided into two categories. One category deals with personal law issues, including such matters as marriage, inheritance and custody of children. The other concerns public law issues, notably freedom of religion and expression, and penal law. This distinction is in line with the historical varying level of application of personal and public aspects of religious legal traditions by Muslims, or as Schacht states: "In terms of subject matter the hold of *Shariah* was and is strongest in the area of personal status (marriage, divorce, maintenance, matters of minors such as custody and guardianship, and inheritance), and weakest or non-existent in areas such as penal law, taxation, and constitutional law."[4] Bielfieldt has a similar view:

> While traditional *Shariah* norms continue to mark family structures all over the Islamic world, the *Shariah* criminal law is applied only in a few Islamic countries today.... The emphasis of the *Shariah* has always been much more on family matters than on criminal law. The portrayal of the *Shariah* as primarily consisting of a set of cruel punishments, as it is sometimes presented in Western media, therefore, is at least one-sided.[5]

Consistent with the historical trend of abandonment of public Muslim legal traditions, the study argues that this category of traditions, in comparison with personal Muslim legal traditions, is more capable of being ignored in practice when facing conflicting modern human rights standards.

This study is devoted to an analysis of the three above mentioned areas of Muslim legal traditions, i.e. *irtidad, Dhimmah*, and rights of the child, which will be studied separately in three parts of the book, A, B and C. In each part the relevant personal and public rules of Muslim legal traditions along with their connected human rights issues will be introduced first. Then the effects of religious legal traditions on legislation and legal practices of states in each

---

3 Tore Lindholm, 'Human Rights in Christianity and in Islam', in Silvennoinen Suvikki & Markku Suksi (eds.) *Human Rights and Religion: the Case of the Sudan* (Institute for Human Rights, Abo Akademi University, Turku/Abo, Finland, 1997), p. 82.

4 Joseph Schacht. *An Introduction to Islamic Law* (Oxford At the Clarendon Press, 1964), p. 76.

5 Heiner Bielefeldt, 'Muslim Voice in the Human Rights Debate' 17 *Human Rights Quarterly* 4 (1995), p. 612.

area with regard to related human rights standards will be examined. Finally some comments will be set forth in the concluding remarks to each part for resolving the problematic features of the related issues.

The reason for selecting these three areas is that the legislation and legal practices of states in these subjects have been mainly ignored in the Islam and human rights discourse. For example there is an extensive amount of literature in this field on women's rights, but very little on the rights of the child.[6] Furthermore, as each of these three areas is composed of public and personal aspects of religious legal traditions, a comparison of the effects of the two categories in legislation and state legal practice is more feasible.

While the main sources of parts A and B of this study are the legislation and related reports on states legal practices, part C is mostly based on UN documentation related to the Convention on the Rights of the Child (CRC).[7] The issue of religious based reservations of Muslim states to the CRC will be examined in this part as well.

In searching for common approaches by Muslim states facing problematic religious legal traditions, this study argues that a distinction should be made between official references to *Shariah* and statutory laws affected by religious traditions on the one hand, and the effects of these traditions on the states legal practices on the other. The phenomenon of impracticality of some legislation affected by public Muslim legal traditions is another issue with regard to this argument. Finally the study introduces a new conception of *Shariah* which in fact is not necessarily a matter of law, but a reference to 'Islam'.

There is a wealth of literature in English on the issue of Islam and human rights mainly focusing on its theoretical aspects.[8] Abdulahi An-Na'im is the leading scholar in this field and his major work is a theoretical study on public

---

6 For example with regard to the issue of Muslim legal traditions and women's rights a long list of articles is available in the website of Emory School of law at: <http://www.law.emory.edu/IHR/tp14.html.>.Yet, the only article on Islam and children's rights is: Syed Safir, 'The Impact of Islamic Law on the Implementation of the Convention on the Right of the Child: The Plight of Non-marital Children under *Shariah*' 6 *The International Journal of Children's Rights* (1998). Also for a list of literature on theoretical aspects of *dhimmah* and *irtidad* see the bibliography attached.

7 Convention on the Rights of the Child (CRC), G.A. res. 44/25, annex, 44 U.N. GAOR Supp. (No. 49) at 167, U.N.Doc.A/44/49 (1989), entered into force, 2 Sept. 1990.

8 For an analysis of related literature on Islam and human rights also see Eva Brems 'Islam and Human Rights Views', in Eva Brems, *Human Rights: Universality and Diversity* (Kluwer Law International, the Hague, 2001), pp. 183–293.

Muslim legal traditions.[9] Among legal studies, the book written by Shaheen Sardar Ali on the situation of women in Pakistan, which examines both the theoretical and practical aspects of the issue, deserves special attention.[10] There are also some comparative studies whose main areas of focus are not necessarily legal aspects, among which the book written by Anne Elisabeth Mayer,[11] who is one of the pioneers in the field. Her work is a political-legal study focusing on conflict between Muslim legal traditions and human rights.

This book is complimentary to other works that have been already conducted and it aims to address those areas of the debate which have been ignored in the previous literature. Along with its practical vision, the study has two other specific characteristics.

First, the project has been conducted within the scope of international law. Therefore, its focus is on the official application of religious legal traditions, rather than on those traditions that are applied by individuals. In this respect, special attention will be devoted to the ways Muslim states deal with their international commitments under the related human rights treaties. With regard to this issue, a secondary focus of the study is to what extent these commitments have pushed or encouraged Muslim states to abandon or modify problematic aspects of their legal traditions.

Second, this is the first comparative study on the effects of Muslim legal traditions that addresses the legislation and legal practices of related Muslim states with respect to *irtidad*, *Dhimmah*, and rights of the child. This comparison will also include differing official interpretations of Muslim legal traditions on the same issue, or differing solutions by Muslim states for the resolution of particularly problematic traditions. Through this approach, the study presents the successful polices of some states for the attention of others and furthermore sets forth appropriate commentary where applicable.

MUSLIM LEGAL TRADITIONS

The Prophet Muhammad was born in Mecca in 570 A.D. and in 610 A.D. received the first verses of the Koran. After ten years in Mecca he immigrated

---

9 It is: Abdullahi Ahmed An-Na'im, *Toward an Islamic Reformation: Civil Liberties, Human Rights and International Law* (Syracuse, NY: Syracuse University Press, 1990).

10 It is: Shaheen Sardar Ali, *Gender and Human Rights in Islam and International Law, Equal before Allah (Unequal before Man?)* (Kluwer Law International, the Hague, 2000).

11 It is: Anne Elizabeth Mayer, *Islam and Human Rights, Tradition and Politics*, Third Edition (Westview Press, London, 1999).

to Medina in 622, where he established the first Muslim community. The situation of Arabs before Islam is described by Mahmasani as follows: "The Arabs in *jahilyah* (the pre-Islamic era) lived a simple – almost primitive existence on their peninsula and the areas adjacent to it. Their society was a composite of disunited tribes with no central authority to bind them together in a coherent whole."[12] Considering the Arab law in *jahilyah*, Schacht states:

> The positive law of the ancient Arabs is decidedly profane, matter-of-fact, and informal; even their penal law is reduced to questions of compensation and payment.... The law of personal status and family, of inheritance, and criminal law were dominated, both among the Bedouins and among the sedentary population, by the ancient Arabian tribal system. This system implied the absence of legal protection for the individuals outside his tribe, the absence of a developed concept of criminal justice and the reduction of crimes to torts, the responsibility of the tribal group for the acts of its members, and therefore blood feuds, mitigated by the institution of blood-money.... The relations of sexes in pre-Islamic Arabia were characterized not so much by polygamy, which certainly existed, as by the frequency of divorce, loose unions, and promiscuity, which sometimes make it difficult to draw a line between marriage and prostitution. Slavery and concubinage with slave women were taken for granted. The absence of an organized political authority in Arab society, both Bedouin and sedentary, implied the absence of an organized judicial system.[13]

The basic purpose of Islam and indeed of all religions according to the Koran is humanistic, ethical, moral and spiritual.[14] Therefore, "[t]he primary reason for sending the prophets was to proclaim truths and lay down eternal values, not to make laws."[15] Mohammad, however, in line with his mission, had to apply the eternal values in his message into the daily law and politics of Medina, where he, like Moses and unlike Jesus, faced new responsibilities as the ruler and legislator.

---

12 Subhi Mahmasani, *Falsafat Al-Tashri fi Al-Islam, the Philosophy of Jurisprudence in Islam* (trans. F. Ziadeh, Brill, Leiden, Netherlands, 1961), p. 15.

13 Schacht, *supra* note 4, pp. 6–7.

14 See The Koran, for example, 2:151 and 62:2.

15 Mohammad Mojtahed Shabestari, Interview with: 42 *Howzeh* (1991), quoted in, Asghar Shirazi, 'Criticism from Outside' Chapter 16, in *The Constitution of Iran*, available at the website of Dr. Abdolkarim Soroush at: <http://www.seraj.org/schirazi.htm>.

After the death of the Prophet, with the speedy expansion of Muslim territories, medieval scholars had to address the vast and variable legal requirements of the new Muslim territories. Muslim jurists had two sources available for accomplishing this task, the Koran and the *Sunnah* (sayings and deeds of the Prophet); both sources, however, provided mainly general guidance. Vessey-Fitzgerald states the Koran "is not and does not profess to be a code of law or even a law book, nor Muhammad a lawgiver in any Western sense."[16] This fact is evident in considering the number of verses of the Koran devoted to legal issues: "Out of 6666 verses of the Koran, about 500 have a legal element, the vast majority of which deal with worship rituals, leaving about 80 verses of legal subject matter in the strict sense of the term."[17] The development of Muslim law therefore was based on the endeavours of Muslim jurists through the exercise of legal reasoning (*ijtihad*) and using specific jurisdictional methods.[18]

"With the expansion of Islam and its establishment within different cultures outside Arabia, about 500 schools of legal reasoning developed in the early years, but most of them disappeared and others merged by the beginning of the third century of Islam."[19] From that time on, a consensus arose among Sunni scholars that all essential jurisprudential questions had been thoroughly discussed and finally settled. So, around the beginning of the tenth century A.D., mainstream Muslim jurisprudence formally recognized the finality of formulated legal opinion in the recognition of the four major schools of law, Hanafi, Maliki, Shafi'i and Hanbali. It was believed that no one could have attained the same level of knowledge as the early *ulama* (or scholars); therefore their formulations were final and binding and the gates of *ijtihad* for future generations were 'closed'. This phase is called 'the closing

16 S.G. Vessey-Fitzgerald, 'Nature and Sources of the *Shariah*' in Majid Khadduri & Herbert J. Liebesny, (eds.) *Law in the Middle East, Volume I, Origin and Development of Islamic Law* (The Middle East Institute, Washington, D.C., 1995), p. 87.

17 Vesey-Fitzgerald, *ibid.*; Also see, Fazlur Rahman, *Islam*, Second Edition (London: University of Chicago Press, 1979), p. 69; and Noel J. Coulson, *A History of Islamic Law* (Edinburgh University Press, Edinburg, 1964), p. 12.

18 The two main jurisprudential methods according to Sunnis are *ijma* and *qiyas*. *Ijma* is consensus of opinions, and *qiyas* means reasoning by juristic analogy. The science of law is called *fiqh* and the body of Muslim law is in fact a creation of *fiqh*.

19 Mashood A. Baderin, 'Establishing Areas of Common Ground between Islamic Law and International Human Rights' 5 *the International Journal of Human Right* 2 (2001), p. 77.

of the door of *ijtihad*'.[20] In fact from this time, which proceeded from the starting point of the decline of Muslim civilizations, Muslim law has not had any measurable development.

Muslim law "was at the time of introduction no doubt a major step forwards."[21] It entailed "a highly developed awareness of rights and obligations, a combination of which enabled Islam to formulate a system which would seek to safeguard the rights of individuals to an extent which was not common in the legal thinking of many cultures and civilizations."[22] An-Na'im states:

> In my view, by securing a relatively advanced degree of protection for the rights of women and non-Muslims, historical formulations of *Shariah* did provide for better protection of human rights than other normative systems in [the] past. For example from the very beginning, *Shariah* was understood to require an independent legal personality for the women, and the protection of certain minimum rights for them in inheritance and family relations, beyond what was possible under other major normative systems until the nineteenth century. Similarly, *Shariah* guarantees specific rights for the so-called People of the Book (mainly Christians and Jews), more than what had been provided for under other major normative systems in the past.[23]

Similarly, Ostrog points out:

> Considered from the point of view of its logical structure, the system [Muslim law] is one of rare perfection. Those Eastern thinkers of the ninth century laid down on the basis of theology, the principle of the

---

20 Recent scholarships, in particular that of W. Montgomery Watt and Wael B. Hallaq, has indicated that the door was never fully closed; the expression was only used as a majority view among Muslim scholars. There was also always a minority that claimed that the closing of the door is wrong, and a properly qualified scholar must have the right to perform *ijtihad*, at all times, not only up until the four schools of law were defined. See Knut S. Vikor, 'The Development of *Ijtihad* and Islamic Reform, 1750–1850', in *The Third Nordic Conference on Middle Eastern Studies: Ethnic Encounter and Culture Change*, Joensun, Finland, 19–22 June 1992 available at: <www.hf-fak.uib.no/institutter/smi/paj/Vikor.html>.

21 Lindholm, *supra* note 3, p. 82.

22 See B. Breiner, 'A Christian View of Human Rights in Islam', in B. Breiner (ed.) *Two Papers on Shariah* (Birmingham: CSIC papers), p. 1 at 3, quoted in Baderin, *supra* note 19, p. 85.

23 Abdullahi Ahmed An-Na'im, 'Islam and Human Rights: Beyond the Universal Debate', in Asil, *Proceedings of the 94th Annual Meeting*, April 5–8 2000, Washington, D.C., pp. 95–103.

> rights of Man, in those very terms, comprehending the rights of individual liberty, and inviolability of person and property, elaborated a law of war of which the humanist, chivalrous prescriptions would have put to the blush certain belligerents in the Great War; expounded a doctrine of toleration of non-Muslim creeds so liberal that our West had to wait a thousand years before seeing equivalent principles adopted.[24]

The subjects of Muslim law are divided into three categories; *ibadat* which means worship issues and address relations between God and man, such as the rules for praying, fasting and hajj pilgrimage; *muamilat*, which means transactions, mainly legal acts between individuals, such as marriage, divorce, custody and inheritance; finally *siasiyat*, which literally means politics, and addresses issues related to inter-state and state-individual relations, such as laws of war and penal law. It is important to note that "[t]he rules in none of these categories, even the worship rules, are mysterious ones, but they are all based on reason."[25] In this study *muamilat* and *siasiyat* are identified as personal and public Muslim legal traditions respectively.[26]

---

24 C.L. Ostrong, 'The Angora Reform', three Lectures delivered at the centenary celebrations of University College on June 27, 28, & 29 (London, University of London Press, 1927), pp. 30–31, cited in Asef A.A. Fyzee, *Outlines of Muhammadan Law*, Third Edition (London: Oxford University Press, 1964), pp. 53–54, quoted in Baderin, *supra* note 19, p. 86.

25 Mohammad Mojtahed Shabestari, *A Critique of the Official Reading of Religion (Crises, Challenges and Solutions)*, Second Edition (Tarh-e No Publisher, Tehran, Iran, 2002) in Persian, p. 166.

26 For the list of issues under personal Muslim legal traditions see generally Jamal J. Nasir, *The Islamic Law of Personal Status*, Third Edition (Kluwer Law International, the Hague, 1990). On Muslim personal (family) law also see Ghibli Mallat & Jane Connors (eds.) *Islamic Family Law* (Graham & Trotman, 1993). And on Muslim public law see Ghibli Mallat & Jane Connors (eds.) *Islam and Public Law, Classical and Contemporary Studies* (Graham & Trotman, 1993). Among the subjects of public Muslim legal traditions, the issues related to Muslim traditional penal code are not of special focus in this study and will be discussed selectively. Muslim traditional penal code consists of four systems or categories. In the first, that of *hadd* or *hudood*, the most important crimes, which threaten the very basic of the community are punishable pursuant to penalties are said to be set by the Koran, or by *Sunnah*. *Hudood* crimes consist of adultery, defamation, theft, robbery, rebellion, drunkenness, and apostasy. The second system, *qisas*, concerns intentional crimes against the person. Its fundamental premise is the *lex talionis*, that is, 'eye for eye, tooth for tooth', and is set out in the Koran, in verse 5:32 and further developed by verse 17:33. The third is *diyah*, which prescribes restitution or compensation for the victim, and the fourth *tazir*, by which public authorities set their own punishment and in which the judge has wide discretion. For a critical study on Muslim traditional penal code see Mostafa Mohaghegh Damad, *The Rules of Islamic Jurisprudence, Penal Section*, Fourth Edition (Markaz-e Nashr-e Olum-e Eslami Publisher, Tehran, 2004) in Persian.

Finally, for the purpose of this study, when a reference to early (classical, historical or traditional) Muslim law is made, the terms 'Muslim law', 'Islamic law' or 'Muslim legal traditions' all have a similar meaning. The noun 'Islam' in this study, however, is reserved for when a reference is being made to the essential elements of the religion, as will be explained further. The study thus makes an intentional differentiation between 'Muslim' and 'Islam', with the former being used to indicate the generic concept, and to 'Muslim legal traditions' or 'Muslim law' rather than 'Islamic law'. This is in order to distinguish between subordinate aspects of the religion and its essential elements. For the same purpose, because the term *Shariah*[27] for ordinary Muslims and some readers might imply 'Islam', this term is not used as a synonym for Muslim law, unless in quoted texts.

'Legal traditions' or 'religious legal traditions' are also more familiar terms for non-Muslim readers, because other religions and civilizations have such traditions as well.[28] Furthermore, by using the term 'traditions' as will be discussed later, it is easier to remember that, when comparing Muslim legal traditions with modern human rights norms, the former date from before the tenth century, while the latter are the achievement of the last six decades of modernity and post-modernity; Bielfieldt states: "The emancipatory principle has been articulated only in the modern era. By comparison, the Islamic *Shariah*, the normative tradition commonly known as Islamic law, is much older."[29]

DISTINCTION BETWEEN THE ESSENCE AND THE SUBORDINATES OF ISLAM AND THEIR RELEVANCE TO HUMAN RIGHTS

The conflict between the immutability of Muslim law and the universality of human rights has been one of the main issues of debate in the Islam and human rights discourse. It seems that on both sides of the debate a distinction should be made between the essence and the subordinate, or in other words, between the principles and the legal standards that implement them. While the former is universal and immutable, the latter is variable and subject

27 *Shariah*, literally means 'the way' or 'road' to follow.

28 For study of other legal traditions such as Chthonic, Talmudic, common law and Hindu, see for example, Patrick Glenn H., *Legal Traditions of the World, Sustainable Diversity in Law* (Oxford University Press, 2000).

29 Bielefeldt, *supra* note 5, p. 595.

to change based on the relevant temporal and social context. This approach provides a more appropriate ground for a better understanding of the interaction of religion and human rights.

The concept of cultural relativism in human rights can also be defined based on this distinction, according to which different human rights standards should be considered for different times, cultures and social developments. This approach can also be named as localization of human rights principles; bringing heavenly ideals down to earth, a similar task as that performed by Muhammad when he tested the divine values of his message with the real life of Bedouin Arabs of Medina. Similar to other progressive ideals, when the Koranic divine principles were put into practice at the time of their emergence in underdeveloped Bedouin societies, they had to be limited and modified under the pressure of their historical and social contexts.

Shestack states: "[H]uman rights are a set of moral principles and their justification lies in the province of moral philosophy."[30] Thus the principles of religion and of human rights could both be considered as eternal and in no need of reconciliation; they need only to be identified. The major common principle between human rights and Islam, as well as other monotheist religions, is human dignity. Shestack states:

> If one accepts the premise of the Old Testament that Adam was created in the 'image of God', this implies that the divine stamp gives human beings a high value of worth.[31] In a similar vein the Koran says: 'Surely we have accorded dignity to the sons of man.'... In a religious context every human being is considered sacred. Accepting a universal common father gives rise to a common humanity, and from this flows a universality of certain rights. Because rights stem from a divine source, they are inalienable by mortal authority. This concept is found not only in the Judeo-Christian tradition, but also in Islam and other religions with a deistic base.[32]

---

30 Jerome J. Shestack, 'The Philosophic Foundations of Human Rights' 20 *Human Rights Quarterly* 2 (1998) p. 202.

31 An appealing expression of this comes from the Talmud: "A man may coin several coins with the same matrix and all will be similar, but the King of Kings, the Almighty, has coined every man with the same matrix of Adam and no one is similar to the other. Therefore, every man ought to say the whole world has been created for me." See Sanhedrin 38:1 (Adin Steinsaltz ed., Random House, 1989).

32 Shestack, *supra* note 30, p. 205.

According to McDougal, Lasswell, and Chen:

> The contemporary image of man as capable of respecting himself and others, and of constructively participating in the shaping and sharing of all human dignity values, is the culmination of many different trends in thought, secular as well as religious, with origins extending far back into antiquity and coming down through the centuries with vast cultural and geographic reach.[33]

By searching the Koran and *Sunnah* many scholars have tried to extract other divine principles of Islam relevant to human rights. According to Baderin:

> Major moral principles that serve as basic postulates for the concept of human rights can be listed as "dignity (*karamah*), freedom (*hurriyah*), humaneness (*insaniyah*), equality (*musawah*), beneficence (*ihsan*), responsibility (*masuliyyah*), co-operation (*ta'awun*) and justice (*adalah*). [They] evolved, and were embodied in the general doctrine of Islamic theology, law and governance.[34]

Bassiouni has also referred to some relevant Islamic principles for human rights including "brotherhood, mercy and compassion."[35] In the same sense, Khadduri has listed the five principles of Islamic human rights as, "(1) dignity and brotherhood; (2) equality among members of the community, without distinction on the basis of race, colour or class; (3) respect for the honour, reputation and family of everyone; (4) the presumption of innocence; and (5) individual freedom."[36]

---

33 See Myres S. McDougal & Harold D. Lasswell, & Lung-Chu Chen, *Human Rights and the World Public Order* (New Haven, Yale University Press, 1980), pp 376–377, quoted in Baderin, *supra* note 19, p. 90.

34 Baderin, *supra* note 19, p. 86. There are some other principles mentioned by Baderin: cooperation for goodness and seek knowledge. *Ibid.*, p. 82. He also names the fundamental principles underlying the *Shariah* as: (i) the removal of difficulties (ii) the realization of welfare and (iii) the realization of universal justice, which are all relevant postulates of international human rights. See *ibid.*, p. 100.

35 M. Cherif Bassiouni, 'Sources of Islamic Law, and the Protection of Human Rights In the Islamic Criminal Justice System' in, M. Cherif Bassiouni (ed.) *The Islamic Criminal Justice System* (Oceana Publications, Inc, London, Rome, New York, 1982), p. 13.

36 Majid Khadduri, *The Islamic Conception of Justice* (Johns Hopkins University Press, U.S.A., 1984), pp. 236–37.

With regard to the essential elements of religion and human rights on the one hand, and their subordinate aspects on the other, the presumption of this study is that the main principles of religion and its moral foundation form an immutable core; similarly, on this plane, human rights principles could be considered eternal, unchanging or natural. All other aspects of religion and human rights, such as bans and ordinances of Muslim law and international and regional standards of human rights, are subordinate applications of this essence, and in this regard, respond to their social context and are subject to change.

The above mentioned presumption on mutability of Muslim law is based on the viewpoints of eminent Muslim scholars. Sardar Ali states: "Muslim scholars including Mohammad Arkoun, Abdullahi An-Naʾim, Bassam Tibi and Riffat Hassan among others, have argued that any discussion of human rights in Islam must take into account the historical context within which the *Shariah* was constructed and applied by the early Muslims".[37] In fact, "in keeping with the Koranic promise that 'God intends every facility for you; he does not want to put you to difficulties'[38] the Islamic tradition appears capable of dealing flexibly with human needs and shortcomings. Such pragmatism also has shaped the *Shariah* from its very beginning."[39]

It is not only the critical literature that argues for the influence of social contexts on Muslim law; such an argument was presented, for example, in an official document by Iran:

> In the case of criminal offences, the blood-money was payable by the father or paternal relative, who was not, however, himself regarded as an offender. That system had its origins in the need to maintain ties between tribes in the era of the dawn of Islam. The system had proved effective in practice, but nevertheless was under review.[40]

Coulson has a reference to the effects of social context in the time of the development of Muslim law in the early centuries of Islam: "It is also important to understand how early Muslims' interpretations of Islam were affected by their culture and in the social and political climates, even decades after the

---

37 Shaheen Sardar Ali, 'The Conceptual Foundation of Human Rights: A Comparative Perspective' 3 *European Public Law* 1 (1997), p. 278.

38 The Koran, 2:185.

39 Schacht, *supra* note 4, pp. 76–77.

40 See Human Rights Committee: Summary record of the 1251st meeting (Iran), U.N.Doc. CCPR/C/SR.1251 (29 July 1993).

death of the Prophet for example, there were vast differences in the way the two early Islamic intellectual centres interpreted law."[41]

According to the Sudanese Muslim reformer, *Ustadh* Mahmud Muhammad Taha, "much of what had come to be regarded as timeless *Shariah* rules were actually legislation that had been intended only to guide the early Muslim community in Medina."[42] In this sense, An-Naʾim denies the divinity of Muslim law. He argues that, "*Shariah* is not the whole of Islam but instead is an interpretation of its fundamental sources as understood in a particular historical context."[43]

Among Iranian scholars the viewpoints of Mohammad Mojtahed Shabestari command special attention. In his book 'Hermeneutics of the Book and *Sunnah*', he argues that according to the science of hermeneutics any interpretation of a text relies on personal knowledge and presumptions of the interpreter. These presumptions and personal knowledge are in fact the connecting linkages between the interpreter and the text. Religion, therefore, cannot be defined by a mere abstraction of a jurist or theologist as an interpreter of the text. In this sense there is no single text in religion that is not open to different interpretations. Shabestari further questions the assertion that God has a legislative function, as God only establishes values, not laws.[44]

There is a phrase in Muslim jurisprudence that states, '*ijtihad* against the text is not allowed', which is similar to the phrase 'if something is expressed in the text, there is no room for implication (*Expressum facit cessare tacitum*)'. Shabestari in this regard argues that whatever exists in the *Sunnah* and the Koran (the text) is what was conceived as being best to provide for the benefit of the human being of that time, and not the best possible interpretation for all times. What was done by the Prophet and the Book shows only the direction. Muslims of each time should strive to remain in this direction.[45] Abdolkarim Sorush, another Iranian scholar, has a similar opinion:

---

41 Coulson, *supra* note 17, pp. 47–50.

42 Mayer, Islam and Human Rights, Tradition and Politics, *supra* note 11, p. 169. It was argued by Taha that the Koranic verses revealed during the Meccan era were more egalitarian and democratic in sprit while the Medinese verses display a hierarchical trend. See generally Mahmud Muhammad Taha, *Second Message of Islam* (trans. Abdullahi Ahmed An-Naʾim, Syracuse: Syracuse University Press, 1987).

43 An-Naʾim, Toward an Islamic Reformation, *supra* note 9, p. xiv.

44 Mohammad Mojtahed Shabestari, *Hermeneutic, the Scripture and the Tradition* (Tarh-e No Publisher, Tehran, Iran, 2000) in Persian, p. 114.

45 Mohammad Mojtahed Shabestari, A Critique of the Official Reading of Religion, *supra* note 15, p. 76. Also see Mohammad Mojtahed Shabestari, *Faith and Freedom* (Tarh-e No Publisher, Tehran, Iran, 2000) in Persian, p. 160.

> It would seem that the social commands stipulated in religious law are temporary in nature unless proven otherwise.... the Prophet basically endorsed the rules and commands current at the time in Arab society and they became the measures of justice in their own day. And there is no reason why we should consider the regulations current at that time in Arab society as the best possible regulations for all times.[46]

Sorush further refers to the humanitarian resources of the religion and reiterates the principle of humanity as a criterion for approving a law:

> Mining the humanitarian resources of a religion is more important than ascertaining its privileged divinity. In fact, it is humanity's right to reject inhuman religions and even to contest their claim to true religiosity. Natural rights simply mean principles whose observance promotes a more humane, rational, secure, prosperous, and fulfilling life. Rational ends such as justice, order and welfare and deliverance from discrimination, strife, prejudice, fratricide, ignorance, hunger, and oppression are the result of the long historic experience of humanity and a matter of consensus among all reasonable people. It is not as though any of these principles could be set aside for the sake of some religious dogma.[47]

To sum up, one might argue that 'the text' (the Koran and the *Sunnah*) are the source of principles, general guidance and examples. In fact, for Muslims, what is not allowed is not '*'ijtihad* against the text', as understood in usual sense, but '*'ijtihad* against the essential principles provided by the text'.

MUSLIM STATES AND MUSLIM LEGAL TRADITIONS

The term Muslim states in this study refers to the fifty-seven member states of the Organization of Islamic Conference (OIC), with mostly predominant

46 Abdolkarim Soroush, 'Contraction and Expansion of Women's Rights, An Interview with Dr. Abdolkarim Soroush' (2000), available at available at the website of Dr. Abdolkarim Soroush at: <http://www.seraj.org/zanan.htm>. Soroush' major critical work on traditional Muslim law is: *Theoretical Contraction and Expansion of Shariah* (Serat Cultural Institution, Tehran, 1995) in Persian.

47 Abdolkarim Sorush, 'Reason and Revelation, Reason Defines Truth, Public Interest, and Humanity', in Abdolkarim Soroush, *Reason, Freedom and Democracy in Islam: Essential Writings of Abdolkarim Soroush* (Oxford University Press, 2000), available at the Iranian website at: <http://www.iranian.com/Opinion/2001/February/Soroush/>.

Muslim population.[48] In the Constitutions, legislation and other legislative sources of Muslim states, there are different categories of references to Islam, *Shariah* and similar terms, each with a different purpose. The majority of Muslim states today have officially proclaimed Islam to be the state religion.[49] Such a reference to Islam by itself bears no legal attribute, but is a reference to national identity.

There are other references to Islam, *Shariah* or similar terms, which display legal features. These references may address personal Muslim legal traditions, public Muslim legal traditions or have some other purpose. Before discussing these categories, it should be noted that while personal Muslim legal traditions and part of public Muslim legal traditions used to constitute the basic law of Muslim countries for more than twelve centuries, a trend of withdrawal from part of those traditions started in almost all Muslim countries from around the mid nineteenth century. It is worth adding that the reform of law in Muslim countries took place in two different phases, for public and personal aspects. An-Na'im states:

> The first [reform] involved replacing *Shariah* with secular legislation in commercial, civil, constitutional, and penal matters. In most parts of the Muslim world, only family law and inheritance were left to the jurisdiction of *Shariah*. The second reform was undertaken in respect to the *Shariah*... as applied to family law and inheritance for Muslims.[50]

---

48 The list of members of the Organization of the Islamic Conference is available at the website of the organization at: <http://www.oic-oci.org>. Because of their different political and legal system, Albania and the six Muslim states of former Soviet Union, Azerbaijan, Kazakhstan, Kyrgyz Republic, Tajikistan, Turkmenistan, and Uzbekistan are excluded from this study.

49 See e.g., Oman (Chapter 1, Art. 2 of the Basic Law); Saudi Arabia (Art. 1 of the Basic Law), and the current Constitutions of Bahrain (Art. 2); Egypt (Art. 2); Iran (Art. 12); Jordan (Art. 2); Kuwait (Art. 2); Malaysia (Art. 3); Morocco (Art. 6); Tunisia (Art. 1); Egypt (Art. 2); Algeria (Art. 2); Bahrain (Art. 2); Bangladesh (Art. 2 A); Brunei (Art. 3); Iran (Art. 12); Jordan (Art. 2); Kuwait (Art. 2); Libya (Art. 2); Malaysia (Art. 3.1); Maldives (Art. 1 and 7); Morocco (Art. 6); Pakistan (Art. 1 and 2); Qatar (Art. 1); Somalia (Section 1, Chapter 1, Art. 3); United Arab Emirates (Art. 7); Yemen (Art. 2).

50 An-Na'im, Toward an Islamic Reformation, *supra* note 9, p. 44.

References Mainly Address Personal Muslim Legal Traditions

First, Muslim Legal Traditions as a Source of Legislation

In the Constitutions of several Muslim countries, Islam, *Shariah* or similar terms are introduced as the main source of legislation.[51] For example, according to Article 7(A) of the Constitution of Iraq, "Islam is the official religion of the state and is to be considered a source of legislation."[52]

Despite the indicated reform of Muslim law, personal Muslim legal traditions or Muslim family law, with some degree of modification, have remained in force in almost all Muslim countries. While in most non-Muslim states religious family law is incorporated in the state civil code, in the majority of Muslim states, family law still is considered as religious law. In these cases, *Shariah* as a source of law is something similar to religious law as a source of the civil code in secular states or as customary law in common law systems. Therefore, whether the existence of a linkage between legislation and *Shariah* or Islam is officially referred to by a state or not, the legislation of almost all Muslim states is more or less influenced by personal Muslim legal traditions.[53]

Second, Un-codified Muslim Legal Traditions as a Source of Jurisdiction

In the legislation of Afghanistan, Kuwait, Egypt Algeria and Iran,[54] Islam, *Shariah* or similar terms are introduced as a source of judgment. For example,

---

51 For example the current Constitutions of Egypt (Art. 2); Bahrain (Art. 2); Iran (Art. 4); Kuwait (Art. 2); Maldives (Art. 156); Qatar (Art. 1); Sudan (Art. 65); Syria (Art. 3.2); United Arab Emirates (Art. 7); Yemen (Art. 3); Oman (Chapter 1, Art. 2 of the Basic Law); and Palestine (Arts. 4/2 and 92/1 of the draft Basic Law for the Transitional Period).

52 Constitution of Iraq, approved by a referendum on 15 Oct. 2005.

53 With regard to application of personal Muslim legal traditions in different Muslim countries it should be added that among the four Sunni schools of jurisprudence the Hanafi school is followed in Turkey, Syria, Lebanon, Jordan, India, Pakistan, Bangladesh, Afghanistan, Iraq, Egypt, Palestine, and Libya; the Maliki school is followed in North and West Africa (Algeria, Gambia, Ghana, Libya, Morocco, Senegal, Sudan, Tunisia) and Kuwait; the Shafi'i school is followed in lower Egypt, Yemen, East Africa (Ethiopia, Maldives) and East Asia (Indonesia, Malaysia, Philippines, Brunei); and the Hanbali school is followed in Saudi Arabia and Qatar. Among the Shiite schools, the major one being the Ithna-ashari (Ja'fari) is followed in Iran, Southern Iraq, South Lebanon and Bahrain; the Zaydi is followed in Yemen; the Ismaili is followed in India and Pakistan; and the Ibadi is followed in Oman and parts of North Africa.

54 According to a report by Iran, "[r]esort to *fatwa*, to the age-old body of Islamic law, principle and precedent, was also admitted in the Civil Codes of Algeria, Egypt and Syria (all of which had ratified or acceded to the Covenant), as well as in that of Kuwait." See Summary

Article 1(2) of the Civil Code of Kuwait directs that, in the absence of a specific legislative provision, judges are to adjudicate according to custom (*urf*) and in the absence of an applicable principle of custom, be guided by the principles of Islamic jurisprudence (*fiqh*) most appropriate under the general and particular circumstances.[55]

Similarly, according to Article 167 of the Constitution of Iran, in the absence of statutory law the judge has to "deliver his judgment on the basis of authoritative Islamic sources and authentic *fatwa* (rulings issued by qualified jurists)."[56] Yet, while in Algeria and Kuwait un-codified Muslim legal traditions can be applied only for family law matters, in Iran and Egypt the authority of these un-codified traditions in practice has been extended to public law as well.[57]

Third, Application of Muslim Legal Traditions by Shariah *Courts*

In a number of Muslim and non-Muslim states, *Shariah* courts are part of the judiciary.[58] Jurisdiction of *Shariah* courts in Muslim countries, with two exceptions, is in family law matters. The first exception is Saudi Arabia, where *Shariah* courts have general and residual jurisdiction, i.e. jurisdiction over any case or matter the jurisdiction over which has not been expressly assigned to another tribunal. The second is Malaysia, where the jurisdiction of *Shariah* courts is extended to religious offences as well, which is somehow deemed an issue of public law.[59]

---

record, 1993 (Iran) *supra* note 40. For the case of Afghanistan see Article 130(2) of the Constitution and the relevant discussion in section 2.4.2 of this book.

55 Civil Code of Kuwait, cited in the website of Emory School of law, *supra* note 6.

56 According to one official report of Iran, "[*f*]*atawa* [plural of *fatwa*], which could also be invoked in the personal domain (e.g. with regard to the rules for prayer and fasting), as well as in commercial affairs, amounted to doctrine, in other words, to the body of instruction handed down by the great jurisconsults of Islam; it could be of help to modern judges in the absence of codified law." See Summary record, 1993 (Iran) *supra* note 40, para. 11.

57 Two relevant cases in Iran, Eshkevari and Aghajari, and one in Egypt, Hamed Abu Zayd, will be discussed in part A of this book.

58 Some of these states include: Bahrain, Brunei, Ethiopia, Gambia, Indonesia, Iraq, Jordan, Kenya, Lebanon, Malaysia, Palestine, Philippines, Qatar, Singapore, Somalia, Srilanka, Sudan, Syria, United Arab Emirates, Morocco, Nigeria, Oman, Pakistan, Qatar and Saudi Arabia. Rabbinical courts in Israel have also similar jurisdiction to *Shariah* courts in Muslim countries.

59 This issue will be discussed with regard to apostasy in part A of this book.

Constitutional References That Address Personal Muslim Legal Traditions or the Legal System in General

There are some references in the Constitutions of Pakistan, Iran and Afghanistan, and in the Basic Law of Saudi Arabia, which introduce Islam, *Shariah* or similar terms as a criterion for approving the legislation. It is beyond the scope of this study to examine this issue in detail, but it is sufficient to note that two kinds of purposes are identified from the wordings of these references. First, with regard to Pakistan and Saudi Arabia, where references are made to the Koran and *Sunnah*, the legislation addresses mainly personal Muslim legal traditions to be considered as a criterion for family law matters. Article 2A of the Constitution of Pakistan requires all laws to be brought into consonance with the Koran and *Sunnah*. Similarly in Saudi Arabia, the Basic Law states that the administration of justice is based on "*Shariah* rules according to the teachings of the holy Koran, the *Sunnah*, and the regulations set by the ruler provided that they do not contradict the holy Koran and *Sunnah*".

Second, references to 'Islam' and 'Islamic criteria', which appear in the Constitutions of Iran and Afghanistan, are not necessarily a reference to legal aspects of the religion. These are in fact references to the religion as a whole or its divine principles. According to Article 3 of the Constitution of Afghanistan: "No law shall contravene the tenets and provisions of the holy religion of Islam in Afghanistan."[60]

The reference to 'Islamic criteria' in Article 4 of the Constitution of Iran, similar to the above mentioned reference to Islam in the Constitution of Afghanistan, addresses the whole body of legislation. The article reads as follows: "All civil, criminal, financial, economic, administrative, cultural, military, political and other laws and regulations must be based on Islamic criteria. This principle applies generally to all articles of the Constitution, as well as to the other laws and regulations...."

'Islamic criteria' is a translation of the Persian term '*mavazin-e eslami*'. What is understood in Persian by this is that this term and similar terms[61] do not have legal effect, but rather represent a reference to Islamic principles which form the eternal essence of the religion. Therefore, as this term reappears in other articles of the Constitution with regard to other activities of

60 Constitution of the Islamic Republic of Afghanistan, ratified 26 Jan. 2004.

61 See other references to 'Islam', 'Islamic criteria', 'fundamental principles of Islam' and 'Islamic ideology' in Articles 20, 21, 24, 26, 28, 61, 72, 144 and 168 of the Constitution of Iran.

the state, one might conclude that the scope of the application of this term as a criterion not only applies to the judicial system, but extends to the whole activities of the state.

References that Address Public Muslim Legal Traditions

'Islamization of law' has been a political demand during the last three decades by some Muslim movements seeking the revival of Muslim law. As Muslim traditional personal law was never abandoned, this demand has focused on public aspects of the religious legal traditions. Also, with regard to the numerous aspects of public Muslim legal traditions, the only area which was regarded as Muslim law in need of revival was part of traditional penal code. In this sense, though Iran and Pakistan have incorporated part of this code in their legislation, in practice they have faced a number of difficulties.[62]

Interestingly, with the exception of Pakistan, there is no term in the legislation of other Muslim states referring to islamization of legislation, or calling for the revival of public Muslim law. In Pakistan, Part IX of the Constitution is entitled 'Islamic provisions' and provides for the islamization of all existing laws, reiterating that no laws shall be enacted which are 'repugnant' to the injunctions of Islam.[63]

Finally to sum up, considering the different levels of application of public and personal Muslim legal traditions, one might presume that any general reference to the temporary application of '*Shariah*' or Muslim law is in fact a reference to personal Muslim legal traditions or family law matters, unless a related area of Muslim legal traditions is explicitly pointed out.

---

62 It is also important to distinguish between the moaning demands for revival of Islam in last two centuries with the demands for islamization of law in recent decades. Interestingly enough, though the main demand in Iran Islamic revolution of 1979 was revival of Islam, rarely revival of traditional Muslim law was claimed by the rhetoricians and leader of the revolution.

63 On islamization of Law in Pakistan see generally Mehdi Rubya, *The Islamization of the Law in Pakistan* (Richmond, Surrey: Curzon Press, 1994).

Part A
Apostasy (*IRTIDAD*)

Introductory Remarks

In evaluating the effects of Muslim legal traditions of apostasy this part distinguishes between the three different phenomena of apostasy, which can be listed as conversion, heresy and *sabb* (blasphemy). While these three phenomena may overlap in some ways, for Muslim jurists the term *irtidad* (*ridda*) is generally used to describe the act of a convert, a blasphemer or a heretic. To present some more recent examples for each phenomenon: charging Abdul Rahman in March 2006 for rejecting Islam in a lower court in Kabul is an issue of conversion; the famous controversial case of the Danish Cartoons in September 2005 is a matter of *sabb*; and declaring Shiites as apostates in Iraq by some militant extremist is an issue of heresy.

The study makes a distinction between the public aspects of these traditions and their personal aspects. Public rules of the legal traditions of apostasy which have been embodied partly in the legislation of some Muslim states include prohibition and punishment of the three different alleged offences, conversion, blasphemy and heresy, along with the civil consequences of these offences, such as confiscation of the property of the offender. Despite their partial insertion in legislation, public rules of Muslim traditions of apostasy are not applicable anymore and therefore have been gradually abandoned in case law. Yet, the remnants of personal aspects of these traditions, notably the family law consequences of apostasy, such as dissolving the marriage of the convert, though they might not be incorporated in legislation, can be found in domestic case law.

Considering the practice of those legal consequences of apostasy that are not embodied in the legislation on the one hand, and impracticality of related legislation on prohibition and punishment of apostasy-related offences on the other, the study will argue that states practices of traditional rules of apostasy are not necessarily a reflection of their related statutory laws.

Part A is divided into four chapters. The first chapter is devoted to an introduction to the three different phenomena of apostasy in Muslim legal traditions and the international human rights norms relevant to each of them. The main focus of the study is on intra-religious freedoms, or freedoms of followers of a religion within their religious community, rather than inter-religious issues which involve the relations between different religions.

Within the broad scope of freedom of religion, opinion and expression, this study addresses only those aspects of the issues which are directly linked to the effects of Muslim traditions of apostasy. In this regard, the phenomenon of conversion in Muslim legal traditions engages the right to change religion under Article 18 of the Universal Declaration of Human Rights (UDHR)[1] and Article 18 of the International Covenant on Civil and Political Rights (ICCPR).[2] Similarly, the phenomena of *sabb* and heresy will be examined with regard to the legitimacy of limitations on freedom of religion, opinion and expression under Articles 18(3), 19(3) and 20 of the ICCPR.

Part A further provides, in the other three chapters, a comprehensive analysis of the effects of each phenomenon of apostasy on the legislation and legal practices of Muslim states. The second chapter starts with a survey of the legislation of Muslim states on conversion and proselytizing. Subsequently, the extent to which Muslim states impose legal consequences in relation to apostasy are examined. In this sense, the possibility of use or abuse of family law consequences of apostasy by individuals will be discussed. Then, in order to examine the practical effects of related legislation, a case study on the practice of conversion in Malaysia is presented. Finally, the case of Abdul Rahman illustrates the possibility of the imposition of the death sentence or the legal consequence of apostasy on the accused under the current legislation of Afghanistan.

Based on UN documentation, the last section of the second chapter is allocated to the official position of Muslim states on conversion. First, the position of Muslim states in drafting the relevant provisions of the UDHR, the ICCPR, the Declaration on the Elimination of All Forms of Intolerance Based on Religion or Belief (the Religion Declaration)[3] and the Convention on the Rights of the Child (the CRC)[4] will be discussed. Furthermore, imple-

---

1 Universal Declaration of Human Rights (UDHR), G.A. res. 217A (III), U.N.Doc.A/810 at 71 (1948).

2 International Covenant on Civil and Political Rights (ICCR), G.A. res. 2200A (XXI), 21 U.N. GAOR Supp. (No. 16) at 52, U.N.Doc.A/6316 (1966), 999 U.N.T.S. 171, entered into force, 23 March 1976.

3 Declaration on Elimination of All Forms of of Intolerance and Discrimination Based on Religion or Belief, G.A. res. 36/55, 36 U.N. GAOR Supp. (No. 51) at 171, U.N.Doc.A/36/684 (1981).

4 The Convention on the Rights of the Child (CRC), G.A. res. 44/25, annex, 44 U.N. GAOR Supp. (No. 49) at 167, U.N.Doc.A/44/49 (1989), entered into force, 2 Sept. 1990.

mentation of the related provisions of the ICCPR and the CRC by Muslim states will be examined.

The third chapter is allocated to the issue of blasphemy (*sabb*). It is a common policy among the majority of states to pass legislation on insulting religions and religious feelings. With regard to the effects of Muslim traditions of apostasy, Pakistan and Iran are the only Muslim states that have inserted the identical traditional punishment of *sabb* in their legislation. The third chapter starts with a survey on the related legislation of these two countries. Then, the *Rushdie* case as the most famous apostasy case in recent history will be discussed. The crisis of the Danish Cartoons can also be considered as a case of *sabb*.[5] Yet, as this study is limited to the examination of Muslim states practices, it will not address this case in detail.

The fourth chapter examines the phenomenon of heresy. To ensure government control over religions and religious groups, states resort to legislation or policies that might give rise to the investigation of the religious opinions and practices of individuals or groups. These policies are revealed in three different categories. In the first category one might find legislation and policies against blasphemy that contain anti-heretic elements. In this regard two kinds of legislation, in Iran and Malaysia, will be studied. The second category covers legislation and policies against so-called heretic religious groups. While the only example of statutory legislation against heretic groups is the one in Pakistan against the Ahmadies, there are some other groups that have been constantly under pressure from anti-heresy policies. The third category contains those security laws that target both individuals and groups. While these laws mainly have been passed for a justifiable purpose, including controlling

5 The twelve cartoons of the Prophet Muhammad were published on 30 Sept. 2005 by the Danish newspaper Jyllands-Posten, and showed the Prophet in a variety of humorous or satirical situations. The cartoons were further republished in Austria in January 2006, and then at the beginning of February 2006 in a number of European newspapers in France, Germany, Italy and Spain. Publishing these cartoons caused outrage among some Muslims and led to a crisis in EU-Muslim relations. There was at least one *fatwa* of the death sentence against the cartoonist by one *Shariah* court in India which fortunately didn't cause to violence. For more information about the Danish Cartoons see for example the Annual Report of the UN Special Rapporteur on Contemporary Forms of Racism, Racial Discrimination, Xenophobia and Related Intolerance: 'Situation of Muslims and Arab Peoples in Various Parts of the World, Section III: The Cartoons of the Prophet Muhammad Published in A Danish Newspaper', U.N.Doc.E/CN.4/2006/17. In his report the Special Rapporteur makes some excellent comments on the hypocrisy of the 'freedom of expression' argument used in that case.

hostile, extremist or terrorist groups (such as the Al-Qaeda), they might also target peaceful individuals or groups, which merely have different religious opinions from those of the orthodoxy.

Along with these three kinds of legislation, the chapter examines *takfir*, or declaring a Muslim fellow individual or group 'heretics', as a violation of freedom of opinion, and as a major source of religious intolerance and violence in Muslim countries and some other parts of the world. *Takfir* has been practiced quite common not only in Muslim history, but also among other religious groups such as Christians. In current times, two kinds of issuing *takfir* can be distinguished among Muslims; the authorized and the arbitrary. While the present authority of *Shariah* courts does not include declaring *takfir*, the best known example of authorized declarations of *takfir* are those by Al-Azhar against Muslim scholars in Egypt, which caused the murder of some noted scholars. The most dangerous instances of arbitrary declarations of *takfir* are those by Muslim extremists against a differing sect that caused massive killings of people in Algeria, and later in Afghanistan and Iraq.

Finally, this chapter examines the four major recent cases of heresy which were filed against four eminent Muslim scholars, Taha in Sudan, Abu Zayd in Egypt, and Eshkevari and Aghajari in Iran. These are cases in which the four scholars have been accused by the court of *irtidad*, in essence heresy, because their religious opinions were different from those of the orthodoxy.

CHAPTER ONE

Muslim Legal Traditions of Apostasy and Relevant Human Rights Law

1.1. Related Legal Traditions and Their Three Different Phenomena

1.1.1. *Conversion*

According to the Koranic principle of 'free choice' every human being is free to choose his or her religion or belief based upon his or her own will: "Duress is not permissible in religion, as the path has become clear from falsehood".[6] Kaidivar numerates different Koranic principles on freedom of religion among which are the denial of duress and force in religion and faith, and freedom as a means of guidance and manifestation.[7]

Yet, similar to many other progressive ideals, the Koranic principles on freedom of religion have been dramatically modified to be compatible with the social context of their elaboration, and the situations of war in early centuries of Muslim history. In fact, when studying the concept of freedom of religion in early Muslim communities, "one needs to avoid thinking in [post modern] twentieth century terms [of the West], that is, from an individualistic perspective, which tends to interpret religious creed as an entirely personal matter."[8]

To briefly elaborate on the reasoning for this contradiction, it seems that despite the Koranic principle of freedom to choose one's religion, in practice early Muslim jurisprudence had to consider protection of the newly emerged Muslim community. While early Muslims were in a state of war with surrounding unbeliever enemies, conversion by any member of their community

6 The Koran, 2:256.

7 See Mohsen Kadivar, 'Freedom of Thought and Religion in Islam', in Mofid University, *Collected Papers of the International Conference on Human Rights and Dialogue of Civilization*, May 2001 (Mofid University Publication Institute, Qom – Iran, 2001).

8 Donna E. Arzt, 'The Role of Compulsion in Islamic Conversion: *Jihad*, *Dhimmi* and *Ridda*' 8 *Buffalo Human Rights Law Review* 15 (2002), p. 32.

to the religion of their enemies could be interpreted as joining the enemy camp. As the only fabric of the new Muslim society was religion, for early Muslims conversion was considered not merely matter of faith, but "equal to treason",[9] "submission to foreign domination",[10] "treason against a very basic and all-encompassing group identity and loyalty",[11] and an "act of war against the Muslims".[12]

Rahman notes that: "Apostates involved were not merely renegades from the faith but also in active opposition to the Muslims, having joined the warring disbelievers' camp."[13] In this sense, as will be discussed later, the majority of Muslim schools of law did not consider imposing the death penalty for women apostates, presumably because women would not engage in war against Muslims.[14] Even today concern for the protection of the community is more serious in multi religious communities, where each community has to protect its identity and existence from the threats of other communities.

Despite what was mentioned on the logic of considering conversion as an offence, in later criminalizing conversion, the factor of 'intent' was neglected by Muslim jurists. Therefore, whether conversion took place as a search for truth or as a hostile act to the community, it was considered as a crime, liable to punishment.

By the same token a Muslim child after reaching the age of maturity had to take on the religion of his or her father, i.e. Islam. This again was against the Koranic principles of freedom of religion. In fact, 'obeying parents' as a justification for non-believers to follow the religion of their fathers has been rejected by the Koran.[15] By contrast, according to another rule of Muslim legal traditions, every Muslim from the age of maturity (a boy at fifteen years and

9 Sayyid Muhammad Rizvi, 'Apostasy (*Irtidad*) in Islam', available at the website of al-Islam at: <http://www.al-islam.org/short/apostacy.htm>.

10 Arzt, The Role of Compulsion, *supra* note 8, p. 25.

11 Kanan Makiya, 'Cruelty and Silence: War, Tyranny, Uprising and the Arab World' 90 (1993), quoted in Arzt, *ibid.*, p. 29.

12 Hassan Riffat, 'On Human Rights and the Koranic Perspective', in Arlene Swidler (ed.) *Human Rights in Religious Traditions* (New York: The Pilgrim Press, 1982), p. 61.

13 Senu Abdul Rahman, *Punishment of apostasy in Islam* (Institute of Islamic Culture, Lahore, 1972), p. 70.

14 See Mohammed Talbi, 'Religious Liberty: A Muslim Perspective', in Leonard Swidler (ed.) *Religious Liberty and Human Rights in Nations and Religions* (New York and Philadelphia: Hippocrene Books and Ecumenical Press, 1986), pp. 182–183.

15 See the Koran, 2:170; 5:104; 7:28; 10:78; 21:53–54; 26:74–76; 31: 21; 43:22–23.

a girl at nine-thirteen years of age) should stand for the principles of his or her religion on his or her own findings.[16]

It should be noted that the prohibition of conversion is not merely an issue of Muslim legal traditions. A similar view was held by Thomas Aquinas to the effect that those "who at one time accepted the Faith and professed it; they must be compelled, even by physical force, to carry out what they promised and to hold what they once accepted."[17]

Among the temporary Sunni jurists, Sheikh Yousef Al-Qaradhawi holds a different view to the traditional views on punishment of conversion. He makes a distinction between 'limited conversion' that is merely conversion of an individual, and 'expanded conversion', which is conversion of an individual that is extended to others. While there is no punishment for the former, the latter is subject to punishment:

> Limited *ridda* is the *ridda* of the individual who switches religion and is not interested in others.... [Yet,] one of the freedoms that Islam does not accept is the freedom of *ridda* that expands and threatens the social fabric and its foundations.... [This] is a *ridda* in which the individual who abandons Islam calls [upon others] to do likewise, a group whose path is not the path of society and whose goal is not the goal of the nation, and whose allegiance is not to the Islamic nation. Such [individuals] endanger the social fabric, and they are like the *murtaddoon* [apostates], who were fought by [the first Caliph] Abu Bakr together with the Companions of the Prophet [the *Sahaabi*]. Those *murtaddoon* falsely claimed that they were prophets with the same inspiration as was given to the Prophet Muhammad...[18]

---

16 It is the view of all grand Shiite jurists (*mujtahids*), as proclaimed in the first Article of their main jurisprudential book called '*Resaaleh Tawdhih-al-Masaael*,' that "*taqlid* (imitation) in principles of religion is not permissible, and a Muslim should be certain about principles of the religion [by his or her own findings]". See for example the view of Ayatollah Fazel Lankarani in English, available at his website: <http://www.lankarani.org>.

17 Eric D'Arcy, *Conscience and its Rights to Freedom* (London: Sheed & Ward, 1961), quoted in Tad Stahnke, 'Proselytism and the Freedom to Change Religion in International Human Rights Law', *Brigham Young University Law Review* 251 (1999), p. 282.

18 Al-Ahram al-Arabi (Egypt), 'Accusing Muslim Intellectuals of Apostasy', July 3, 2004, translation in English in Aluma Dankowitz, cited in *Inquiry and Analysis Series*, No. 208, Feb. 18, 2005, available at the website of "Inquiry and Analysis, The Middle East Media Research Institute" at: <http://memri.org/bin/articles.cgi?Page=archives&Area=ia&ID=IA20805#_edn3>.

As with the most prominent Shiite jurists, the majority identically repeat the traditional apostasy rules on converts.[19] Yet, according to Ayatollah Makarem Shirazi, if a *murtad* (apostate) does not declare his or her unbelief he will not be punished.[20] Ayatollah Jannaati also does not give his opinion on apostate on grounds that the issue requires scrutiny.[21]

Among grand Shiite jurists Ayatollah Montazeri has a unique opinion with special focus on the issue of intention of convert. He refers to those who in the past had converted from Islam and reiterates that the penalty for such *murtads* used to be applied to those who were Muslim and "then on ground of hostility and with the intent to damage Islam" became unbelievers. Ayatollah Montazeri does not state whether, if such a hostile conversion happens in current times, the punishment should be applied or not. Yet, according to him, "merely doubting or changing one's belief, if it happens after research, does not result in the death penalty". He reiterates that for accusing somebody of *irtidad*, obtaining assurance (*ihraz*) is obligatory for the judge. In this sense he refers to a main principle of Islamic jurisprudence (*fiqh*), which holds: "Don't enforce punishment (*hudood*) in case of doubt."[22]

Considering the issue of proselytising it should be noted that different religions have different views on the practice of proselytism. While for Christians proselytizing is an 'essential mission' of the religion and linked to conversion,[23] for Muslims this issue is different. Though inviting non-believers to Islam is

---

19 For Ayatollah Fazel Lankarani see page 438, Questions 1152–1154 at his website in Persian at: <http://www.lankarani.com/Persian/ahkam/jm2/j20.html#432>. For Ayatollah Musavi Ardabili see his website in Persian at: <http://www.ardebili.org/Per/FAQ/NewFAQ/>. For Ayatollah Sistani see his website in Persian at: <http://www.sistani.org/html/far/main/index-istifta.php?page=4&lang=far&part=4>.

20 For the views of Ayatollah Makarem Shirazi see his website in Persian at: <http://www.makaremshirazi.org/persian/modules.php?name=es&p=2&id=119>. Also for his views about some heretic group see: <http://www.makaremshirazi.org/persian/modules.php?name=es&p=2&id=122>.

21 See (Ayatollah) Mohammad Ebrahim Jannaati, *Periods of Jurisprudence and Its Manner of Explanation* (Kayhan Publisher, Tehran, 1995) in Persian, pp. 438–439.

22 For the views of Ayatollah Hoseinali Montazeri, see questions 885–891 and 2506–2509 in his website in Persian at: <http://www.amontazeri.com>. For his views also see a report at BBC website in Persian: <http://www.bbc.co.uk/persian/iran/story/2005/02/050202_mj-montzari-renegade.shtml>.

23 See *Kokkinakis* v. *Greece* Case, 260-A Eur. Ct. H.R. (ser.A) (1993). In this case court referred to a report by the World Council of Churches to determine that proselytism was part of the 'essential mission' of all Christians and that improper proselytism was a corruption of the mission of Christians. Consequently, the majority of the court held that the attempt to convert non-believers was an essential part of the religious obligations of many Christians.

generally encouraged in accordance with Muslim religious teaching, unlike Christians, proselytizing for Muslims is not considered as one of the religious obligations or practices. On the other hand, while conversion from Islam was considered an offence according to the legal traditions, in the same sense Muslims did not tolerate proselytizing by other fellow religions targeting Muslims. It was also one of the *Dhimmah* conditions that non-Muslims were not allowed to propagate their religions among Muslims.[24]

1.1.2. *Blasphemy* (Sabb)

'*Sabb*' means 'insulting', and in the legal traditions, the offence of insulting God and the Prophet are called '*sabb-Allah*' and '*sabb-al Rasul*' (or *sabb-al Nabi*) respectively. According to Saeed: "In the discussion on apostasy there is a special category in which the jurists explore the use of foul language primarily with regard to the Prophet. This is known as *sabb-al Rasul*. Later on this was considered to include the use of foul language with regard to *Allah* (*sabb-Allah*)".[25]

Despite the explicit statement of the Bible that "blaspheming the Holy Spirit is unforgivable",[26] "neither the Koran nor the Prophet stated clearly the existence of an offence called blasphemy or a specific temporal punishment for it".[27] According to the Koran a good Muslim is one who does not care about others behaving badly: "And they who do not bear witness to what is false, and when they pass by what is vain, they pass by nobly."[28] The Koran also explicitly prohibits Muslims insulting non-believers and their sacred things: "Don't insult those who call on other than God (non believers), for then they may insult [your] God openly in their ignorance."[29]

However, in the early Muslim times during the wars of the Prophet, few cases of punishment of militant enemies for *sabb* have been reported, the most famous one of which was the case of Ka'b ben al-Ashraf, who in his composed *poetry* denigrated the Prophet and his followers. In the time of war all adult

---

24 See Kadivar *supra* note 7. *Dhimmah* conditions will be discussed in more detail in part B of this book.

25 Abdullah Saeed & Hassan Saeed, *Freedom of Religion, Apostasy, and Islam* (Aldershot, Hants, England; Burlington, VT: Ashgatee, 2004), pp. 37–38.

26 Luke, 12:10.

27 Saeed, *supra* note 25, p. 38.

28 The *Koran*, 25:72.

29 *Ibid.*, 6:108.

enemy men were considered combatants, and Ka'b was attacked and killed by some solders from the Muslim camp.[30]

While in a few early cases of *sabb* the punishment was merely carried out against enemy combatants, in later codifications of the law, the offence along with its instant punishment was extended to Muslim offenders as well. In this regard, while in cases of conversion an authorized judge decided on the offence and its punishment, for *sabb* any individual Muslim was capable of realizing the offence and also allowed, or according to some jurists even religiously obliged,[31] to an instant implementation of the punishment, the killing of the offender.

According to Sunni jurists, along with God and the Prophet, the list of the religious sacred things, insulting which are subject to death punishment might extend to angels and the Prophet's Companions (*sahaabis*). According to the majority of contemporary major Shiite jurists, the death penalty is applied to insulters of the Prophet and the twelve Shiite *Imams*. Some other Shiite jurists have added to the list Fatemeh (the daughter of the Prophet), and all other prophets as well.[32]

Finally it should be noted that according to the Muslim jurists, insult is a matter of relativism. Therefore, the customs (*urf*) of each society is the criterion for recognizing the offence. Baghi states, "even the custom among scholars is different from those of ordinary people in the same society."[33] This means that while the expression of an opinion by a scholar in public might be considered *sabb*, the same expression in an academic atmosphere may not be, and may even be encouraged.

1.1.3. *Heresy*

Historically, blasphemy laws have been used for punishment of heretics or those whose beliefs were considered a threat to the dominant religion. Thus, Jesus was convicted under the Jewish blasphemy laws. Matthew's account of

---

30 On case of Ka'b see Hosein Torbatinejad, *Islam and Violence* (Haram Publication, Qom, Iran, 2003) in Persian, pp. 262–265.

31 See Ayatollah Montazeri, *supra* note 22.

32 See Hosein Mirmohammadsadeghi, *Offences against Security of the State and Public Tranquillity*, Fourth Edition (Mizaan Publisher, Tehran, Iran, 2004) in Persian, p. 166. For more information about the list of sacred personalities for Shiites and Sunnis see also section 3.1 of this book on legislation of Iran and Pakistan.

33 Emadeddin Baghi, 'Where is the Crisis?', 13 Feb. 2006, in Persian, available at Emrouz website at: <http://www.emrouz.info/archives/2006/02/00247_24.php>.

this trial reports that after Jesus had confessed his claim to divinity before the Jewish Sanhedrin, the High Priest Caiphas, was so outraged that he tore his clothes and said: "He has blasphemed! There, you have just heard the blasphemy, what is your opinion? To which the other members of the council replied 'He deserves to die.'"[34]

According to Muslim jurists a heretic or '*zandiq*' is, "an unbeliever who hides his unbelief and pretends to be Muslim".[35] Yet, to survey the practical aspects of the matter, this study has reserved a specific concept of heresy. While conversion, refers to a Muslim who has formally renounced Islam, according to the definition of heresy a Muslim is accused of unbelief on grounds of his opinion being different from that of the majority or orthodoxy. On difference of convesion and heresy Arzt states, "the former applies to Muslims who have rejected Islamic belief, while the latter is used to refer to Muslim believers who advocate internal reform or a heterodox interpretation of Islam."[36]

The concept of heresy chosen for this study is also a familiar one in Western literature. According to the Oxford English Dictionary, heresy is a "theological or religious opinion or doctrine maintained in opposition, or held to be contrary, to the 'catholic' or orthodox doctrine of the Christian Church, or, by extension, to that of any church, creed, or religious system, considered as orthodox."[37]

The deeds of the Prophet and his successors showed great tolerance with all their religious and political dissidents who believed in a different version of the religion. Ali's deed showed that *Khavarij*, as his main political and religious opponents, were free to express their views and argue about their beliefs in public, as long as they did not take up their sword against the Caliph. While Muslims have a brilliant history of scientific dialogue among different religious opinions and even between Muslims and atheists, nevertheless, in the history of Muslims, cases of charging people with heresy have not been rare, particularly where the rulers used heresy as a pretext for oppressing their opponents. Saeed points out that "[s]tate involvement in theological matters

---

34 Mt. 26:64–66, quoted in N. Cox, *Blasphemy and the Law in Ireland* (The Edwin Mellen Press, LTD, 2000), p. 3.

35 Ayatollah Jannaati, *supra* note 21, pp. 438–439.

36 Donna E. Arzt, 'Religious Human Rights in the Middle East and North Africa' 10 *Emory International law Review* 1 (1996), available at: <http://www.law.emory.edu/EILR/volumes/spring96/arzt.html>.

37 Wikipedia, The Free Encyclopaedia, available at: <http://www.reference.com/browse/wiki/Heresy>.

began during the Umayyad period. Some rulers took a particularly harsh stand against thinkers with a Qadari orientation."[38]

For Muslims jurists, the concept of heresy emerged from the concept of conversion. According to all Muslim jurists, denying one of the main principles of Islam leads to apostasy. Muslim jurists have reached consensus on at least two of these principles, believing in one God, and the prophet-hood of Muhammad. However, according to some jurists, denying, and even doubting the essential requirements of the religion (*dharuriyat-e din*) also lead to apostasy. According to this view a Muslim is not free to deny the affairs that are indispensable to religion. The list of these affairs, however, varies according to different jurists and might be considered as narrow as opposing one rule of traditional Muslim law.[39]

Heresy is defined by Thomas Aquinas as "a species of infidelity in men who, having professed the faith of Christ, corrupt its dogmas."[40] The concept of dogma, as it exists in Catholicism, is not familiar to Muslims, and no official institution or authorized person has been introduced in the Koran or by the Prophet as the final interpreter of the text or the authority for the identification of heretic beliefs. While this phenomenon can help in exploring the new scientific era, where the issue of heresy is concerned, it might happen that even a *mufti* or *mujtahid*, or even an ordinary person who doesn't have the authority from the ruler, considers himself to have this right to declare a *fatwa* with which to label an individual, an opinion or a sect as heretic. This act

38 Saeed, *supra* note 25, p. 28. The author refers to Ma'bad al-Juhani who was executed for his views by order of the Umayyad Caliph Abdal-Malik Marwan (705 A.D.) and Ghaylan b. Muslim al-Dimashqi who was put to death for the same reason by Caliph Hisham b. Abd al-Malik. Saeed also provides information about a list of very famous Muslim scholars, respected and recognized today as major contributors to Islamic civilizations, who were accused in their times for heresy, some of whom were prosecuted and even executed. Among these scholars are: Abu Hanifa, the *Imam* of Hanafi school of law, Ahmad b. Hanbal, the *Imam* of Hanbali school of law, Muhammad b. Isma'il al-Bukhari, al-Hussayn b. Mansur al-Hallaj, Abu Hamid Muhamamd al-Ghazali, Avicenna (Ibn Sina), Ibn Hazm, Farabi, Ibn Rushd, Sarakhsi. *Ibid.*, pp. 30–31. Kadivar also provides another list of some prominent Muslim scholars whether sophist or philosopher who have been charged for their views. The list includes Avicenna, Sohrevardi, Sad ol'Moteahelin, Mohiedin ebn Arabi and Sheikh Haadi Najm Aabaadi (Known as Mokafer). See Kadivar, *supra* note 7. On heresy in Muslim history also see Johannes J.G. Jansen, 'Muslim Victims of *Jihad*', Utrecht University, the Netherlands, 2005, available at: <http://www.iheu.org/node/1545>.

39 For different opinions of Sunni jurists on these instances see Saeed, *supra* note 25, pp. 43–48.

40 Wikipedia, The Free Encyclopaedia, available at: <http://www.reference.com/browse/wiki/Heresy>.

of declaring other Muslims heretic or unbelievers is called '*takfir*'. Though a *fatwa* by itself lacks the power of enforcement, it might be enforced against an accused heretic arbitrarily by the followers of the *mufti* as a religious duty.

The broad definition of heresy has sometimes been the cause of the situation where a whole Muslim sect or a religious group has become the subject of *takfir*, or has been called heretic by another sect. This labelling of another religious group as heretic has resonances among Christians as well:

> 'Heresy' has no purely objective meaning: the category exists only from the point-of-view of a position within a sect that has been previously defined as 'orthodox'. Heresy is a value-judgment and the expression of a view from within an established belief system. For instance, Roman Catholics held Protestantism as a heresy while some non-Catholics considered Catholicism the 'Great Apostasy'.[41]

Among Shiite jurists Ayatollah Montazeri has tried to clarify the ambiguities of the issue:

> If for a Muslim any of the commandments of the religion have not been proven as necessities of the religion and therefore he or she denies such commandments on the grounds of his or her doubt (for example if he or she finds that prayer was obligatory exclusively for the early Muslims, or if he or she does not believe in the obligation of *hijab* hair dress for women), he or she is not to be considered a *murtad*, and therefore the rules of *murtad* will not be applied on him or her.[42]

Ayatollah Sistani apparently has a similar view. In response to a question on the consequences for a person who denies the necessity of the 'morning prayer', Ayatollah Sistani states: "Such denying is denying the necessities of religion". Yet, he further reiterates that "denying the necessities of religion, [only] if it results in the denying of God and the Prophet, such act is to be considered *irtidad*".[43] That means if the denying of morning prayer, though a necessity of religion, does not result in a denial of God and the Prophet, the person is not considered a *murtad*.

---

41 Wikipedia, The Free Encyclopaedia, available at: <http://www.reference.com/browse/wiki/Heresy>.

42 See Ayatollah Montazeri, *supra* note 22.

43 *See* the website of Ayatollah Sistani in Persian, *supra* note 19.

1.1.4. *Punishment of Apostasy*

No verse in the Koran prescribes punishment for conversion.[44] Yet, according to Muslim legal traditions, in the case of conversion, the death penalty for males and life imprisonment for females is imposed under certain conditions. For blasphemy the death penalty might also be extended to females as well. Prescriptions of rules for such punishment by Muslim jurists were apparently based on the rules of preceding religions or customs of the time. For example, for the punishment of blasphemy, the Bible states: "He who blasphemes the name of the Lord shall be put to death. The entire assembly must stone him, whether an alien or a native born, when he blasphemes the Name, he must be put to death."[45] There is also another biblical basis for such a punishment that states:

> If your brother, the son of your mother, or your son, or your daughter, or the wife of your bosom, or your friend who is as your own soul, entices you secretly saying, 'Let us go and serve other gods', which neither you nor your father have known, some of the gods of the people that are round about you, whether near you, or far off from you, from the one end of the earth to the other, you shall not yield to him or listen to him, nor shall your eye pity him, nor shall you spare him, nor shall you conceal him; but you shall kill him; your hand shall be first against him to put him to death, and afterwards the hands of all people.[46]

According to the majority of Sunni jurists the punishment for a male apostate under some conditions is death. Yet, most of the Sunni jurists believe that a period of at least three days must be given the apostate to repent.[47] Upon repenting, no punishment is applied to the apostate.[48] Shiite jurists, however,

---

44 See for example the Koran, 2:256; 3:72; 3:90; 4:48; 4:137; 5:54.

45 Leviticus, 24:16.

46 Deuteronomy, 13:6–9, Revised Standard Version. Saeed says that in the medieval period this verse was the Biblical basis for punishment of apostasy and heresy that was often death. See Saeed, *supra* note 25, p. 35.

47 The Al-Azhar Creed and Philosophy Committee affiliated to Al-Azhar Islamic Research Institute recommended a change in the application of the apostasy law by giving the accused apostate a whole lifetime to renounce his apostasy instead of the three-day period laid down in traditional Muslim law. See 'The Application of the Apostasy Law in the World Today', Barnabas Fund, May 2003, available at: <http://www.barnabasfund.org/Apostasy/_edn2#_edn2.>.

48 Regarding Sunni views on punishment of apostasy see Saeed, *supra* note 25, pp. 51–68.

divide converts into two groups: those who were born Muslim and then became converts or *murtads* (*murtad fitri*) and those who were born non-Muslims and converted to Islam, then after their conversion renounced Islam (*murtad milli*).[49] According to the majority of Shiite jurists a male *murtad fitri* has no right to repent, though a male or female *murtad milli* has such a right. Both Sunni and Shiite jurists prescribe lifelong imprisonment for a female *murtad*. During the imprisonment any time a female *murtad* repents, her repent would be accepted and she will be released upon repenting.[50]

While the punishment for heresy apparently is similar to the punishment for conversion, the punishment of *sabb* is different. There are also different views on the possibility of affording the opportunity to repent to blasphemers. *Sabb*, according to some jurists is an offence that leads to *irtidad* (apostasy), thus the offence is liable to death. Based on this argument the same opportunity to repent as described above is considered for the offender. For some other jurists, *sabb* is a separate offence liable to death. Therefore, whether *sabb* is carried out by a male or apparently even a female Muslim, or non-Muslim, the offender is liable to death. That seems the reason why, according to some jurists, repenting is not accepted for *sabb*.[51]

As mentioned in part 1.1.2, another difference between punishment of *sabb* and conversion is that according to the majority of Shiite jurists, in cases of *sabb*, instant punishment (killing) of the offender, either Muslim or non-Muslim, is not only permissible, but also a religious obligation for any Muslim who realizes the offence or any other who comes to know about it. In this sense, as soon as the offence takes place, the offender must be killed immediately by any one who does not fear for his own life to be endangered.[52]

A concept of Muslim traditional penal code that is linked to the punishment of a *murtad* is that of '*mahduroddam*' or outlaw. Outlaw means one whose life and safety is not protected by the law, for example an attacker. If someone is considered *mahduroddam* by mistake, his or her arbitrary killing

---

49 On *murtad fitri* and *milli* see Kadivar *supra* note 7.

50 *Ibid.*

51 On this issue see also Saeed, *supra* note 25, pp. 37–39.

52 There is consensus among all cotemporary Shiite jurists on the instant punishment of an offender in cases of *sabb*. For example in response to a question Ayatollah Montazeri makes a reference to this issue: "In cases of *sabb-al Nabi*.... if the witness doses not have fear of his or her life and also there is no fear of mischief (*mafsadeh*) it is obligatory for him or her to kill the insulter". See Ayatollah Montazeri, *supra* note 22, question 885.

is not considered a murder, and therefore liable to *qisas* (retaliation), or blood money, but it is an offence of a lesser degree, liable to *tazir*, where the judge has room for determining the punishment.[53]

1.1.5. *Legal Consequences of Apostasy*

As mentioned before, according to Muslim legal traditions, two kinds of legal consequences could be expected for an act of apostasy; those pertaining to family law matters and to civil law matters. Considering the application of different religious family laws for Muslims and non-Muslims in traditional Muslim law, not only conversion from Islam, but conversion to Islam, automatically leads to a change in the personal law of the convert. Yet, as in cases of conflicts of religious laws, where Muslim law prevails, converts from Islam have to expect to be deprived of some of their rights, such as custody of children, inheritance from Muslim relatives and dissolution of marriage.

On the other hand, for converts from Islam the change of personal law is not the only legal consequence of apostasy. As the majority of Sunni jurists consider an apostate an outlaw, even if the death penalty is not imposed on him or her, civil consequences of death (so called civil death), such as confiscation of property by the ruler or its distribution among inhabitants could be imposed on him or her. Civil consequences of apostasy are as follows:

- The apostate is not allowed to marry a Muslim or a non-Muslim;
- When a married person becomes an apostate, the marriage is dissolved no matter whether the wife or husband converts with him or her;
- The apostate's right to exercise custody over his or her children is waived, no matter if his or her children convert with him or her;
- Right of inheritance of apostate will be waived;

53 The more problematic cases of *mahuroddam* that happen mainly in tribal areas nowadays are those of honour killing for adultery. There are also a number of other controversial cases of murder in Iranian jurisprudence, the last of which is so called 'Group Murder' in 2002 in Kerman (Iran). While the brutal murders by a group of vigilantes in this southern city of Iran had shocked the country the killers claimed that the victims were *mahuroddam* and therefore liable to death. For more information about this case for example see Iran Daily (Islamic Republic News Agency), available at: <http://www.iran-daily.com/1384/2318/html/national.htm> in Persian. For other cases of *mahduroddam* in Iran also see Nur Mohammad Sabri, *A Selection of the Judgments of Criminal Courts*, Second Edition (Ferdowsi Press, Tehran, 2002) in Persian, pp. 32–37, 67–68 & 94–95.

- The apostate's right to dispose of his property is in abeyance and the legal effects of his or her acts are suspended.[54]

Regarding the legal consequences of conversion for blasphemy, the viewpoint of Muslim jurists is not clear. Considering what was mentioned on the relevance of *sabb* and *irtidad*, it is logical to conclude that according to those jurists for whom blasphemy results in *irtidad* of a Muslim, the legal consequence of *irtidad* is imposed on the blasphemer as well; and for those jurists who believe in blasphemy as a different offence, the legal consequences are not necessarily imposed.

1.2. RELATED INTERNATIONAL HUMAN RIGHTS LAW

1.2.1. *Conversion and Proselytizing*

In contrast to the Muslim legal traditions of apostasy, freedom to change one's religion is explicitly recognized in Article 18 of the UDHR,[55] Article 9(1) of the European Convention for the Protection of Human Rights and Fundamental Freedoms, (the ECHR)[56] and Article 12(1) of the American Convention on Human Rights.[57] The related article of the UDHR reads as follows: "Everyone has the right to freedom of thought, conscience and religion; this right includes freedom to change his religion or belief, and freedom, either alone or in community with others and in public or private, to manifest his religion or belief in teaching, practice, worship and observance."[58]

This right is not explicitly recognized in Article 18 of the ICCPR, the African Charter of Human Rights,[59] and the Religion Declaration.[60] However,

54 See Rudolph Peters & Gert J.J. De Vries, 'Apostasy in Islam', in *Die Welt des Islams*, New Ser., Vol. 17, Issue 1/4. (1976–1977), p. 7.

55 UDHR, *supra* note 1.

56 The European Convention for the Protection of Human Rights and Fundamental Freedoms (ECHR), 213 U.N.T.S. 222, entered into force, 3 Sept. 1953, as amended by Protocols Nos 3, 5, 8, and 11 which entered into force, 21 Sept. 1970, 20 Dec. 1971, 1 Jan. 1990, and 1 Nov. 1998 respectively.

57 The American Convention on Human Rights, O.A.S. Treaty Series No. 36, 1144 U.N.T.S. 123, entered into force, 18 July 1978, reprinted in Basic Documents Pertaining to Human Rights in the Inter-American System, OEA/Ser.L.V/II.82 doc.6 rev.1 at 25 (1992).

58 UDHR, *supra* note 1.

59 The African [Banjul] Charter on Human and Peoples' Rights, adopted, 27 June 1981, OAU Doc. CAB/LEG/67/3 rev. 5, 21 I.L.M. 58 (1982), entered into force, 12 Oct. 1986.

60 The Religion Declaration, *supra* note 3.

the Human Rights Committee in its General Comment 22 on Article 18 of the ICCPR observes that "the freedom to 'have or to adopt a religion' or belief necessarily entails the freedom to choose a religion or belief, including the right to 'replace one's current religion or belief with another' or to adopt atheistic views, as well as the right to retain one's religion or belief."[61] Furthermore, Article 8 of the Religion Declaration reiterates that "[n]othing in the present Declaration shall be construed as restricting or derogating from any right defined in the Universal Declaration of Human Rights and the International Covenants on Human Rights."[62]

On the other hand, as stated generally in Article 29(2) of the UDHR, and more clearly in Article 18(3) of the ICCPR, freedom to manifest one's religion or beliefs may be subject to limitations when they are necessary to protect, among others, public order, moral values, and rights and freedoms of others.[63] Yet, when imposing these limitations, the three principles of non-discrimination, proportionality, and legality have to be considered by states. According to General Comment 22 of the Human Rights Committee: "Limitations may be applied only for those purposes for which they were prescribed and must be directly related and proportionate to the specific need on which they are predicated. Restrictions may not be imposed for discriminatory purposes or applied in a discriminatory manner."[64]

On imposing the limitations, Article 18 of the ICCPR distinguishes freedom of thought, conscience, religion or belief from the freedom to manifest

---

61 Human Rights Committee, General Comment 22, Article 18 (Forty-eighth session, 1993), U.N.Doc.CCPR/C/21/Rev.1/Add.4 (1993), reprinted in Compilation of General Comments and General Recommendations Adopted by Human Rights Treaty Bodies, U.N.Doc. HRI/GEN/1/Rev.6 at 155 (2003).

62 Religion Declaration, *supra* note 3.

63 According to Article 29(2) of the UDHR: "In the exercise of his rights and freedoms, everyone shall be subject only to such limitations as are determined by law solely for the purpose of securing due recognition and respect for the rights and freedoms of others and of meeting the just requirements of morality, public order and the general welfare in a democratic society." UDHR, *supra* note 1. Article 18(3) of the ICCPR states that: "Freedom to manifest to one's religion or beliefs may be subject only to such limitations as are prescribed by law and are necessary to protect public safety, order, health or morals or the fundamental rights and freedoms of others." ICCPR, *supra* note 2. Also Article 9(2) of the ECHR states that: "Freedom to manifest one's religion or beliefs shall be subject only to such limitations as are prescribed by law and are necessary in a democratic society in the interests of public safety, for the protection of public order, health or morals, or for the protection of the rights and freedoms of others." ECHR, *supra* note 54.

64 General Comment 22, *supra* note 61, para. 4.

religion or belief. According to General Comment 22: "The article does not permit any limitations whatsoever on the freedom of thought and conscience or on the freedom to have or adopt a religion or belief of one's choice. These freedoms are protected unconditionally."[65]

Based on this General Comment, changing of religion is an unconditional right as far as it does not contain elements of manifestation of religion, such as propagating for the new religion, or against the previous religion. Such manifestations might fall under the limitation clause of not only Article 18(3) of the ICCPR, but also, as will be discussed in chapter 4, Articles 19(3) and 20 of the ICCPR on freedom of expression.

Freedom to have or change one's religion is linked to the right to proselytize, a form of manifestation of religion, which itself is conducted mainly through expression. As Stahnke explains:

> ...proselytism may take different forms, such as religious discussions, preaching, teaching, the publication, distribution or sale of printed and electronic works, broadcasting, solicitation of funds, or provision of humanitarian or social services. All of these actions can be proselytism depending upon the intent with which they are undertaken. Therefore, regulation of any of these activities may intentionally or unintentionally restrict proselytism.[66]

Neither proselytism nor propagation of a new religion has been an explicit subject of international instruments of human rights. Yet according to the General Comment 22: "The freedom to manifest religion or belief in worship, observance, practice and teaching encompasses a broad range of acts,"[67] which easily can include many elements of proselytizing and propagating for a new religion. The American Convention explicitly states in Article 12(1) that the right to freedom of religion includes the freedom to "disseminate one's religion or beliefs".[68] Also, despite an explicit prohibition of proselytism in the Constitution of Greece,[69] in the *Kokkinakis* v. *Greece* case, the majority

65 *Ibid.*

66 Stahnke, *supra* note 17, p. 262.

67 General Comment 22, *supra* note 61, para. 4.

68 The American Convention on Human Rights, *supra* note 57.

69 Article 13(2) of the Constitution of Greece states: "All known religions shall be free and their rites of worship shall be performed unhindered and under the protection of the law. The practice of rites of worship is not allowed to offend public order or the good usages. Proselytism is prohibited." Constitution of Greece, adopted on 11 June 1975.

of the European Court of Human Rights, without giving a definition on proselytising, held that the attempt to convert non-believers was an essential part of the religious obligations of many Christians. The Court further stated that "the freedom to change religion would likely be a dead letter if the freedom to manifest religion did not include 'the right to try to convince one's neighbour'."[70]

Similar to other aspects of the manifestation of religion, states have had an open hand to impose limitations against proselytizing. Yet, according to Krishnaswami the problem of proselytizing is different from other forms of manifestations of religion as it "presents intensity and a sharpness not to be found in any of the others."[71] He adds:

> The attempt to convert individuals from one faith to another may conflict with their freedom to maintain their own religion or belief, and tends to meet with resistance not only from the individuals concerned but from group as well. And even the propagation of a message may affect the peaceful coexistence of various faiths and lead to clashes between them, either because of the contents of the message or the methods used in spreading it.[72]

'Prohibition of coercion' is a further ground for restrictions against proselytizing which is provided by Article 18(2) of the ICCPR. This article reads as follows: "No one shall be subject to coercion which would impair his freedom to have or to adopt a religion or belief of his choice."[73] Similarly, Article 1(2) of the Religion Declaration prohibits coercion: "No one shall be subject to

70 *Kokkinakis* v. *Greece*, *supra* note 22. Minos Kokkinakis was an elderly Jehovah's Witness, who was convicted of breaching the prohibition against proselytism in Greek law. The court referred to a report by the World Council of Churches to determine that proselytism was part of the 'essential mission' of all Christians and that improper proselytism was a corruption of the mission of Christians. Consequently, the majority of the court held that the attempt to convert non-believers was an essential part of the religious obligations of many Christians. See also Carolyn Evans, 'Religious Freedom in European Human Rights Law, The Search for a Guiding Conception', in Mark W. Janis & Carolyn Evans (eds.) *Religion and International Law* (Kluwer Law International, the Hague, 1999) pp. 121 & 163.

71 Arcot Krishnaswami, Special Rapporteur of the Sub-Commission on Prevention of Discrimination and Protection of Minorities, *Study of Discrimination in the Matter of Religious Rights and Practices* (United Nations publication, Sales No. 60. XIV. 2, New York, 1960) (Krishnaswami Study), p. 40.

72 *Ibid.*

73 ICCPR, *supra* note 2.

coercion which would impair his freedom to have a religion or belief of his choice."[74]

Similar to the cases of publicizing conversion, proselytizing might also include criticism or attacking the beliefs of targeted religions. As will be discussed in the following sections, if such criticism of a religion is not conducted in a proper way, it might stand against the followers of targeted religions. These acts are sometimes restricted under the regulations on offences against religions such as blasphemy laws, which give the state an open hand to limit proselytism, especially in sensitive multi-religious societies.

1.2.2. *Offences against Religion, and Religious Hatred Speech*

In connection with the phenomena of *sabb* and heresy in Muslim legal traditions of apostasy, the legitimacy of limitations on freedom of expression will be discussed in this section. Article 19(1) of the ICCPR states: "Everyone shall have the right to hold opinions without interference."[75] According to the Human Rights Committee General Comment 10: "This is a right to which the Covenant permits no exception or restriction."[76] On the other hand, every one is free to express his opinions. According to Article 19(2) of the ICCPR: "Everyone shall have the right to freedom of expression; this right shall include freedom to seek, receive and impart information and ideas of all kinds, regardless of frontiers, either orally, in writing or in print, in the form of art, or through any other media of his choice."[77]

Unlike freedom of opinion, freedom of expression is subject to responsibilities and duties and therefore subject to limitations. According to Article 19(3) of the ICCPR: "The exercise of the rights provided for in paragraph 2 of this article carries with it special duties and responsibilities. It may therefore be subject to certain restrictions."[78] According to the same article these limitations, however, "shall only be such as are provided for by law and are necessary: (a) For the respect of the rights or reputations of others; (b) For the protection of national security or public order (order public), or of public

74 The Religion Declaration, *supra* note 3.

75 ICCPR, *supra* note 2.

76 Human Rights Committee, General Comment 10, Article 19 (Nineteenth session, 1983), Compilation of General Comments and General Recommendations Adopted by Human Rights Treaty Bodies, U.N.Doc.HRI/GEN/1/Rev.6 at 132 (2003).

77 ICCPR, *supra* note 2.

78 *Ibid.*

health or morals."[79] There is a similar limitation clause for freedom of expression in Article 13(2) of American Convention on Human Rights[80] and Article 10(2) of the European Convention on Human Rights.[81] In a comparison with Article 19(2) of the ICCPR the limitation clause in Article 10(2) of the European Convention provides more grounds for limitations on freedom of expression:

> The exercise of these freedoms, since it carries with it duties and responsibilities, may be subject to such formalities, conditions, restrictions or penalties as are prescribed by law and are necessary in a democratic society, in the interests of national security, territorial integrity or public safety, for the prevention of disorder or crime, for the protection of health or morals, for the protection of the reputation or rights of others, for preventing the disclosure of information received in confidence, or for maintaining the authority and impartiality of the judiciary.[82]

It is a common policy among the majority of states to pass legislation on insulting religions and religious feelings. Some Muslim states have incorporated such restricting measures either in their Press Code and/or Penal Code. As an example from a Muslim state, Article 160(3) of the Penal Code of Algeria provides penalties for those who deface, destroy or profane any places of worship whatsoever, and Article 160(4) provides penalties for those who mutilate, destroy or defile "monuments, statues, pictures or other objects that may be used for the purposes of religious worship." Likewise, Article 77 of the Act of 3 April 1990 on information provides penalties for anyone who, in writing, or by sounds, images, drawings or any other direct or indirect means, offends against Islam and the other celestial religions.[83]

Religious related limitations against freedom of expression in some European states are found in laws against blasphemy or insulting religion.[84] As an example, Austrian law reads as follows:

---

79 *Ibid.*

80 The American Convention on Human Rights, *supra* note 57.

81 ECHR, *supra* note 56.

82 *Ibid.*

83 Human Rights Committee: Consideration of Reports Submitted by States Parties, Second periodic report (Algeria), para. 160, U.N.Doc.CCPR.C.101.Add.1 (18 May 1998). The legislation of Iran and Pakistan will be discussed in section 3.1 of this book. For another example see Article 103 of 1990 Yemen Law on the Press and Publications, Law No 25, signed in Dec. 1990.

84 Such laws still exist in legislation of several Western countries, such as in Austria (Articles 188, 189 of the criminal code), Finland (Section 10 of Chapter 17 of the penal code), Germany (Article 166 of the criminal code), Ireland (Article 40/6.1.i of the Constitution), The

> Whoever, in circumstances where his behaviour is likely to arouse justified indignation, disparages or insults a person who, or an object which, is an object of veneration of a church or religious community established within the country, or a dogma, a lawful custom or a lawful institution of such a church or religious community, shall be liable to a prison sentence of up to six months or a fine of up to 360 daily rates.[85]

The following definition of blasphemous libel in the UK was given by the trial judge in the case of *Whitehouse* v. *Lemon* (The Gay News case), "Blasphemous libel is committed if there is published any writing concerning God or Christ, the Christian religion, the Bible, or some sacred subject, using words which are scurrilous, abusive or offensive and which tend to vilify the Christian religion (and therefore have a tendency to lead to a breach of the peace).[86]

While the Austrian blasphemy law criminalizes insulting against all recognized religions, in the United Kingdom, as well as in some other Western and Muslim countries,[87] the subject of blasphemy law is only insulting the dominant religion. The European Commission has stated that the "main purpose" of the English common law offence of blasphemous libel is "to protect the rights of citizens not to be offended in their religious feelings."[88] However, the *Rushdie* case supported an opposite view. Members of the Muslim community in Britain referred the case of *Rushdie* to court in order to complain about the blasphemies in the Satanic Verses. The complaint was dismissed for the reason that the protection provided by English blasphemy law is only to the Church of England, and in some respects to Christianity as a whole.[89] The European Court of Human Rights also refused the case, saying that there was no positive obligation for the UK to protect Muslims from blasphemy.[90]

Netherlands (Article 147 of the criminal code), Spain (Article 525 of the criminal code). Yet, there has been a tendency in Western countries towards the repeal or reform of blasphemy laws, and these laws are only infrequently enforced where they exist.

85 Section 188 of Austrian Penal Code, reprinted in Otto-Preminger, 295 Eur. Ct. H.R. (Ser. A) at 12.

86 *R.* v. *Lemon, R.* v. *Gay News Ltd.* Central Criminal Court, 11 July 1977 (transcript, p. 9), quoted in Great Britain, Law Commission, *Offences against Religion and Public Worship* (London: H.M.S.O., 1981), pp. 2–3.

87 For Muslim countries see section 3.1 of this book.

88 *Gay News Ltd.* v. *United Kingdom*, 5 Eur. H.R. Rep. 123, P11 (1983) (Commission report).

89 *R.* v. *Chief Metropolitan Stipendairy Magistrate, ex parte Choudhury*, 1 All E.R. 306 (Q.B. 1991). Also *quoted in* Wingrove v. United Kingdom, 24 EHRR (1997) 1, para. 28.

90 The European Commission determined that the protection provided by English blasphemy law only to Christianity, was not discrimination on the grounds of religion in violation

Similarly, blasphemy law in Massachusetts only addresses Christianity. Section 36 of Chapter 272 of the Massachusetts General Laws reads as follows:

> Whoever wilfully blasphemes the holy name of God by denying, cursing or contumeliously reproaching God, his creation, government or final judging of the world, or by cursing or contumeliously reproaching Jesus Christ or the Holy Ghost, or by cursing or contumeliously reproaching or exposing to contempt and ridicule, the holy word of God contained in the holy scriptures shall be punished by imprisonment in jail for not more than one year or by a fine of not more than three hundred dollars, and may also be bound to good behaviour.[91]

Article 20 of the ICCPR introduces a new area for limitations against freedom of expression. It also obliges states to adopt legislative measures against such expressions. The article reads as follows: "1. Any propaganda for war shall be prohibited by law. 2. Any advocacy of national, racial or religious hatred that constitutes incitement to discrimination, hostility or violence shall be prohibited by law."[92]

In the ECHR there is no article similar to Article 20 of the ICCPR, but Article 13(5) of American Convention on Human Rights is equivalent to it. Article 13(5) of the American Convention reads as follows: "Any propaganda for war and any advocacy of national, racial, or religious hatred that constitute incitements to lawless violence or to any other similar action against any person or group of persons on any grounds including those of race, colour, religion, language, or national origin shall be considered as offences punishable by law."[93] However, "while Article 13(5) requires the prohibition of advocacy that constitutes incitement to violence, Article 20 of the ICCPR requires the much broader prohibition of advocacy that constitutes incitement to discrimination, hostility or violence."[94] Nevertheless the American Convention

---

of Art. 14 of the European Convention. See *Choudhury* v. *U. Kappliction* No. 17439/1990 reprinted in 12 Hum. R.L.J. 172–73 (1991).

91 Wikipedia, The Free Encyclopaedia, available at: <http://www.reference.com/browse/wiki/Blasphemy>.

92 ICCPR, *supra* note 2.

93 The American Convention on Human Rights, *supra* note 57.

94 Jonna Oyediran, 'Article 13(5) of the American Convention on Human Rights', in Sandra Coliver (ed.) *Striking a Balance: Hate Speech, Freedom of Expression and Non- discrimination, Article 19* (London and Human Rights Centre, University of Essex, 1992), p. 33.

offers protection to a broader range of groups than Article 20, as indicated in Article 13(5), which states, "the enumerated grounds for protection are illustrative only."[95]

Finally it should be noted that despite the earlier drafts of the Religion Declaration, it contains no similar article to that of Article 20(2) of the ICCPR on religious hatred, as Boyle states:

> Although the 1981 [Religion] Declaration couples intolerance with discrimination in its title, it is primarily concerned with the question of discrimination. Thus it has no clause equivalent to Article 4 of the ICERD Convention [Convention on the Elimination of All Forms of Racial Discrimination][96] on incitement to religious discrimination or hatred, although in other respects it follows the structure of that treaty. The draft Convention and early drafts prepared by the Sub-commission of what became the 1981 [Religion] Declaration did have an anti-incitement clause.[97]

---

95 *Ibid.*

96 Convention on the Elimination of All Forms of Racial Discrimination (ICERD), G.A. res. 2106 (XX), Annex, 20 U.N. GAOR Supp. (No. 14) at 47, U.N.Doc.A/6014 (1966), 660 U.N.T.S. 195, entered into force, 4 Jan. 1969. Article 4 of the Convention reads as follows: "States Parties condemn all propaganda and all organizations which are based on ideas or theories of superiority of one race or group of persons of one colour or ethnic origin, or which attempt to justify or promote racial hatred and discrimination in any form, and undertake to adopt immediate and positive measures designed to eradicate all incitement to, or acts of, such discrimination and, to this end, with due regard to the principles embodied in the Universal Declaration of Human Rights and the rights expressly set forth in Article 5 of this Convention, inter alia:

(a) Shall declare an offence punishable by law all dissemination of ideas based on racial superiority or hatred, incitement to racial discrimination, as well as all acts of violence or incitement to such acts against any race or group of persons of another colour or ethnic origin, and also the provision of any assistance to racist activities, including the financing thereof;

(b) Shall declare illegal and prohibit organizations, and also organized and all other propaganda activities, which promote and incite racial discrimination, and shall recognize participation in such organizations or activities as an offence punishable by law;

(c) Shall not permit public authorities or public institutions, national or local, to promote or incite racial discrimination."

97 Kevin Boyle, 'Religious Intolerance and the Incitement of Hatred', in Coliver, *supra* note 94, p. 64. For further information on the issue of religious hatred speech on Draft Convention and Draft Declaration see Boyle, *ibid.*, pp. 64–65.

The main purpose of Article 20(1) is protection of peace worldwide.[98] Article 20(2) has another major purpose equivalent to Article 4 of the ICERD, which is protection of vulnerable 'others' to live free from fear. In this sense, it is similar to the purposes of provisions of other international and regional instruments on protection of vulnerable peoples, for which affirmative measures have to be undertaken. These purposes are different from 'rights of others' or 'public order' under Article 19(3) of the ICCPR, or other limitation clauses in international and regional instruments.

However, according to Boyle, "while this obligation [in the Article 20] should constitute an adequate international guarantee, comments made by [the Human Rights] Committee members suggest that many countries do not appear to take their obligations under Article 20 seriously."[99] In other words, those states which have not resorted to affirmative measures against religious hatred will continue to be in breach of their international obligations under Article 20(2).

Finally, there are many more circumstances under Articles 19(3) and Article 20 of the ICCPR in which freedom of expression can be circumscribed than there are under the limitations against freedom of religion under Article 18(3) of the ICCPR.[100] However, when freedom of religion overlaps with freedom of expression, those restrictions against the latter might encroach upon the former. In this sense, the provision of Article 20 is reiterated in the Human Rights Committee General Comment 22 on freedom of religion: "In accordance with Article 20, no manifestation of religion or belief may amount to propaganda for war or advocacy of national, racial or religious hatred that constitutes incitement to discrimination, hostility or violence."[101]

Criticizing a Religion

Criticizing a religion or part of its elements should be respected in a democratic society. Yet, such criticism, if it is not conducted in a proper way, might face some limitations under Article 19(3). Furthermore, if such criticism includes elements of hate speech or violence, such expression should be prohibited under Article 20 of the ICCPR.

---

98 Also see Michael Kearney, *Freedom from Fear: Prohibition of Propaganda for War in International law* (PhD dissertation, Irish Centre for Human Rights – National University of Ireland, Galway, defended in April 2006, Forthcoming, Oxford University Press).

99 Boyle, *supra* note 97, p. 65.

100 ICCPR, *supra* note 2.

101 General Comment No. 22, *supra* note 61, para. 7.

An important relevant issue that will be discussed in chapter 5 in more detail under the subject of heresy is that blasphemy law might be used as a pretext to limit criticism against religion or restrict other religious opinions different from the orthodox version of the religion. Krishnaswami states:

> Unfortunately, in some cases the laws against blasphemy have been framed in such a manner that they characterize any pronouncement not in conformity with the predominant faith as blasphemous. [They] have sometimes been used to limit unduly – or even to prohibit altogether – the dissemination of beliefs other than those of the predominant religion or philosophy.[102]

In fact the distinction between a legal and illegal expression against a religion is not the substantive question, but rather the manner in which the expression is presented. According to the English court in the *Wingrove* v. *United Kingdom* case, which was confirmed by the European Court of Human Rights,[103] the distinction between an illegal blasphemy act and legal criticism against a religion is the manner the criticism is presented and not the substances of a criticism. The European Court held: "It is not blasphemous to speak or publish opinions hostile to the Christian religion, or to deny the existence of God, if the publication is couched in decent and temperate language. The test to be applied is as to the manner in which the doctrines are advocated and not to the substance of the doctrines themselves."[104]

In another case, in which the Austrian law was applied to seize a film entitled '*Das Liebeskonzil*' (Council in Heaven),[105] the court stated that followers of a religion cannot be exempted from general criticism of others:

> Those who choose to exercise the freedom to manifest their religion, irrespective of whether they do so as members of a religious majority or a minority, cannot reasonably expect to be exempt from all criticism. They must tolerate and accept the denial of their religious beliefs by others and even the propagation of doctrines hostile to their faith.[106]

---

102 Krishnaswami Study, *supra* note 71, p. 35.

103 24 Eur. H.R. Rep. 1 (1996).

104 *Ibid.*, at 14 (emphasis added) (quoting Art. 214 of Stephen's Digest of the Criminal Law (9th ed. 1950).

105 See Otto-Preminger, 295 Eur. Ct. H.R. (Ser. A) at 8–9. According to the report of the case, the film was based on a play written by Oskar Panizza that was published in 1894. Panizza was later imprisoned by a German court for 'crimes against religion', and the play was banned in Germany. *Ibid.*, at 11.

106 *Ibid.*, at 28.

Similarly, the view point of the United States Supreme Court in *United States* v. *Ballard* represented a valuable insight, that contents of a religion or an individual's beliefs cannot be considered as a ground for referring them to trial:[107]

> Men may believe what they cannot prove. They may not be put to the proof of their religious doctrines or beliefs. Religious experiences which are as real as life to some may be incomprehensible to others. Yet the fact that they may be beyond the ken of mortals does not mean that they can be made suspect before the law. Many take their gospel from the New Testament. But it would hardly be supposed that they could be tried before a jury charged with the duty of determining whether those teachings contained false representations. The miracles of the New Testament, the Divinity of Christ, life after death, the power of prayer are deep in the religious convictions of many. If one could be sent to jail because a jury in a hostile environment found those teachings false, little indeed would be left of religious freedom. The Fathers of the Constitution were not unaware of the varied and extreme views of religious sects, of the violence of disagreement among them, and of the lack of any one religious creed on which all men would agree. They fashioned a charter of government which envisaged the widest possible tolerance of conflicting views. The religious views espoused by [the movement's leaders] might seem incredible, if not preposterous, to most people. But if those doctrines are subject to trial before a jury charged with finding their truth or falsity, then the same can be done with the religious beliefs of any sect. When the tiers of fact undertake that task, they enter a forbidden domain.[108]

In *Das Liebeskonzil*, the court pointed out how criticism of a religion might interfere with an adherent's right to freedom of religion: "Indeed, in extreme cases the effect of particular methods of opposing or denying religious beliefs

107 322 U.S. 78 (1944), at 79. In that case, the leaders of a religious movement called 'I Am' were charged with selling literature and soliciting funds and memberships "by means of false and fraudulent representations, pretences and promises". The Supreme Court was faced with the issue of whether the trial court was correct to withhold from the jury any question as to the truth of the asserted religious beliefs and limit the jury question to whether the movement's leaders "honestly and in good faith believed" those beliefs. The Court upheld the trial court's decision on the grounds that the First Amendment precludes courts from deciding the truth or falsity of religious doctrines and beliefs.

108 *Ibid.*, at 86–87.

can be such as to inhibit those who hold such beliefs from exercising their freedom to hold and express them."[109]

The court further stated that the duties and responsibilities of those who are expressing their opinions on religious matters, are to avoid expressions that are gratuitously offensive to others and therefore do not contribute to any form of public debate:

> Whoever exercises the rights and freedoms enshrined in the first paragraph of that article undertakes 'duties and responsibilities'. Amongst them – in the context of religious opinions and beliefs – may legitimately be included an obligation to avoid as far as possible expressions that are gratuitously offensive to others and thus an infringement of their rights, and which therefore do not contribute to any form of public debate capable of furthering progress in human affairs.[110]

1.3. SUMMARY

In this chapter the three different phenomena of Muslim legal traditions of apostasy, conversion, blasphemy and heresy, along with the relevant human rights standards, have been discussed in detail. Firstly, with regard to conversion it should be noted that despite what was mentioned on the logic of considering conversion as an offence in earlier Muslim history, in later criminalizing the conversion, the factor of 'intent' has been neglected by the majority of Muslim jurists. Accordingly, whether the conversion has taken place as a search for truth or as hostile to the community, it was considered a crime, liable to punishment. Not only was conversion from Islam considered an offence according to traditional Muslim law, as will be discussed later, it was also part of the *Dhimmah* conditions that non-Muslims were not allowed to propagate their religions among Muslims.[111]

Under Article 18 of both the UDHR and the ICCPR, changing one's religion when it does not contain elements of manifestation of religion is an unconditional right and subject to no restrictions. Yet, if conversion contains elements of manifestation of religion, such as propagating for the new religion or against the previous religion, such manifestations might fall under

109 *Ibid.*, at 28.
110 Otto-Preminger, 295 Eur. Ct. H.R. (ser. A) at 19.
111 On the issue of *dhimmah* conditions see section 5.1.1 of this book.

the limitation clause of not only Article 18(3) of the ICCPR on freedom of religion but also Articles 19(3) and 20 of the ICCPR on freedom of expression. Similarly, proselytizing as a kind of manifestation of religion, which is conducted mainly through expression, might fall under the same limitations on freedom of religion and expression.

States can resort to legitimate restrictions against manifestations of religion, among which restrictions against some special kinds of proselytizing in sensitive multi-religious communities seems logical. In these societies, the activities of foreign missionaries in particular may remain under control. However, as reiterated in the General Comment 22, when imposing any limitation on human rights, the three principles of non-discrimination, proportionality and legality have to be considered by states.

While in the Koran there is no verse prescribing punishment for conversion, according to traditional Muslim law, the death penalty for males and life imprisonment for females converts are imposed under certain conditions. Considering modern standards of human rights, even if the conversion is conducted as a hostile act towards the community, prescribing the death penalty for such an offence is not justifiable.[112]

Also, whether a penalty is imposed on an apostate or not, the act of apostasy automatically leads to some civil and family law consequences, such as dissolving the marriage of the apostate, depriving him or her of the custody of his or her children and confiscation of his or her property. Imposing the legal consequences of apostasy is a violation of the fundamental rights of the apostate, such as the right to property, right to inherit, right to family and right to custody of children. Furthermore, as changing a religion in theory causes a change in the applicable religious personal law, in cases of conflict of religious laws between the new religious law and the Muslim law, the latter prevails, which can be discriminatory against the convert.

Secondly, *sabb* means insulting, and in Muslim legal traditions the offence of insulting God and the Prophet are called *sabb-Allah* and *sabb-al Rasul* (*sabb- al Nabi*) respectively. Insulting religious sacred things is one of the major sources of violence in sensitive multi-religious communities. While the religious sensibilities of the dominant religion are an issue of public order and of more concern for the governments, similar provisions for insulting

112 According to Article 6.2 of the ICCPR: "In countries which have not abolished the death penalty, sentence of death may be imposed only for the most serious crimes." ICCPR, *supra* note 2.

the religious feelings of followers of minority religions and beliefs are also required. For Muslims, insulting other religions and beliefs has been explicitly prohibited in the Koran.

The distinction between an illegal blasphemy act and a legal criticism of a religion is the manner in which the criticism is presented, and not the substance of the criticism. Criticizing a religion or part of its elements should be respected in a democratic society. Yet such criticism, if it is not conducted in a proper way, might face some limitations under Article 19(3) of the ICCPR. Furthermore if such criticism includes elements of hate speech or violence, such expression should be prohibited, as according to Article 20 of the ICCPR, states are obliged to adopt legislation against advocacy of religious hatred that might be conducted against individuals or a religious group as a whole.

Among the three phenomena of apostasy, only prohibition and punishment of *sabb* can be justifiable under modern human rights standards. However, imposing the death penalty and legal consequence of apostasy for the offender of *sabb*, as discussed above, is in conflict with international human rights law.

On the other hand, according to Muslim jurists, insult is a matter of relativism and the customs (*urf*) of each society are the criterion for recognizing the offence. Therefore as the act of insult might be comprehended differently in different times and places and in accordance with different views, the necessity for a jury to realize the offence of blasphemy or *sabb* is evident. A case of *sabb*, according to traditional Muslim law, can be recognized by an ordinary, reasonable person and not necessarily by a *mufti* or *mujtahid*. Therefore, in the cases of *sabb*, the jury should not, as suggested by an Iranian lawyer, consist of religious jurists,[113] but as prescribed in Iranian Press Code, consist of representatives of ordinary people.[114]

---

113 While according to Muslim legal traditions insulting can be recognized by ordinary people, the well-known Iranian lawyer Seyed Mohammad Seyfzaadeh, in some cases has enquired the opinion of some grand *mujtahids* in recognizing the offence. See for example, Seyed Mohammad Seyfzaadeh, 'Rereading the Case of Samiei-nezad' in Persian, available at Roozonline Electronic Daily at: <http://roozonline.com/02article/010301.shtml>. Also for the trial of Neshat Daily against two well-know journalists, Emadeddin Baghi and Latif Safari see the interview by the lawyer in Persian, available at the website of Shargh Daily, at <http://www.sharghnewspaper.com/831220/html/online.htm#s198606>.

114 Ratified on 19 March 1986 and is in force since 31 Jan. 1987, available at the website of Embassy of Iran in Hungary at: <http://www.iranembassy.hu/political_press.html>, and the website of Autopars at: <http://www.autopars.com/state/l_press.htm>.

Finally, the ambiguous concept of heresy in Muslim legal traditions is a matter of investigating beliefs and opinions. This concept is also linked to the concept of conversion and the same punishment is applied for both. Yet, while a convert formally renounces Islam, a heretic is a Muslim who is accused of unbelief on grounds of his or her opinion being different from that of the majority or orthodoxy. Criminalizing heresy is even worse than criminalizing conversion, as the freedom of opinion of the accused would be at stake as well as his or her freedom of conscience. Freedom to hold an opinion which is guaranteed under Article 19 of the ICCPR is an unconditional right to which the Covenant permits no limitation or restriction. There is no need to say that the duty of the state is to determine the existence of fraud or misrepresentation by an individual or religious group. The state is not in the position of determining the truth or falsity of religious beliefs. The state should recognize offences and not investigate beliefs and opinions.

Among all aspects of the three phenomena of apostasy in Muslim legal traditions the major problematic issue which is linked to heresy is *takfir*, or declaring other Muslim individuals or religious groups to be infidel. *Takfir* has had a destructive impact on freedom of religion, opinion and expression in Muslim societies and arbitrary *takfir* has been the main source of intra-religious violence within Muslim communities, the best examples of which is mass killings of innocent people in Algeria, Iraq and other Muslim countries by militant extremist groups. *Takfir* in fact legitimizes murder against those who exercise freedom of opinion. It not only should be prohibited but also should be considered a criminal act subject to punishment. One ground for such legislative measures against the practice of *takfir* is Article 20(2) of the ICCPR, according to which *takfir* can be considered as a clear example of religious hatred speech.

CHAPTER TWO

Current Application of Traditional Rules of Conversion and Proselytizing

2.1. Legislation on Conversion

National legislation of all Muslim and non-Muslim states generally permits citizens to change one's religion. This fact was acknowledged by the UN Special Rapporteur of the Sub-Commission on Prevention of Discrimination and Protection of Minorities, Francesco Capotorti, who stated that "almost in all countries surveyed, including those in which a religion has been declared the state religion, the Constitution or the law proclaims the principle of freedom of religion and generally guarantees to everyone the freedom to change his religion or belief."[115]

Nigeria, despite its multi-religious population, is the only Muslim state whose Constitution explicitly provides for freedom of conversion. Article 38(1) of the Nigerian Constitution reads as follows: "Every person shall be entitled to freedom of thought, conscience and religion, including freedom to change his religion or belief, and freedom (either alone or in community with others, and in public or in private) to manifest and propagate his religion or belief in worship, teaching, practice and observance."[116]

On the other hand, the Sudan Penal Code of 1991 prescribes the death penalty for an offence related to conversion. Article 126(1) of the Sudan Penal Code, categorized under *hudood* offences,[117] interestingly does not prohibit any of the three phenomena of apostasy described in the preceding chapter, but proscribes declaring one's own conversion and advocating others to renounce Islam as a criminal offence. It reads as follows: "Every Muslim who advocates

---

115 Francesco Capotorti, Special Rapporteur of the Sub-commission on Prevention of Discriminating and Protection of Minorities, *Study on the Rights of Persons Belonging to Ethnic, Religious and Linguistic Minorities* (Centre for Human Rights, Geneva, United Nations, New York, 1991), p. 72.

116 Constitution of the Federal Republic of Nigeria, 1999.

117 According to the Muslim traditional penal code crimes classified under *hudood* are the most severe of crimes, such as murder, theft, and adultery. See Introduction of this book, footnote 26.

the renunciation of the creed of Islam, or who publicly declares his renouncement thereof by an express statement or conclusive act, shall be deemed to commit the offence of apostasy".[118]

According to Article 126(2), a form of repent opportunity is provided whereby "whoever commits apostasy shall be given a chance to repent during a period to be determined by the court". However, where a person accused of an offence of apostasy persists in his or her offence, and "is not a recent convert to Islam", the accused will be sentenced to death.[119] As the offence mentioned in Article 126(1) is not equivalent to apostasy, it is not clear of what the accused should repent. Further, unlike traditional Muslim law that allows three days for repent, this law leaves it to the court to decide the length of the period. The concept of "recent convert" is also not clear in the legal traditions. Furthermore, while the death penalty is applied only for males in traditional Muslim law, Article 126(2) does not distinguish between males and females. The only similarity to the traditions of apostasy is where, according to the Sudanese Penal Code, the death penalty "shall be remitted whenever the apostate recants his apostasy before execution."[120]

Along with the Sudan Penal Code there is other legislation in some Malaysian states which incorporate some forms of punishments against alleged converts. These laws are not in compliance with Muslim legal traditions either. According to section 201 of the Administration of Islamic Religious Affairs (Trengganu)[121] Enactment 1986, expressing renouncement of Islam is an offence, but with a lesser punishment than provided under Sudanese legislation. This section describes that a Muslim who says he is no longer a Muslim treats the religion with contempt, which is punishable by a fine not exceeding RM3000 or imprisonment not exceeding one year, or both.[122]

Also according to the legislation in some other Malaysian states, a form of detention, known under the title of 'rehabilitation period', is provided for converts:

---

118 Abdelfattah Amor, Special Rapporteur of the Commission on Human Rights, Implementation of the Declaration on the Elimination of All Forms of Intolerance and Discrimination Based on Religion or Belief, Interim Report Relating to Visit to the Sudan, para. 20, U.N.Doc.A/51/542/Add.2, (11 Nov. 1996) (hereinafter Abdelfattah Amor, Visit to Sudan).

119 *Ibid.*

120 *Ibid.*

121 Trengganu is a Malaysian state.

122 Quoted in Saeed, *supra* note 25, p. 147.

> Under the *Syariah* [*Shariah*] Offences (Malacca) Enactment 1991, if a Muslim admits that he has left the religion of Islam or declares himself a non-Muslim, and the court is satisfied that he has indeed done something that can be interpreted as an attempt to change his religion, the court should order him to be detained in the Islamic Faith Rehabilitation Centre for a period not exceeding six months. He will be required to undergo a course of education and asked to repent.[123]

2.2. LEGISLATION ON PROSELYTIZING

Laws or policies against proselytizing are not necessarily an issue of traditional Muslim law, or even solely a phenomenon in Muslim states. In fact such policies are followed in countries with religious sensibilities. For example Article 13(2) of the Constitution of Greece reads as follows:

> All known religions shall be free and their rites of worship shall be performed unhindered and under the protection of the law. The practice of rites of worship is not allowed to offend public order or the good usages. Proselytism is prohibited.[124]

Similarly Article 19(1) of the Constitution of Nepal states that: "Every person shall have the freedom to profess and practise his own religion as handed down to him from ancient times having due regard to traditional practices; provided that no person shall be entitled to convert another person from one religion to another."[125] Also in India, the two Indian states of Orissa and Madhya Pradesh criminalize the conversion of a person to another religion under certain circumstances.[126]

---

123 *Ibid.*, pp. 139–140. Also according to Saeed: "Identical provisions are found in several other state laws including the Council of the Religion of Islam and Malay Custom (Kelantan) Enactment, 1994, Section 102(3) and the *Syariah* [*Shariah*] Criminal Offences (Sabah) Enactment 1995, Section 63(1). These two enactments allow detention for up to 36 months." *Ibid.*

124 Constitution of Greece, *supra* note 69.

125 Constitution of the Kingdom of Nepal, 1990. Apparently, citizens are no longer prohibited from changing their religion by virtue of their own free will, as a law penalizing self-conversion was repealed in 1992. See Stahnke, *supra* note 17, p. 281.

126 The relevant section of the Orissa Freedom of Religion Act 2 of 1968 provides: "No person shall convert or attempt to convert, either directly or otherwise, any person from one religious faith to another by the use of force or by inducement or by any fraudulent means nor shall any person abet any such conversion." Quoted in Stahnke, *supra* note 17, p. 317.

Malaysia is the only Muslim state where the Constitution includes a provision restricting proselytizing. According to Article 11(1) of the Constitution of Malaysia, "every person has the right to profess and practice his religion and, subject to clause (4), to propagate it."[127] Clause (4) of Article 11 reads as follows: "State law and in respect of the Federal Territories of Kuala Lumpur and Lubuan, federal law may control or restrict the propagation of any religious doctrine or belief among persons professing the religion of Islam."[128] This limitation clause is additional or explanatory to clause (5) of Article 11, which, similar to other international and national legislation, introduces general limitations against the freedom of professing and practicing religion on grounds of public order, moral values and freedom of others. This clause reads as follows: "This article does not authorize any act contrary to any general law relating to public order, public health or morality."[129]

Pursuant to the provision of the Constitution of Malaysia, states governments as well as the federal government have enacted laws prohibiting the propagation of non-Muslim doctrines among Muslims.[130] Saeed notes that such laws create "an offence to persuade, influence or incite a Muslim to be a follower or a member of another religion,[131] to subject a Muslim under the age of eighteen to the influence of a non-Islamic religion,[132] and to send or

---

127 Constitution of Malaysia, 31 Aug. 1957, amended 16 Sept. 1963.

128 *Ibid.*

129 *Ibid.*

130 See for instance, Control and Restriction (The Propagation of Non-Islamic Religions among Muslims) (Negeri Sembilan) Bill, 1991; Non-Islamic Religions (Control of Propagations among Muslims) (Selangor) Enactment 1988; Control and Restriction of the Propagation of Non-Islamic Religions to Muslims (Malacca) Enactment 1998; Control and Restriction of the Propagation of Non-Islamic Religions (Kelantan) Enactment 1981, quoted in Saeed, *supra* note 25, p. 126.

131 Section 4, Control and Restriction (The Propagation of Non-Islamic Religions among Muslims) (Negeri Sembilan) Bill, 1991; Section 4, Non-Islamic Religions (Control of Propagations among Muslims) (Selangor) Enactment 1988; Section 4, Control and Restriction of the Propagation of Non-Islamic Religions to Muslims (Malacca) Enactment 1998; Section 4, Control and Restriction of the Propagation of Non-Islamic Religions (Kelantan) Enactment 1981.

132 Section 5, Control and Restriction (The Propagation of Non-Islamic Religions among Muslims) (Negeri Sembilan) Bill, 1991; Section 5, Non-Islamic Religions (Control of Propagations among Muslims) (Selangor) Enactment 1988; Section 5, Control and Restriction of the Propagation of Non-Islamic Religions to Muslims (Malacca) Enactment 1998; Section 5, Control and Restriction of the Propagation of Non-Islamic Religions (Kelantan) Enactment 1981.

deliver publications concerning non-Islamic religions to a Muslim,[133] especially in a public place."[134]

A similar provision against proselytizing activities targeting Muslims exists in Article 220 of the Morocco Criminal Code.[135] Indonesia, a country with a multi-religious population, has also passed legislation on restricting proselytizing. Such restrictions are against proselytizing activities targeting not only Muslims, but followers of other recognized religions, especially the dominant religion. For example "a joint decree issued by the Ministries of Religion and Home Affairs in 1979 remains in effect, which prohibits members of one religion from trying to convert members of other faiths, including through bribes, persuasion, or distribution of religious materials."[136]

In other states, restrictions might be imposed on activities of a particular religious group. Stahnke observes that:

> [Such restrictions] may accompany, or be an intended consequence of a ban on the existence or limitations on the activities of that group in its organizational form. Examples of this type of restriction have included the Ahmadies in Pakistan, Baha'is in Iran, and Jehovah's Witnesses in Argentina, Singapore, Gabon and the Central African Republic.[137]

Among these examples, Article 298-C of the Pakistani blasphemy law is the only legislation in Muslim states on prohibition and punishment of proselytizing by a special group, in this case the Ahmadies. According to this article: "An Ahmadi who preaches or propagates his faith, or invites others to accept his faith, by words, either spoken or written, or by visible representation or

---

133 Section 7, Control and Restriction (The Propagation of Non-Islamic Religions among Muslims) (Negeri Sembilan) Bill, 1991; Section 7, Non-Islamic Religions (Control of Propagations Among Muslims) (Selangor) Enactment 1988; Section 7, Control and Restriction of the Propagation of Non-Islamic Religions to Muslims (Malacca) Enactment 1998; Section 7, Control and Restriction of the Propagation of Non-Islamic Religions (Kelantan) Enactment 1981.

134 Section 8, Control and Restriction (The Propagation of Non-Islamic Religions Among Muslims) (Negeri Sembilan) Bill, 1991; Section 8, Non-Islamic Religions (Control of Propagations Among Muslims) (Selangor) Enactment 1988; Section 8, Control and Restriction of the Propagation of Non-Islamic Religions to Muslims (Malacca) Enactment 1998; Section 8, Control and Restriction of the Propagation of Non-Islamic Religions (Kelantan) Enactment 1981. Quoted in Saeed, *supra* note 25, p. 126.

135 Human Rights Committee: Consideration of Reports Submitted by States Parties, Fifth periodic report (Morocco), para. 219, U.N.Doc.CCPR/C/MAR/2004/5, (11 May 2004).

136 U.S. Department of State, International Religious Freedom Report on Jordan, 2003.

137 Stahnke, *supra* note 17, p. 268.

in any manner whatsoever outrages the religious feelings of Muslims, shall be punished with imprisonment of either description for a term which may extend to three years and shall also be liable to fine."[138]

2.3. LEGAL CONSEQUENCES OF CONVERSION

2.3.1. *Legislation on Legal Consequences of Conversion*

As explained above, according to Muslim legal traditions two kinds of legal consequences can arise for an act of apostasy, those of civil matters and the others on family law matters.[139] However, with the exception of *Syariah* [*Shariah*] Criminal Code of Kelantan (the Kelantan Code) in Malaysia[140] which was not approved by the federal government, there is no example of civil consequences of apostasy in the legislation of Muslim states. The Kelantan Code, as will be discussed in more detail in section 4.1 regarding legislation on heresy, suggested confiscation of the property of the apostate.

With regard to family law consequences of apostasy, the issue mainly arises in case law. There are, however, provisions in the legislation of a number of Muslim states relevant to these family law consequences. While according to the legal traditions in cases of conflict of religious laws Muslim law prevails, in Egypt when changing one's religion "[i]n cases of personal status and family status, the traditions of the religion in question would apply."[141] Such a provision, though it seems non-discriminatory between different religions, does not protect the convert from undesirable family law consequences of conversion which will be imposed on him or her either by Muslim legal traditions or the traditions of the other religion in question.

The rules on the dissolution of marriage in cases of changing religion have been incorporated in the legislation of some Muslim states. "If a Muslim husband apostasies, or if a non-Muslim husband refuses to adopt Islam after his wife has done so, the marriage shall be automatically dissolved. This ruling is

---

138 *Ibid.*

139 See section 2.1.5 of this book.

140 *Syariah* [*Shariah*] Criminal Code (II) (Kelantan), Enactment 1993, Section 23(21). Quoted in M.H. Kamali, 'Islamic Law: a Critique of The *Hudood* Bill of Kelantan, Malaysia', 13 *Arab Law Quarterly* 3 (1998) available at the website of Fiqh at: <http://www.thefiqh.org/article.php/18>, visited June 2003.

141 Human Rights Committee: Summary record of the 1247th meeting (Egypt), para. 13, U.N.Doc.CCPR/C/SR.1247 (29/07/93).

held in Yemeni Civil Code Article 49."[142] Legislation in Kuwait addresses the issue in more detail in Article 143 of the Civil Code under the heading "Annulment on the Grounds of Religious Differences", which reads as follows:

> a– If the two non-Muslim spouses together convert to Islam, their marriage shall continue.
> b– If the husband only adopts Islam, if his wife is a *Kitabi* [Jew or Christian] marriage shall continue. If she is not, she shall be offered the opportunity to convert to Islam. If she accepts or becomes a *Kitabi*, they shall remain married otherwise the marriage is nullified.
> c– If the wife only adopts Islam, the husband shall be invited to the same; the marriage shall continue if he consents, and become nullified if he does not. If he lacks legal capacity, the marriage shall be dissolved forthwith if the wife has converted to Islam before consumption; if the marriage has been consummated, then the *iddat* [a specific period for Muslim woman, after divorce or the death of her husband, during which she should avoid a new marriage] has to be observed....[143]

However, according to the legislation in Pakistan, neither a marriage of a Muslim man converting from Islam, nor the marriage of a non-Muslim woman converting to Islam with his or her spouse is annulled, but the marriage of a non-Muslim man converting to Islam with his non-Muslim wife will be dissolved.[144]

The rules of inheritance between non-Muslims and Muslims are also applied differently in various countries. According to "Egyptian inheritance law, in testate succession between Muslims and non-Muslims is not allowed."[145] In Iran, the law is even more discriminatory against non-Muslims. According to Article 881(bis) of the Civil Code: "An infidel [Non-Muslim] does not inherit from a Muslim; and if there be a Muslim among the heirs of an infidel

---

142 Jamal J. Nasir, *The Islamic Law of Personal Status*, Third Edition (Kluwer Law International, the Hague, 1990), p. 134.

143 Quoted in Nasir, *Ibid.*

144 See Abdelfattah Amor, Special Rapporteur of the Commission on Human Rights, Implementation of the Declaration on the Elimination of All Forms of of Intolerance and Discrimination Based on Religion or Belief, Report Relating to Visit to Pakistan, para. 32, U.N.Doc.E/CN.4/1996/95/Add.1 (2 Jan. 1996) (hereinafter Abdelfattah Amor, Visit to Pakistan).

145 Law 73, Art. 6(1) (1947), quoted in Maurits S. Berger, 'Apostasy and Public Policy in Contemporary Egypt: An Evaluation of Recent Cases from Egypt's Highest Courts' 25 *Human Rights Quarterly* 3 (2003), p. 724.

deceased, the infidel heirs do not inherit, even if they belong to a class and degree closer to the deceased than the Muslim heir."[146] However, currently the above mentioned discriminatory article is under review.[147] Also in Malaysia and Pakistan, the discriminatory rules of religious legal traditions on inheritance have been abandoned and therefore Muslims and non-Muslims inherit from each other.

Another legal consequence of conversion may arise with respect to the right of custody and guardianship of children. In Malaysia, laws discriminate between men and women in regard to custody. Islamic family laws prohibit awarding custody "to a woman who has renounced Islam."[148] According to the Islamic Family Law (Negeri Sembilan) Enactment 1983, "[i]f the mother was disqualified from having custody [of her children], the right would pass to the maternal grandmother or maternal-great-grandmother. Only in the absence of a maternal grandmother would the father be considered for the purpose of the custody [of the children]."[149] While the right to custody of children after a certain age is submitted to the father in Malaysia, apparently, these laws do not prescribe steps for situations where a father is considered unqualified.

2.3.2. *Legal Consequences of Conversion in Practice*

As there are few reported decisions on apostasy, it is not possible to investigate the extent to which the civil or family law consequences of apostasy have been imposed on converts and other apostates in Muslim states. Berger reiterates that in Egypt "consequences are related mostly to marriage and inheritance."[150] Further, he lists some of the civil consequences in the case law of the Court

---

146 Civil Code of Iran, (trans. M.A.R. Taleghany, Fred B. Rothman & Co, U.S., 1995). For further information on inheritance of non-Muslim from Muslim in legislation of Iran see Shirin Ebadi, *History and Documentation of Human Rights in Iran* (trans. Nazila Fathi, Bibliotheca Persica Press, New York, NY, 2000).

147 An amendment to Article 881 of the Civil Code is under discussion in Iranian parliament. See the statement by Morris Motamed the representative of Assyrians in the parliament on 16 Nov. 2005, in Persian, available at Iranian Student News Agency, at: <http://www.isna.ir/Main/NewsView.aspx?ID=News-615541>.

148 Section 89(d), Islamic Family Law (Saban) Enactment 1992; Section 83(d) Islamic Family Law (Perlis), Enactment 1991; Section 83(d), Islamic Family Law (Selanagor) Enactment 1984; Section 84(d), Islamic Family Law (Johor) Enactment 1990; Section 83(d) Islamic Family Law (Negeri Sembilan) Enactment 1983; Section 83(d), Islamic Family Law (Kedah) Enactment 1979; Section 84(d), Islamic Family Law (Pahang) Enactment 1987; Section 72(d), Islamic Family Law (Malacca) Enactment 1983, quoted in Saeed, *supra* note 25, p. 145.

149 Section 81 Islamic Family Law (Negeri Sembilan) Enactment 1983, quoted in Saeed, *ibid.*

150 Berger, *supra* note 145, pp. 723–4.

of Cassation in Egypt:[151] "According to the court's opinion apostasy prevents the apostate from entering into a (new) marriage, even with a non-Muslim[152] and all blood ties with his or her children will be considered non-existent, regardless of whether the apostasy of the parent took place before or after their birth."[153]

If the civil code in a Muslim state is not amended, theoretically some family law consequences of conversion are unavoidable, as when a convert changes religion, this automatically leads to change the applicable family law. This situation is explained by Berger as follows: "Religion – and hence conversion – therefore are not private matters of the individual, but bearing significant legal consequences. Conversion does not only allow a person to take part in sermons in another church, but also implies the application of the family law of that church."[154]

On the other hand, in some Muslim countries, when religious laws conflict, Muslim law or state law, which is itself, rooted in Muslim law, prevails over other religious laws. Hence, in theory, all converts from Islam will be deprived of some of their rights, such as inheritance from Muslim relatives and dissolving of their marriage. For example, in those countries which do not recognize civil marriage, conversion, if registered officially, could result in dissolving the marriage of the converted husband, since Muslim legal traditions do not recognizes the marriage of a Muslim woman to a non-Muslim man.[155] However, where the religion or conversion is not registered in a country, such conflict of religious laws will not appear. Berger provides a list of family law consequences of conversion in Egyptian case law:[156]

> According to the related case law succession between Muslims and non-Muslims is not allowed[157] so an apostate is excluded from inheritance.[158] Also apostasy renders the marriage of the apostate null and void (*batil*),

151 Cases No. 9, Year 44, 24 Dec. 1975; No. 162, Year 62, 16 May 1995.

152 Such marriage is "considered as not concluded." Cases No. 20, Year 34, 30 Mar. 1966; No. 9, Year 44, 24 Dec. 1975; No. 162, Year 62, 16 May 1995.

153 Berger, *supra* note 145, pp. 273–4.

154 *Ibid.*, p. 273.

155 The subject of personal law autonomy regimes and the issue of conflicts of religious family laws will be discussed in more detail in Part B.

156 Cases No. 34, Year 55, 27 Nov. 1990; Nos. 475, 478, 481, Year 65, 5 Aug. 1996.

157 Law 73, Art. 6(1) (1947).

158 Cases No. 28, Year 33, 19 Jan. 1966; No. 17, Year 39, 10 Apr. 1974; No. 162, Year 62, 16 May 1995. Also Legal Ruling (*Fatwa*) Nr. 804 of 2 Dec. 1962 by the Advisory Section of the State Council and Supreme Administrative Court No. 240, Year 22, 13 May 1973.

> results in the separation (*tafriq*) of the spouses.[159] According to the Court of Cassation, an apostate should be given the opportunity to repent and return to Islam, in which case a new marriage contract and dowry are required to resume marital life.[160]

The most relevant Egyptian case is the Abu Zayd case in 1995, which will be discussed in more detail in section 4.4.2. In that case the Appeal Court in Cairo ruled that Professor Abu-Zayd was an apostate and ordered his separation from his wife but did not impose other consequences of apostasy on him. This decision was later upheld by the Supreme Court.

With regards to the issue of inheritance, it should be noted that even if the family law does not recognize the inheritance of Muslim and non-Muslims from each other, in the instance where the conversion is not registered in that country, such conflicts of law on inheritance will not be apparent. This may be the main reason why conflicts of religious family laws have not been reported from Muslim countries. There is, however, one exception, namely the Case of a Christian Widow in Egypt, in which:

> [the] Supreme Administrative Court was asked to look into the case of a Christian widow of a Christian university professor. She was considered an apostate for having previously converted to Islam and then reverted to Christianity in order to marry her husband. The fact that the civil court case had been filed by the deceased's sister gave reason to believe that it was her intention to exclude her brother's wife from the inheritance.[161]

---

159 Court of Cassation No. 20, Year 34, 30 Mar. 1966; No. 25, Year 37, 29 May 1968; Nos. 475, 478, 481, Year 65, 5 Aug. 1996; No. 25, Year 37, 29 May 1969. Also Supreme Administrative Court No. 240, Year 22, 13 May 1973, discussed by Hamad Seif al- Islam 'Legal Plurality and Legislation of Human Rights Abuses: A Case Study of State Council Ruling Concerning the Right of Apostates', in Maurits Berger & Laila Al-Zwaini (eds.) *Legal Pluralism in the Arab World* (Kluwer Law International, the Hague, 1999), pp. 225–28.

160 Berger, *supra* note 145, p. 723. There is another report of restriction on conversion in Egypt which is not necessarily an issue of Muslim legal traditions. An Egyptian Copt converted to Islam in 1953, and accordingly changed his name and his religion in his identification document. In 1974 he reversed to Christianity and requested the competent state authority to issue him new documents with his original Christian name, stating his religion as Christian. The Office replied that it was legal to change his name but not his religion since Islam does not allow its adherence to apostatize." Case 20/29, State Council, 8 April 1980,quoted in Seif al-Islam, *supra* note 159, pp. 225–28.

161 (Case No. 240, Year 22, 13 May 1973.), quoted in Berger, *supra* note 145 pp. 723–724. In this case her husband died on 1 May 1963. As widow, she received a pension from the university until 31 Dec. 1966 when the sister of the deceased presented the university with the

With regard to right to custody of children in cases of conversion a controversial case has been reported from Jordan:

> In 2002, the *Shariah* and civil court systems adjudicated a dispute concerning custody of two minors raised as Christians, whose father allegedly converted to Islam shortly before his death. The widow contends that her husband's signature on the conversion certificate is a forgery. The courts assigned legal custody to the Christian widow's brother, who is a convert to Islam. However, the children remained in the mother's physical custody pending the result of a counter suit she filed against her brother, alleging disinterest in the children and misuse of the children's trust funds. In April 2005 a court ruled in the mother's favour and assigned her legal custody of the children. In May, the widow's brother appealed against the ruling, but an appellate court rejected the petition.[162]

In general, either with regard to the civil consequences or the family law consequences, it is not clear to which extent in practice these consequences have been imposed on apostates. For example, despite the two lists provided by Berger on civil and family law consequences of apostasy in Egypt, there are only two reported cases – the case of Abu Zayd and the case of a Christian Widow – which led to dissolution of marriage and deprivation of inheritance, with none of the other listed consequences being applied.

2.3.3. *Use or Abuse of Legal Consequences of Conversion*

Considering that Muslim law prevails in cases of conflict between religious laws, the legal consequences of apostasy may become subject of use or abuse by individuals in some Muslim countries. With regard to marriage and divorce Berger states:

> Due to the impossibility under Christian laws to obtain a divorce, a woman may resort to converting to Islam to render the marriage with her

---

ruling number 36/83 of the Cairo Court of Appeal, which had upheld the ruling of the Cairo Primary Court on family affairs (Lawsuit 111/1964). The latter had ruled that the marriage was invalid since the wife was an apostate having previously converted to Islam, then reverted to Christianity. Therefore she had no right to the inheritance.

162 See U.S. Department of State, International Religious Freedom Report on Jordan, 2005, See also Abdelfattah Amor, Special Rapporteur of the Commission on Human Rights, Report Submitted on Freedom of Religion and Belief, in accordance with Commission on Human Rights resolution 2002/40, U.N.Doc.E/CN.4/2003/66 (2003).

> Christian husband void. And a Christian husband, who is faced with the same legal obstacles to divorce, may opt for conversion to Islam to obtain the right to divorce his wife by means of repudiation (*talaq*).[163]

And the following case in Malaysia indicates the ways in which the rules on legal consequences of apostasy might by abused:

> The plaintiff (wife) petitioned for divorce in the *Syariah* [*Shariah*] court of Kuala Lumpur. She subsequently filed a suit in the High Court in Kuala Lumpur against her husband, claiming damages and an injunction to restrain the defendant from assaulting, harassing or molesting her and members of her family. Apparently she believed that the *Syariah* [*Shariah*] court would not grant such remedies to a Muslim wife. [So], in an apparent attempt to avoid *Syariah* [*Shariah*] court jurisdiction, she allegedly renounced her faith.[164]

Sanasarian also refers to a case between two brothers in Iran:

> [T]wo brothers were in conflict over their inheritance from their father. One converted to Islam and married a Muslim woman, thereby winning for himself the entire inheritance. After a long court battle, [and] realizing that the Muslim brother would inherit everything, the other brother also converted, ending up with his half of the inheritance.[165]

Changing religion to benefit from marriage or divorce opportunities, however, may have problematic disadvantages. Such was the case of the Christian widow mentioned above.[166] On this regard Berger states:

> Since it is both socially and legally impossible for the [Muslim] woman to denounce Islam and adopt Christianity, it is usually the man who will convert to Islam in order to marry his fiancée. However, in the case when he merely converted to fulfil the condition for marriage, remaining truthful to his Christian faith renders him an apostate.[167]

---

163 Berger, *supra* note 145, pp. 723–724.

164 *Mohamed Habibullah Bin Mahmood* v. *Faridah Bte Dato Talib* [1992] 2 MLJ 793, quoted in Saeed, *supra* note 25, p. 147.

165 Eliz Sanasarian, *Religious Minorities in Iran* (Cambridge University Press, 2000), p. 131.

166 (Case No. 240, Year 22, 13 May 1973), *supra* note 141.

167 Berger, *supra* note 145, p. 724.

In Malaysia, federal and state laws have tried to address the issue of abusing the family law consequences by passing legislative measures. For example, the Islamic Family Law (Federal Territories) Act of 1984 has made this abuse an offence punishable by up to six months imprisonment. The Negeri Sembilan Islamic Family Law Enactment, as amended in September 1991, increased punishments for attempting dissolution of marriage through apostasy from six months imprisonment to one year's imprisonment.[168] Similarly Section 12 of the Crimes (*Syariah*) (Perak) Enactment 1992 provides that:

> Any Muslim who declares himself to be a non-Muslim so as to avoid any action being taken against him under this Enactment or any other law in force, is guilty of an offence and shall, on conviction, be liable to a fine not exceeding 1,000 Ringgit or to imprisonment for a term not exceeding three years or to both.[169]

The disadvantages of the legal consequences of conversion have been considered by Israel as a justifiable ground for limiting freedom of religion in favour of the convert's family:

> Freedom of religion may be curtailed on the grounds of pressing public interests. One example of such regulation concerns religious conversion. Each individual enjoys the right to change his or her religion. However, since such a change may affect the personal law and family law governing the neophyte, the rights of other members of the neophyte's family are given special protection.[170]

Thus, the unilateral change of one's religion will not affect the validity of his marriage and the applicable law in matters of marriage, divorce, and alimony.[171]

Legal consequences of conversion and subsequent conflicts of religious personal laws are so complicated that some countries, such as Jordan, have preferred simply not to recognize the conversion from Islam:

168 Section 130, Islamic Family Law (Amendment) (Negeri Sembilan) Enactment No. 4, 1992, quoted in Saeed, *supra* note 25, p. 145.

169 *Ibid.*, p. 147.

170 Asher Maoz, 'Religious Human Rights in the State of Israel' in John D. Van der Vyver & John Witte Jr (eds.) *Religious Human Rights in Global Perspective: Legal Perspective* (Kluwer Law International, the Hague, 1996) p. 360.

171 According to Religious Community Ordinance, 1927, quoted in Maoz *ibid.*

> The government [of Jordan] does not fully recognize the legality of such conversions. Under *Shariah* converts are regarded as apostates and legally may be denied their property and other rights; however, in practice this principle is not applied.... Converts from Islam do not fall under the jurisdiction of their new religion's laws in matters of personal status and still are considered Muslims under *Shariah*. Converts to Islam remain under the jurisdiction of the *Shariah* courts.[172]

2.4. CASE STUDIES

2.4.1. *Legislation on Conversion and Proselytizing in Practice: The Case of Malaysia*

In states where the cases of conversion are not registered, there are no statistics available on their extent. Also, no case of punishment for conversion has been reported in any Muslim states. For example, according to a report on Mauritania: "The small number of known converts from Islam suffered no social ostracism, and there were no reports of societal or governmental attempts to punish them during the period covered by this report."[173]

Malaysia is the only Muslim state, from which some informal statistics have been reported. According to a report between 1991 and 1998, 689 Malays, 425 women and 264 men, had applied to change their religion at the National Registration Department.[174] Further, according to another report between 1994 and 1997, 519 Muslims in the country applied to change their religion, while over 11,000 persons in Malaysia converted to Islam.[175]

On the other hand, administrative procedural laws regarding conversion in Malaysia make it evident that such conversions are occurring. As an example, the Administration of Islamic Law (Negeri Sembilan) Enactment 1991, as amended in 1995, provides a comprehensive procedure for renouncing Islam. Under the law, application has to be made *ex parte* before a judge of the *Syariah* [*Shariah*] High Court in open court. Upon receiving the application the judge may postpone the hearing for a period of thirty days and refer the

---

172 U.S. Department of State, International Religious Freedom Report on Jordan, 2003.

173 U.S. Department of State, International Religious Freedom Report on Mauritania, 2005.

174 Provided by Roslan Kassim, the head of the UMNO Youth Movement, Straits Times (Singapore), 19 June 1998, p. 43 (Online Lexis, 9 Dec. 2000), quoted in Saeed, *supra* note 25, p. 145.

175 Straits Times (Singapore), 17 June 1998, (Online Lexis, 9 Dec. 2000), quoted in Saeed, *supra* note 25, p. 146.

applicant to the *mufti*. It is not clear what procedure occurs subsequent to this decision, but if the judge is satisfied that it is in the interest of the applicant and Islam generally to proceed immediately, he may hear the applicant and make an order as he thinks fit. Once a person has obtained an order declaring that he or she has renounced Islam as his or her religion, he or she will then register the order with the Registrar of New Converts.[176]

Yet, apparently in practice, the relevant procedure for conversion in Malaysia, especially for a majority of ethnic Malays, is not an easy task. As already mentioned, in those countries where apostasy results in dissolving of marriage and other legal consequences, the related administrative procedure for registering the conversion is very complicated and lengthy. This is more difficult for Muslims such as Malays that bear the element of ethnicity as well. According to a report on Malaysia:

> Muslims who wish to convert from Islam face severe obstacles. For Muslims, particularly ethnic Malays, the right to leave the Islamic faith and adhere to another religion is a controversial question, and in practice it is very difficult for Muslims to change [their] religions. The legal process of conversion is unclear; in practice it is very difficult for Muslims to change their religion legally.[177]

While, according to the legal traditions, apostasy automatically dissolves a marriage, in Malaysia the dissolution must be confirmed by the *Shariah* court.[178] As a result, several state governments have also enacted laws prohibiting Muslims from renouncing Islam before obtaining a declaration from the *Shariah* court allowing such a renunciation.[179] This might have some advantages as it leaves the complicated legal and administrative measures of conversion to a particular specialist judiciary body. It prevents the abuse of

---

176 Sections 90 A(2) and 90 A(4)(a), 90 (6) and (7), Administration of Islamic Law (Negeri Sembilan) Enactment 1991, quoted in Saeed, *supra* note 25, p. 140.

177 U.S. Department of State, International Religious Freedom Report on Malaysia, 2001.

178 Section 46, Islamic Family Law (Saban) Enactment 1992; Section 46 Islamic Family Law (Perlis), Enactment 1991; Section 46, Islamic Family Law (Selanagor) Enactment 1984; Section 45, Islamic Family Law (Johor) Enactment 1990; Section 46, Islamic Family Law (Federal Territories) Act 1984; Section 46, Islamic Family Law (Negeri Sembilan) Enactment 1983; Section 39, Islamic Family Law (Kedah) Enactment 1979; Section 46, Islamic Family Law (Pahang) Enactment 1987; Section 33, Islamic Family Law (Malacca) Enactment 1983; Section 34, Islamic Family Law (Kelantan) Enactment 1987. See Saeed, *supra* note 25, p. 145.

179 Section 90 A(1), Administration of Islamic Law (Negeri Sembilan) Enactment 1991; Section 102(1), Council of the Religion of Islam and Malay Custom (Kelantan) Enactment 1994, quoted in Saeed, *supra* note 25, p. 139.

conversion and also protects individuals from arbitrary interference of others in the realm of their belief. Yet, imposing such period under the title of 'repent period' is in no way justifiable. Furthermore the question remains as to whether such a period is similarly imposed on those who are converting to Islam.

Considering the provisions of the Constitution and other legislation on restriction of proselytizing in Malaysia, the Malaysian case law does not consider all forms of proselytizing as a breach of law. For example, in the case of *Minister for Home Affairs v. Othman*[180] the petitioner, a Christian, was detained by the Minister of Home Affairs under a statute that permitted such detentions in order to prevent persons from "acting in any manner prejudicial to the security of Malaysia."[181] The Minister supported the detention on the grounds that the petitioner "was involved in a plan or programme for the dissemination of Christianity amongst Malays."[182] It was alleged that the petitioner had attended a series of meetings and seminars and had caused the conversion of six Malays to Christianity. The lower court, on a petition of habeas corpus, ruled that the detention was unlawful,[183] and the Supreme Court affirmed that decision.[184]

The Supreme Court recognized that under the Malaysian Constitution, the article protecting the right of freedom of religion "does not authorize any act contrary to any general law relating to public order, public health or morality."[185] However, the Supreme Court determined that the extent of the petitioner's activities, as alleged by the Minister, did not fall within that provision:

> We do not think that mere participation in meetings and seminars can make a person a threat to the security of the country. As regards the alleged conversion of six Malays, even if it was true, it cannot in our opinion by itself be regarded as a threat to the security of the country.... The guarantee provided by Article 11 of the Constitution, i.e. the freedom to profess and practice one's religion, must be given effect unless the actions of a person go well beyond what can normally be regarded as professing and practising one's religion.[186]

180 [1989] 1 M.L.J. 418 (Sup. Ct.).
181 *Ibid.* at 419.
182 *Ibid.* at 420. See Stahnke, *supra* note 17, p. 309.
183 The lower court decision is reported at [1989] 1 M.L.J. 368 (High Ct.).
184 Orhman, 1 M.L.J. 418, cited in Stahnke, *supra* note 17, p. 310.
185 Orhman, 1 M.L.J. 419, cited in Stahnke, *ibid.*
186 Orhman, 1 M.L.J. 420, cited in Stahnke, *ibid.*

It should be added that neither the Minister for Home Affairs nor the court has made any reference to the commitments of the state to Muslim law on the issue of proselytizing. Furthermore, based on the decision of the court, despite what might appear at the first sight, clause (4) of Article 11 of the Constitution of Malaysia by itself does not provide a new area of restriction against freedom of religion, but it is explanatory to clause (5) of Article 11, which, similar to other international and national legislation, introduces general limitations against the freedom to profess and practice religion on grounds of public order, moral values and the freedom of others.

2.4.2. *Case of Abdul Rahman in Afghanistan*

In March 2006, Abdul Rahman was charged in a lower court in Kabul with rejecting Islam. His case, however, was dismissed after he was deemed mentally unfit to stand trial. Consequently he was freed after a period of around two weeks detention. Although at no time were the prosecutor or other Afghan judiciary officials quoted as explicitly referring to the conversion as an offence or to the death sentence as its punishment, it was argued widely by the media that the accused could face the death sentence. The event, therefore, aroused much debate about the impact of so called *Shariah* law on criminal justice in Afghanistan and the issue of freedom of religion in this country.

According to the reports Abdul Rahman converted to Christianity sixteen years before in Pakistan. His problems began when he returned to Afghanistan in 2002 and tried to recover his two daughters, now aged thirteen and fourteen, who were living with his parents in Kabul. His parents refused to return them and referred the case to the police, with the complaint that their son had become violent. Rahman's father then denounced him as a convert, based on which Rahman was promptly arrested.[187]

To examine the case, a distinction should be made between the conversion as a crime in legislation of Afghanistan and the possibility of imposing the legal consequences of conversion in that country. In the new Constitution of Afghanistan several provisions are against criminalizing the conversion. According to Article 7(1): "The state shall abide by the UN charter, international treaties, international conventions that Afghanistan has signed, and the

---

187 See for example BBC at: <http://news.bbc.co.uk/2/hi/south_asia/4832872.stm>, <http://news.bbc.co.uk/2/hi/south_asia/4851666.stm>, CNN at: <http://www.cnn.com/2006/WORLD/meast/03/21/afghan.christian/index.html?section=cnn_topstories>, and Amnesty International, Public Statement, AI Index: ASA 11/008/2006 (Public), News Service No: 071, 22 March 2006, available at: <http://www.amnestyusa.org/news/document.do?id=ENGASA110082006>

Universal Declaration of Human Rights". Also according to Article 27(1) of the Constitution of Afghanistan, no act is considered a crime, unless determined by a law adopted prior to the date the offence is committed.[188]

As according to Muslim legal traditions, conversion might be considered as a *hadd* crime, a legislation that can be referred to for criminalizing conversion is Article 1 of the 1976 Penal Code, which is still in force. The article reads as follows: "This law regulates the '*tazir*' crimes and penalties. Those committing crimes of '*hudood*' and '*qisas*' and '*diat*' [blood money] shall be punished in accordance with the provisions of Islamic religious law (the Hanafi religious jurisprudence)."[189]

On the other hand, the only reference of the Constitution to Islamic law (*Shariah*) is in Article 130(2), according to which any application of Hanafi jurisprudence should be within the limits of the Constitution. The article reads as follows: "When there is no provision in the Constitution or other laws regarding ruling on an issue, the courts' decisions shall be within the limits of this Constitution in accord with the Hanafi jurisprudence and in a way to serve justice in the best possible manner."[190]

Even by ignoring the provisions of the Constitution mentioned above, some other articles of the 1976 Penal Code are contradictory to its Article 1. For example, based on Article 2, "no act shall be considered crime, but in accordance with the law".[191] Similarly Article 3 states: "No one can be punished but in accordance with the provisions of the law which has been enforced before commitment of the act under reference."[192] According to these two articles, conversion may not be considered an offence. On the other hand, despite the provisions of Article 1, other provisions of the Code, for example Chapter 8 of Section 2 on adultery, consider crimes that are in fact part of *hudood* crimes.[193]

188 Constitution of the Islamic Republic of Afghanistan, ratified 26 Jan. 2004.

189 Penal Code, issue No. 13, Section No. 347, 7 Oct. 1976, available at BBC at: <http://news.bbc.co.uk/2/hi/south_asia/4832872.stm>, and International Committee of the Red Cross at: <http://www.icrc.ch/ihlat.nsf/6fa4d35e5e3025394125673e00508143/845809a497304d8fc12571140033ac69/$FILE/Penal%20Code%20-%20Afghanistan%20-%20EN.pdf>.

190 *Ibid.*

191 *Ibid.*

192 *Ibid.*

193 *Ibid.* On the other hand, if the judge in the lower court would have imposed the death penalty, Abdul Rahman still had two avenues of appeal under Afghan law – the Provincial Court and the Supreme Court. Furthermore, according to Article 129(2) of the Constitution the death penalty has to be approved by the president.

Importantly, the part of the case that was completely ignored by observers concerned the legal consequences of the conversion. In fact, the only reason for filing the case against Abdul Rahman by his father was the dispute over the custody of the children and not Rahman's committing a crime. As apparently there is no statutory law in Afghanistan on cases of conflicts of law, the dispute over the custody of the children is the only area where Hanafi jurisprudence could be applied based on Article 130(2) of the Constitution. According to the Hanafi School, along with other Muslim schools of law, in cases of conflicts of religious laws the Muslim law prevails, where a convert from Islam is deprived of custody of his or her children.

2.5. THE STATES OFFICIAL POSITIONS

2.5.1. *Drafting of the Related International Instruments*

In the preparatory discussions of the UDHR, the main arguments of states against explicit reference to the right to change one's religion was on the grounds of preventing the abuse thereof by missionaries. Egypt, Saudi Arabia and some non Muslim states had brought forward such an argument.[194] Their concern was that this right gave too much scope to missionaries who had often been involved in the colonization of developing states. Yet, apparently only Saudi Arabia made a reference that such a right is against the tenets of Islam.[195]

Unlike Saudi Arabia, the representatives of Lebanon and Pakistan were in favour of entering a reference to the right to change one's religion in the Declaration. According to the representative of Lebanon, "there is no real freedom, if one is not free to change his mind."[196] Similarly the representative of Pakistan, quoting the Koran stated:

---

194 E.g. Saudi Arabia (in: A/C.3/SR.127, p. 3, A/C.3/SR.563, p. 106, para. 11, A/C.3/SR.2009, p. 14, para. 7, A/C.3/SR.2093, p. 14, A/C.3/SR.289, p. 115, paras. 43 and 46, A/C.3/SR.367, p. 124, para. 41, A/C.3/SR.566, p. 125, para. 34, A/C.3/SR.1021, p. 198, para. 11), Egypt (in A/PV.183, p. 913 and E/CN.4/SR.117, p. 8), Brazil (in A/C.3/SR.1023, p. 206, paras. 14–16), Costa Rica (in: A/C.3/SR.576, p. 181, para. 37) and Halpern (in: E/CN.4/Sub.2/162, p. 6, para. 11c). For the comments of Saudi Arabian delegate also see 3(1) U.N. GAOR C.3 (127th mtg) 391, 392, U.N.Doc.A/C.3/SR.127 (1948).

195 See the discussion within the Drafting Committee on an International Convention on Human Rights, (E/CN.4/AC.3/SR.5, p. 8) and (A/C.3/SR.565, p. 116, paras. 12, 13 and 15).

196 E/CN.4/AC.1/SR.3, p. 3.

> 'Let he who chooses to believe, believe, and he who choose to disbelieve, disbelieve.'[197] The Muslim... strove to persuade men to change their faith and alter their way of living, so as to follow the faith and way of living it preached, but it recognized the same right of conversion for other religions as for itself.[198]

Finally, the Saudi Arabian proposal to amend the Universal Declaration to remove the words 'freedom to change his religion or belief' was defeated twenty two to twelve with eight abstentions.[199] Among the Muslim states, Pakistan, Afghanistan, Iraq, Iran, Lebanon and Syria voted in favour of the adoption of the Declaration, while Saudi Arabia abstained, and Yemen did not participate in the vote.[200] Egypt, while voting in favour of the Declaration, made an explanatory statement.[201]

The draft ICCPR included a similar reference as the UHDR to the freedom to change one's religion or belief. In 1952, Egypt submitted an amendment not relevant to traditional Muslim law, in which, interestingly, on the one hand it emphasized on preserving the reference to the right to change one's religion in the draft, and on the other hand suggested a reference to the prohibition of coercion on ground of preventing the abusive activities of missionaries. Later on in 1960, Saudi Arabia insisted on the deletion of the reference to changing one's religion[202] which finally led to the deletion of the phrase.

Similar to the ICCPR, no reference was made to the right to change one's religion in the Religion Declaration.[203] De Jong states: "This change was agreed to only at the very end of the drafting process... after strong pressure by [some] Islamic states."[204] However, as mentioned in section 1.2.1 of this book the right to change one's religion was guaranteed in Article 8 of the Religion Declaration by reiterating the provisions of the UHDR and the International Covenants.

---

197 The Koran, 18:29.

198 A/PV.182, p. 890. Similarly, in A/C.3/SR.571, p. 152, para. 45 and A/C.3/SR.1024, p. 211. paras. 21–23.

199 U.N.Doc.A/C.3/247/Rev.1 (1948).

200 See the report of Reynaldo Galindo Pohl, Special Representative on the Situation of Human Rights in Iran, para. 42, U.N.Doc.E/CN.4/1988/24: p. 11.

201 See A/PV.183: pp. 912–913.

202 See A/4625: p. 16 para. 48 and A/C.3/L.876.

203 The Religion Declaration, *supra* note 3.

204 Cornelis D. de Jong, *The freedom of Thought, Conscience and Religion or Belief in the United Nations (1946–1992)* (School of Human Rights Research, Antwerpen: Intersentia; Oxford: Hart, c, 2000), p. 48.

With regard to the CRC, during the preparatory discussion of the treaty, inclusion of a phrase on freedom of a child to choose his or her religion was an issue of concern for some Muslim states.[205] Unlike the preparatory discussions of the previous international human rights instruments, this time the concern was introduced mainly by reference to the requirements of Muslim law. As an example, the permanent representative of Bangladesh submitted a paper to the conference according to which, "Article 7(bis) [Article 14] appears to run counter to the traditions of the major religious systems of the world and in particular to Islam... It appears to infringe upon the sanctioned practice of a child being reached in the religion of his parents."[206]

Finally, in the preparatory discussions of the Convention, no explicit reference to the right of the child to choose his or her religion was accepted for this article. Furthermore, a paragraph on respecting the rights and duties of parents in providing direction for their children's religion was included in the article.[207]

Despite the modified version of Article 14 as explained above, ten Muslim states, namely Bangladesh, Maldives, Morocco, United Arab Emirates, Brunei, Syria, Malaysia, Oman, Jordan, and Iraq, entered reservations to this article and Algeria entered a declaration on it.[208] The other three states with general reservations based on *Shariah*, i.e. Qatar, Iran and Saudi Arabia can be considered as reserving states to this article as well.[209]

However, it should be noted that among the 57 Muslim states, 44 of them are parties to the ICCPR and none of them have entered reservations to its Article 18 on freedom of religion.[210] Among reserving states to Article 14 of

---

205 For more information see Sharon Detrick, *The United Nations Convention on the Rights of the Child: A Guide to the Travaux Preparatoires* (Dordrecht, London: M. Nijhoff Publishers, 1992) pp. 238–24, David Johnson, 'Cultural and Regional Pluralism in the Drafting of the UN Convention on the Rights of the Child', in Michael Freman & Philip Veerman (eds.) *The Ideologies of Children's Rights* (Martinus Nijhoff Publishers, 1992) pp. 99–103.

206 Paper Submitted by the Permanent Representative of Bangladesh, U.N.Doc.E/CN.4/1986/39, Annex IV, at 2, quoted in Detrick, *supra* note 205, p. 244.

207 See the final version of Article 14 in section 8.4 of this book.

208 Similarly some non-Muslim states such as Poland and the Holy See have entered declarations to the effect that a child's right to freedom of religion, as defined in Article 14, shall be exercised with respect for parental authority.

209 On Muslim states and the CRC see part C of this book.

210 Thirteen Muslim states that are not signatories to the ICCPR are including Bahrain, Brunei, Comoros, Guinea-Bissau, Kazakhstan, Indonesia, Malaysia, Maldives, Oman, Pakistan, Qatar, Saudi Arabia and United Arab Emirates.

the CRC seven states, i.e. Maldives, United Arab Emirates, Brunei, Malaysia, Oman, Qatar, and Saudi Arabia, are not states parties of the ICCPR. The six other reserving states, i.e. Bangladesh, Morocco, Syria, Jordan, Iraq and Iran, despite their reservations to the CRC, are states parties to the ICCPR and therefore committed to Article 18 of that instrument.

Unlike other reserving states, Jordan and Iraq are the only states that in their reservations insist on the conflicting areas of traditional Muslim law with the provisions of the Article 14. Iraq's reservation to this article reads as follows: "The government of Iraq has seen fit to accept [the Convention]... subject to a reservation in respect to Article 14, paragraph 1, concerning the child's freedom of religion, as allowing a child to change his or her religion runs counter to the provisions of the Islamic *Shariah*."[211] Jordan, in its reservation, declares that Article 14, which "grant[s] the child the right to freedom of choice of religion" along with Articles 20 and 21, "are at variance with the precepts of the tolerant Islamic *Shariah*" and excluded itself from commitment to these three articles.[212]

2.5.2. *Implementation of the International Covenant on Civil and Political Rights and the Declaration on the Elimination of All Forms of Intolerance Based on Religion or Belief*

With respect to the implementation of Article 18 of the ICCPR, some Muslim states have reiterated their commitment to the right to choose one's religion and related activities. For example, the Malaysian government argued that prohibition on proselytism of Muslims by non-Muslims does not interfere with the ability of Muslims to change their religion:

> If any Muslim desires to seek knowledge about another religion or even to possess another religion of his own free will and on his own initiative, laws are not capable of deterring him. Those laws are merely aimed at protecting Muslims from being subjected to attempts to convert them to another religion.[213]

211 For the reservations and the Declarations to the CRC see Office of the United Nations High Commissioner for Human Rights, Ratifications and Reservations: Convention on the Rights of the Child, at <http://www.ohchr.org/english/countries/ratification/11.htm>, last updated May 8, 2006.

212 *Ibid.*

213 Abdelfattah Amor, Special Rapporteur of the Commission on Human Rights, Implementation of the Declaration on the Elimination of All Forms of Intolerance and of

Also, Kuwait, in its initial report on the implementation of the ICCPR referred to the case of conversion by a Kuwaiti citizen, Robert Kambar, as evidence of its full commitments to the freedom to change one's religion:

> Kuwait wishes to note the case of Robert Kambar, a Kuwaiti citizen who announced his apostasy from Islam. The case has had far-reaching domestic and international ramifications. However, the person concerned has not been subject to any threats from the state or from ordinary citizens. This incident serves as concrete evidence of the respect for the full freedom to adopt, observe and practice any form of religious worship in the state of Kuwait.[214]

Other Muslim states that have questioned the right to choose one's religion and the issue of proselytizing, have tried to justify their positions less by reiterating the requirements of Muslim law, and far more on the ground of protection of public order.

In one of the reports, a representative of Sudan reiterated recognition of the right to choose the religion in his country. According to the report of Abdelfattah Amor: "Turabi [a member of Sudanese delegation] and the [Sudan] Consultative Human Rights Council stated that conversion for Muslims was accepted but could not be manifested for fear of disturbing public order."[215]

In their discussions with the Human Rights Committee, the two members of the Sudanese delegation expressed interesting views on punishment of converts in Islam. First, El *Mufti* began by reiterating the importance of obeying mandatory Islamic rules by Muslims. He stated: "With regard to the Islamic punishments for apostasy and other similar offences (known as *hudood* or *qisas*), they had not been invented by the Sudanese government but were mandatory under a true interpretation of Islam, even if some Islamic countries were not applying them."[216] Still, despite his earlier views on the requirements of Islam and while in Muslim legal traditions mere conversion was liable to punishment, the Sudanese Penal Code, according to El-*Mufti*, does not punish mere conversion, but the manifestation of conversion when it

---

Discrimination Based on Religion or Belief, U.N.Doc.E/CN.4/1990/46 (1990), para. 58, cited in Stahnke, *supra* note 17, p. 285.

214 Human Rights Committee: Consideration of Reports Submitted by States Parties, Initial report (Kuwait), para. 236, U.N.Doc.CCPR/C/120/Add.1 (3 Dec. 1999).

215 Abdelfattah Amor, Visit to Sudan, *supra* note 118, para. 49.

216 Human Rights Committee: Summary record of the 1629th meeting (Sudan), para. 14, U.N.Doc.CCPR/C/SR.1629 (31 Oct. 1997).

threatens public order: "Under the Criminal Act of 1991, apostasy or the act of conversion was not punishable as such. But any manifestation of apostasy that threatened public order was punishable."[217]

Elradi, another member of the Sudanese delegation had an interesting explanation, based on his personal research on punishment of converts according to Islam. However, his findings were neither consistent with the traditional Muslim law, nor with the provisions of the Sudanese Penal Code: "A person could change his religion, provided he did so without causing a danger to the state or to the public welfare. If that line was crossed, he could be prosecuted. Thus, the offence became more like high treason, which was recognized as punishable all over the world."[218]

On the other hand, while representatives of Muslim states rarely did make explicit references to the requirements of Muslim law on the matter of changing the religion, Egypt by implicit reference to these requirements has shown reluctance regarding recognition of this right. In 2000, in its report to the Human Rights Committee, Egypt started by reiterating its stand on the right to adopt a religion or belief of one's choice according to the state's legislation:

> Every Egyptian Constitution has embodied the principle of freedom of belief and freedom of religious observance, which are established constitutional principles in every civilized country. This means that everyone has the right to adopt a religion or belief of his choice that satisfies his conscience and gives him comfort. It is not permissible for any authority to condemn him for the choice he makes based on his deepest feelings.[219]

Yet, in its further explanation, while the report first prescribed the legitimate restrictions on the practice of the religion, it then, by referring to rulings of the Supreme Court and Supreme Constitutional Court, extended the scope of the limitations to the right to have or choose a religion. Furthermore the report ignored, or seemingly, denied generally the issue of choosing other beliefs or converting to religions other than those of "recognized sacred religions". The report reads as follows:

---

217 *Ibid.*

218 *Ibid.*, para. 39.

219 Human Rights Committee: Consideration of Reports Submitted by States Parties, Combined third and fourth periodic reports (Egypt), para. 478, U.N.Doc.CCPR/C/EGY/2001/3 (15 April 2002).

> ...Restrictions relating to matters of public safety, order, health and morals as well as the rights and freedoms of others are constraints which must be observed by all in their exercise of freedom of religious expression and freedom of belief...This principle was elucidated in a ruling of the Supreme Court, later replaced by the Supreme Constitutional Court, which stipulated that the freedom to have or to adopt any of the recognized sacred religions is limited by the condition that public order and morals in the country in which it is adopted must not be jeopardized thereby (Constitutional Case No. 7, judicial year 2, hearing of 1 March 1975).[220]

Along with the above mentioned implicit reference of Egypt to the requirements of Muslim law, there are few cases in which a representative of Muslim states has an explicit argument on non-recognition of the right to change one's religion. The report of Mauritania in 1991 is one example, in which it has explicitly defended the provisions of traditional Muslim law against the freedom to choose religion, though the argument again has ultimately been linked to the issue of the protection of public order:

> The Islamic religion, which plays an important role in the maintenance of security and stability, is an integrated religious faith and any person who embraces it of his own free will must be assumed to have accepted all its teachings, including the rules governing apostasy, which strengthen the foundations of the society based upon it.
>
> Apostasy from this religion, which guarantees so many freedoms and so much security, stability and social justice, is regarded as high treason and everyone is aware of the penalties that states impose for this type of offence, which threatens their stability and their very existence.

---

220 *Ibid.*, para. 483. On relevance of public order and Muslim legal traditions in Egyptian case law see Berger, *supra* note 145. Similarly, the relevance of requirements of religion and public order is mentioned in the judgment of an English court with regard to blasphemy: "Indeed, all offences of this kind are not only offences to God, but crimes against the law of the land, and are punishable as such, inasmuch as they tend to destroy those obligations whereby civil society is bound together; and it is upon this ground that the Christian religion constitutes part of the law of England..." Choudhury [1991] 1 All E.R. at 313 (quoting R. v. Williams [1797] 26 State Tr. 654, 714), quoted in Stahnke, *supra* note 17, p. 292.

> While this religion does not compel anyone to embrace it, it does not tolerate duplicity in this respect or apostasy, which is incompatible with its sacrosanct nature as a divinely-revealed religion based on immutable principles.
>
> The precepts of this religion cannot be changed, since the holy law on which it is based comprises moral principles in which our society believes and any person who violates them arouses social indignation. Consequently, apostasy constitutes one of the most serious offences against the public order and morality established by this religion....[221]

Also, in the report by Abdelfattah Amor on Iran, a reference has been made by the representative of Iran, in which he denied the right to change one's religion on the ground of reservation of Muslim states to this right:

> With regard to recognition of the right to change [one's] religion, the government representatives said that Article 18 of the Universal Declaration of Human Rights expressly recognized conversion, that the Islamic countries had expressed reservations about it and that Article 18 of the International Covenant on Civil and Political Rights did not refer to conversion.[222]

Yet, according to the report the same authority stated that, under the Civil Code, conversion was not a crime and that no one had been punished for converting.[223]

More recently, Yemen, in both its third and fourth periodic reports on the implementation of the ICCPR, has implicitly rejected the freedom to change one's religion. In both reports, however, it does not refer to the requirements of Muslim law to support its position, but rather to the necessities of public order. Furthermore, in both reports Yemen links its position to the position of other Muslim states. For example, the fourth periodic report indicates: "Yemen's position is thus the same as that of other Islamic states: while it believes in freedom of creed and conscience, it holds that to change one's

---

221 UN Commission on Human Rights, Implementation of the Declaration on the Elimination of All Forms of of Intolerance and Discrimination Based on Religion or Belief, para. 76, U.N.Doc.E/CN.4/1991/56 (1991), quoted in Stahnke *supra* note 17, p. 283.

222 Abdelfattah Amor, Special Rapporteur of the Commission on Human Rights, Implementation of the Declaration on the Elimination of All forms of Intolerance and Discrimination Based on Religion or Belief, Report Relating to Visit to Iran, para. 21, U.N.Doc. E/CN.4/1996/95/Add.2 (9 Feb. 1996) (hereinafter Abdelfattah Amor, Visit to Iran).

223 *Ibid.*

religion and to proclaim such change would be to create discord that would be highly detrimental to social stability and security."[224]

By reiterating that the religion of God is Islam and by referring to the conditions therein for entering and leaving the faith, it is implied that Muslims are not allowed to leave their religion: "Given the belief of the government of Yemen in the importance of devotion to the Islamic religion, freedom of religion and conscience resides within the individual himself, who is aware that the religion of God is Islam. Islam specifies conditions for entering and leaving the faith."[225]

In 1988, the United Nations Special Rapporteur on Freedom of Religion alleged that the provisions of the Constitution of Malaysia on proselytizing and the laws enacted pursuant to it had a negative impact on religious freedom. In response, the Malaysian government articulated certain problems inherent in maintaining social stability in a multi-religious state that is nevertheless dominated by a particular religious tradition.[226] From the perspective of the Malaysian government, "the unity and stability of the multiethnic, multi-religious state of Malaysia is dependent upon the preservation and strengthening of the Islamic character of the state and Muslim institutions."[227] According to this perspective, rather than maintaining commitments to Muslim law, the goal of the legislation in restricting proselytizing is the protection of the unity and stability of the state.

Similarly, to justify its legislation against proselytizing, Morocco, in its fifth periodic report on the implementation of the ICCPR, resorted to the requirement to protect public order:

---

224 Human Rights Committee: Consideration of Reports Submitted by States Parties, Fourth periodic report (Yemen), para. 354, U.N.Doc.CCPR/C/YEM/2004/4 (3 Dec. 2004).

225 *Ibid.* Similar wording exists in the third periodic report of Yemen on the implementation of the ICCPR. See Human Rights Committee: Consideration of Reports Submitted by States Parties, Third periodic report (Yemen), para. 106, U.N.Doc.CCPR/C/YEM/2001/3 (18 Oct. 2001).

226 Implementation of the Declaration on the Elimination of All Forms of Intolerance and Discrimination Based on Religion or Belief, U.N. ESCOR, 45th Sess., Provisional Agenda Item 22, Commission on Human Rights, para. 51, U.N.Doc.E/CN.4/1989/44 (1988), quoted in Stahnke, *supra* note 17, p. 308.

227 Implementation of the Declaration on the Elimination of All Forms of Intolerance and Discrimination Based on Religion or Belief, U.N. ESCOR, 46th Sess., Capital Provisional Agenda Item 24, Committee on Human Rights, para. 58, U.N.Doc.E/CN.4/1990/46 (1990), quoted in Stahnke, *supra* note 17, p. 309.

> Islam is the state religion, as established in Article 6 of the Constitution, and Muslim religious values are thus part of the public order. For that reason, Moroccan law has always sought to protect the faith from anything that might offend Muslims' religious sensibilities. Thus, any attempt to weaken Muslims' faith or convert them to another religion is punishable under criminal law.[228]

2.5.3. *Implementation of the Convention on the Rights of the Child*

Jordan is the only Muslim state which, in its report, has had an explicit reference to the prohibition of freedom to choose or abandon a religion by a child. Part of a report by a non-governmental organization which is attached to the second report of Jordan, found 'freedom to choose a religion' not only in conflict with Islam, but also with Christianity.[229] However, the same report correctly referred further to a real reason for ignoring this right i.e. the family system of the country. The report stated: "Moreover, the individual's family links and the religious and ideological upbringing that individuals receive within their families in Jordan do not permit the renunciation of religion."[230] Similarly, Syria, when explaining its reservation, did not refer to the requirement of traditional Muslim law but to the "family law concerns".[231]

2.6. SUMMARY

With regard to the effects of public aspects of Muslim legal traditions of apostasy, it should be noted that not one single state has included a literal provision of these traditions on prohibition and punishment of conversion in its legislation. Yet, the legislation in Sudan has prescribed the death penalty not for conversion but for conversion related offences. Legislation in some Malaysian states also incorporates some forms of punishment against converts

---

228 Consideration of Reports, 2004 (Morocco), *supra* note 135, para. 219.

229 Committee on the Rights of the Child: Consideration of Reports Submitted by States Parties, Second periodic report (Jordan), Appendix, National Task Force for Children, Periodic report by the non-governmental organizations in Jordan on the implementation of the Convention on the Rights of the Child during the period 1993–1998, para. 9(33), U.N.Doc. CRC/C/70/Add.4 (17 Sept. 1999). See section 8.4 of this book for more details.

230 *Ibid.*

231 Committee on the Rights of the Child: Consideration of Reports Submitted by States Parties, initial report (Syria), para. 82, U.N.Doc.CRC/C/28/Add.2 (14 Feb. 1996). See section 8.4 of this book for more details.

such as fines and short terms of imprisonment. According to the legislation in some other Malaysian states, a form of short detention period, under the title of 'rehabilitation period', is imposed on converts. Fortunately in practice no case has been reported on the imposing of these punishments in Sudan or in Malaysia. Similarly, the legislation of none of the Muslim states imposes civil consequences of apostasy, such as confiscation of property of the apostate.

With regard to proselytizing, Malaysia is the only Muslim state whose Constitution includes a provision restricting proselytizing. Also it should be noted that in practice policies against proselytizing are neither an impact of Muslim legal traditions nor merely a phenomenon in Muslim states. In fact such policies are followed in areas with sensible religious diversities.

On the other hand, the personal aspects of Muslim legal traditions of apostasy, which are family law consequences of conversion, may lead to loss of custody of children, deprivation of inheritance and divorce of an apostate. While these aspects can be found mainly in case law, legislation of some Muslim countries on matters such as inheritance and marriage can affect these consequences. For example, with regard to inheritance whereas in Iran and Egypt a non-Muslim does not inherit from a Muslim, in Malaysia and Pakistan the problematic rule of traditional Muslim law on inheritance has been abandoned.

Considering official positions of Muslim states with regard to the right to change one's religion, it should be added that during the preparatory discussions of international human rights instruments, especially the CRC, many Muslim states have shown reluctance to make an explicit recognition of the right to change one's religion. In this regard, some Muslim states played a clear role in excluding an explicit reference to this right in the ICCPR, the Religion Declaration, and the CRC.

With respect to implementation of the international instruments there are few cases in which a representative of Muslim states has had an explicit argument on non-recognition of the right to change one's religion or denying the right of children to choose the religion. Finally, while the issue of changing one's religion has been addressed by the Human Rights Committee, the family law consequences of conversion has been mostly neglected by that Committee and other related UN bodies.

CHAPTER THREE

Current Application of Traditional Rules of Blasphemy (*Sabb*)

3.1. Related Legislation

There is a reference to apostasy (*irtidad*) in Article 26 of the 1986 Press Code of Iran, which in fact addresses *sabb*. The article states: "Whoever insults Islam and its sacred things through the press and his or her guilt amount to apostasy, shall be sentenced as an apostate and should his or her offence fall short of apostasy he or she be subject to the Islamic Penal Code".[232] On the other hand, as "there was no relevant article in the Penal Code to Article 26 of the Press Code, this shortcoming was addressed in 1996 by the new Article 513 of the Penal Code."[233] The article, which was included under the category of *tazir*, explicitly prescribed the death penalty for *sabb*. The article states: "Anyone who insults sacred things of Islam or any of the great prophets, or pious *Imams* [twelve Shiite *Imams*] or Highness Fatima [the daughter of the Prophet] if the offence is liable to *sabb*-al *Nabi* the offender will be executed and otherwise he or she will be imprisoned from one to five years."[234]

Despite the earlier aim of the legislators to link this article to the relevant provision of the Press Code, the article by its general wording is capable of addressing offences of insulting under the scope of both the media and elsewhere. Furthermore, while an act of insult varies in different times and places, there is no legal base for realizing *sabb*-al *Nabi* or offence of lesser degree in the Code or other laws.[235] Also, as will be discussed in the next section, Article 6 of the Press Code has extended the scope of the Code to the offences based on heresy.[236]

---

232 The Press Code of Iran, *supra* note 114.

233 Mirmohammadsadeghi, *supra* note 32, p. 47.

234 Iran Penal Code (Islamic Punishment Act), approved on 30 July 1991, amended on 11 May 1996, Book 5 under '*Tazirat* [plural of *tazir*] and Preventive Punishments', First Chapter, Offences against Internal and External Security, Article 513.

235 Also see introduction of this book, footnote 56.

236 See section 4.1 of this book for more details.

Inheriting from the era of colonialism,[237] Pakistan has embodied its blasphemy law in Articles 298A, 295B and 295C of its Penal Code. Unlike Iran, these articles have provided a long list of instances of *sabb* or other insulting offences. Article 295C, which prescribes the definition and punishments of *sabb*, along with the death penalty for the offence, suggests other alternative punishments, i.e. life imprisonment and a fine. Yet, similar to the legislation of Iran and apparently in line with the traditional Muslim law on punishment of *sabb*, no distinction has been made between the punishment of a male or a female offender. The article defines the offence as, use of derogatory remarks, etc. in respect of the Holy Prophet. The article adds: "Whoever by words, either spoken or written or by visible representation, or by any imputation, innuendo, or insinuation, directly or indirectly, defiles the sacred name of the Holy Prophet Mohammad shall be punished with death, or imprisonment for life, and shall also be liable to fine."[238]

The two other articles of the Pakistani Penal Code address the other blasphemy offences lesser than *sabb* with lighter punishments. Article 295-B is related to defiling of a printed copy of the Holy Koran: "Whoever will fully defiles, damages or desecrates a copy of the Holy Koran or of an extract there from or uses it in any derogatory manner or for any unlawful purpose shall be punishable for imprisonment for life."[239]

---

237 Sections 295 and 298 of the Pakistan Penal Code (1861) were aimed at preventing and limiting religious violence. In 1980, Section 298 was inserted in the Penal Code and in 1982 Section 295B was added to it. In 1986, the 'Criminal Law Amendment Act' amended the Penal Code and inserted the blasphemy law in Section 295C. Section 295C of the Penal Code was amended on 29 July 1991 as a result of the entry into force of the 1991 *Shariah* Act. In the spring of 1991 the Supreme Court, following the precepts of the *Shariah*, issued an order, subsequently confirmed by the Senate, declaring any person henceforth found guilty of blasphemy under Section 295C of the Penal Code, liable to the death penalty, without any possible form of appeal. In 1991 Ordinance XXI, promulgated on 7 July, amended Section 295 A of the Penal Code and the Code of Penal Procedure by raising from two to ten years the maximum prison sentence for outraging the religious feelings of any group. Finally in 1992, Section 123 A of the Penal Code was amended to declare any act prejudicial to the ideology of Pakistan a criminal offence. See Abdelfattah Amor: Visit to Pakistan, *supra* note 144, paras. 10–16.

In this part Sections 295B, 295C and 298A of Pakistan Penal Code will be discussed and compared with similar provisions of other Muslim states. Sections 289B and 298C of Pakistan Penal Code on Ahmadies will be left to the next part.

238 Pakistan Blasphemy law *ibid.*

239 *Ibid.*

Article 298-A is concerned with insulting holy persons other than the Prophet Muhammad. While taking into consideration the sensitivities of both the Shiite and Sunni citizens of the country, this provision provides a longer list of the holy persons in comparison with its equivalent Article 513 of Penal Code of Iran. Article 298-A reads as follows:

> Use of derogatory remarks, etc…., in respect of holy personages. Whoever by words, either spoken or written, or by visible representation, or by any imputation, innuendo or insinuation, directly or indirectly defiles a sacred name of any wife (*Ummul Mumineen*), or members of the family (*Ahle-bait*), of the Holy Prophet, or any of the righteous Caliphs (*Khulafa-e-Rashideen*) or Companions (*Sahaabi*) of the Holy Prophet description for a term which may extend to three years, or with fine, or with both.[240]

The blasphemy law of Pakistan has been a subject of wide criticism inside and outside the country as stated by Abdelfattah Amor in his report:

> …More generally speaking, blasphemy as an offence against belief may be subject to special legislation. However, such legislation should not be discriminatory and should not give rise to abuse. Nor should it be so vague as to jeopardize human rights, especially those of minorities. If offences against belief are made punishable under ordinary law, then procedural guarantees must be introduced and a balanced attitude must be maintained. While protecting freedom of conscience and freedom of worship is clearly a necessity, applying the death penalty for blasphemy appears disproportionate and even unacceptable, especially in view of the fact that blasphemy is very often the reflection of a very low standard of education and culture, for which the blasphemer is never solely to blame.[241]

Finally, to make a comparison between the legislation on *sabb* in Pakistan and Iran with that of Sudan, which has prescribed the death penalty in its legislation for a conversion related offence, it is worth mentioning that, according to Article 125 of the Sudan Criminal Code, the punishment for insulting the religion, which apparently includes *sabb*, is imprisonment for a term not exceeding one year or by a fine or whipping, which may not exceed 40 lashes. Furthermore, unlike the legislation of Iran that merely covers the sacred things of Islam, the Criminal Code of Sudan, similar to the blasphemy

240 *Ibid.*
241 Abdelfattah Amor, Visit to Pakistan, *supra* note 144, para. 82.

law in Pakistan, addresses insulting other religions as well. Article 125 reads as follows: "Whoever by any means publicly abuses or insults any of the religions, their rites or beliefs or ceremonies, or seeks to excite feelings of contempt and disrespect against the believers therein, shall be punished by imprisonment for a term not exceeding one year or by a fine or a whipping, which may not exceed forty lashes."[242]

With regard to the extent in which the *sabb* cases have been applied in Pakistan and Iran, it should be added that in Iran few cases of *sabb* have been filed under the Press Code,[243] fortunately none of them have been accepted as *sabb* by the court. Yet, there was a famous controversial case, that of Professor Aghajari, which contained more heretical elements than insulting ones and therefore will be discussed in chapter 5 under the subject of heresy.

Pakistan, unlike Iran, has faced very problematic experiences in the application of its blasphemy law and especially filing *sabb* cases against Muslims and non-Muslims. In this country no case of the death penalty or life imprisonment has been imposed for *sabb*. However, a handful of cases have remained unresolved because the courts have repeatedly postponed hearings. As the reports show, these cases mainly concern offences of simply expressing an opinion rather than insulting and are therefore more correctly categorized as heresy rather than blasphemy cases.[244]

3.2. RUSHDIE: A *SABB* CASE?

The most controversial case of apostasy in the recent century is the one of a Muslim British novelist, Salman Rushdie, and his novel the Satanic Verses,

242 Abdelfattah Amor, Visit to Sudan, *supra* note 118, para. 23.

243 One case was against Samiei-nezad, a journalist, who was first charged for *sabb*, though, the court further dismissed the allegation. For more information about this case and other *sabb* cases against two well-know Iranian journalists see the reports by the lawyer, Seyed Mohammad Seyfzaadeh, *supra* note 113.

244 See for example the U.S. Department of State, International Religious Freedom Reports on Pakistan. Among the relevant cases, that of Binazir Butto, the former prime minister of Pakistan, is a clear example of allegation based on heresy which was filed under blasphemy law. When Binazir Bhutto, then leader of the opposition, criticized the *Shariah* Courts in 1992 for increasing the severity of the penalties for blasphemy, the Federal Minister for Religious Affairs, Mawlana Abadu Sitar Niazi issued a *fatwa* against her, declaring her to be a kafir liable to the death penalty. A year later when she was prime minister, a case was brought against her to the Lahore High Court under Section 295-C by Zia ul-Islam, leader of the Pakistan Movement for Workers, for criticizing the blasphemy law.

which was published in 1988. Rushdie in his book "refers to the Companions of the Prophet as 'fucking clowns', identifies the Prophet's wives with whores, refers to the Prophet as '*Mahound*', a medieval Christian expression, denigrating Mohammad as an agent of the devil, and calls Mecca the city of '*Jahilia*', or ignorance."[245]

Following the publication of the novel which provoked outrage among Muslims worldwide, Ayatollah Khomeini of Iran issued a *fatwa* on the death of Rushdie and all persons involved in the publication the work. The *fatwa* stated the following:

> ....I would like to inform all the intrepid Muslims in the world that the author of the book entitled the Satanic Verses, which has been compiled, printed and published in opposition to Islam, the Prophet and the Koran, as well as those publishers who were aware of its contents, have been sentenced to death.
>
> I call on all zealous Muslims to execute them quickly, wherever they find them, so that no one will dare to insult the Islamic sanctions. Whoever is killed on this path will be regarded as a martyr....
>
> In addition, anyone who has access to the author of the book, and does not possess the power to execute him, should refer him to the people so that he may be punished for his actions....[246]

Later, when the president (now leader) of Iran, Ayatollah Khamenehei, suggested that Salman Rushdie apologize and when Rushdie consequently did so, Ayatollah Khomeini announced that "even if Salman Rushdie repents and becomes the most pious man of time, it is incumbent on every Muslim to employ everything he has got, his life and his wealth, to send him to hell."[247]

Regarding the compliance of the *fatwa* with Muslim legal traditions of apostasy many questions have been raised, as Chase states:

> In looking at the *fatwa*, one must begin by defining some narrow points which remain vague on a first reading. The actual crime, with which

245 Salman Rushdie, *The Satanic Verses* (1992) at 359–94, quoted in Anthony Chase, 'Legal Guardians: Islamic Law, International Law, Human Rights Law, and the Salman Rushdie Affair' 11 *The American University Journal of International Law and Policy* 375 (1996), p. 416.

246 Observer, 19 Feb. 1989, quoted in Lisa Appignanesi & Sara Maitland, *The Rushdie File* (London: ICA: Fourth Estate, 1989), p. 84.

247 IRNA, Iranian News Agency, 19 Feb. 1989, quoted in Appignanesi & Maitland, *Ibid.*, p. 122.

> Rushdie is charged, for example, is not stated. Is the crime insult? Heresy? Blasphemy? Apostasy? Are the publishers of the Satanic Verses sentenced to death for the same reason or for a different crime? None of this is stated, making for a rather peculiar legal statement, particularly given the specificity which normally characterizes *fatwas*.[248]

Giving an answer to the related questions is not difficult, if the distinction lines between conversion, *sabb* and heresy, discussed in the first chapter, is taken into consideration. According to Muslim legal traditions using the aforementioned mocking terms in the Satanic Verses can be considered as *sabb-al Rasul* in the eyes of any ordinary Muslim. Based on Muslim traditional law, the punishment of this offence was death for both males and females, and for Muslims and non-Muslim offenders, and, according to the majority of Muslim jurists, with no possibility of repenting for it. This is why Rushdie's right to repent was further refused by Ayatollah Khomeini. On the extent of the *fatwa* to the publishers of the book, it can be added that anybody who knowingly engaged in the disseminating *sabb-al Rasul*, according to Ayatollah Khomeini was committing the same offence as Rushdie had.

In addition to the above mentioned issues of the *fatwa*, some other aspects are still not clear. As discussed before, unlike the heresy cases in which the offence of apostasy needs to be recognized by a *mujtahid* or *mufti*, in cases of *sabb* the offence can be realized by any ordinary Muslim. Therefore, one might correctly ask what was the requirement of the issuing the *fatwa* by Ayatollah Khomeini or any other *mujtahid*? In fact, there was no need for a *fatwa* in the case of Rushdie, unless a *mujtahid* like Ayatollah Khomeini needs to reiterate the importance of the offence and its punishment.

Above all the most controversial aspect related to the *fatwa* was its extraterritorial feature which led to the rupture of diplomatic relations of Iran and Western European states. While it is obvious that the extraterritorial feature of the *fatwa* was in sharp contrast with the international commitments of Iran, considering the importance of principle of sanctity of treaties in Islam, the legality of extraterritorial feature of *fatwa* under Muslim law was also questioned by some scholars.[249]

---

248 Chase, *supra* note 244, p. 396.

249 One should also remember another specific feature of Shiite jurisprudence, i.e. the extraordinary political authority of Shiite *mujtahid* which led to the introducing the doctrine of *Velaayat-e Faqih* (the guardianship of competent Muslim jurists over the people) by Ayatollah Khomeini. This doctrine later became the foundation of the political system of Iran

Arzt states: "*Shariah* applies only within the Muslim world and can only be administered by Muslim rulers within their own communities. Muslims living outside the *dar-al-Islam* [Muslim's territories] are not subject to Islamic law."[250] In this frame, even some later governmental publications in Iran argued that Ayatollah Khomeini's *fatwa* did not refer to implementation of the punishment but merely held a political position.[251]

Finally, international pressure against the *fatwa* led the Iranian government to disassociate itself from punishment of Rushdie, at least in the territory of other states, as is stated in the report by the UN Special Rapporteur on Freedom of Expression:

> During his visit, the Special Rapporteur was informed by the government that *fatwas* are issued by the religious authorities and not by state organizations *per se* and that it did not seek or encourage the killing of Mr. Rushdie or any persons involved in the publishing of the Satanic Verses. The government stressed it did not associate itself with any attack on anyone outside its jurisdiction and did not interfere in the internal affairs of other states.[252]

3.3. SUMMARY

The death sentence for *sabb* in the legislation of Pakistan and Iran is the only examples of identical incorporation of religious legal traditions for punishment of apostasy in the legislation of Muslim states. Yet with regard to the practice,

---

after the 1979 revolution. Having this doctrine in mind, Ayatollah Khomeini, neither in the time of issuing the *fatwa* nor in statements afterwards, referred to the legal bases of his *fatwa* under Muslim law, as for him a *mujtahid*, and especially the leading one, who is *Vali-ye Faqih* (the competent jurist), has much more authority than to be restricted by the limited scope of traditional Muslim law. Even there is no evidence that he himself has called his statement against Rushdie a '*fatwa*', a term which is commonly used in traditional Muslim law terminology.

250 Donna E. Arzt, 'Heroes or Heretics: Religious Dissidents under Islamic Law' 14 *Wisconsin International Law Journal, University of Wisconsin* (1996) p. 402. On the principle of sanctity of treaties in Islam and the contradictory aspect of the *fatwa* with this principle see Chase, *supra* note 244, p. 412, and Majid Khadduri, *War and Peace in the Law of Islam* (Johns Hopkins Press, 1955), p. 204; also see section 5.1.1 of this book.

251 See Mehdi Montazer Gha'em, *Personal and Opinion Freedoms according to Imam Khomeini, and Its Fiqhi Bases*, (Moassese-ye Tanzim va Nashr-e Asar-e Emam Khomeyni Publication, Tehran, Iran, 2002), in Persian, p. 116.

252 Special Rapporteur on the Promotion and Protection of the Right to Freedom of Opinion and Expression, Report Relating to Visit to Iran, U.N.Doc.E/CN.4/2004/62/Add.2, para. 17 (12 Jan. 2004) (Special Rapporteur on Freedom of Expression, Visit to Iran).

it should be added that in Iran few cases of *sabb* have been filed under the Press Code, and none of the cases were accepted as *sabb* by the court. Pakistan, unlike Iran, has faced very problematic allegations under its blasphemy law, though fortunately still none of them has resulted in severe punishment. As the reports indicate, these cases are mainly not for offences of insulting but simply expressing an opinion; in other words, more than being a blasphemy case, they are heresy cases. The blasphemy law of Pakistan has been a subject of wide criticism inside and outside the country.

On the issue of *fatwa* by Ayatollah Khomeini against Salman Rushdie, it was discussed that the contents of the *fatwa* were mainly in compliance with Muslim legal traditions of apostasy. Yet, considering the importance of principle of sanctity of treaties in Islam, the extraterritorial aspect of the *fatwa* was not justifiable under traditional Muslim law.

It is worth mentioning at this juncture that, in its later reaction towards the *fatwa*, the Iranian government in fact did distinguish between the issuing a *fatwa* by a religious authority and the acts of the government. This was apparently the first time that the Iranian government officially made a clear distinction between a government act and requirements of Muslim law.[253]

---

253 This new approach of Iranian government can be justified under the doctrine of *Masalih* (or consideration of public interests) in traditional Muslim law, based on which the interests of the public prevails the religious commitments.

CHAPTER FOUR

Current Application of Traditional Rules of Heresy

4.1. Related Legislation

Article 23 of the Iranian Constitution states: "The investigation of individuals' beliefs is forbidden, and no one may be molested or taken to task simply for holding a certain belief."[254] Yet, as will be discussed further, Article 6 of the Press Code of Iran has an opposite tendency.

Article 24 of the Iranian Constitution is quoted at the heading of the Iranian Press Code: "Publications and the press have freedom of expression except when it is detrimental to *mabaani-ye Islami* (the fundamental principles of Islam) or the rights of the public. The details of this exception will be specified by law."[255]

Based on this article of the Constitution, Article 6 of the Press Code had to specify fundamental Islamic principles. Instead, as mentioned in section 3.1 of this book, it has extended the scope of the limitation of Article 24 of the Constitution to include a wide scope from atheistic articles to publications prejudicial to *ahkaam-e Islam* (Islamic code) which is equivalent to Muslim legal traditions. Part of Article 6 reads as follows:

> The print media are permitted to publish news items except in cases when they violate Islamic principles and codes and public rights as outlined in this chapter:
>
> 1. Publishing atheistic articles or issues which are prejudicial to Islamic codes, or promoting subjects which might damage the foundation of the Islamic Republic;
>
> 2. Propagating obscene and religiously forbidden acts...;
>
> 7. Insulting Islam and its sacred things, or offending the Leader of the Revolution and recognized religious authorities (senior Muslim jurists);

254 Constitution of Islamic Republic of Iran, 1979, amended on 28 July 1989.
255 Press Code of Iran, *supra* note 114.

9. Committing plagiarism or quoting articles from the deviant press, parties and groups which oppose Islam (inside and outside the country) in such a manner as to propagate such ideas (the limits of such offences shall be defined by the executive by-law).[256]

Using such terms as "atheistic articles", "issues prejudicial to Islamic codes", "promoting subjects which might damage the foundation of the Islamic Republic", "propagating obscene and religiously forbidden acts", "committing plagiarism or quoting articles from the deviant press", in itself makes the law even more ambiguous and subject to a broader interpretation based on heresy. With regard to the terms "Islamic principles" and "Islamic code", Aakhundi states, "while 'Islamic principles' is not more than three issues: unity of God (*tawhid*), prophet-hood (*nabovvat*) and the day after (*ma'ad*), the press law has added another term, 'Islamic code' (*ahkaam-e Islam*), a broad area that can include whatever we are doing."[257]

The UN Special Rapporteur on Freedom of Expression considered that many of the limitations provided for in the Press Code of Iran do not confirm to the permissible restrictions under Article 19(3) of the ICCPR, because, "in most cases the grounds for these limitations lack any objective criteria and clear definition, and are therefore open to subjective and arbitrary interpretation by the judges implementing them."[258]

The Malaysian states also have legislation on insulting Islam. Yet, similar to the Iranian Press Code, the scope of prohibitions have at times been extended to issues relating to '*Syariah* law' [*Shariah* law], which is another name for 'Islamic code', referred to in the legislation of Iran.[259]

In Malaysia, Sunni Islam is the official branch of Islam; propagating other branches of Islam or any criticism against the prevailing interpretation of

---

256 *Ibid.*

257 Iranian Student News Agency (ISNA), 'Dr. Mehrpour and Dr. Aakhundi in An Interview with ISNA (Iranian Student News Agency)', 1 Dec. 2005, in Persian, available at Iranian Student News Agency at: <http://www.isna.ir/Main/NewsView.aspx?ID=News-624539>. This Code has been subject to widespread criticism. Shirin Ebadi states: "The Iranian press law is a compilation of confusing principles, legal contradictions, and items limiting the freedom of expression, through which 'criticism' can be interpreted as a 'crime'". See Shirin Ebadi, 'Ganji, Hostage of Iran's Press Law', 5 Dec. 2005, available at: Roozonline Electronic Daily at: <http://roozonline.com/11english/009049.shtml>.

258 Special Rapporteur on Freedom of Expression, Visit to Iran, *supra* note 252, para. 95.

259 See Section 22, Crimes (*Syariah*) (Perak) Enactment 1992; Section 169 Administration of Muslim Law (Selangor) Enactment 1952; Section 128, Administration of Muslim Law (Perlis) Enactment 1964, quoted in Saeed, *supra* note 25, p. 140.

Muslim law is prohibited under some state laws. For example, Section 163(1) of the Kedah Administration of Muslim Law Enactment 1962, makes it an offence to be in possession of any book or document or to give any instruction or ruling on Islamic law that is contrary to the belief of *Ahl-al-Sunnah wa al-jama'ah* (Sunnis) or to the tenets of the Shafi'i, Hanafi, Maliki or Hanbali schools. Contravention of this law can lead to imprisonment for a term not exceeding six months or a fine not exceeding 1,000 Ringgit, or both.[260]

Legislation in some Malaysian states also forbids the use by non-Muslims of certain Arabic or Islamic words and phrases in any publications or in a speech during organized gatherings which the person knew or ought to have known, at the time, would be published or broadcast.[261]

Muslims who engage in non-Sunni teachings or practices are often labelled 'deviant' in the legislation of some Malaysian states.[262] With regard to the reasoning for the use of the term 'deviant' in place of 'apostasy', '*ridda*' or '*irtidad*', Saeed states:

> Government and religious authorities avoid using the term 'apostasy' or similar terms to describe such people and their activities. The authorities probably feel that the use of such terms implies that the people so described are no longer Muslims. On the other hand, assumption of deviation or deviant teaching categorize them as straying Muslims, which leaves

260 Identical provisions are found in Section 159, Administration of Muslim Law (Malacca) Enactment 1959 and Section 160, Administration of Muslim Law (Penang) Enactment 1959. See Saeed, *supra* note 25, p. 128.

261 Schedule Parts I and II of 1981 Kelantan Enactment on Control and Restriction of the Propagation of Non-Islamic Religions ban the following words and phrases: *Allah, firman Allah, ulama, hadith, ibadah, ka'bah, kadi, ilahi, wahyu, mubaligh, syariah, giblah, hajj, mufti, rasul, iman, da'wah, salat, khalifah, wali, fatwa, imam, nabi, sheikh, subhannallah, alhamdulillah, lailahaillallah, walillahilhamd, allahu akbar, insyallah, astaghfirullahal azim, tabarak Allah, masyaallah, lahaula wala quata illabillah.* Similar restrictions are found in several other state laws for instance, Schedule, Parts I and II, Control and Restriction (The Propagation of Non-Islamic Religions Among Muslims) (Negeri Sembilan) Bill, 1991. See Saeed, *supra* note 25, p. 127.

262 Generally state laws use the phrase 'false doctrine'. See for example Section 167, Administration of Muslim Law (Selangor) Enactment 1952; Section 204, Administration of Islamic Religious Affairs (Trengganu), Enactment 1986; Section 119, Council of Religion of Islam and Malay Custom (Kelantan) Enactment 1994; Section 157, Administration of Muslim Law (Malacca) Enactment 1959; Section 161, Administration of Muslim Law (Keldah) Enactment 1962; Section 158, Administration of Muslim Law (Pahang), Enactment 1959. On the other hand, Section 13, Crimes (*Syariah*) (Perak) Bill, 1992, uses the word 'apostasy', while section 102, Council of the Religion of Islam and Malay Custom (Kelantan), Enactment 1994 uses the word '*murtad*'. See Saeed, *supra* note 25, p. 128.

> open the possibility of rehabilitation. There is also the issue of jurisdiction. Islamic law is applicable only to citizens professing the religion of Islam. Therefore, once the government has declared a particular individual an apostate or a particular activity equivalent to apostasy, it may no longer be able to take action against them, as they are no longer Muslims.[263]

Another example of heresy laws is the *Syariah* [*Shariah*] Criminal Offences (Takzir) (Trengganu) Enactment 2001. This law does not use such terms as deviant teaching or beliefs, assuming other beliefs to be false. Instead it considers some other heresy offences which include opinions contrary to *fatwa* (Art. 12), issuing of *fatwa* (Art. 13), religious publications contrary to *hukum Syariah* [*Shariah* rules] (Art. 14), manipulating the teachings of Islam or the Islamic law (Art. 15) and Friday prayers in unauthorized places.[264]

The law, in Articles 16 and 18, governs a very new area of religious offences. Article 16 makes a part of religious practices, i.e. prayer and Friday prayer, obligatory by law and it makes the failure to undertake these practices an offence. Interestingly, the law only addresses prayer and no other Muslim obligatory religious practice, such as fasting, *zakaat* (religious tax), and hajj pilgrimage. Article 16, under the title "failure to perform Friday prayer", obliges all Muslim men to attend Friday prayer. As Friday prayer is not an obligatory religious practice for Muslim women, the law distinguishes between male and female Muslims:

> Any male person, being *mukallaf* [eighteen years old according to Malaysian law], who fails to perform the Friday prayers in a mosque within his *mukim masjid* [the mosque in the vicinity of his residence) for three consecutive weeks without *uzur Syariah* [religiously justifiable excuse], or without any reasonable case shall be guilty of an offence and shall in conversion be liable to a fine not exceeding 1,000 Ringgit or to imprisonment for a term not exceeding six months or to both.[265]

Article 18, under the title "failure to perform *fardhu* prayer [religiously obligatory five times daily prayers]", obliges by law every Muslim to practice his or

---

263 *Ibid.*, pp. 130–131.

264 The Code reprinted in Patricia A. Martinez, 'The Politics of Power over the *Shariah* in Malaysia,' paper presented at the conference: *Reframing Islam: Politics into Law*: 10–11 Sept. 2005 at Irish Centre for Human Rights, National University of Ireland, Galway, available at: <http://www.nuigalway.ie/human_rights/reframing_Islam/Docs/Papers/Martinez.pdf>.

265 *Ibid.*

her prayers. However, the way in which the performance of prayer is to be monitored by the authorities is not clear: "Any person who, being *mukallaf*, fails to perform the *fardhu* prayer without *uzur Syariah* shall be guilty of an offence and shall on conviction be liable to a fine not exceeding 5,000 Ringgit or imprisonment for a term not exceeding three years or both."[266]

It is worth mentioning that Muslim religious practices are mainly made singly and should not necessarily be manifested in public. This phenomenon has made Muslim religious practices a personal matter. Nonetheless, there are two exceptions to this rule: the practice of hajj pilgrimage, according to all major Muslim sects; and attending Friday prayer, according to the majority of Sunni schools and some Shiite jurists, are religious obligations. Also, it has been encouraged that daily prayers be practiced in *jama'ah* (with a group).

The only legislation which prescribes the death penalty for heresy is the *Syariah* [*Shariah*] Criminal Code of Kelantan (the Kelantan Code) in Malaysia.[267] This code, however, was not approved by the Federal Government of Malaysia and therefore did not come into force.[268] This code, similar to the related article of the Sudan Penal Code on conversion, is part of a *hudood* code, yet, it does not have a reference to the prohibition of conversion.

Section 23(1) of the Kelantan Code, in defining the offence of *irtidad* does not refer to intentionally renouncing Islam, but to the act of heresy: "Any act done or any word uttered by a Muslim who is a *mukallaf*, being an act or word which according to *Syariah* [*Shariah*] law, affects or which is against the *aqidah* (belief) in the Islamic religion."[269] *Shariah* law is not a codified law in Malaysia and can be interpreted differently according to the opinion of any *mufti*. Also the scope of heretical acts which affect fundamental aspects of one's religion is ambiguous and can be extended to any single act or word, as it is surprisingly widened to various matters of *halaal* (religiously allowed acts) and *haraam* (religiously prohibited acts):

---

266 *Ibid.*

267 *Syariah* [*Shariah*] Criminal Code (II) (Kelantan), Enactment 1993, Section 23(21), quoted in Kamali, *supra* note 140.

268 Under the Constitution [Federal List, Item 4(h)] the parliament has exclusive jurisdiction in respect of criminal law, including the creation of offences in respect of any of the matters included in the Federal List or dealt with by federal law. Furthermore, Criminal Jurisdiction Act, 1965 limits the jurisdiction of the *Syariah* [*Shariah*]court to pass sentences of up to three year or fine not exceeding 5,000 Ringgit or six stokes of the whip or any combination of thereof.

269 The Kelantan Code, *supra* note 140.

> Acts or words which affect the *aqidah* (belief) are those which deal with the fundamental aspects of the Islamic religion, which are deemed to have been known and believed by every Muslim as part of their general knowledge about being a Muslim such as matters pertaining to the pillars of Islam (*rukn* Islam), pillars of belief (*rukn iman*) and matters of *halaal* and *haraam*.[270]

Regarding punishment of an apostate, the Kelantan Code, in Section 23(3), differs somewhat compared with the provisions of the Sudan Penal Code. According to this section, along with the death penalty, the property of the offender will be forfeited, which is in fact the unique example of incorporation of traditional rules on civil consequences of apostasy in a legislation. The time for repenting is three days, but even if the offender repents, a different punishment which has no base in legal traditions, i.e. imprisonment, will be imposed on him or her. Furthermore, while the offence is not conversion, the offender apparently should repent his or her heretic beliefs. Similar to the Sudan Penal Code, the Kelantan Code, inconsistent with traditional Muslim law, does not distinguish between male and female apostates, regarding their punishment. The section reads as follows:

> A Muslim (adult and sane) who is accused of apostasy is required to repent within three days and failure to do so makes him or her liable to the punishment of death as well as the forfeiture of his or her property. The offender will be free of the death sentence, even if it has been passed, if he or she repents; the property will be returned but the defendant would still be liable to imprisonment, not exceeding five years.[271]

In practice, however, allegations based on heresy have rarely been reported in Malaysia. According to reports, an Islamic court in 2000 sentenced four persons to three year prison terms for "not recanting their alleged heretical beliefs and returning to the true teachings of Islam."[272] The court rejected their argument that they were not subject to Islamic *Shariah* law because they had ceased to be Muslims. Dismissing their appeal, the Court of Appeal ruled in 2002 that only the Islamic court is qualified to determine whether a Muslim

---

270 *Ibid.*
271 *Ibid.*
272 U.S. Department of State, International Religious Freedom Report on Malaysia, 2001–2005.

has become an apostate. In July 2004, the Federal Court upheld the lower court ruling that only the Islamic court is qualified to determine whether a Muslim has become an apostate.[273]

In Egypt, the case law has provided a broad interpretation of the issue of insulting religious sacred things, thus giving a wide scope for allegations based on heresy. According to the Court of Cassation, not only derogating from the Koran and the Prophet, but even claiming anything contradictory to them or doubting in them, can result in unbelief:

> Scorning the Koran or the Prophetic *Sunnah*, or mocking, repudiating, or disavowing them, or intentionally claiming anything contradicting them publicly or haughtily, or doubting any of it,... denying God's existence or His creation as mentioned in the Koran,... repudiating the prophecy of Mohammad or in general his prophecy to all people, or doubting his sincerity.[274]

Egypt's case law on heresy will be discussed in more detail when examining the case of Abu Zayd in section 4.4.2 of this book.

4.2. HERETIC RELIGIOUS GROUPS

4.2.1. *The Ahmadies*[275]

The Ahmadies (Ahmadiyya) is a Muslim sect founded by Ghulam Ahmad of Qadian (Punjab) in the nineteenth century. The number of Ahmadies in Pakistan, according to different sources, varies from 286,000[276] to more than two million.[277] In 1974, a constitutional amendment declared the Ahmadies – who consider themselves Muslims but have been looked upon as heretics in Pakistan owing to their attitude regarding the finality of the Prophet Mohammad –

273 *Ibid.*

274 Court of Cassation, Nos. 475, 478, 481, Year 65, 5 Aug. 1996 on Abu Zayd, quoted in Berger, *supra* note 145, pp. 731–732.

275 The source of Information in this part is, Abdelfattah Amor, Visit to Pakistan, *supra* note 144, unless other sources stated.

276 Reuters Foundation, Pakistan: Mob violence heightens insecurity among minorities, 20 Feb 2006, available at: <http://www.alertnet.org/thenews/newsdesk/IRIN/20780947c8744d8bf3f4fac8c28e3509.htm>.

277 U.S. Department of State, International Religious Freedom Report on Pakistan, 2005.

a non-Muslim minority. Following the 1974 constitutional amendment, in 1984, Ordinance XX added Sections 298 B and 298 C to the Penal Code, expressly referring to the Ahmadies and forbidding them to profess to be Muslims and to use Muslim practices in their worship or in the propagation of their faith. Sections B and C read as follows:

> 298-B
> "Misuse of epithet, descriptions and titles, etc. reserved for certain holy personages or places."
>
> 1. Any person of the Qadiani group or the Lahori group (who call themselves Ahmadies or by any other name) who by words, either spoken or written or by visible representation:
>
> a. refers to or addresses, any person, other than a Caliph or Companion of the Holy Prophet Mohammad, as '*Ameerul Momineen*', '*Khalifat-ul-Momineen*', '*Khalifat-ul-Muslimeen*', '*Sahaabi*' or '*Razi Allah Anho*',
>
> b. refers to or addresses, any person, other than a wife of the Holy Prophet Mohammad, as *Ummul-Mumineen*;
>
> c. refers to, or addresses any person, other than a member of the family (*Ahle-Bait*) of the Holy Prophet Mohammad as *Ahle-Bait*; or
>
> d. refers to or names, or calls, his place of worship as *Masjid* [Mosque];
>
> Shall be punished with imprisonment of either description for a term which may extend to three years, and shall also be liable to fine.
>
> 2. Any person of the Qadiani group or Lahore group, (who call themselves Ahmadies or by any other names), who by words, either spoken or written, or by visible representations, refers to the mode or form of call to prayers followed by his faith as '*Azan*' or recites *Azan* as used by the Muslims, shall be punished with imprisonment of either description for a term which may extend to three years and shall also be liable to fine.
>
> 298-C
> "Persons of the Qadiani group, etc., calling himself a Muslim or preaching or propagating his faith."
> Any person of the Qadiani group or the Lahori group (who call themselves Ahmadies or any other name), who directly or indirectly, professes himself as a Muslim, or calls, or refers to, his faith as Islam, or preaches or propagates his faith, or invites others to accept his faith, by words,

> either spoken or written, or by visible representation or in any manner whatsoever outrages the religious feelings of Muslims, shall be punished with imprisonment of either description for a term which may extend to three years and shall also be liable to fine.[278]

The Ahmadies, who have been seriously affected by the new legislation, appealed to the courts against the way in which they were being treated. On 3 July 1993, the Supreme Court issued a judgment in which it interpreted the reference to the law in Article 20 of the Constitution on religious freedom as a reference to Islamic law. It also found that any claim by Ahmadies to be Muslims constituted a provocation against Muslims, which made it difficult to ensure their protection.[279]

With regard to the blasphemy laws of Pakistan on the Ahmadies, Abdelfattah Amor, in his report, concluded: "The present state laws related to religious minorities, and more generally speaking the subject of tolerance and non-discrimination based on religion or belief, are likely to favour or foster intolerance in society. The law applied specifically to the Ahmadi minority is particularly questionable and in some respects frankly unwarranted."[280]

According to many non-governmental sources, the religious activities of the Ahmadi community have been seriously restricted, especially as a result of the 1974 constitutional amendment declaring them to be a non-Muslim minority, the Ordinance XX of 1984 and the blasphemy law. Many Ahmadies are reported to have been prosecuted under Section 298 C of the Penal Code for the following offences: saying daily prayers, referring to *Kalimat Tayyaba* (holy words), calling to prayer (*Azan*), preaching, using Muslim epithets and verses of the Koran, and professing to be Muslims. It is also reported that Ahmadies have been accused of claiming to be Muslims under the terms of Section 295 C, which authorises the death penalty for the offender. In addition, it has been reported that Ahmadies are not allowed to bury their dead in Muslim cemeteries.[281]

The Pakistani authorities, however, have insisted on the respect of freedom of religion of Ahmadies in Pakistan, on the condition that they withdraw their claims of being Muslim. Abdelfattah Amor in his report states:

---

278 Quoted in Saeed, *supra* note 25, pp. 184–185.
279 Abdelfattah Amor, Visit to Pakistan, *supra* note 144, para. 21.
280 *Ibid.*, para. 82.
281 *Ibid.*, para. 41.

> While Ahmadies were not authorized to propagate and practice their religion as Muslims, all their religious activities as non-Muslims were authorized. With regard to cases of prosecution against the Ahmadies, the official sources explained that they arose from the propagation of religious views by Ahmadies claiming to be Muslims; the religious activities of the Ahmadies might be interfered with, on the other hand, for reasons which were not religious but purely personal, arising from infringements of the law, especially the law on blasphemy.[282]

4.2.2. *Other Heretic Religious Groups*

With the exception of the Ahmadies who have been targeted by law in Pakistan, in other cases, heretic religious groups and sects have been the targets of state policies. One important case, which will be discussed further in section 4.4.1 of this book, is that of the Sudanese Republican Party or the Republican Brotherhood (*Ikhwan Jamhouriyeen*). The Court of Appeal, when it accused Mahmud Muhammad Taha, the leader of the group, of apostasy, extended its judgment to all members of the Republican Brotherhood or the followers of Taha. They were "equally held to be apostates and to be treated as such in all interactions with Muslims. The Republicans' books, pamphlets and all other publications were called on to be collected and destroyed. Any future publications and distribution of information containing the issues they dealt with were banned, along with any other activity of the Republicans."[283]

In Malaysia, according to a report, in November 1999, the Parliamentary Secretary to the Prime Minister's Department, Mohamed Abdullah, revealed that there were 51 groups active in preaching deviant teaching to more than 16,000 followers.[284] According to another report:

> The government is concerned that 'deviationist' teachings could cause divisions among Muslims. Members of such groups can be arrested and detained, with the consent of the Islamic court, to be 'rehabilitated' and returned to the 'true path of Islam.' The Selangor Religious Department detained 66 members of a 'deviationist' group in 2003 and arrested 96

---

282 *Ibid.*, para. 43.

283 Declan O'Sulivan, 'The Death Sentence for Mahmud Muhammad Taha: Misuse of the Sudanese Legal System and Islamic *Shariah*' 15 *The International Journal of Human Rights* 3 (2001), p. 55.

284 Bernama, 17 Nov. 1998 (Online Lexis, 9 Dec. 2000), quoted in Saeed, *supra* note 25, p. 129.

> followers of another 'deviationist' sect in April. In 2002, the government revealed that the Malaysian Islamic Development Department 'rehabilitated' hundreds of followers from 125 'deviationist' groups after they underwent 'counselling' at a faith rehabilitation centre in the state of Negeri Sembilan.[285]

Among banned or 'deviant' religious groups in Malaysia, there is no reference to Shiites, Ahmadies or a well known Muslim religious group, either in federal government or state government sources. Two others, however, have been named as banned religious groups. First, there was a religious movement called Arqam that was banned in 1991. Before this ban, in early 1986, the government banned one book of Ashaari, the movement founder. In this book, Ashaari announced his belief in the imminent appearance of the Mahdi, who according to widely held Muslim belief would one day rule the world and restore religion and justice.[286]

Second, despite not using such terms as *irtidad* or *ridda* for 'deviant' religious groups in Malaysia, Saeed refers to another case in which the opinions of a religious group were declared equivalent to *irtidad* by *mufti*s:

> In August 1995 *mufti*s throughout the country made a joint statement saying that expressing an anti-*hadith*[287] view was equivalent to becoming *murtad* or committing an act of apostasy. This was in response to the anti-*hadith* movement of 1980s and 1990s led by Kassim Ahmad, the former secretary general of the Malaysian Socialist Party.[288]

Unlike smaller or short-lived Malaysian heretic religious groups, there are other deep-rooted, well-known heretic sects in other Muslim countries. The

---

285 U.S. Department of State, International Religious Freedom Report on Malaysia, 2004.

286 See Saeed, *supra* note 25, pp. 128–130.

287 *Hadith* is narration by the Prophet Muhammad and anti-*hadith* is one who questions the validity of *hadith* as a source of Muslim law.

288 Saeed, *supra* note 25, p. 131. Ahmad wrote a book in 1986 entitled '*Hadith*: A Re-evaluation', where he argued than *hadith* was not necessary because the Koran is complete, authoritative and transmitted directly from *Allah*. Further, he argued that *hadith*, being a human product, lacked revelation validity. He also claimed that *hadith* contributed to the disunity of the Muslim *ummah* (nation), arguing that during the Umayyad rule political parties had invented *hadith* to justify their own position. See Raymond L.M. Lee & Susan E. Ackerman, *Sacred Tensions: Modernity and Religious Transformation in Malaysia* (Columbia, SC: University of South Carolina Press, 1997), pp. 51–53.

biggest and most frequently targeted by anti-heresy policies are the Shiites.[289] Shiites in Saudi Arabia, Iraq, Afghanistan and Bahrain have been subjected to persecution and discrimination by the governments. In Saudi Arabia, for example, their practices are considered heretic. "According to Saudi officialdom, Islam is Wahabism, and members of the large Shiite minority in Saudi Arabia are exposed to persecution, often being treated like heretics."[290] With regard to the religious practices of Shiites in Saudi Arabia, Arzt notes:

> Objects used in Shiite prayer are confiscated and their users beaten, while the Shiite calls to prayer is considered 'contrary to pure Islam' and punishable 'with no leniency'. Public school textbooks and officially sanctioned *fatwa*s routinely denigrate the Shiite faith....[291]

Also, a restricting situation against Alavies exists in some Muslim countries. Although the Alavies constitute a big religious minority in Turkey and Syria, they have been considered heretic by some Muslim religious leaders. "A formal ruling handed down by Shaykh al-Islam Ibn Taymiyya (1263–1328) determined that spilling Alavi blood is permissible if the Alavies fail to repent and return to Islam."[292] Unlike Syria, where president Asad is an Alavi, in Turkey, as stated in the following report, the religious rights of Alavies have been subject to discrimination and ignorance:

> In addition to the country's Sunni Muslim majority, there are an estimated five to twelve million Alavies, followers of a belief system that incorporates

289 Shiites comprise about 10% of the current more than one billion Muslim populations worldwide and are found in significant numbers in Pakistan and southern Lebanon, as well as predominating in Iran, Iraq, Azerbaijan, and Bahrain. Smaller communities also exist in Yemen, Syria, Saudi Arabia, northern Israel, India, Oman, Afghanistan, the United Arab Emirates, and Somalia. See Introduction of this book, footnote 54.

290 Anne Elizabeth Mayer, *Islam and Human Rights, Tradition and Politics*, Third Edition (Westview Press, London, 1999), p. 147. Also see Amnesty International, 'Saudi Arabia: Religious Intolerance' (New York: Amnesty International, 1993).

291 Arzt, Religious Human Rights, *supra* note, 36.

292 Matti Moosa, *Extremist Shiites: The Ghulat Sects* (Syracus, N.Y.: Syracus University Press, 1987), p. 414; Martin Kramer, 'Syria's Alavies and the Shi'ism', in Martin Kramer (ed.) *Shi'ism: Resistance and Revolution* (Boulder, Colo.: Westview, 198), p. 238, quoted in Eyal Zisser, 'The Alavies, Lords of Syria: From Ethnic Minority to Ruling Sect', in Orfa Bengio & Gabriel Ben-Dor (eds.) *Minorities and the State in the Arab World* (Lynne Rienner Publishers, USA, UK, 1999), p. 130.

> aspects of both Shiite and Sunni Islam and draws on the traditions of other religions found in Anatolia as well.... The Turkish government considers Alavism a heterodox Muslim sect; however, some Turkish Alavies and radical Sunnis maintain Alavies are not Muslims.... Many Alavies allege discrimination in the state's failure to include any of their doctrines or beliefs in religious instruction classes in public schools, which reflect Sunni Muslim doctrines. They also charge a bias in the *Diyanet*,[293] which views Alavies as a cultural rather than religious group; the *Diyanet* does not allocate specific funds for Alavi activities or religious leadership. However, some Sunni Islamic political activists charge that the state favours and is under the influence of the Alavies.[294]

Also different Sufi sects have been banned and restricted as heretic in some countries. According to a report: "in Turkey mystical Sufi religious-social orders (*tariqat*s) have been banned officially since the 1920s. The military ranks *tariqat*s among the most harmful threats to secularism; however, *tariqat*s remain active and widespread."[295] In Iran, one popular Sufi sect is Nematollahi. Although this sect strictly observes Islamic practices and beliefs, some conservative Muslim clerics see it as a danger to Islam. On 13 February 2006, hundreds of demonstrators belonging to this sect, including women and children, were injured, when the police and some extremist groups broke up the protest, and as many as 1200 were arrested. Iran's hard-line daily 'Kayhan', on 14 February, quoted senior clerics in Qom as saying that Sufism should be eradicated in the city, while it was reported that in September one of Iran's Grand Ayatollahs called for a clampdown on Sufis in Qom.[296] This city is the major Shiite clerical centre in Iran.

The Zikris is another Sufi sect. In Pakistan "200,000 Zikris are found in Gwadar, Balochistan. Most Sunnis consider Zikris to be non-Muslims due to their unique religious ceremonies, including a separate hajj held in Turbat,

---

293 The Government's Directorate of Religious Affairs.

294 U.S. Department of State, International Religious Freedom Report on Turkey, 2003.

295 *Ibid.*

296 See for example Golnaz Esfandiari, 'Iran: Qom Authorities Crack Down On Sufis', Payvand's Iran News, available at the website of Payvand at: <http://www.payvand.com/news/06/feb/1135.html>.

Balochistan."[297] "As in the case of the Ahmadies, there is said to be a campaign to have the Zikris declared non-Muslim."[298]

4.2.3. *Security Laws against Heretic Religious Groups*

With the increase of religious extremism in recent decades, a number of security laws against the activities of these groups have been passed in some Muslim countries. As an example, the following part was added to the Penal Code of Egypt in 1992:

> A penalty of imprisonment for a period of not less that six months and not more than five years or a fine of not less than LE 500 and not more than LE 1000 shall be imposed on any person who exploits religion in order to promote or advocate extremist ideologies by word of mouths, in writing or any other manner with a view to stirring up sedition, disparaging or belittling any divine religion or its adherents or prejudicing national unity or social harmony.[299]

The legislation in some Muslim states, however, has been subject to abuse by governmental authorities in targeting peaceful unauthorized religious groups. For example, according to one report about Egypt: "Mohamed El-Derini, one of a group of nine Shiite Muslims, was arrested by the State Security Intelligence Service (SSIS) in 2003 and again in March 2004 apparently because of [his] religious beliefs; then was released in June 2005 after having spent fifteen months in administrative detention."[300] In another example, in Malaysia under the Internal Security Act, 1960 (ISA),[301] "between October 2000 and January 2001 the federal government detained six followers of Shiite teaching.... The

---

297 U.S. Department of State, International Religious Freedom Report on Pakistan, 2005.

298 Abdelfattah Amor, Visit to Pakistan, *supra* note 144, para. 46.

299 Report submitted to the Commission of Human Rights by Angelo Riberio, Special Rapporteur on Implementation of the Declaration on the Elimination of All forms of Intolerance and Discrimination Based on Religion or Belief, paras. 11–15, U.N.Doc.E/CN.4/1992/25 (18 Dec. 1981), quoted in Boyle, *supra* note 97, p. 68.

300 U.S. Department of State, International Religious Freedom Report on Egypt, 2005.

301 This law allows indefinite detention without trial that apparently can be extended for an unlimited time by the police. For more information about the ISA Practice and relevant Malaysian court judgement, see the related website of the Anti-ISA Movement at: <http://www.suaram.org/isa/>.

police released one of them, two were sent to restricted residence and the rest were detained for a two-year period."[302] However, according to another report during the period 2002–2003, "no individuals were detained under the ISA for religious reasons."[303]

4.3. SOURCES OF *TAKFIR* (DECLARING OTHER MUSLIMS AS INFIDEL)

4.3.1. *Authorized (Official) Sources*

In current times, the Islamic Research Institute at Al-Azhar is the most well-known authorized source for declaring *takfir*. On the practice of *takfir* by Al-Azhar, Berger states:

> One of the first accusations was made against the – nowadays renown scholar – Taha Hussain for the contents of his Ph.D. dissertation written at the [Al-]Azhar University in the 1930s. Such an accusation cost the life of the Egyptian writer and human rights activist Farag Foda, who was very critical of the Islamic establishment. He was shot dead by an Islamic extremist in 1992, one week after he had been branded an apostate by the Al-Azhar. In 1997, the Al-Azhar Front for Scholars accused Hassan Hanafi, a philosophy professor at Cairo University, of apostasy, but the case was never pursued and faded away without any repercussions…., the latest accusation of apostasy and heresy was made against the abovementioned Nawal al-Saadawy by the Egyptian Grand *Mufti*.[304]

There are other non-religious official institutions that have declared *takfir*. As mentioned above, in the case of the Ahmadies in Pakistan, the parliament and the courts made a judgment on the heresy of the Ahmadies. Similarly, as will be discussed further in section 4.4 of this book, in the cases of Ostadh Taha, Abu Zayd, Eshkevari and Aghajari, the courts charged the accused with apostasy. In another case, in September 2005, Latif Pedram, a candidate for

---

302 SURAM (Malaysia), Abolish ISA Movement, <http://www.suaram.org/isa/list_deatinees.htm>, quoted in Saeed, *supra* note 25, p. 128.

303 U.S. Department of State, International Religious Freedom Report on Malaysia, 2003.

304 Berger, *supra* note 145, p. 730.

the Afghanistan presidency, was accused of apostasy (*kofr -guei*) – in fact of heresy – by the Supreme Court of Afghanistan and was asked to withdraw his name as a candidate, as he had announced an opinion about polygamy and the right of divorce in Muslim law.[305]

An interesting and unusual case of *takfir* is the one made by the Organization of the Islamic Conference (OIC) against Rushdie. The foreign ministers of 44 member states of the organization held a meeting in Riyadh in March 1989 where they announced: "The conference declared that blasphemy cannot be justified on the basis of freedom of expression and opinion. The conference strongly condemned the book 'the Satanic Verses', whose author is regarded as a heretic. It appeals to all members of society to impose a ban on the book and to take the necessary legislation to insure the protection of the religious beliefs of others."[306]

Finally, it is important to notice that institutions such as parliaments, courts or the Organization of the Islamic Conference are not qualified for declaring *takfir*, unless their declarations are based on an earlier declaration of *takfir* by an authorized *mufti* or *mujtahid*. However, if the offence of Rushdie is considered *sabb*, as mentioned in sections 1.1.2 and 3.2 of this book, such a prior declaration is not needed, as *sabb* can be identified by ordinary Muslims as well. As will be discussed in the next section, such earlier declarations of *takfir* were revealed in the two major cases of heresy against Taha and Aghajari, though in other cases, such as the case of Abu Zayd, the earlier declaration might remain undisclosed.

4.3.2. *Semi-authorized and Arbitrary Sources*

Other sources of *takfir* are semi-authorized and arbitrary ones. Semi-authorized sources are those *mufti*s or *mujtahid*s whose opinions or declarations of *takfir* might affect court decisions, governmental institutions or governmental policies. These sources are mainly funded or supported by the governments as well. As mentioned above, and as will be discussed further, in the cases of the

---

305 After international community questioned the constitutionality of this ruling, Latif Pedram was allowed to remain in the race. See U.S. Department of State, International Religious Freedom Report on Afghanistan, 2004. Also see a report by BBC in Persian, available at: <http//www.bbc.co.uk/Persian/afganistan/story/200…/040901_a_afg_latif_pedram.shtm>.

306 Quoted in Daniel Pipes, 'The Ayatollah, the Novelist, and the West, Commentary', June 1989, available at: <http://www.danielpipes.org/article/186>.

Ahmadies, Rushdie, Latif Pedram, Taha, Abu Zayd and Aghajari, the parliaments, courts or the Organization of Islamic Conference are not qualified to declare *takfir*, unless their declarations are based on an earlier declaration of *takfir* by such authorized or semi-authorized sources.

As mentioned in the above mentioned example of Al-Azhar, sometimes the declaration of semi-authorized sources will lead to violence or arbitrary killings of heretics or unbelievers. As another example shows, in 1996 in Iran, such declarations were used as the justification for the arbitrary killing of two Iranian political opponents and three writers by members of Iran's intelligence forces in an event known as 'Serial Murder'.[307] The other famous case of *takfir* by Shiite *mujtahid*s before the 1979 Iranian revolution was the one against Ahmad Kasravi, a famous Iranian scholar, which led to his assassination in Tehran in 1956.[308]

Arbitrary sources of *takfir* are those *mufti*s, *mujtahid*s or even ordinary individuals who belong to illegal groups and normally neither their existence nor their declarations are in line with governmental policies. It is beyond the scope of this study to examine arbitrary cases of *takfir* and its dangerous role in creating violence and mass killing among Muslims.

It is worth mentioning, however, that such practices are less common among Shiite groups than among Sunnis, at least in recent decades. One reason for this is that, in recent years, mainly Sunni militant groups have been active, and therefore, like some other political groups have resorted to religious justifications such as *takfir* for the elimination of their opponents.

Furthermore, although any Shiite *mujtahid* is qualified to issue a *fatwa*, among Shiites, only the *fatwa*s of well-known grand *mujtahid*s, of whom there

---

307 In 1998 agents of Iranian Ministry of Intelligence killed Darioush Foroohar and his wife Parvaneh Foroohar, Majid Sharif, Mohammad Mokhtari, and Jafar Payandeh. Darioush and Parvaneh Foroohar were long-time political activist and had been leaders of the Mellat Party of Iran since 1951. Sharif, Mokhtari and Payandeh were well known journalists and writers. Under pressure from president Khatami, in January 1999, the Ministry of intelligence acknowledged that its agents had perpetrated the murders. Subsequently, the authorities arrested eighteen people and tried them in connection with the killing. Later it was announced that a high ranking official of the ministry, Saeed Emami, was the mastermind behind the serial killings. Emami committed suicide while in custody and the involvement of other officials, especially those qualified *mujtahid*s who issued the declaration of *takfir*, remained a mystery.

308 For more information about Kasravi, See for example, Iraj Bashiri, 'A Brief Note on the Life of Ahmad Kasravi', (2000), available at: <http://www.angelfire.com/rnb/bashiri/Authors/Kasravi.html>.

are not, normally, more than a dozen, are listened to or obeyed by ordinary Shiites. This held true in the case of Moqtada Sadr in the early years of the occupation of Iraq. He could not continue with his military activities, as he did not succeed in gaining the support of Ayatollah Sistani or any other grand Shiite *mujtahids*. For Sunni groups, however, systematic institutions such as Al-Azhar do not exist everywhere and oftentimes *fatwas* which are issued by unqualified individuals are obeyed by ordinary people. Controlling the sources of these *fatwas* and their numerous religious schools, known as *madresah*, has been an issue of concern particularly for the Pakistani government in the last decade.

Following the intra-religious violations in Iraq, Pakistan and some other Muslim states, in which religious extremists were declaring other Muslim individuals or groups to be unbelievers, a statement was issued in accordance with the *fatwas* of major Sunni and Shiite jurists (both Ja'fari and Zaydi) by their representatives at a conference held in Amman in July 2005. This body of major jurists included the Grand *Imam* Shaykh Al-Azhar, the Grand Ayatollah Sistani, the Grand *Mufti* of Egypt, the Grand *Mufti* of the Sultanate of Oman, the Islamic *Fiqh* Academy in the Kingdom of Saudi Arabia, the Grand Council for Religious Affairs of Turkey, the Grand *Mufti* of the Hashemite Kingdom of Jordan and the Members of its National *Fatwa* Committee, and Shaykh Dr. Yusuf Al-Qaradawi.[309]

To protect different sects from being labelled as heretic, the first part of that statement provides a list of some famous Muslim sects, whose beliefs in Islam were found to be in accordance with the main principles of Islam by the conference:

> Whosoever is an adherent of one of the four Sunni schools of jurisprudence (Hanafi, Maliki, Shafi'i and Hanbali), the Ja'fari (Shi'i) school of jurisprudence, the Zaydi school of jurisprudence, the Ibadi school of jurisprudence, or the Thahiri school of jurisprudence is a Muslim. Declaring that person an apostate is impossible. Verily his (or her) blood, honour, and property are sacrosanct.[310]

309 International Islamic Conference, 'True Islam and its Role in Modern Society', 4–6 July 2005. The final statement is available at the website of Embassy of Jordan in Washington: <http://www.jordanembassyus.org/new/pr/pr07062005.shtml>. Translation of the statement in Persian is available at the Baztzb website at: <http://www.baztab.com/news/26749.php>. Visited on 27.12.2006.

310 *Ibid.*

Apparently, consensus over including other Muslim sects in the list was not achieved by the conference; for example, with regard to Ash'ari, Sufism and Salafi not being apostate, it was only declared by the *fatwa* of Shaykh Al-Azhar, and not other participants in the conference: "Moreover, in accordance with what appeared in the *fatwa* of the Honourable and Respectable Shaykh Al-Azhar, it is not possible to declare that anyone who subscribes to the Ash'ari creed or who practices true Sufism is an apostate. Likewise, it is not possible to declare whosoever subscribes to true Salafi thought an apostate."[311]

In listing the minimum elements of belief that save a Muslim individual or sect from being labelled as an apostate, the statement failed to reach consensus and referred to ambiguous terms such as "necessary article of religion": "Equally, it is not possible to declare as apostates any group of Muslims who believe in *Allah* the Mighty and Sublime and His Messenger and the pillars of faith, and respect the pillars of Islam and do not deny any necessary article of religion."

With regard to arbitrary sources of *takfir*, the statement pointed out:

> Acknowledgement of the schools of jurisprudence within Islam means adhering to a fundamental methodology in the issuance of *fatwa*s. No one may issue a *fatwa* without the requisite personal qualifications which each school of jurisprudence defines. No one may issue a *fatwa* without adhering to the methodology of the schools of jurisprudence. No one may claim to do absolute *ijtihad* and create a new school of jurisprudence or to issue unacceptable *fatwa*s that take Muslims out of the principles and certainties of the *Shariah* and what has been established in respect of its schools of jurisprudence.[312]

The statement, however, seems very conservative in holding a position against any labelling of apostasy. One reason for this failure is that all participants in the conference, as the religious official authorities, had to give their opinions under the limits of traditional Muslim law.

---

311 *Ibid.*
312 *Ibid.*

4.4. THE MAJOR HERESY CASES

4.4.1. *The Case of Ostadh Mahmud Muhammad Taha (Sudan)*

In January 1985, Mahmud Muhammad Taha, leader of the Sudanese Republican Party or the Republican Brotherhood (*Ikhwan Jamhouriyeen*) and four of his followers were accused in court of offences against the state.[313] Regarding the opinion of the court on offences against the state, O'Sulivan notes:

> The judge did not, at any time, describe the details of the offence against state, which the accused were being charged with and convicted of, but he emphasized certain parts of a pamphlet that pointed towards the need for an Islamic revival and reform of *Shariah* law that was sought after by the Republican Brotherhood. The judge declared, without producing any evidence to contest the views and beliefs stated within the pamphlet, that the information provided within would include social upheaval if it was allowed to be publicly distributed.[314]

According to An Na'im, the judgment of the court, however, for some reason implied accusations of apostasy:

> The trial judge stated that the death sentence would not be carried out if the accused were to repent and recant at any time before execution. As the notion of stay of execution on the grounds of repentance and recanting of one's beliefs or views is completely alien to Sudanese criminal law, the judge must have had the *Shariah* offences of apostasy in mind although he refused to mention it, presumably because of the obvious constitutional objections.[315]

The Court of Appeal, in the absence of the accused, confirmed the original conviction for offences against state, and further added a new explicit convic-

313 Taha called for a liberal, openly-debated, and humanistic revision of traditional Muslim law. He called his approach the 'Second Message of Islam', as it distinguished between the Koranic passages revealed in Medina, which he argued dealt only with circumstances in Arabia at that time, and the Koranic passages revealed in Mecca, which contained an eternal message. This allowed him to justify discarding Muslim legal traditions which were inconsistence with modern human rights norms. See Mahmud Muhammad Taha, *Second Message of Islam* (trans. Abdullahi Ahmed An-Na'im, Syracuse: Syracuse University Press, 1987).

314 O'Sulivan, *supra* note 283, p. 54.

315 Abdullahi Ahmed An-Na'im, 'The Islamic Law of Apostasy and its Modern Applicability: A Case from The Sudan' *Religion* 16 (1986), p. 208.

tion and sentence for the separate crime of apostasy.[316] The court ordered Taha "to be executed immediately, without the opportunity to repent and recant, because he had persisted in advocating his 'heretical' view for many years and refused to heed judicial and other pronouncements."[317]

Furthermore, as mentioned in section 4.2.2, the Court of Appeal extended its judgment to all members of the Republicans or the followers of Taha declaring them equally to be apostates and to be treated as such in all interactions with Muslims.[318] The other four accused were allowed one month to repent and the 76 year old Taha was publicly hanged on 19 January, 1985. In addition, as he was not considered a Muslim, his body was not allowed to be buried in a Muslim cemetery and his property was also confiscated.[319] Numaire announced his support for the execution "on the basis of *Shariah* law to protect the nation from the danger of Mahmud Muhammad Taha and his slander of God and his insolence towards Him and to protect this homeland from heresy."[320]

As mentioned in section 4.3.1, a civil court is not a qualified source of *takfir*. Therefore, its judgments on apostasy, if made, should be based on a qualified source of *takfir*, such as a *mufti* or a religious court. This held true with the accusation against Taha of heresy. O'Sullivan names two previous declarations that the Court of Appeal referred to in its judgment:

> One was a previous conviction in *Shariah* court in Khartoum on 18 November 1986, some seventeen years earlier, by some private plaintiffs who were offended by Taha's opinion on Islam. During this trial, Taha and the movement were declared *kafir* [infidel], heathen or non-Muslim. On the second point, the Court of Appeal cited the opinions of the Al-Azhar University in Egypt and the Muslim World League. Both argued that Taha was an apostate and proceeded to tell the Sudanese court to treat him as such.[321]

316 O'Sulivan, *supra* note 283, p. 55.

317 An-Na'im, *supra* note 315, p. 208.

318 O'Sulivan, *supra* note 283, p. 55.

319 *Ibid.*

320 Mayer, *supra* note 290, p. 185. Numaire's stance backfired, however, as an international outcry led to his toppling by a popular coalition only three months later. See Arzt, Heroes or Heretics, *supra* note 250, p. 406.

321 O'Sulivan, *supra* note 283, p. 56.

4.4.2. *The Case of Professor Nasr Hamed Abu Zayd (Egypt)*

Nasr Hamed Abu Zayd, a former Professor of Arabic literature at Cairo University, currently leads the Chair of 'Islam and Humanism' at the University for Humanistics in Utrecht, the Netherlands. In 1996, the Egyptian Court of Cassation ruled that the writings of Abu Zayd on Islam constituted an act of apostasy or unbelief.[322] As a result of this rule Abu Zayd's marriage with his wife was dissolved. According to the court Abud Zayd's writings included:

> scorning the Koran or the Prophetic *Sunnah*, or mocking, repudiating, or disavowing them, or intentionally claiming anything contradicting them publicly or haughtily, or doubting any of it,...denying God's existence or His creation as mentioned in the Koran,...repudiating the prophecy of Mohammad or in general his prophecy to all people, or doubting his sincerity.[323]

The above list of offences mentioned by the court includes the three phenomena of apostasy. First, "denying God's existence" results in conversion or renouncing Islam. Second, "scorning the Koran or the Prophetic *Sunnah*, or mocking, repudiating, or disavowing them" are blasphemy offences. Finally, "claiming anything, contradicting them publicly or haughtily, or doubting any of it, denying God's creation as mentioned in the Koran, and doubting the Prophet's sincerity" are the issues of different interpretation of religion and therefore heresy offences.

In the court's judgment, no reference was made to the intentional renouncing of Islam or *sabb*, therefore, Abu Zayd was in fact guilty of heresy. The details of the judgment provide more elaboration on the offence and it even calls Abu Zayd a heretic (*zandiq*):

> ...because he has revealed his unbelief after having been a believer, even if he claims to be a Muslim. An apostate cannot be excused when he claims to be a Muslim, because he has adopted a stance contrary to Islam. But

322 Abu Zayd criticizes the traditional way of reading the Koran as being outdated and calls for a scientifically founded interpretation which places the text into historical context and distinguishes the real meaning from contemporary ideas arising from the spirit of the times. According to Abu Zayd a modern interpretation of Islam is to be developed by applying historic and linguistic methods, since the Koran itself is open to diverse interpretations. For Abu Zayd's view see Nasr Hamed Abu Zayd, *Rethinking the Koran: Towards a Humanistic Hermeneutics* (Humanistics University Press, Utrecht, 2004).

323 Court of Cassation, Nos. 475, 478, 481, Year 65, 5 Aug. 1996, quoted in Berger, *supra* note 145, p. 720.

then a heretic (*zandiq*) usually talks about his infidelity and proclaims his wrong faith while at the same time claiming that he is a Muslim.[324]

The court made its conclusion of apostasy or unbelief of Abu Zayd after examining his teachings, publications, and his critical views on traditional Muslim law. According to the court:

- He denounces that the Koran is the word of God, describing it as 'a cultural product,' and as being affiliated to a human culture, rendering it an incarnated human text.
- He describes [Islam] as an Arabic religion, denying its universality and availability to everybody.
- He attacks the application of the *Shariah* by describing it as backward and reactionary.
- He claims that the *Shariah* is the reason behind the backwardness of Muslims and their degradation.
- He states that abiding by *Shariah* texts is contradictory to civilization and progress and hinders the proceeding of life.
- He accuses the theological method as clashing with the mind by stating that 'there is a battle being fought by the powers of the superstition and myth in the name of religion and literal meanings of religious texts and by the intellectual powers of progress trying to fight sometimes with superstition on its own ground.' This is clear unbelief!
- He goes as far as calling for liberation from *Shariah* texts, claiming that they lack any essential and fixed elements, and that they only express a historic phase which has passed. This is an accusation that the law of God is not suitable for all times....
- He denies that God Almighty is [physically] on His great Throne and that His Chair encompasses the Heavens and Earth, and that He created Paradise, Hell, Angels and Demons, although the Koranic verses categorically stipulate all that....
- He boldly proceeded in this approach, which is opposed to Islam in its meaning, dogmas and fundamentals, denying the main fundamentals of its sacredness. He did not hesitate to contradict established truths, even historic ones.... while he was fully aware of its meaning and truth within the balance of the *Shariah*.[325]

324 *Ibid.*, p. 732.
325 *Ibid.*, quoted in Berger, *supra* note 145, pp. 731–732.

Apart from its declarations on apostasy, the court revealed another area that is different from that of traditional law of apostasy, namely the issue of public order. According to the court, Abu Zayd had failed to prove his loyalty to the orthodoxy of religion, to *Shariah* as a source of law, and to the state as the foundations of the public order:

> To depart from Islam is to revolt against it, and this necessarily finds its reflection in the loyalty of the individual to the *Shariah*, the state, and his ties with the society. This is what no law or state tolerates... No individual has the right to proclaim that which contradicts the public policy or morals (*al-nizam al-ammawal-adab*), use his opinion to harm the fundamentals upon which the society is built, to revile the sacred things, or to disdain Islam or any other heavenly religion.[326]

Although the court insisted on referring to this disloyalty as a threat to public order, interestingly enough, it does not suggest any punishment for the alleged offence, but merely resorted to a kind of indirect punishment that is dissolving the marriage of the accused based on traditional apostasy rules. Furthermore, similar to the case of Taha, Abu Zayd was not afforded the right to repent and, apparently, it was also not requested by him. It is not clear whether such ignorance of the right to repent was based on the legal traditions or on a fault by the court.

It is worth mentioning that, unlike the case of Taha, in the case of Abu Zayd, the court did not refer in its judgment to the earlier declaration of *takfir* by a qualified source of *takfir*, such as Al-Azhar. Yet, as the court's declaration of *takfir* was not challenged by Al-Azhar, apparently the court has either gained the consent of Al-Azhar unofficially, or the silence of Al-Azhar has been considered to constitute consent.

Finally, the controversial debate on the case of Abu Zayd caused the Egyptian legislation to withdraw from a problematic aspect of the legal traditions. The case brought to the court by the complaint of a third party was based on traditional Muslim law on *hisba* which allows an individual to sue on behalf of the community.[327] After the judgment on Abu Zayd, Egypt

---

326 *Ibid.*, p. 733.

327 In the case of Abu Zayd, a referee reader of the committee, in charge of evaluating Abu Zayd's work in order to grant him the position of professor, had deemed his work anti-Islamic. It was upon the instigation of Abu Zayd's accuser that his alleged apostasy was brought before the court. See *ibid.*, pp. 727–728.

subsequently changed its laws to prevent private parties from bringing such suits to court in the future. However, it did not protect Abu Zayd and his wife from the consequences of the judgment and they were obliged to seek asylum in Europe.[328]

4.4.3. *The Case of Hasan Yousefi Eshkevari (Iran)*

Hasan Yausefi Eshkevari, a researcher, journalist, cleric, and director of the 'Ali Shariati Research Centre', was arrested on 5 August 2000 on his return from a controversial conference in Berlin on charge of, among others, insult of sacred things of the holy religion and denial of essential requirements of the religion. In response to a question following his lecture during the Berlin conference, he stated that in his view veiling and the enforcement of a strict dress code for women had cultural and historical origins in Iran but is not required by Islam. Islamic principles relating to social issues were adaptable to change as the Prophet had only sanctioned them for the needs of his time.

These remarks were considered by a court as denying the essential requirements of the religion, which can lead to apostasy of Eshkevari. Later the court dismissed the charge of apostasy and, finally, in May 2001 Eshkevari was sentenced for other lesser offences to seven years' imprisonment and his status as a cleric was removed. He was released in February 2005 after more than four years of imprisonment as he was eligible for release after serving two-thirds of his sentence.[329]

4.4.4. *The Case of Professor Hashem Aghajari (Iran)*

Hashem Aghajari is a professor of history at Tabiat-e-Modarres University in Tehran as well as head of its history department. Following a public speech,[330] he was tried in October 2002 by the Fourteenth District Court in Hamadaan,

---

328 In July 2001, the Cairo Personal Status Court rejected a private complaint made by a hardliner attorney Nabih al-Wahsh against Nawal al-Sa'adawi, world well-known 70 year old Egyptian feminist writer, accusing her of apostasy for comments she had made on religious issues in the Egyptian weekly *al-Midan*. In his compliant the attorney sought to force the divorce of al-Sa'adawi from her husband.

329 On Eshkevari see for example website of Payvand at: <http://www.payvand.com/news/00/aug/1022.html>, Amnesty International at: <http://web.amnesty.org/library/Index/ENGMDE130222000?open&of=ENG-IRN>, and Pen American Centre at: <http://www.pen.org/freedom/hm/eshkevari.htm>.

330 For a translation of his speech in English see: <http://www.sullivan-country.com/id4/ip.htm>.

behind closed doors, on a variety of charges, including *sabb*-al *Nabi*, insulting the Shiite *Imams* and top state religious authorities. The judge later handed down a sentence of death, in addition to 74 lashes, eight years imprisonment and internal exile, and a ten year prohibition from teaching. However, unlike the case of Abu Zayd the court did not order dissolving the marriage of Aghajari and his wife as a legal consequence of the act of apostasy.

Later on the district court in Hamadaan failed to answer several questions of the Supreme National Court concerning its judgment. According to the Supreme Court, the judgment did not distinguish between *sabb*-al *Nabi* and unbelief. While *sabb*-al *Nabi* is an issue of Article 513 of the Penal Code, unbelief is not considered an offence according to the same code. Furthermore, the judgment did not provide sufficient reasoning with regard to the parts of the accused' speech which had led to the conclusion of his unbelief. In addition, it was not clear from the judgment, which *usul* (the fundamental principles) or *frue* (the major commandments or practices) of the religion have been denied by the accused. It was also not clear from the term 'insulting the clerics' to whom or to what part of their writings reference is being made.[331]

After a period of approximately 23 months, the death sentence was revoked by the Supreme Court and, in July 2005, the case was sent to another lower court for retrial in Tehran. The judge in the new court announced that after primary consultations, he had concluded that *irtidad* based on *Sabb*-al *Nabi* (in fact blasphemy), or denying the necessities of Islam (in fact heresy) is not relevant to the case of Aghajari but only insulting sacred things of the religion.[332] This time the court kept a distance from the heresy accusations as the general prosecutor's representative repeatedly stated that the duty of the court is not to investigate the opinions of the accused but to meet the issue of insulting the sacred things.

Finally, Aghajari was sentenced to five years in prison (two years suspended) and five years deprivation of social rights on grounds of insulting religious sacred things. As Aghajari had already served three years in prison, he was thus released after the final trial. His lawyer, however, did not accept the judgment on the grounds that it was not based on a jury opinion. The lawyer believed that such a jury for realizing insulting should consist of experts

331 See the websites of Shargh Daily at: <http://www.sharghnewspaper.com/830216/index.htm> and Iranian Student News Agency at: <http://www.isna.ir/news/NewsPrint.asp?id=376787>.

332 See the website of Iranian Student News Agency at: <http://www.isna.co.ir/news/NewsPrint.asp?id=399884>.

in law, history, sociology, *fiqh* (Islamic jurisprudence) and *kalaam* (theology). He also insisted that an intention to insult was a necessary factor.[333]

The case of Aghajari revealed some crucial questions facing the Iranian judiciary. Regarding the sources of the declaration of *takfir*, according to the information later released by Aghajari's lawyer, the judgment on *irtidad* by the Hamadaan court was based on the judge's reliance on the opinion of a few hardliner *mujtahids*.[334]

On the other hand, according to Muslim legal traditions, when an apostasy verdict is issued by a *mujtahid*, no other court or *mujtahid* can render it null. This fact was reiterated by Elham, currently the minister of justice and the cabinet spokesman, and at that time the spokesman of the Guardian Council. He said, "Nobody can announce a verdict on *irtidad* void. *Irtidad* if it is *fitri* may not be repented. If the verdict is issued as a primary rule no one can cancel it. I either doubt if *sabb-al Nabi* can be forgivable."[335]

Yet, despite this fact, the lawyer and some other officials sought the opinion of other *mujtahids*, such as the Leader and the Chief of the Judiciary, who, in contradiction to the hardliner's opinions, reasoned that Aghajari's offence was not considered apostasy.[336] Announcing these differing opinions

---

333 See the final statement of Aghajari's lawyer, Seyed Mohammad Seyfzaadeh, (20 July 2004) in Persian, available at the website of Iranian Student News Agency at: <http://www.isna.co.ir/news/NewsPrint.asp?id=408719>.

334 For more information about these declaration of *takfir* see Hosein Baastaani, 'He Should be Killed, without Trial', (10 Jan. 2006) in Persian, available at Roozonline Electronic Daily at: <http://roozonline.com/02article/013282.shtml>. Also see Hosein Baastaani, 'The Meeting of the Expert Assembly and Meaningful Points', in Persian, available at Roozonline Electronic Daily at: <http://roozonline.com/02article/012478.shtm>.

335 Hamshahri Daily, 8 Dec. 2002, quoted in Hosein Baastaani, 'The Role of Ostadh in the Death Sentences' (15 Nov. 2005) in Persian, available at Roozonline Electronic Daily at: <http://roozonline.com/02article/011721.shtml>.

336 See the final statement of Seyfzaadeh, *supra* note 333. It seems that Seyfzaadeh did not distinguish between *sabb* and heresy as for both he has enquired the opinions of major *mujtahids*. Yet, based on Muslim legal traditions, for realizing *sabb* an opinion of *mujtahid* is not required. Apart from the Aghajari case, in subsequent journalist cases Seyfzaadeh sought similarly the opinion of *mujtahids* on whether they consider the contents of articles *sabb* or an offence of insult of lesser degree. See for example the interview of Seyfzaadeh with ISNA regarding articles on *qisas* (Retaliation) in Neshat Daily. In this interview Seyfzaadeh mentions that he has enquired from eleven *mujtahids* on whether the articles contained an element of insulting pious *Imams*. Quoted in Shargh Online (11 March 2005), in Persian available at the website of Shargh Daily at: <http://www.sharghnewspaper.com/831220/html/s198606>. However, as *mujtahids* themselves are known as outstanding jurists in Iran, this policy might have been followed by the lawyer for convincing the judges or putting pressures on them.

provided the grounds for transferring the case from Hamadaan to another court in Tehran.

The issue of religious duties of Muslims regarding a *takfir* declaration which conflicts with a court decision was also questioned by a journal, belonging to Ayatollah Mesbah Yazdi, before the death sentence was issued by the Hamadaan Court. The journal asked: "Does Ayatollah Mesbah or other grand *mujtahid*s consider Aghajari as a *murtad*?" And the journal continued, "If according to the grand *mujtahid*s Aghajari is a *murtad* but the court has a different opinion and releases him, what is the religious duty of Muslims?"[337] The journal implied that if the court has a different opinion on *takfir* from that of *mujtahid*s, the duty of Muslims is to obey the opinion of the *mujtahid* and not that of the court.

4.5. SUMMARY

Article 6 of the Press Code of Iran has extended the scope of the limitation of freedom of expression to those statements against the Islamic Code (*ahkaam-e Islam*), and other ambiguous areas, subject to a broad interpretation based on heresy. Similarly, some Malaysian states have enforced legislation on insulting Islam, in which, similar to the Iranian Press Code, the scope of the prohibitions are sometimes extended to issues contrary to traditional Muslim law and other ambiguous areas. Furthermore, in Malaysia, as Sunni Islam is the official branch of Islam, propagating other branches of Islam or any criticism against the prevailing interpretation of Muslim law is prohibited under some state laws.

In Egypt, while there is no statutory law against heresy, the case law demonstrates a broad interpretation of the issue of insulting religious sacred things, which could potentially allow for allegations based on heresy. In practice, however, fortunately, very few cases of allegations based on heresy have been reported in Iran, Malaysia and Egypt; the most important of those which have come before the courts are the cases of Eshkevari and Aghajari in Iran and Abu Zayd in Egypt.

On the other hand, while restrictive policies are adopted for many different minority Muslim sects in different Muslim countries, the Ahmadies

337 Partow-e Sokhan Journal, (31 July 2002), quoted in Hosein Baastaani, the Role of Ostadh, *supra* note 335.

is the only Muslim group which has been targeted in legislation and thus severely affected.

With regard to heresy, the main issue of concern in Muslim countries is *takfir* or declaring other Muslim individuals or groups apostate. There are different sources of *takfir*, authorised, semi-authorised and arbitrary. While the Islamic Research Institute at Al-Azhar is the most famous authorised or semi-authorised one, arbitrary sources of *takfir* are those *mufti*s, *mujtahid*s or even individual Muslims who may belong to illegal groups.

Among the four major cases of heresy discussed here, the case of Abu Zayd was purely heretic, in which his marriage was dissolved by the court. However, in the case of Abu Zayd, apart from what was considered as apostasy in the first judgment, the court further revealed another area of concern for the case which is different from that of traditional Muslim law, i.e. the issue of public order.

It is worth mentioning that for both cases of Taha and Aghajari, the judgments of the courts on apostasy were based on an earlier or simultaneous declaration of *takfir* by some semi-authorised sources. For the case of Abu Zayd, although apparently such an earlier declaration existed, it was not referred to by the court.

Concluding Remarks

In evaluating the impacts of Muslim legal traditions of apostasy on legislation and legal practices of Muslim states, the study distinguished between the three different phenomena of apostasy namely conversion, blasphemy and heresy. Moreover, to the extent in which the traditional rules of apostasy have been practiced or embodied in the legislation, a dividing line was drawn between the public aspects of these traditions and their personal aspects. Furthermore, since "there is a difference between the principle of having a law, and the effectiveness of its enforcement, which may depend basically on how judgment is exercised",[254] another distinction should be made between the written legislative sources and the legal practice of Muslim states with regard to their religious legal traditions.

The Extent of Inclusion of Muslim Legal Traditions of Apostasy in Legislation

The personal aspects of legal traditions of apostasy which are the family law consequences such as dissolving the marriage of the convert, are primarily found in legal practices and not in legislation. With regard to the effects of the public aspects of legal traditions of apostasy on the legislation, it should be noted that no state has included in its legislation a literal provision of these traditions on the prohibition and punishment of conversion. Similarly, the legislation of non-Muslim state imposes civil consequences for apostasy, such as confiscation of property of the apostate.

Nonetheless, the legislation in Sudan is the only legislation in force that has prescribed the death penalty not for conversion but for a conversion related offences. Also legislation in several Malaysian states incorporates some forms of punishment against converts including fines and short terms of imprisonment. Additionally, a form of short detention period, under the title of 'rehabilitation period', might be imposed on converts.

---

254 CRE, Second Review of the Race Relations Act 1976 (1991) at 60, quoted in Theresa Murphy, 'Incitement to Hatred; Lessons from Northern Ireland' in Coliver, *supra* note 94, p. 65.

The only public aspect of Muslim legal traditions of apostasy which has literally been embodied in the legislation of Muslim states is the death sentence as a punishment of *sabb* in Pakistan and Iran. With regard to heresy, the legislation on insulting religious sacred things in Iran, Pakistan and some Malaysian states is capable of being subject to wide interpretation so as to include critical opinions on the orthodox version of the religion such as criticism of problematic religious traditions and other ambiguous religious areas. With respect to religious groups, the Ahmadies in Pakistan is the only Muslim group that has been labelled as non-Muslim by a statutory law.

THE EXTENT OF APPLICATION OF MUSLIM LEGAL TRADITIONS OF APOSTASY IN LEGAL PRACTICES

Although administrative obstacles and social pressure may exist for converts in Muslim communities, no case of governmental punishment for conversion in Muslim countries has been reported. With regard to blasphemy and the application of relevant legislation in Pakistan and Iran, it should be added that in Iran while few cases of *sabb* have been filed under the Press Code, fortunately none of them were accepted as *sabb* by the court. Pakistan, unlike Iran, has been faced with very problematic allegations of *sabb* under the blasphemy law, though there have not been any reports of courts imposing a severe punishment.

The blasphemy law in Pakistan has been abused for allegations of heresy. Apart from Pakistan, four major heresy cases in Sudan, Egypt and Iran were discussed in detail in this part. Among these cases only the case of Abu Zayd in Egypt was a purely heretic one, which resulted not in a criminal punishment, but rather, in the dissolution of his marriage. In Egypt, while there is no statutory law against heresy, the case law has provided a broad interpretation of the issue of insulting religious sacred things that can give an open hand for allegations based on heresy.

The Sudanese case of Taha which took place in 1985 during the time of Numaire, is the only case of execution and at the same time the only case of imposing the civil consequences of apostasy for an apostasy related offence in recent Muslim history. In a further two major cases in Iran, namely the Eshkevari and Aghajari, apostasy (in fact heresy) was one of the charges against the accused. However, in both cases the allegation of heresy was dismissed by the court and both scholars were sentenced to prison for other offences. Finally, with regard to heretic religious groups, while restricting policies against these groups have been reported in some Muslim countries, the Ahmadies in Pakistan is the only Muslim group that has been severely affected by legislation.

With regard to the family consequences of conversion, it is not possible to investigate the extent to which these consequences have been imposed on converts. In this respect, however, cases affecting the custody of children have been reported in Malaysia, Jordan and finally the famous case of Abdul Rahman in Afghanistan. In the case of Abdul Rahman it was argued that while his punishment of conversion according to the current legislation of Afghanistan was very unlikely, depriving him of the custody of his two children seemed unavoidable. Also in the only two reported cases of apostasy from Egypt, i.e. Abu Zayd and the Christian Widow, dissolution of the marriage and deprivation of inherence were imposed respectively.

IMPRACTICAL LEGISLATION AND THE DISTINCTION BETWEEN WRITTEN LAWS AND LEGAL PRACTICES

Legislation on the prohibition and punishment of apostasy related offences has mainly disclosed impracticality. Yet, considering the important role of religion in Muslim societies, the related Muslim states are either reluctant or have failed in modifying this problematic legislation. Therefore, these laws can be considered as written but impractical, which address not the real jurisdictional requirements of the societies, but the states local policies with regard to religious sensitivities and general public concerns. On this duality Bielefeldt states:

> One should take into account that many Muslims still might feel insecure about the relationship between traditional religious norms on the one hand and modern legal standards on the other. That is why many Muslims assert the validity of the traditional Islamic *Shariah* in principle and at the same time seems prepared to accommodate pragmatically some political and legal reforms. For instance, even those who defend the legitimacy of *hadd* punishment in theory frequently prefer to avoid the actual implementation of these punishments, invoking practical obstacles to their reintroduction.[255]

255 Heiner Bielefeldt, 'Muslim Voice in the Human Rights Debate', 17 *Human Rights Quarterly* 4 (1995), p. 613.

Regarding this approach of Muslim states towards problematic religious traditions An-Na'im notes that "the psychological rational behind the displacement of *Shariah* seems to have been that Muslims preferred to keep *Shariah* intact and inviolable in theory even if that was not possible in practice."[256] Anderson founds logic for this duality in theory and practice:

> To a Muslim, it has always been a far more heinous sin to deny or question the divine revelation than to fail to obey it. So it seemed preferable to continue to play lip-service to an inviolate *Shariah*, as the only law of fundamental authority, and to excuse departure from much of it in practice by appealing to the doctrine of necessity (*dharura*), rather than to make any attempt to adapt that law to the circumstances and needs of contemporary life.[257]

Apart from the issue of religious sensitivities, another concern of Muslim states in explicit recognition of the right to change the religion is the very complicated family law consequences of apostasy on the converts.

As elaborated above on the impracticality of written legislation on prohibition and punishment of apostasy on the one hand, and on the practice of unwritten family law consequences of apostasy on the other hand, one might conclude that the practices of traditional Muslim law by Muslim states are not necessarily a reflection of their statutory laws.

WITHDRAWING FROM PROBLEMATIC TRADITIONS OF APOSTASY

It is not possible to identify clearly the trend of abandonment of problematic traditions of apostasy by Muslim states. With regard to the family law consequences of apostasy it was interesting to see that whereas in Iran and Egypt a non-Muslim can not inherit from a Muslim, in Malaysia and Pakistan the discriminatory rules of traditional Muslim law on inheritance have been abandoned and therefore Muslims and non-Muslims may inherit from each other.

Considering the case of Rushdie, it was important that in an effort to disassociate Iranian government from the death sentence of Rushdie, at least

256 Abdullahi Ahmed An-Na'im, *Toward an Islamic Reformation: Civil Liberties, Human Rights and International Law* (Syracuse, NY: Syracuse University Press, 1990), p. 6.

257 J. Norman D. Anderson, *Law Reform in the Muslim World* (London: Athlone Press, 1976), p. 6.

in the territory of other states, the Iranian authorities, apparently for the first time, made a clear distinction between government acts and religious rules.

On the issue of heresy, in the aftermath of the critical debate raised on the four major heresy cases, seemingly the judiciary in Sudan, Egypt, Iran and in other Muslim countries appeared to distance themselves from engaging in similar cases and the incumbent controversies. After the execution of Taha and the fall of Numaire some time later, the Sudan judiciary apologized for the judgment. Also as the case of Abu Zayd was brought to the court by a third party, based on legal traditions of *hisba* which allows an individual to sue on behalf of the community, subsequent to the judgment on Abu Zayd, Egypt altered its laws to prevent private parties from bringing such suits to court in the future.

COMMENTS ON INTRA-RELIGIOUS RIGHTS AND TOLERANCE

On the issue of freedom of religion and religious intolerance, the focus of international human rights law is on inter-religious issues rather than intra-religious ones. While inter-religious rights address freedom to followers of a religion in connection with other religions, the intra-religious rights are a matter of freedom of individuals and smaller religious groups within the same larger religious community. Intra-religious rights appear in three different categories. First is the freedom to criticise a religion as a whole or in part, especially the orthodox version of a religion. Second is the right to practice the religion in a different way than the majority or to be excluded from part of religious practices including its legal traditions, such as the family law. Third is the right of those who wish to exclude themselves from the domain of their religion or their religious community as a whole or in other words renounce their religion.

Among the three intra-religious issues, only the third category, the right to change or renounce the religion, has been brought into special focus of related international instruments, and the two other categories have been insufficiently treated. For these two categories a distinction should be made between intra-religious intolerance and intra-religious freedoms. While the issue of intra-religious intolerance has become a subject of special attention after the rise of militant extremism in Muslim countries during the last decades,[258] the intra-religious rights are still neglected. In this sense, while the

258 See for example Abdelfattah Amor, Special Rapporteur of the Commission on Human Rights, Implementation of the Declaration on the Elimination of All Forms of Intolerance

right to criticise a religion is partly considered under Article 19 of the ICCPR on freedom of expression, the right to be excluded from part of religious practices or perform it in a different way from the majority has been omitted from the discourse. This needs to be rectified since as noted by Eltayeb: "What is particularly necessary is to secure and guarantee the right of dissent within a religious community."[259]

COMMENTS ON CONVERSION AND PROSELYTIZING

States can resort to legitimate restrictions against manifestations of religion, among which restrictions against some special kinds of proselytizing in sensitive multi-religious communities appear reasonable. In these societies particularly the activities of foreign missionaries may be regulated by the state. Yet the right to change one's religion, when it does not contain the elements of manifestations of religion is an unconditional right and subject to no restrictions.

As mentioned above, given the religious sensitivities among the majority of Muslim communities, for some Muslim states it is difficult to explicitly recognize the right to change one's religion in their formal position, though at least in practice they should lift the restrictions in fulfilment of this right. In this sense the first priority is to minimize the role of the government and governmental institutions in the process of conversion.

Legislation in some Malaysian states has provided the widest engagement of the government in the process of conversion. Nevertheless, as mentioned above, it is not easy to asses the extent of practice under this legislation. Administrative measures for conversion, such as changing the family law, a rehabilitation period, the approval of *Shariah* courts, and finally registration of the new religion, at least in theory, make the process long and complicated. In fact, from the initiation of the process of conversion until the conversion is registered into the new religious community, the religious rights of a converted person are ignored by the government, as the convert is neither included in the new religion, nor excluded from the previous one.

---

and Discrimination Based on Religion or Belief, Report Relating to Visit to Algeria, U.N.Doc. E/CN.4/2003/66/Add.1 (9 Jan. 2003).

259 Mohammed S.M. Eltayeb, 'A Human Rights Framework for Defining and Understanding Intra-religious Persecutions in Muslim Countries', in Nazila Ghanea (ed.) *The Challenge of Religious Discrimination at the Dawn of the New Millennium* (Martinus Nijhoff Publishers, Leiden/Boston, 2003), p. 85.

Furthermore, since changing a religion causes a change in the applicable religious personal law, in cases of conflict between the new religious law and the Muslim law, the latter prevails, which can be discriminatory against the convert. In practice, such discrimination varies in different Muslim countries, depending on the modification of the related provisions of the civil code. Yet the best solution for avoiding the discriminatory aspects of conflicts of religious laws is by adopting an optional civil code that can be applied in cases of conflicts of laws. This issue will be discussed in more detail in part B of this book.

Cases of conversion are very rare among Muslims; hence the right to change one's religion has not been a priority of the UN related bodies responsible for setting relevant international standards. Furthermore, it seems that the existence of such controversial laws, so long as they are not put into practice, has not been of special concern for human rights observers and the international community. Still, the cases of unwritten family law consequences of conversion deserve more attention.

COMMENTS ON *SABB* AND BLASPHEMY LAWS

Insulting religious sacred things is one of the major sources of violence in sensitive multi-religious communities. While the religious sensibilities of the dominant religion are an issue of public order and of more concern for the governments, similar provisions for insulting the religious feelings of followers of minor religions and beliefs are also required. Fortunately for Muslims, insulting other religions and beliefs has been explicitly prohibited in the Koran.

On the other hand, an act of insult might be comprehended differently in different times and places and in accordance with different views. Yet, the necessity for a jury to be present in cases concerning the offence of blasphemy or *sabb* is apparently still under question in legislation and legal practices of some Muslim states. A case of *sabb* according to Muslim legal traditions can be recognized by an ordinary, reasonable person and not necessarily by a *mufti* or *mujtahid*. Therefore, in these cases the jury should not consist of qualified religious jurists, but as prescribed in the Iranian Press Code, should consist of representatives of ordinary people.[260]

260 Iranian Press Code, *supra* note 94, Article 34.

COMMENTS ON HERESY AND *TAKFIR*

The duty of the state is to determine the existence of fraud or misrepresentation by an individual or religious group. The state is not in the position of determining the truth or falsity of religious beliefs. The state should recognize offences and not investigate beliefs and opinions. Legislation in Iran, Pakistan and Malaysia on blasphemy or insulting religious sanctities can easily be interpreted against critical religious opinions; a similar problem exists in Egypt's jurisprudence.

Article 20(2) of the ICCPR obliges states to adopt legislative measures against hate speech. On the other hand, Muslim countries, as compared to European countries, have experienced less sensitivities on ethnic matters but more often on religious matters.[261] Yet, such sensitivities, as shown in their reports to the UN treaty bodies, have not led them to legislate against religious hate speech. Jordan, Egypt, and Sudan are among few Muslims states that have referred in their reports to the prohibition of religious hate speech in their legislation but with no further information on the implementation of the related law. For example, according to a report by Sudan:

> The necessary measures [have been] taken to fulfil the obligations contained in Article 20 Section 64 of the Criminal Act of 1991 which incriminates any advocacy of national, racial or religious hatred that constitutes incitement to discrimination, hostility or violence, and the amendment proposed by the government to incriminate racial discrimination as an offence.[262]

---

261 A comprehensive study on racial discrimination and religious discrimination, and the relevance of ethnic to religion has been presented in 2000 by Abdelfattah Amor. See Abdelfattah Amor, Special Rapporteur of the Commission on Human Rights, 'Racial Discrimination and Religious Discrimination: Identification and Measures', presented at the World Conference against Racism, Racial Discrimination, Xenophobia and Related Intolerance at Geneva, 1–5 May 2000, U.N.Doc.A/CONF.189/PC.1/7 (13 April 2000). This issue will also be addressed in part B of this book.

262 Human Rights Committee: Consideration of Reports Submitted by States Parties, Third periodic report (Sudan), para. 138, U.N.Doc.CCPR/C/75/Add.2 (13 March 1997) For Jordan see Human Rights Committee: Consideration of Reports Submitted by States Parties, Second periodic report (Jordan), para. 25, U.N.Doc.CCPR/C/76/Add.1 (18 Jan. 1993). For Egypt see Committee on the Elimination of Racial Discrimination: Consideration of Reports Submitted by States Parties, Sixteenth periodic reports (Egypt), paras. 100–101, U.N.Doc. CERD/C/384/Add.3 (11 April 2001).

It seems that such legislation is crucial with regard to vulnerable minority religious groups such as the Ahmadies and against the practice of *takfir* or declaring other Muslims individuals or religious groups as infidel. *Takfir* can be considered as a clear example of speech which constitutes incitement to violence on grounds of religious hatred.

Among all aspects of the three phenomena of apostasy in the legal traditions the major problematic issue is *takfir*. This phenomenon has had a destructive impact on freedom of religion, opinion and expression in Muslim societies. Arbitrary *takfir* has been the main source of intra-religious violence within Muslim communities, the most egregious examples of which have been the mass killings of innocent people in Algeria, Iraq and other Muslim countries by militant extremist groups.

As was mentioned in section 4.3.2, according to the final declaration of an international conference in Amman, only a learned person like a *mujtahid* or *mufti* is entitled to declare *takfir*. Though these comments are useful in limiting the extent of violence raised by arbitrary declarations of *takfir*, they seem very conservative as well. In fact such views imply that the right to declare *takfir* is reserved for religious authorities. This includes the declarations of *takfir* by such authorised *mufti*s which led to execution of Taha, dissolving the marriage of Abu Zayd and charging Aghajari with the death sentence.

In Malaysia labelling a Muslim an apostate, an infidel and so on, is in itself an offence.[263] Such a regulation has to be included in the legislation of all related Muslim countries. Surely the initiative for such prohibition should first address official religious centres, since the declaring of *takfir* by such centres gives justifications for other unofficial and arbitrary cases. *Takfir* not only should be prohibited but also should be considered a criminal act subject to punishment, as it legitimizes murder as a reaction to an individual having exercised their right to freedom of opinion and expression.

---

263 See for instance Section 205, Administration of Islamic Religion Affairs (Trengganu) Enactment 1986, *supra* note 121.

Part B

Protection of Minorities (*Dhimmah*)

Introductory Remarks

Dhimmah, as part of the Muslim legal traditions comprising public and personal rules, has experienced a long history of regulating the status of minorities in Muslim territories. Parts of *Dhimmah* public rules, i.e. recognition of Christians and Jews as religious minorities and the main part of *Dhimmah* personal rules, i.e. recognition of the personal law of religious minorities, are still applied widely by almost all Muslim states.

Part B is divided into chapters 5, 6 and 7. Chapter 5 starts with a short contextual and historical background of the Muslim legal traditions of *Dhimmah*, along with their public and personal rules. It further provides a short survey of the application of *Dhimmah* in the recent history of Muslim countries. In the second section of the chapter, the relevant international human rights law on the 'right of minorities to identity' and the 'principle of non-discrimination' will be discussed.

In international human rights law there is no specific definition for culture, identity, right to identity, and right to culture, nor is there such a definition in the binding treaties affecting religious minorities. Yet, the application of the principle of 'equality' along with the 'preservation of characteristics' have been considered as the corner stones of a system for the protection of minorities.[1] These two elements are referred to in the 1935 advisory opinion of the Permanent Court of International Justice on *Minority Schools in Albania* (PCIJ Opinion):

> The idea underlying the treaties for the protection of minorities was to secure for them the possibility of living peaceably alongside of the population, while preserving their own characteristics. In order to attain this objective, two things were regarded as particularly necessary. The first was to ensure that members of racial, religious and linguistic minorities should be placed in every respect on a footing of perfect equality with the other nationals of the state. The second was to ensure for the minority

1 In the homepage of the UN website on minorities the three issues in focus are listed as follows: non-discrimination, recognition of identity and cultural diversity. See <www.unhchr.ch/minorities/documentation.htm>.

> elements suitable means for the preservation of their own characteristics and traditions.[2]

Then, to show how far the two elements are interrelated, the court further states: "These two requirements are indeed closely interlocked, for these there would be no true equality between a majority and a minority if the latter were deprived of its own institutions, and were consequently compelled to renounce that which constitute the very essence of its being as a minority."[3] Yet, as will be discussed further, despite their close interconnection, when implementing the two elements, they should clearly be distinguished from each other.

Regarding the 'right of minorities to identity', relevant to *Dhimmah* traditions, two issues of 'recognition of minorities' and the concept of 'personal legal autonomy' will be of special interest to this study. On the concept of non-discrimination the study makes a distinction between discrimination on the ground of religion and discrimination in religious rights. A similar distinction can be made between discrimination on the ground of identity and discrimination in identity rights.

In Chapters 6 and 7, the effects of the public and personal *Dhimmah* rules on the legislation and legal practices of Muslim states will be examined respectively. In Muslim countries two kinds of positive measures for protection of recognized religious minorities can be identified. The first, which is an issue of public *Dhimmah* rules, is the recognition of religious minorities. While this phenomenon in non-Muslim countries is very rare, it is a common policy in the majority of Muslim countries. In this regard differences and commonalities among Muslim states in the recognition of religious minorities and the extent to which the *Dhimmah* traditions have affected these policies will be studied in chapter 6.

The chapter further investigates whether this recognition has led to some advantages for the recognized minorities or conversely some disadvantages for them and for other non-recognized minorities. Considering the issue of recognition, a survey of the relevant provisions in the Constitution of Iran

---

2 *Minority Schools in Albania*, advisory opinion of 6 April 1935, P.C.I.J., Publication series A–B, No. 64, p. 17. Though not directly linked to the purpose of this study, it is worth mentioning that a third requirement should be considered with regard to religious minorities, namely, freedom of religion. Consequently, the necessity to consider religious minorities' rights to freedom of religion makes their issue of human rights a more complicated issue than that of other minorities.

3 *Ibid.*

on the rights of followers of non-recognized religions will be discussed. The legal status of the Baha'is in Iran and in some other Muslim countries will then be examined.

A favourable policy with regard to religious minorities which is applied in some Muslim countries is the allocation of special seats in parliament for representatives of recognized religious minorities. This policy is a new phenomenon of modern states and does not have any roots in the *Dhimmah* traditions, though it can be linked to public *Dhimmah* rules and therefore will be discussed in chapter 6. Another kind of positive measure for the protection of religious minorities is the recognition of their personal law in Muslim countries. This issue which is relevant to personal *Dhimmah* rules will be discussed in chapter 7.

On the issue of discrimination, the study is limited to a survey of discrimination on the ground of religion in the legislation and legal practices of some Muslim states. Such discrimination which is in fact the result of the identical application of problematic *Dhimmah* traditions may occur in either public or personal law and will be discussed in chapters 6 and 7 respectively.

This part also investigates the conditions in which the cotemporary application of *Dhimmah* traditions could be considered as contributing to the protection of minorities, or in contrast, violating principles of their human rights. Finally, in the absence of any other distinctly binding international or regional contractual or customary law for the preservation of minorities' right to identity, part B, in its concluding remarks, proposes a strengthening of the contributing aspects of Muslim legal traditions of *Dhimmah*, as a stable regional customary system. On the other hand, the study suggests eliminating the discriminatory and problematic dimensions of these traditions.

CHAPTER FIVE

MUSLIM LEGAL TRADITIONS OF *DHIMMAH* AND RELEVANT HUMAN RIGHTS LAW

5.1. *DHIMMAH* AND ITS PRACTICE IN RECENT HISTORY

5.1.1. *Dhimmah*

The Koran says: "O Mankind, we created you from a single pair of a male and a female, and made you into nations and tribes that you may know each other."[4] It also affirms that "among God's signs are the creation of the heavens and the earth, and the difference of your languages and colours. Verily in that are indeed signs for those who know".[5] The Koran further recognizes diversity in belief and religion as it reads: "And if your God wished, it would certainly have created all people as one single nation, yet they still have their differences..."[6] By these verses not only is the diversity of people clearly recognized as a divine principle in the Koran, but also "human diversity is indicated as a basis or identification and appreciation of the power and divine wisdom of God, the creator of humanity."[7]

Similar to other progressive ideals, when the Koranic divine principles were put into practice at the time of their emergence in underdeveloped Bedouin societies, they had to be limited and modified under the pressure of their historical and social contexts. Rules affecting the status of non-Muslims among Muslims were not exceptional. Mayer points out:

> The pre-modern *Shariah* rules affecting the status of non-Muslims... reflect the circumstances of that era. The nascent community was weak and beleaguered, faced with the difficult task of the absorbing non-Muslim

4 The Koran, 49:13.

5 *Ibid.*, 30:22.

6 *Ibid.*, 11:118.

7 Mashood A. Baderin, 'Establishing Areas of Common Ground between Islamic Law and International Human Rights' 5 *the International Journal of Human Right* 2 (2001), pp. 164–165.

communities in newly won territories while having to meet the military threat of powerful non-Muslim foes.[8]

To understand the situation of early Muslims "one needs to avoid thinking in twentieth century terms, that is, from an individualistic perspective, which tends to interpret religious creed as an entirely personal matter".[9] After early Muslims had been unified by the new religion and established their new community they remained at war for several decades with the non-believer enemies surrounding them. The situation of Christians and Jews living among these Muslims was unique. They were neither Muslim, nor enemy, and were respected as *Ahlil-Kitab* (People of the Book). But from a security and political point, there was suspicion they were helping the enemy. Hence, they were not considered as full citizens of the newly established community.

The first political society of Muslims was shaped in Medina and was based upon a new progressive system of social links – a shared belief in God and the prophet hood of Muhammad – which replaced the traditional tribal/ethnic links-based system. While according to tribal links, similar to temporary modern national links, other tribes or nationals were considered aliens or even enemies, according to the new belief-based system, citizens were categorized as Muslims or full citizens; People of the Book or the recognized minorities who could live permanently among Muslim under a contract called *Dhimmah*; or, finally, other non-believers or those who could reside in Muslim territories temporarily based on other contracts such as '*Aman*'[10] or 'peace'. Non-Muslims who resided among Muslims under a contact were called *Muahids*. "Other people were considered enemies or *harbi*. *Harbi* in classical Shi'i literature means those who do not obey God and his Prophet and have not made the *Dhimmah* or other agreement with *Darul-Islam* (the territory of Islam)."[11]

Islam emphasizes the necessity of abiding by contracts and treaties, known as "promises to God" or "*Ahd-Allah*", and reiterates that: "When you have

8 Anne Elizabeth Mayer, *Islam and Human Rights, Tradition and Politics*, Third Edition (Westview Press, London, 1999), pp. 134–135.

9 Donna E. Arzt, 'The Role of Compulsion in Islamic Conversion: *Jihad*, *Dhimmi* and *Ridda*' 8 *Buffalo Human Rights Law Review* 15 (2002), p. 32.

10 For further information on *Aman* See Majid Khadduri, *War and Peace in the Law of Islam* (Johns Hopkins Press, 1955), pp. 162–169.

11 Seyed Mohammad Ghari Seyed Fatemi 'Nationality or Citizenship? A Normative Appraisal of International Law, Shi'i *Fiqh* and the Iranian Legal System', in Mofid University, *Collected Papers of the International Conference on Human Rights and Dialogue of Civilization, May 2001* (Mofid University Publication Institute, Qom – Iran, 2001), p. 260.

made a promise to God be loyal to it."[12] The verses of the Koran that may be referred to in the necessity of being loyal to nations that Muslims have concluded contracts with are as follows:

- "Fulfil the covenant of God when you have covenanted and break not oaths after their confirmation."[13]
- "And fulfil the covenant, for the covenant entails responsibility."[14]
- "Fulfil your commitments and keep your promises until your contract is over and remember that God likes those of you who are virtuous."[15]
- "Abide by your commitments to those who have signed an agreement with you at Masjid-al-haram[16] but only until they have not breached their promise."[17]

With regard to the *Aman* the Koran says: "And if anyone of the non-believers seeks your protection, protect him, so that he may hear the word of *Allah*, and afterwards conduct him to his place of safety."[18]As defined by the jurisconsults: "*Aman* means to restrain oneself, for the sake of God or to please God, from attacking the belligerents with the intention of killing or taking them hostage."[19] The definition of *Dhimmah* according to Ghari Seyed Fatemi is as follows:

> The permission given to *Ahlil-Kitab* including to reside in *Darul-Islam*, provided that they respect Islamic rules. *Darul-Islam*, indeed, by accepting them in the light of such an agreement, grants to them the Muslims' protection, in return for the payment of *Jizya* [protection tax].[20] In fact

12 The Koran, 6:91. Some Koranic verses on importance of keeping one's promise are as follows: 5:1; 2:27, 80, 100, 177; 3:75, 76; 13:20, 25; 16:94, 95; 23:8; 33:15.

13 The Koran, 16:91.

14 *Ibid.*, 17:34.

15 *Ibid.*, 9:4.

16 Masjid-al-haram is the Muslim's holiest place which is located in Mecca. The meaning of Masjid-al-haram in Arabic is "Prohibited Mosque" and means that anything which is not peaceful is prohibited there.

17 The Koran, 9:7.

18 *Ibid.*, 9:6.

19 Sarakhsi, *The description of Seir-al-Kabir, Vol. 1*, p. 44, quoted in Seyed Mostafa Mohaghegh Damad, 'Compiling the International Humanitarian Law and its Islamic Concept' *Journal of Juridical Researches* 18 (1996) in Persian, p. 189.

20 *Jizyah* is generally translated as poll tax, but since poll taxes were unilaterally based on the will of the ruler, a more accurate translation may be 'a protection and security tax'. See Abd al-Rahman Awang, *The status of the Dhimmi in Islamic Law* (PhD thesis, University of

> by this agreement they will be recognized as legitimate religious minorities who are granted the protection of *Darul-Islam* which is guaranteed to Muslims in matters of peace and security.[21]

Using contemporary legal terminology, *Dhimmah* traditions had two dimensions, public and personal. According to *Dhimmah* public conditions, only People of the Book could legitimately enter into *Dhimmah* contracts with Muslims. Those non-Muslims that entered into *Dhimmah* contracts were called *Dhimmis.*[22] They had to pay a special tax called *Jizya*, and for this tax, they were exempted from military services and also were supported by Muslims against their enemies. They had the right to conduct the internal affairs of their community. They enjoyed general freedoms and equal justice, but as will be discussed later, were discriminated against on the issues of evidence and punishment in litigation involving Muslims. *Dhimmis* also were discriminated against in some aspects of their public life. For example, they "could be either excluded from serving in government altogether or excluded only from high government positions".[23] They did not have equal rights with Muslims in practicing their religions either.[24]

According to the *Dhimmah* personal aspects, *Dhimmis* were ruled "under their personal laws in marriage, divorce, inheritance, the selling of wine and the eating and trading of pork".[25] Yet, "in a civil suit between a Muslim and a non-Muslim, the Muslim judge was required to apply his own law."[26] This could be discriminatory against non-Muslims in mixed cases. For example a Muslim man was allowed to marry a *Dhimmi* woman, but marriage of a

---

Edinburgh, 1988), p. 60, quoted in Eliz Sanasarian, *Religious Minorities in Iran* (Cambridge University Press, 2000), p. 22.

21 Ghari Seyed Fatemi, *supra* note 11, p. 261. This definition is based on the traditional Shiite *fiqh*, but there is no special difference in this view with those of Sunnis.

22 They were also called "*mu'ahidun*", which means the contractees, or the holders of covenant.

23 Mayer, *supra* note 8, p. 135.

24 See generally Abdur Rahman I Doi, *Non-Muslims under Shariah (Islamic Law)*, Third Edition (Ta ha Publishers Ltd., London, 1983).

25 *Ibid.*, pp. 50–51.

26 Cardahi Chourci, 'Conflict of Law', in Majid Khadduri & Herbert J. Liebesny (eds.) *Law in the Middle East, Volume 1, Origin and Development of Islamic Law* (The Middle East Institute, Washington, D.C., 1995), p. 337. On the issue of conflict of religious laws in Muslim legal traditions also see Maurits S Berger, 'Conflicts Law and Public Policy in Egyptian Family Law: Islamic Law through the Backdoor' 50 *American Journal of Comparative Law, Summer* 3(2002), pp. 556–557.

Muslim woman with a *Dhimmi* man was not allowed. Also, in general non-Muslims were not allowed to inherit from Muslims, and most schools of law did not accept Muslims inheriting from non-Muslims either; "yet, testamentary succession remain[ed] possible".[27]

5.1.2. *DHIMMAH* SYSTEM IN RECENT CENTURIES

With regard to *Dhimmah* public rules, it seems that after the decline of the 'the state of war' in the early history of Muslims, when the territories of the new Muslim empire were sufficiently stabilized, the significance of *jizya* as a form of reciprocity for providing security to non-Muslims was reduced. Yet, as mentioned before, two main aspects of *Dhimmah*, i.e. recognition of major religious groups and recognition of their religious family law, have survived until the present.

In Persia, for instance, there was a new era of application of *Dhimmah* personal rules, at least from about 1600, when the new Armenian communities settled in larger cities of Iran. During this period, similar to other non-Muslims, Armenians had autonomy over their internal affairs including their personal family law. For example in New Julfa, a suburb of the Safavid capital of Isfahan, "they elected their own mayor, or *kalantar*, rang church bells, had public religious processions, established their own courts, and had no restrictions on clothing or the production of wine."[28] On the relation of Armenian with the central government, Sanasarian states:

The relationship between the Armenian community and the Safavid state was shaped by *Millet*-type administration. The New Julfa Armenians had internal autonomy; their relationship to the state was mediated through the patriarchs of the church and individuals appointed as the shah's representatives in the administration of the community's affairs.[29]

---

27 Eva Brems, 'Islam and Human Rights Views', in Eva Brems, *Human Rights: Universality and Diversity* (Kluwer Law International, the Hague, 2001) p. 213. As stated by Berger, "According to Islamic law, the will (*wasiya*) is the sole possibility for Muslims and non-Muslims to succeed to each other's properties. The only limitation is that the testator may not bequeath more than one third of his property. The remaining two thirds (or more, of course) are to be divided according to the rules of intestate succession law." See Berger, *supra* note 25, pp. 581–582.

28 Parstimes, available at the website of Parstime at: <http://www.parstimes.com/history/armenians.html>.

29 Sanasarian, *supra* note 20, p. 29. On situation of Armenians in Iran Also see Carl Skutsch, *Encyclopaedia of the World's Minorities*, Vol. 1 (New York: Routledge, 2005) p. 135,

In comparison to Iran, the other great Muslim empire, that of the Ottomans, had a clearer history of practicing a *Dhimmah*-descended rule, called *Millet*, with regard to numerous religious groups all over their territories.

> Before conquering Syria and Egypt, the Ottomans had reigned over a mostly European and Christian Empire. In the Balkans and in Istanbul, they had devised a new system, the *Millet* based on *Dhimmah* tradition, for the coexistence of religions, which they simply extended to their newly seized Arab provinces. As *Millet*, a term usually translated as nations.[30]

According to Fargues, recognition of personal laws of religious groups by the *Millet* system was as follows:

> The main non-Muslim communities were given legal recognition. In their private lives, marriage, inheritance, and education Christians and Jews were no longer direct subjects of the Sultan. Instead they were now subject to an authority from their own religion, to which Istanbul delegated power in matters pertaining to personal status. Non-Muslim communities were thus made stable components of a multi-religious society.[31]

Consistent with the traditional application of *Dhimmah*, in the *Millet* system minorities "were subject to *Shariah* in mixed cases".[32]

Considering the high efficiency that the *Millet* system showed during the Ottomans reign, after the collapse of that empire, it has been followed not only by succeeding Muslim states, but also by Israel:

> The religious court system in Israel is based on [the] *Millet* system, a legacy of the Ottoman empire that collapsed in the First World War. Ottoman law granted an important degree of autonomy to the Christian and Jewish communities living under its control, particularly with respect to personal law. This heritage of religious pluralism was continued under

---

and Vera B. Moreen, 'The Status of Religious Minorities in Safavid Iran, 1617–1661' 40 *Journal of New Eastern Studies* (1981).

30 Philippe Fargues, 'Demographic Islamization: Non-Muslims in Muslim Countries' 21 *SAIS Review* 2 (2001). On situation of religious minorities during Ottomans also see Bruce Masters, *Christians and Jews in the Ottoman Arab World* (New York: Cambridge University Press, 2001).

31 Fargues, *ibid.*

32 Mayer, *supra* note 8, p. 140.

> British Mandatory Rule that succeeded Ottoman Rule and continued almost until the foundation of the state of Israel.[33]

On the privileges of the *Millet* system Rehman says:

> The *Millet* system as practiced by Ottomans allowed the various religious minorities to enjoy a generous measure of social, civil and religious autonomy. The positive features and benevolence of the system have been applauded by Western jurists and commentators; one leading authority comparing it to an application of the right to self-determination in advance of Woodrow Wilson.[34]

With regard to other areas further from the Peninsula, it has to be added that from the time of the emergence of Islam the only known religions to early Muslims were Christianity, Judaism and Sabi.[35] These are the religions that are listed in the Koran.[36] Later, when the Muslims were faced with new religions in the north, Zoroastrians were also included as *Dhimmis*. Subsequently, "in practice, as Islam expanded eastward, the pre-modern doctrine had to be adjusted and Muslims had to learn to coexist with Hindus and other polytheists."[37] And later with the spread of Islam westward "for practical reasons even the title...of the protected people was extended to non-Zoroastrians such as the Scandinavians and the Berbers."[38]

It is not possible within the scope of this study to examine the extent and effects of *Dhimmah* in all Muslim territories. Yet, it is sufficient to say, "[w]hile in historical terms [a] crucial distinction existed between the *Ahlil-Kitab* and

---

33 Henry J. Steiner & Phillip Alston, 'Comments on State, Religion, and Personal Law in Israel', in Henry J. Steiner & Phillip Alston (eds.) *International Human Rights in Context, Law, Politics, Morals*, Second Edition (Oxford University Press, 2000), p. 495.

34 Vernon Van Dyke, *Human Rights, Ethnicity and Discrimination* (Wetport, Conn./ London: Greenwood Press 1985), p. 85, quoted in Javid Rehman, 'Accommodating Religious Identities in An Islamic State: International Law, Freedom of Religion and the Rights of Religious Minorities' 7 *International Journal on Minority and Group Rights* 2 (2000), p. 151.

35 Sabis or Sabians is a sect between Christianity and Judaism.

36 The Koran, 2:62. "Surely those who believe, and those who are Jews, and the Christians, and the Sabians, whoever believes in *Allah* and the Last Day and does good, they shall have their reward from their Lord, and there is no fear for them, nor shall they grieve."

37 Mayer, *supra* note 8, p. 135.

38 H. A. R. Gibb & J. H. Kramers (eds.) *Shorter Encyclopaedia of Islam* (Ithaca: Cornell University Press, 1953), p. 300, quoted in Sanasarian, *supra* note 20, p. 21.

the pagans, the tolerance which was shown towards the *Ahlil-Kitab* was frequently extended to the latter".[39]

5.2. RELATED HUMAN RIGHTS LAW ON RELIGIOUS MINORITIES

5.2.1. *Protection of Religious Minorities in Their Right to Identity (Identity Rights)*

Definition of Religious Minorities

As already mentioned, there is little agreement on the definition of minorities. Because it is not possible to explain religion in a definitive manner, consensus on the definition of religious minorities is an even harder task. Yet, there are some definitions for minorities, though not unanimously accepted, that could be considered for working purposes in this study.

Concentrating on the preservation of the traditions of minorities, the PCIJ interpreted the concept of a minority as follows:

> The existence of a group of persons living in a given country or locality having a race, religion, language and traditions in a sentiment of solidarity, with a view to preserve their traditions, maintaining their form of worship, securing the instruction and upbringing of their children in accordance with the spirit and traditions of their race and mutually assisting one another.[40]

Another widely accepted definition for minorities is the one suggested by the Special Rapporteur of the Sub-Commission on Prevention of Discrimination and Protection of Minorities (the Sub-Commission on Minorities), Francesco Capotorti in 1977. Capotorti, basing himself on the PCIJ opinion and other relevant proposals, stressed 'the different characteristics of minorities from the rest of population', as the main element of his definition, which reads as follows:

> [A] group numerically inferior to the rest of the population of a state, in a non-dominant position, whose members... possess ethnic, religious or linguistic characteristics differing from those of the rest of the popula-

39 Rehman, *supra* note 34, p. 151.
40 PCIJ Opinion, *supra* note 2, p. 17.

tion and show, if only implicitly, a sense of solidarity, directed towards preserving their culture, traditions, religion or language.[41]

References to Identity in International Human Rights Treaties

Explicit reference to identity is made in four international human rights treaties. According to Article 29(1) of the Convention on the Rights of the Child (the CRC), states parties agree that the education of the child shall be directed to, "the development of respect for the child's parents, his or her own cultural identity... language and values, for the national values of the country in which the child is living, the country from which he or she may originate, and for civilizations different from his or her own".[42] Yet, this article is not specifically directed at minorities, but addresses the related issues of the child within majorities or minorities.

The other international treaties consider specifically the identity of three specific minority groups, namely indigenous and tribal peoples, migrant workers and national minorities. First, the preamble of the ILO Convention Concerning Indigenous and Tribal Peoples in Independent Countries (No. 169) of 1991 (ILO Convention No. 169) recognizes "the aspirations of these peoples to exercise control over their own institutions, ways of life and economic development and to maintain and develop their identities, languages and religions, within the framework of the states in which they live". Article 2 of the Convention affirms that governments' actions to protect indigenous peoples shall include measures for "promoting the full realization of the social, economic and cultural rights of these peoples with respect for their social and cultural identity, their customs and traditions and their institutions".[43]

The International Convention on the Protection of the Rights of All Migrant Workers and Members of Their Families makes clear reference to cultural identity in three of its articles:

> Article 17(1): Migrant workers and members of their families who are deprived of their liberty shall be treated with humanity and with respect

41 Francesco Capotorti, Special Rapporteur of the Sub-commission on Prevention of Discriminating and Protection of Minorities, *Study on the Rights of Persons Belonging to Ethnic, Religious and Linguistic Minorities* (Centre for Human Rights, Geneva, United Nations, New York, 1991), p. 568. (Capotorti Study)

42 The Convention on the Rights of the Child (CRC), G.A. res. 44/25, annex, 44 U.N. GAOR Supp. (No. 49) at 167, U.N.Doc.A/44/49 (1989), entered into force, 2 Sept. 1990.

43 The ILO Convention Concerning Indigenous and Tribal Peoples in Independent Countries (ILO No. 169), 72 ILO Official Bull. 59, entered into force, 5 Sept. 1991.

> for the inherent dignity of the human person and for their cultural identity....
>
> Article 31(1): States parties shall ensure respect for the cultural identity of migrant workers and members of their families and shall not prevent them from maintaining their cultural links with their state of origin.
>
> (2): States parties may take appropriate measures to assist and encourage efforts in this respect...
>
> Article 34: Nothing in the present part of the Convention shall have the effect of relieving migrant workers and the members of their families from either the obligation to comply with the laws and regulations of any state of transit and the state of employment or the obligation to respect the cultural identity of the inhabitants of such states.[44]

Finally, Article 5(1) of the Framework Convention for the Protection of National Minorities has numerated religion, language, traditions and cultural heritage as the four essential elements of the identity of national minorities: "The parties undertake to promote the conditions necessary for persons belonging to national minorities to maintain and develop their culture, and to preserve the essential elements of their identity, namely their religion, language, traditions and cultural heritage."[45]

Yet, the only obligatory norm on the preservation of the characteristics of religious minorities within the international human rights system is Article 27 of the International Covenant on Civil and Political Rights (ICCPR). This Article reads as follows: "In those states in which ethnic, religious or linguistic minorities exist, persons belonging to such minorities shall not be denied the right, in community with the other members of their group, to enjoy their own culture, to profess and practice their own religion, or to use their own language."[46]

---

44 The International Convention on the Protection of the Rights of All Migrant Workers and Members of Their Families, G.A. res. 45/158, annex, 45 U.N. GAOR Supp. (No. 49A) at 262, U.N.Doc.A/45/49 (1990), entered into force, 1 July 2003.

45 The Framework Convention for the Protection of National Minorities, ETS No. 157, entered into force, 2 Jan. 1998.

46 The International Covenant on Civil and Political Rights (ICCPR), G.A. res. 2200A (XXI), 21 U.N. GAOR Supp. (No. 16) at 52, U.N.Doc.A/6316 (1966), 999 U.N.T.S. 171, entered into force, 23 March 1976. This Article later reappeared as Article 30 of the CRC and its scope was extended to persons of indigenous origin. Article 30 of the CRC reads as follows: "In

Identity Rights or Characteristics Rights?

There is no specific distinction between 'characteristics' and 'identities' in the UN documents surveyed; for example, Article 1 of the Declaration on the Rights of Persons Belonging to National or Ethnic, Religious and Linguistic Minorities (the Minority Declaration)[47] uses 'identity', while Article 4(2) refers to 'characteristics'.[48] By the same token, while both the PCIJ opinion and the Capotorti definition refer to 'characteristics of minorities', the Human Rights Committee in its General Comment 23 uses 'identity'.[49] Hence, one might conclude that both terms are referring to the same thing and that the 'right to identity' is equivalent to the 'right to characteristics'.

Which Sort of Minorities and Which Type of Rights: Areas of Overlap in Article 27 of the International Covenant on Civil and Political Rights

There are wide overlapping areas between different types of identities. For instance, with regard to 'religious identity', where the example of Islam is concerned, this identity sometimes is combined or attached to 'ethnicity'. According to Article 160(2) of the Constitution of Malaysia, "'Malay' means a person who professes the religion of Islam, habitually speaks the Malay language, conforms to Malay custom..."[50] Also, in most Muslim countries, similar to non-Muslim countries, religion is considered a part of the national identity and/or cultural identity.

---

those states in which ethnic, religious or linguistic minorities or persons of indigenous origin exist, a child belonging to such a minority or who is indigenous shall not be denied the right, in community with other members of his or her group, to enjoy his or her own culture, to profess and practice his or her own religion, or to use his or her own language." The CRC, *supra* note 42.

47 A/RES/48/138, adopted by the UN General Assembly resolution 47/135 of 18 Dec. 1992 (The Minority Declaration). Article 1(1) of Minority Declaration spells out that: "States shall protect the existence and the national or ethnic, cultural, religious and linguistic identity of minorities within their respective territories and shall encourage conditions for the promotion of that identity."

48 *Ibid.* Article 4(2) reads as follows: "States shall take measures to create favourable conditions to enable persons belonging to minorities to express their characteristics and to develop their culture, language, religion, traditions and customs, except where specific practices are in violation of national law and contrary to international standards."

49 Human Rights Committee, General Comment 23, Article 27 (Fiftieth session, 1994), U.N.Doc.CCPR/C/21/Rev.1/Add.5 (1994), reprinted in Compilation of General Comments and General Recommendations Adopted by Human Rights Treaty Bodies, U.N.Doc.HRI/GEN/1/Rev.6 at 158 (2003). This General Comments will be discussed in more detail further.

50 Constitution of Malaysia, 31 Aug. 1957, amended 16 Sept. 1963.

In Egypt "Makram Ebeid, a Coptic nationalist leader in the interwar years, liked to say that 'Christianity is my religion, but Islam is my culture.' "[51] However, unlike the Christian Copts in Egypt or in the north of Sudan, Christians in the south of Sudan have been in a minority-majority or south-north conflict with Muslims over previous decades that is in fact a conflict between different identities, as Ronen concludes:

> [It is] essentially a struggle between two starkly different societies to define the state's identity and, as far as the south is concerned, to maintain its own in the face of the rising tide of Islam... It could be defined as a struggle between Africanism and Arabism... Nevertheless, the religious components of identity [are] central to both.[52]

Similarly it is not clear whether European Jews are a religious or an ethnic minority, or incorporate elements of both. In a similar vein, it has been an issue of political and legal struggle by Muslim minorities in the United Kingdom that 'the Race Relations Act' of 1976, affords protection just to Jews and Sikhs as ethnic groups, but not to members of other religions.[53]

The same overlap exists for Bosnians, where the International Criminal Tribunal for the Former Yugoslavia was perplexed about how to define the victims of the Serb 'genocide': 'Muslims', 'Bosnian Muslims', etc.[54] Capotorti states: "The dividing line between culture and language and to a lesser degree between culture and religion is not as clear as it may appear. Therefore, some aspects of the rights relating to culture concern not only persons belonging

51 Fargues, *supra* note 30.

52 Yehudit Ronen, 'Religion and Conflict in Sudan: A Non-Muslim Minority in a Muslim State', in Orfa Bengio & Gabriel Ben-Dor (eds.) *Minorities and the State in the Arab World* (Lynne Rienner Publishers, USA, UK, 1999), p. 85.

53 The text of The Race Relations Act 1976 and the Race Relations (Amendment) Act 2002 is available at: <www.homeoffice.gov.uk/docs/racerel1.html> and <www.hmso.gov.uk/si/si2003/20031626.htm>.With regard to the British Muslims' views on this issue, see for example an interview by the Secretary General of the Muslim Council of Britain (MCB), available at: <www.muslimnews.co.uk/news/news.php?Article=8153>.

54 See *Prosecutor* v. *Radislav Krstic* [2004] ICTY 7 (19 April 2004), Case No: IT-98-33-A, *Prosecutor* v. *Blagojevic*, [2001] ICTY 10 (9 Oct. 2001), Case No. IT-02-60-PT, etc. For a comprehensive study on the areas of overlapping between 'religious' and 'racial' discrimination see Abdelfattah Amor, Special Rapporteur of the Commission on Human Rights, 'Racial Discrimination and Religious Discrimination: Identification and Measures', presented at the World Conference against Racism, Racial Discrimination, Xenophobia and Related Intolerance at Geneva, 1–5 May 2000, U.N. Doc.A/CONF.189/PC.1/7 (13 April 2000).

to ethnic minorities but also to persons belonging to linguistic or religious minorities."[55]

On the other hand, while 'national' minorities were the main concern of the PCIJ opinion,[56] they are not explicitly included in the list of minorities provided by Article 27 of the ICCPR, i.e., 'ethnic', 'religious' or 'linguistic' minorities. There are also 'indigenous peoples', which will be discussed in this study, and other types of minorities that have not been included in any binding instrument. Yet, it is difficult to draw a dividing line between different types of minorities. Dinstein states:

> A religious minority may at the same time be equally regarded as an ethnic and/or a linguistic minority. Even when we consider a strictly religious minority – namely a group different from the majority only in its religious belief, e.g. Catholics in England, we must not lose sight of the link between religion and culture.[57]

Similarly in Article 5(a) of ILO Convention No. 169, 'social', 'cultural', 'religious' and 'spiritual' values and practices of indigenous people are indistinguishable: "[T]he social, cultural, religious and spiritual values and practices of these peoples shall be recognized and protected...."[58]

On the other hand, while 'speaking a language' is not a difficult concept to distinguish, to have an understanding of the scope of each of the two other categories in Article 27 separately is a harder task. Before considering the right to 'profess and practice a religion', the 'right to enjoy a culture' will be examined.

In the same year that the ICCPR and the International Covenant on Economic, Social and Cultural Rights (ICESCR)[59] were adopted, Article 1 of the 1966 Declaration of the UNESCO Principles of International Cultural Cooperation, in explicit wording, recognized the values of all cultures and the

---

55 Capotorti Study, *supra* note 41, p. 99.

56 PCIJ opinion, *supra* note 2.

57 Yoram Dinstein, 'Freedom of Religion and the Protection of Religious Minorities', in Yoram Dinstein, (ed.) *The Protection of Minorities and Human Rights* (Martinus Nijhof Publishers, 1992), p. 159.

58 ILO Convention No. 169, *supra* note 43.

59 International Covenant on Economic, Social and Cultural Rights (ICESCR), G.A. res. 2200A (XXI), 21 U.N. GAOR Supp. (No. 16) at 49, U.N.Doc.A/6316 (1966), 993 U.N.T.S. 3, entered into force, 3 Jan. 1976.

right and the duty of every people to develop its culture. The Article reads as follows:

> 1– Each culture has a dignity and value which must be respected and preserved.
> 2– Every people has the right and the duty to develop its culture.
> 3– In their rich variety and diversity and in the reciprocal influences they exert on one another, all cultures form part of the common heritage belonging to all mankind.[60]

However, despite the recognition of a right to enjoying a culture, cultural rights, or a right to culture in international human rights treaties, the elements of these rights are not well defined. Articles 13 to 15 of the ICESCR,[61] for example, refer merely to 'the right to education'. Patrick Thornberry states: "Contemporary legal instruments do not define 'culture'... They are of limited assistance in elucidating the meaning of 'culture' in the present context, though they point to the importance of education as a prerequisite of any 'culture'."[62]

Again while the Human Rights Committee in its General Comment 23 "observes that culture manifests itself in many forms",[63] the only aspect of culture that is mentioned by this Comment concerns the right of indigenous people to land, which reads as follows: "[A] particular way of life associated with the use of land resources, especially in the case of indigenous peoples. That right may include such traditional activities as fishing or hunting and the right to live in reserves protected by law."[64]

To sum up, there are different areas of overlap between different types of minorities, i.e. ethnic, religious, linguistic and national. In addition, drawing a clear dividing line between the right of minorities to enjoy their culture, and their rights to profess and practice their religion is not as easy at it may appear at the first sight.

---

60 Adopted by the UNESCO General Conference at its fourteenth session, Paris, 4 Nov. 1966, UNESCO's Standard-Setting Instruments, IV.C. (1994).

61 ICESCR, *supra* note 59. It is worth mentioning that, again in this Covenant there is an overlapping between cultural (educational) and religious aspects when Article 13(3) ensures for parents "the religious and moral education of their children in conformity with their own convictions."

62 Patrick Thornberry, *International Law and the Rights of Minorities* (Oxford: Clarendon, 2001), p. 187.

63 General Comment 23 *supra* notes 49.

64 *Ibid.*

Distinguishing between Identity Rights and Principle of Non-discrimination
It should be noted that despite the close connection of the two elements of non-discrimination and identity rights, they should clearly be distinguished from each other. In states reports on the implementation of the ICCPR, the requirements of Article 27 on identity rights are often confused with the requirements of Article 2.1 and 26 on non-discrimination. General Comment 23 addresses this concern as follows:

> The Covenant also distinguishes the rights protected under Article 27 from the guarantees under Articles 2.1 and 26. The entitlement, under Article 2.1, to enjoy the rights under the Covenant without discrimination applies to all individuals within the territory or under the jurisdiction of the state whether or not those persons belong to a minority. In addition, there is a distinct right provided under Article 26 for equality before the law, equal protection of the law, and non-discrimination in respect of rights granted and obligations imposed by the states. It governs the exercise of all rights, whether protected under the Covenant or not, which the state party confers by law on individuals within its territory or under its jurisdiction, irrespective of whether they belong to the minorities specified in Article 27 or not. Some states parties who claim that they do not discriminate on grounds of ethnicity, language or religion, wrongly contend, on that basis alone, that they have no minorities.[65]

Religious Rights or Identity Rights: Distinguishing between the Scope of Article 18 and Article 27 of the International Covenant on Civil and Political Rights in Human Rights Committee General Comments
General Comment 23 points out that the rights to identity in Article 27 of the ICCPR, "should not be confused with other personal rights conferred on one and all under the Covenant."[66] On the other hand, the Article 27 seems to enumerate the three general instances of the right to identity.[67] While among these instances, 'enjoying a culture' and 'using a language' have no explicitly similar or relevant parallel rights within the Covenant,[68] with regard to the

65 General Comment 23, *supra* note 49, para. 4.
66 *Ibid.*, para. 9.
67 ICCPR, *supra* note 46.
68 Though the right to use a language is not explicitly referred to in Article 19 of the ICCPR, the provision has been interpreted in this way by the Human Rights Committee. See

right to 'profess and practice a religion' a similar term expression appears in Article 18(1):

> Everyone shall have the right to freedom of thought, conscience and religion. This right shall include freedom to have or to adopt a religion or belief of his choice, and freedom, either individually or in community with others and in public or private, to manifest his religion or belief in worship, observance, practice and teaching.[69]

The scope of Articles 18 and 27 is not distinguished by the Human Rights Committee General Comments. While General Comment 22 on Article 18 has included 'practice of religion' as one of the instances of 'manifestation of a religion',[70] General Comment 23 confirms that the rights in Article 27 are "distinct from, and additional to, all the other rights which, as individuals in common with everyone else, they are already entitled to enjoy under the Covenant".[71] However, while General Comment 23 tries to draw a line between the rights conferred in Article 27 and those referred to in Articles 1, 2.1, 26, 19, and 14.3 (f), it does not make any effort to distinguish between the rights contained in Article 27 and those in Article 18. Also, as mentioned above, with the one exception of cultural rights relating to the right of indigenous people to land, the General Comment does not refer to other instances of 'enjoying culture'. Hence, the rights contained in Article 27 remain ambiguous.

Furthermore, while instances of manifesting a religion are listed in General Comment 22 and in more detail in Article 6 of the Declaration on Elimination of All Forms of Intolerance Based on Religion or Belief (the Religion Declaration),[72] both of which are related to Article 18, the only UN document containing a detailed development of Article 27 is the one provided by Capotorti in

---

Ballantyne, Davidson, McIntyre v. Canada, Communications Nos. 359/1989 and 385/1989, U.N.Doc.CCPR/C/47/D/359/1989 and 385/1989/Rev.1 (1993).

69 ICCPR, *supra* note 46.

70 Human Rights Committee, General Comment 22, Article 18 (Forty-eighth session, 1993), U.N.Doc.CCPR/C/21/Rev.1/Add.4 (1993), reprinted in Compilation of General Comments and General Recommendations Adopted by Human Rights Treaty Bodies, U.N.Doc. HRI/GEN/1/Rev.6 at 155 (2003).

It reads in para. 4 as follows: "The freedom to manifest religion or belief may be exercised either individually or in community with others and in public or private. The freedom to manifest religion or belief in worship, observance, practice and teaching encompasses a broad range of acts."

71 General Comment 23, *supra* note 49.

72 G.A. res. 36/55, 36 U.N. GAOR Supp. (No. 51) at 171, U.N.Doc.A/36/684 (1981).

his study.[73] Capotorti under the title of "juridical status to a religion professed by a minority" provides a list, which among others, consists of two elements: the question of the recognition and the question of the validity of the laws and customs of the religion professed by a minority.[74] These two elements will be discussed in sections 5.2.3 and 5.2.4 of this book respectively.

Obligation of States with Regard to Identity Rights

With regard to the duty of the state to protect the identity of minorities, Capotorti pointes out: "The objective to be attained is the preservation and natural development of the cultural identity of minorities: The state is therefore called upon to adopt all necessary measures to that end."[75] The Human Rights Committee in its General Comment 23 reiterates the obligation of states to ensure the existence and exercise of identity rights, even through positive measures:

> Although Article 27 is expressed in negative terms, that article, nevertheless, does recognize the existence of a 'right' and requires that it shall not be denied. Consequently, a state party is under an obligation to ensure that the existence and the exercise of this right are protected against their denial or violation. Positive measures of protection are, therefore, required not only against the acts of the state party itself, whether through its legislative, judicial or administrative authorities, but also against the acts of other persons within the state party....Positive measures by states may also be necessary to protect the identity of a minority and the rights of its members to enjoy and develop their culture and language and to practice their religion, in community with the other members of the group.[76]

By the same token regarding the obligations imposed on states for the preservation of cultural, religious and social identity of minorities, General Comment 23 confirms that:

> Article 27 relates to rights whose protection imposes specific obligations on states parties. The protection of these rights is directed towards ensuring the survival and continued development of the cultural, religious and social identity of the minorities concerned....states parties, therefore,

73 Capotorti Study, *supra* note 41.
74 *Ibid.*, pp. 66–72.
75 *Ibid.*, p. 100.
76 General Comment 23, *supra* note 49, paras. 6.1–6.2.

> have an obligation to ensure that the exercise of these rights is fully protected and they should indicate in their reports the measures they have adapted to this end.[77]

Also Article 1(1) of the Minority Declaration spells out: "States shall protect the existence and the national or ethnic, cultural, religious and linguistic identity of minorities within their respective territories and shall encourage conditions for the promotion of that identity."[78] This Article continues: "States shall adopt appropriate legislative and other measures to achieve those ends." The Declaration reaffirms this duty in Article 4: "States shall take measures to create favourable conditions to enable persons belonging to minorities to express their characteristics and to develop their culture, language, religion, traditions and customs."[79]

5.2.2. *Right of Religious Minorities to Be Legally Recognized*

On the importance of official recognition of minorities Capotorti notes that: "...what must be emphasized is the fact that international protection of minorities does depend on official recognition of their existence." He also states:

> It is, of course, acknowledged that, in practice, the recognition of a minority by the state in which it lives improves this situation, facilitates the application of the principles enunciated in Article 27 of the Covenant and gives the members of the minority a solid base for effective protection of the rights guaranteed them at the international level.[80]

However, according to Capotorti the official attitude of states towards recognition of their minority groups varies considerably:

> It might be said that the two extremes are represented by the case of recognition in the Constitution of the existence of a minority and the absence of any recognition at all. Between these two extremes, however, there are some middle positions: recognition of the basis of special legislation or administrative measures or the simple recognition of private institutions representing the interests of minority groups.[81]

---

77 *Ibid.*, para. 9.
78 Minority Declaration, *supra* note 47.
79 *Ibid.*
80 Capotorti Study, *supra* note 41, p. 12.
81 *Ibid.*

As for those countries in which the existence of an ethnic or linguistic minority is not recognized at all in the internal law, Capotorti gives the example of most Latin American countries which maintain that immigrants and their descendants do not constitute minorities.[82] Among European countries, France is the most extreme in non-recognition of any minority in its territory. It entered a declaration with respect to Article 27 of the ICCPR at the time of ratification which states: "In the light of Article 2 of the Constitution of the French Republic, the French government declares that Article 27 is not applicable so far as the Republic is concerned."[83]

By ignoring the requirements of Article 27 of the ICCPR on identity rights and linking it to the requirements of Article 2 on non-discrimination, the justification of France for this policy, as stated in its report, is its commitment to the principle of non-discrimination:

> Since the basic principles of public law prohibit distinctions between citizens on grounds of origin, race or religion, France is a country in which there are no minorities and, as stated in the declaration made by France, Article 27 is not applicable as far as the Republic is concerned.[84]

On the other hand, according to Capotorti, "the word 'recognition' itself does not by any means always have the same meaning."[85] Then, focusing on other minorities than religious minorities he refers to different kinds of recognitions by states:

> The state grants to one or more minorities the status of legal persons, subjects of law, but this is very rarely encountered. It may mean that a coherent set of rights, connected with the principle of protecting the identity of minorities, is granted to members of such minorities. Sometimes, however, the only measure is the granting of some specific rights to the minorities without there being any overall plan. In the last case,

82 *Ibid.*, p. 13.

83 For the reservations and declarations to the ICCPR see Office of the United Nations High Commissioner for Human Rights, Ratifications and Reservations: International Covenant on Civil and Political Rights, at: <http://www.unhchr.ch/html/menu3/b/treaty5_asp.htm>, last updated Feb. 5, 2002.

84 Human Rights Committee: Consideration of Reports Submitted by States Parties, Third periodic report (France), para. 349, U.N.Doc.CCPR/C/76/Add.7 (15 May 1997).

85 Capotorti Study, *supra* note 41, p. 12.

> the recognition of the minority benefiting from the rights is usually implicit and partial.[86]

While Capotorti addresses the question of ethnic and language minorities in detail,[87] surprisingly enough, he leaves the issue of recognition of religious minorities to the scope of Article 18 of the ICCPR: "The question of the recognition of religious minorities as such has lost much of its urgency as a result of the almost universal acceptance of the principle of freedom of conscience and religion which is now incorporated into the domestic law of almost all states."[88] Yet, as mentioned above, under the subject of 'the rights of persons belonging to religious minorities', later he refers to the issue of recognition of religious minorities.[89]

Regarding recognition of religious minorities in European states, it should be noted that while in these countries recognition of a religion other than that of the predominant church, is an uncommon phenomenon, a fortiori, affording such recognition to a minority is even more unlikely. For example, as mentioned above, in the United Kingdom Jews and Sikhs are recognized as ethnic groups but not religious ones. In the same sense, despite the large population of Muslims in many Western European countries, with the exception of Greece Muslims have not been afforded legal status as a religious group in any state.[90]

Furthermore, according to the European Commission of Human Rights recognition as a corporation in Germany dose not imply the recognition of a new religion under Article 9 of the European Convention for the Protection of Human Rights and Fundamental Freedoms, (ECHR):[91] "The commission has decided that Article 9 does not give a right to be formally recognized or registered as a religion in states that still distinguish between recognized

---

86 *Ibid.*

87 *Ibid.*, pp. 12–15.

88 *Ibid.*, p. 13.

89 *Ibid.*, p. 13 and pp. 68–689 under the title of 'juridical status to a religion professed by a minority'.

90 On legal status of Muslims in Europe see Joel S. Fetzer & J. Christopher Soper, *Muslims and the State in Britain, France, and Germany* (Cambridge University Press, 2005). Among European states Greece is an exception. Being affected by the *Millet* system and basing itself on the Treaty of Lausanne of 1923, this country has insisted on calling its Turkish minority the Muslim minority.

91 Convention for the Protection of Human Rights and Fundamental Freedoms, 213 U.N.T.S. 222, entered into force, 3 Sept. 1953, as amended by Protocols Nos. 3, 5, 8, and 11 which entered into force, 21 Sept. 1970, 20 Dec. 1971, 1 Jan. 1990, and 1 Nov. 1998 respectively.

and non-recognized religions."[92] In fact the only minority that is officially recognized by Germany as a subject of Article 27 of the ICCPR is the Danish minority in the north of Schleswig-Holstein:

> In the Federal Republic of Germany as it existed on 2 October 1990, Article 27 of the Covenant was of importance only to the Danish minority in the north of Schleswig-Holstein, a land which borders on Denmark. Following German unification the Sorbian minority resident in Lusatia (Saxony and Brandenburg), a people of Slavonic origins, also became the object of the Federal Republic of Germany's reporting.[93]

The Treaty Based Recognition of Minorities

The current international system of protection of minorities is based predominantly on reciprocity of states. This is evident in the phenomenon amongst European (and some non-European) states of recognition of minorities based on bilateral or multilateral treaties. For example, at the end of the First World War based upon the peace treaties of Versailles, Saint German, Trianon and Neuilly, five special treaties of minority protection were concluded between Poland, Czechoslovakia, Romania, Yugoslavia and Greece respectively, on the one hand, and the allied and associated powers on the other. Very similar provisions were directly included in the peace treaties of Saint German (with Austria), Trianon (with Hungary), Neuilly (with Bulgaria) and Lausanne (with Turkey). Between 1919 and 1940, sixteen countries undertook international obligations on the protection of minorities.[94]

Similarly, after the Second World War, in the agreement between Austria and Italy in Paris, September 1946, 'German-speaking inhabitants' of the Bolzano province and of neighbouring bilingual townships were granted a number of rights. In addition, a special autonomy, comprising legislative and administrative powers, was provided for the province of Bolzano, where German-speaking citizens constituted the majority of the population. Also the

---

92 Xv. Austria, App. No. 8652/79,26 Eur. Comm's H. R. Dec & Rep. 89 (1981), quoted in Carolyn Evans, *Freedom of Religion under the European Convention* (Oxford University Press, New York, 2001), p. 108.

93 Human Rights Committee: Consideration of Reports Submitted by States Parties, Fourth periodic report (Germany), para. 236, U.N.Doc.CCPR/C/84/Add.5 (22 Feb. 1996). Also see the same report, para. 242.

94 See Tore Modeen, 'The International Protection of National Minorities in Europe' (Abo: Abo Akademi, 1969) p. 182.

Memorandum of Understanding between the government of Italy, the UK, the US and Yugoslavia, in London 1954, regarding the free territory of Trieste was signed to safeguard the 'Yugoslav ethnic group' in the Italian-administrated area and the 'Italian ethnic group' in the Yugoslav-administrated area.[95]

Such treaties in fact limit the identity rights of minorities to the interests of states. If identity rights are explicitly recognized in internationally binding instruments, they should be managed and implemented by the state by bestowing individual rights and not through inter-states relations.

The Issue of Old and New Minorities

Generally states are reluctant to extend the scope of identity rights to new minorities. During the debate in the Commission on Human Rights on the draft of Article 27 of the ICCPR, the phrase "In those states in which ethnic, religious, or linguistic minorities exists" was added to the draft article to prevent recognition of new minorities. According to Capotorti:

> It seems that the purpose of the amendment was to restrict the enjoyment of the rights recognized by the article to minorities already long established in the territory of the state, so as to prevent the protection conferred by the new rule from encouraging the formation of new minorities or awakening a 'minority consciousness' in groups formerly assimilated into the population of a state.[96]

For example the report of Germany on the implementation of Article 27 shows its hesitation in recognition of new minorities:

> Problems arise time and again in connection with the protection of minorities, because groups which are not recognized minorities claim to be a privileged protected minority in the sense of Article 27 of the Covenant. In this context the German government attaches particular importance to the *travaux préparatoires* of the Covenant, and especially to the report of 1 July 1955, which states: 'The provisions concerning the

---

95 For similar treaties see for example agreement between India and Pakistan, New Delhi, 8 April 1950; the Austrian State Treaty for the Re-establishment of the Independent and Democratic Austria, Vienna, 15 May 1955; Agreement between the UK and Singapore, London, March-April 1957; Memorandum for the Final Settlement of the Problem of Cyprus, London, Feb. 1959; Unilateral Declarations of Germany and Denmark of 1955 on German and Danish Minorities; The Government Declarations of France and Algeria on Protection of Algerians of French civil status, 19 May 1962, Algeria, See Capotorti Study, *supra* note 41, pp. 12–13.

96 *Ibid.*, p. 35.

> right of minorities, it was understood, should not be applied in such a manner as to encourage the creation of new minorities or to obstruct the process of assimilation.' It was felt that such tendencies could be dangerous for the unity of the state. In view of clarification given on those points, it was thought unnecessary to specify in the article that 'such rights may not be interpreted as entitling any groups settled in the territory of a state, particularly under the terms of immigration laws, to form within that state separate communities which might impair its national unity or security' (A/2929, p. 182, Para. 186).[97]

With respect to new religious minorities some reasons can be assumed for the hesitation of states to recognize the rights of these minorities. The older established minorities are considered less of a threat to state security. While these minorities have already proven their loyalty to the central government, for the new religious groups this process takes time.

Religious sensitivities might also be heightened by the extraterritorial connections that new minorities normally maintain. Politically motivated support afforded to these new religious groups from abroad might intensify the tense situation between these groups and the state. Finally, the new religious groups are generally more active in proselytizing which normally targets the members of the dominant religion; the sort of activities which, as was discussed in part A of this book, are restricted by states in religious societies.

However, the hesitation of states to recognize new minorities should not lead to ignoring the identity rights of new minorities. Capotorti states:

> In view of the general nature of the rules for the protection of human rights adopted within the framework of the United Nations, it is also inadmissible that a distinction could be made between 'old' and 'new' minorities. It is certainly not the function of Article 27 to encourage the formation of new minorities, where a minority exists, however, the Article is applicable to it, regardless of the date of its formation.[98]

Capotorti further adds: "Nevertheless the presence of sufficient elements to indicate that a minority exists is sufficient to make applicable the pertinent international rules, and particularly Article 27 of the ICCPR."[99] By the same

97 Consideration of Reports, Germany (1996), *supra* note 93, para. 242.
98 Capotorti Study, *supra* note 41, p. 35.
99 *Ibid.*, p. 12.

token, General Comment 23 has a different interpretation of the term, 'in which minorities exist' from that of *travaux préparatoires* of the article 27 mentioned above in the report of Germany. According to the General Comment 23 such term guarantees the extension of scope of Article 27 to all the minorities existing in the territory of a state whether 'new' or 'old' and whether recognized or not:

> Article 27 confers rights on persons belonging to minorities which 'exist' in a state party. Given the nature and scope of the rights envisaged under that article, it is not relevant to determine the degree of permanence that the term 'exist' connotes. Those rights simply are that individuals belonging to those minorities should not be denied the right, in community with members of their group, to enjoy their own culture, to practice their religion and speak their language.[100]

The General Comment further extends the scope of the identity rights embodied in Article 27 to those who have only been in the territory of a state for a short period and even to a temporary visitor to a country:

> Just as they need not be nationals or citizens, they need not be permanent residents. Thus, migrant workers or even visitors in a state party constituting such minorities are entitled not to be denied the exercise of those rights. As any other individual in the territory of the state party, they would, also for this purpose, have the general rights, for example, to freedom of association, of assembly, and of expression. The existence of an ethnic, religious or linguistic minority in a given state party does not depend upon a decision by that state party but requires to be established by objective criteria.[101]

Consistent with the above interpretation of the Article 27, Germany later in reply to the Human Rights Committee concerns, modified its previous views on the issue of 'old' and 'new' minorities and reiterated that the rights apply to all minorities in its territory, whether recognized or not:

> The government of the Federal Republic of Germany regrets that the impression has been created that the rights under Article 27 of the Covenant in Germany are granted only to specific minorities (Note 13 of

100 General Comment 23, *supra* note 49, para. 5.2.
101 *Ibid.*

> the Concluding Observations, CCPR/C/79/ dd. 73). All ethnic, religious and linguistic minorities in Germany are protected by the Basic Law as to the rights named in Article 27 of the Covenant. All minorities within the meaning of Article 27 may use their mother tongues and culture and practice their religion. Germany does not exercise any pressure aimed at enforcing assimilation. Accordingly, there are many associations and groupings organized by ethnic, religious or linguistic minorities. These associations serve to maintain cultural identity, the exercise of religious confessions and care for customs and own language. The activities of these associations and groupings are not hindered in any manner. Many individual projects are supported financially by the state.[102]

Finally, in an overlap between the scope of Articles 18 and 27 of the ICCPR, it seems that recognition of a religious community, even under the title of a corporation, which in fact is an issue related to Article 18, can be considered as an implicit recognition of a religious minority in terms of Article 27. Yet, once again concerning the example of Germany one may question the advantage of recognition of the old Danish minority and the disadvantage of non-recognition of the new religious groups in this country. Considering what was quoted above from Capotorti at the beginning of this section, such recognition, reconfirming the identity rights of minorities, may facilitate the implementation of Article 27 by states. While states can choose whether or not to recognise a minority, they are committed to protecting the identity of all minorities in their territory, whether recognized or not, new or old, and permanent residents or short term visitors.

5.2.3. *Right of Minorities to Personal Legal Autonomy*

As mentioned in the previous section according to Capotorti, the second element under the "juridical status to a religion professed by a minority" is "validity of the laws and customs of the religion professed by a minority in the field of private law and in some other matters". For this element Capotorti lists some sub-elements as follows: celebration of marriage, other matters of personal status, observance of religious holidays, conscientious objection to military service, and taking of an oath.[103]

---

102 Human Rights Committee: Consideration of Reports Submitted by States Parties, Fifth periodic report (Germany), para. 373, U.N.Doc.CCPR/C/DEU/2002/5 (4 Dec. 2002).

103 Capotorti Study, *supra* note 41, pp. 66–72.

With regard to the recognition of the marriage of minorities, the Sub-Commission on Minorities in its Draft Declaration on the Elimination of all Forms of Religious Intolerance recommends that: "Everyone shall have the right to have marriage rites performed in accordance with the prescriptions of his religion or belief and no one shall be compelled to undergo a religious marriage ceremony not in conformity with his convictions."[104]

Similarly, regarding the right of minorities to 'enjoying culture', Capotorti refers to the "preservation of their customs and legal traditions". According to him, "[t]here cannot be any doubt that an effective and full protection of the culture of minorities would require the preservation of their customs and legal traditions, which form an integral part of their way of life."[105] In this connection Capotorti further refers to the recognition of private law of different ethnic groups by African states: "It should also be mentioned that, in a very large number of African countries, the customs peculiar to the different ethnic groups have been maintained in force in the field of private law."[106]

For example in South Africa "a custom fulfilling certain requirements can after some time acquire the force of law."[107] The Constitution of South Africa also permits legislation recognizing traditional marriage, or religious, personal or family law. Section 15(3) (1)–(ii) of the Constitution requires that recognition of traditional or religious law must be consistent with the Constitution:[108]

a) This section does not prevent legislation recognizing:
   i– marriages concluded under any tradition, or a system of religious, personal or family law; or
   ii– systems of personal and family law under any tradition, or adhered to by persons professing a particular religion.
b) Recognition in terms of paragraph (a) must be consistent with this section and the other provisions of the Constitution[109]

---

104 Capotorti Study, *supra* note 41, p. 70.

105 *Ibid.*, p. 100.

106 *Ibid.*, 14.

107 Lourens M. Du Plessis, 'Religious Human Rights in South Africa' in John D. Van der Vyver & John Witte Jr (eds.) *Religious Human Rights in Global Perspective: Legal Perspective* (Kluwer Law International, the Hague, 1996), p. 443.

108 Ziyad Motala & Cyril Ramaphosa, *Freedom of Religion, in Constitutional Law* (Oxford University Press, 2002), p. 379.

109 Constitution of the Republic of South Africa 1996, as amended on 11 Oct. 1996. On the courts and religious laws in South Africa see Motala & Ramaphosa, *ibid.*

Yet, the only internationally binding instrument that recognizes personal legal autonomy regimes is the ILO Convention No. 169 Concerning Indigenous and Tribal Peoples, in which this right is reaffirmed in Article 8 and elaborated upon and extended to other non-personal laws such as penal law in subsequent Articles 9–12.[110]

Making no distinction between indigenous people and other minorities, in her working paper on minorities submitted in 1989, Claire Palley, the Special Rapporteur of the Sub-Commission on Minorities, refers to various forms of autonomy as a requirement for the application of Article 27. She states that:

> Especially significant is [the] recent widespread experimentation with various forms of autonomy, devolution or self-government for indigenous peoples and minorities, in countries as diverse as Nicaragua, the Philippines, Bangladesh, Sri Lanka, and Norway. While autonomy is not expressly required by Article 27, it is a mean of protection and promoting the cultural, religious and linguistic rights with which Article 27 deals explicitly.[111]

'Laws and customs of a religion' belonging to religious minorities is a concept similar to the 'legal traditions' belonging to indigenous peoples and ethnic minorities. The validity of marriage and private laws of minorities when recognized by states might be called the 'personal legal autonomy regime' or 'personal law regime' and is defined as follows:

> Members of a defined ethnic [or religious] group will be governed with respect to matters of personal law, marriage, divorce, perhaps adoption, succession, and so on, by a body of law distinctive to it, usually religious in character. Thus all members of a religious community... may be subject to a religious-based personal law system that could be applied by religious courts or by the normal secular courts.[112]

---

110 ILO Convention No. 169, *supra* note 43.

111 E/CN.4/Sub.2/1989/43: p. 5, para. 18, quoted in Cornelis D. de Jong, *The Freedom of Thought, Conscience and Religion or Belief in the United Nations (1946–1992)* (School of Human Rights Research, Antwerpen: Intersentia; Oxford: Hart, c, 2000), p. 257.

112 Henry J. Steiner & Phillip Alston, 'Autonomy Regimes: Religion-based Personal Law, Comments on Autonomy Regimes', in Steiner & Alston, *supra* note 33, p. 491.

Application of a Personal Legal Autonomy Regime and the Issue of Old and New Religions

Not all religious groups have similar identity rights, as they don't have similar religious rights. In a long process of interaction, belief characteristics in traditional religions have been combined with other elements such as ethnicity, law, custom, national, and cultural characteristics of their followers and societies. Furthermore, for the followers of these religions, e.g. 'Irish Catholics', it is not just belief or purely personal belief-related practices that constitute their religion, but religion rather can be traced, among others, in their history, their nationality, ethnicity, and law. For them religion has permeated their identity. For this reason, as discussed earlier, distinguishing between religious, ethnic or national minorities is extremely difficult.

General Comment 22 points out: "Article 18 is not limited in its application to traditional religions or to religions and beliefs with institutional characteristics or practices analogous to those of traditional religions."[113] However, in accordance with the purpose of Article 27, the shaping of a religious based legal system requires a long existence of the religion within the social life of its followers. Therefore as far as the right of minorities to personal legal autonomy is concerned, this right may not extend to followers of all beliefs or religions contemplated by Article 18 of the ICCPR, or all groups referred to in Article 13(1) of ICESCR,[114] but just to those groups with an established personal legal system.

Legitimacy of Limitations on the Right of Minorities to Personal Legal Autonomy

There is no limitation clause in Article 27 of the ICCPR. Yet the General Comment 23 observes that "none of the rights protected under Article 27 of the Covenant may be legitimately exercised in a manner or to an extent inconsistent with the other provisions of the Covenant."[115] With respect to personal legal autonomy regimes, the main issue of concern is the ensuring by states of non- violation of the principle of non-discrimination. Reaffirming this principle, and in connection with the providing of positive measures by states to protect the identity of minorities, the General Comment further warns that "[such positive measures] must respect the provisions of Articles

113 General Comment 22, *supra* note 70.
114 ICESCR, *supra* note 59.
115 General Comment 23, *supra* note 49.

2.1 and 26 of the Covenant both as regards the treatment between different minorities and the treatment between the persons belonging to them and the remaining part of the population."[116]

Another issue of concern is the 'principle of choice' or 'consent' of individual members of the group either to include themselves under the rule of their group's personal legal system or to exclude themselves from this system. In this regard Jones-Pauly, in surveying the issue of marriage contracts in India, insists on the duty of states to ensure that "each person retains the fundamental right to decide her[self or] himself what law shall apply to a marriage contract, whether one wants to be considered a member of a particularistic religious or ethnic legal culture, or as member of a generalized national legal culture applicable to all groups."[117]

Further, de Jong refers to two other important requirements for applying the personal legal autonomy regime as follows:

> First of all, religious law should only be legally binding with respect to persons who profess to be adherents of that particular religion or belief. Secondly, it should be clear and non-ambiguous: if religious norms can be interpreted differently and there is no fixed jurisprudence from religious courts clarifying matters, it would be a violation of the general principle of legal security to introduce religious law without further specification and clarification.[118]

As the right of minorities to identity in general, and to personal legal autonomy in particular, appears to hold an ambiguous status, the areas for imposing limitations on this right are wide and capable of different justifications by

116 *Ibid.* Article 2(1) of the ICCPR reads as follows: "Each state party to the present Covenant undertakes to respect and to ensure to all individuals within its territory and subject to its jurisdiction the rights recognized in the present Covenant, without distinction of any kind, such as race, colour, sex, language, religion, political or other opinion, national or social origin, property, birth or other status."

Article 26 of the ICCPR states that: "All persons are equal before the law and are entitled without any discrimination to the equal protection of the law. In this respect, the law shall prohibit any discrimination and guarantee to all persons equal and effective protection against discrimination on any ground such as race, colour, sex, language, religion, political or other opinion, national or social origin, property, birth or other status." ICCPR, *supra* note 46.

117 Christina Jones-Pauly, 'Tensions between Islamic Law and Human Rights from the Perspective of Comparative law', Seminar, Aug. 1999, rev. 2001 available at: <www.humanrights.ch/cms/pdf/990827_cjp_text.pdf>.

118 De Jong, *supra* note 111, p. 349.

states. On the other hand, the issue of religious personal law is considered by the majority of states as an issue subject to Article 18 and not Article 27 of the ICCPR.[119] Therefore, for these states the limitation clause for freedom to manifest a religion under Article 18(3) is extended to the right of minorities to personal legal autonomy. This clause reads as follows: "Freedom to manifest one's religion or beliefs may be subject only to such limitations as are prescribed by law and are necessary to protect public safety, order, health, or morals or the fundamental rights and freedoms of others."[120]

On conditioning minorities' law Capotorti also refers to the "states' legislative policy". He says: "There is ample justification for the widely expressed view that the maintenance of juridical institutions among minority group ought to be conditioned by the state's legislative policy."[121]

Finally, Article 4(2) of the Minority Declaration introduces two other completely new bases for limitations on the right of minorities to their characteristics, i.e. 'national law' and 'international standards', two ambiguous terms with potential for a wide scope of interpretation. The Article 4(2) reads as follows: "States shall take measures to create favourable conditions to enable persons belonging to minorities to express their characteristics and to develop their culture, language, religion, traditions and customs, except where specific practices are in violation of national law and contrary to international standards."[122]

However, when imposing any limitation on identity rights, the three principles of non-discrimination, proportionality and legality have to be considered by states. According to General Comment 22: "Limitations may be applied only for those purposes for which they were prescribed and must be directly related and proportionate to the specific need on which they are predicated. Restrictions may not be imposed for discriminatory purposes or applied in a discriminatory manner."[123]

---

119 Understanding of states on the relation of personal legal autonomy to the scope of Article 27 of ICCPR will be discussed in more detail in section 7.1 of this book.

120 ICCPR, *supra* note 46.

121 Capotorti Study, *supra* note 41, p. 100.

122 Minority Declaration, *supra* note 47.

123 General Comment 22, *supra* note 70.

5.2.4. *Discrimination on Grounds of Religion and Discrimination in Religious Rights (Discrimination on Grounds of Identity and Discrimination in Identity Rights)*

An-Na'im points out that "[t]he general principle of the rights of the members of religious minorities is to be found in the guarantee against discrimination on grounds of religion or faith. All the relevant international human rights documents and national Constitutions consistently and explicitly provide for this fundamental principle."[124] Article 55(c) of the Charter of the United Nations[125] commits all states to promote "universal respect for, and observance of human rights and fundamental freedoms for all, without discrimination as to race, sex, language or religion." By the same token, the Universal Declaration of Human Rights (UDHR)[126] reiterates this fundamental principle in Article 2: "Everyone is entitled to all rights and freedoms set forth in this Declaration, without distinction of any kind, such as race, colour, sex, language, religion, political or other opinion, national or social origin, property, birth or other status."

Similarly all states are committed under Articles 2(1), 24 and 26 of the ICCPR,[127] Articles 2(2) and 7(c) of the ICESCR[128] to non-discrimination policies towards all persons on their territory and subject to their jurisdiction on grounds such as race, colour, sex, language and religion.

On the other hand, among different grounds for discrimination, to compare the relevance of 'race' and 'religion' on the issue of 'discrimination' one can contrast the purposes of the International Convention on the Elimination of All Forms of Racial Discrimination (ICERD)[129] with those of the Religion Declaration.[130] 'Religion' unlike 'race', is itself a subject of rights which are known as 'religious rights'. Therefore, while the main purposes of the ICERD

---

124 Abdullahi Ahmed An-Na'im, 'Religious Minorities under Islamic Law and the Limits of Cultural Relativism' 9 *Human Rights Quarterly* 1(1987), pp. 7–8.

125 Charter of the United Nations, June 26, 1945, 59 Stat. 1031, T.S. 993, 3 Bevans 1153, entered into force, 24 Oct. 1945.

126 Universal Declaration of Human Rights (UDHR), G.A. res. 217A (III), U.N.Doc. A/810 at 71 (1948). For the text of Articles 2(1) and 26 of the ICCPR see *supra* note 116.

127 ICCPR, *supra* note 46.

128 ICESCR, *supra* note 59.

129 The International Convention on the Elimination of All Forms of Racial Discrimination (ICERD), G.A. res. 2106 (XX), Annex, 20 U.N. GAOR Supp. (No. 14) at 47, U.N.Doc. A/6014 (1966), 660 U.N.T.S. 195, entered into force, 4 Jan. 1969.

130 Religion Declaration, *supra* note 72.

are prevention of 'discrimination on ground of race' and 'racial intolerance', the main purposes of the Religion Declaration are 'prevention of discrimination on ground of religion' and 'religion intolerance' along with an additional purpose which is 'protection of religious rights'. According to Capotorti:

> Even if a state maintains strict neutrality as between various faiths, inequality of treatment is not necessarily excluded. The demands of various religions are different, and a law prohibiting certain acts, or enjoining the performance of others, may prevent one religious group from performing an essential rite or from following a basic observance, but be of no importance at all to another group.[131]

This issue of religious rights makes a study on the relevance of discrimination to religion more complicated. This is the main reason why – while the ICERD is an almost universally accepted treaty against racial discrimination, which has been in force for more than 39 years, there is no international or regional binding instrument against religious based discrimination, apart from the non-binding Religion Declaration. This is despite the fact that the struggle against both kinds of discrimination had a common starting point in the history of the United Nations, as Ghanea states:

> The history of freedom of religion or belief and the elimination of racial discrimination were closely related in the early period. In the late 1940s and early 1950s, United Nations actions in the fields of racial and religious intolerance were not differentiated. This was only to occur after the end of the 1950s when acts of racial and religious intolerance, mainly in Europe, prompted separate and specific United Nations actions in each of these spheres. However, whilst the prohibitions of racial intolerance came to be enshrined in a convention as far back as 1965, the legal status of religious discrimination remains as a Declaration.[132]

Considering the complexity in the concept of religious based discrimination, as mentioned before, this study makes a distinction between 'discrimination on ground of religion and beliefs' and 'discrimination between followers of

131 Capotorti Study, *supra* note 41, pp. 47–48.

132 Nazila Ghanea, "The Right to Freedom of Religion or Belief in International Human Rights Law and Inter-faith Dialogue', in Mofid University, Collected Papers, *supra* note 11, p. 78. On the areas of overlapping between 'religious' and 'racial' discrimination see *also*, Amor, Racial Discrimination and Religious Discrimination, *supra* note 54.

different religions in their religious rights' (discrimination in religious rights). A similar distinction can be made between discrimination on the grounds of identity and discrimination in identity rights. While the former discrimination, namely discrimination on the grounds of religion or identity is contrary to one of the basic universally accepted principles of human rights, the latter, namely, discrimination on religious rights or identity rights can fall subject to different states` policies and legitimate restrictions.

These two kinds of discrimination can also be called explicit or implicit discrimination or, as referred to by Weller, direct or indirect discrimination.[133] Also, as will be discussed further, Krishnaswami, Special Rapporteur of the Sub commission on minorities, has called them *de-jure* discrimination and *de-facto* discrimination. Direct or *de-jure* discrimination can loosely be called, as Krishnaswami notes, "traditional forms of discrimination."[134]

In the majority of countries although the law of the country, especially family law, is equally applicable to everyone, it reflects in certain important matters the concept of the predominant group. Krishnaswami, on the question of religious rights and practices, names this phenomenon the '*de-facto* pre-eminence' of a religion:

> There is no doubt that historically the principle of separation of state and religion emerged as a reaction against the privileged position of the established church or the state religion, and that its purpose was to ensure a large measure of equality to the members of various religions. Within the framework of this principle of separation, however, *de-facto* pre-eminence is sometimes achieved by a particular religion and the law of the country – although equally applicable to everyone – reflects in certain important matters the concept of the predominant group. Thus rules regulating marriage and its dissolution are often taken over from the religious law of the predominant group. Similarly, official holidays

133 On direct and indirect religious discrimination see for example Paul Weller 'The Dimensions and Dynamics of Religious Discrimination: Findings and Analysis from the UK', in Nazila Ghanea (ed.) *The Challenge of Religious Discrimination at the Dawn of the New Millennium* (Martinus Nijhoff Publishers, Leiden/Boston, 2003), pp. 73–75.

134 Arcot Krishnaswami, Special Rapporteur of the Sub-Commission on Prevention of Discrimination and Protection of Minorities, *Study of Discrimination in the Matter of Religious Rights and Practices* (United Nations Publication, Sales No. 60.XIV.2, New York, 1960) (Krishnaswami Study), p. 57.

> and days of rest in many countries correspond to a larger extent to the religious holidays and days of rest of the predominant group.[135]

The state, even when applying the principle of separation, may afford a special status to religious organizations, distinct from that granted to other kinds of associations. But such a status may be granted only on condition that the religious group satisfies certain special conditions – a possibility for some but not for others. By contrast a state may pass legislation with different restricting effects on different religious groups. The most controversial of this type of legislation was the ban on religious symbols which targets Muslim girls more so than others. On the relevant cases in European courts Evans Carolyn states:

> One issue that has caused conceptual difficulties in other jurisdictions that deal with religious freedom but has not been discussed in any detail by the Commission or Court is the interaction between neutral and generally applicable laws and freedom of religion or belief. This is not because of a lack of cases dealing with the issue, but rather because neither the Court nor the Commission has given sophisticated consideration to such cases as a distinct group. The general and neutral law problem arises when a state passes legislation that does not on its face mention religious issues or appears to discriminate against a religious group. Sometimes this neutral appearance is deceptive and the law can either have been passed with the intention of curtailing the religious practices of a particular group or is enforced or applied in a discriminatory manner. These cases merely create the impression of laws that are general and neutral but the reality is otherwise and no particular problem arises in determining that they interfere with religion or belief.[136]

Capotorti also refers to another similar concern with regard to the customs of minority groups with inferior positions in Europe:

> The available information further reveals that some minority groups, in particular those which occupy an inferior position in the society in which they live, confront severe problems in their efforts to maintain their

---

135 Krishnaswami Study *supra* note 134, pp. 47–48.

136 Evans, *supra* note 92, p. 168. For more information about discriminatory natural laws in Europe also see *ibid.*, pp. 118, 119, 125, and 130, 131. On the European approach towards the two kinds of discrimination see Michael Ipgrave, 'Religious Freedom: A Christian Perspective from Britain', in Mofid University, Collected Papers, *supra* note 11.

> customs. The situation of the Gypsies in Europe and of the indigenous population in various countries is illustrative of that point.[137]

Among many different types of direct (traditional forms of) discrimination, the clearest one, which has largely been omitted from the literature, is the one which is imposed in the royal systems. In this system the royal family, king, prince, or princes, on ground of dissent, obtain some special privileges against other members of the nation. Members of the royal family themselves may also be deprived of some of their fundamental rights such as the right to choose a job or the right to marry a person of their own choosing. Considering the existence of this example of direct discrimination several states have entered reservations to the related articles of international human rights treaties.[138]

Articles 8 and 12 of the Constitution of Malaysia refer to these two kinds of discrimination. Article 8 prohibits discrimination on the grounds of religion among others:

> (1) All persons are equal before the law and entitled to the equal protection of the law.
> (2) Except as expressly authorized by this Constitution, there shall be no discrimination against citizens on the ground only of religion, race, descent or place of birth in any law relating to the acquisition, holding or disposition of property or the establishing or carrying on of any trade, business, profession, vocation or employment.[139]

While Article 12 (1) is similar to Article 8 in that it reiterates the principle of non-discrimination on the grounds of religion, Article 12(2) finds it lawful for the Federation or a state to provide special supports for Muslim institutions. The Article reads as follows:

> (1) Without prejudice to the generality of Article 8, there shall be no discrimination against any citizen on the grounds only of religion, race, descent or place of birth;

---

137 Capotorti Study, *supra* note 41, p. 67.

138 For example Belgium, Luxembourg, Morocco, and United Kingdom have entered reservations to Article 7 of the CRC with respect to the succession to the throne. For the reservations and declarations to the CRC see Office of the United Nations High Commissioner for Human Rights, Ratifications and Reservations: Convention on the Rights of the Child, at: <http://www.ohchr.org/english/countries/ratification/11.htm>, last updated May 8, 2006.

139 Constitution of Malaysia, *supra* note 50.

> (a) in the administration of any educational institution maintained by a public authority, and, in particular, the admission of pupils or students or the payment of fees; or
> (b) in providing out of the funds of a public authority financial aid for the maintenance or education of pupils or students in any educational institution (whether or not maintained by a public authority and whether within or outside the Federation).
> (2) Every religious group has the right to establish and maintain institutions for the education of children in its own religion, and there shall be no discrimination on the ground only of religion in any law relating to such institutions or in the administration of any such law; but it shall be lawful for the Federation or a state to establish or maintain or assist in establishing or maintaining Islamic institutions or provide or assist in providing instruction in the religion of Islam and incur such expenditure as may be necessary for the purpose.[140]

With regard to the instances of provisional measures in favour of minorities discussed in this part of the book, according to General Comment 23, "as long as those measures are aimed at correcting conditions which prevent or impair the enjoyment of the rights guaranteed under Article 27, they may constitute a legitimate differentiation under the Covenant, provided that they are based on reasonable and objective criteria."[141] It should be noted that this kind of different treatment or so-called 'positive discrimination' is justified in cases of indirect discrimination and not direct discrimination.

Finally, it also should be added that recognition of some religious groups and non recognition of some others is an issue of discrimination in identity rights and might be justifiable. Yet, if such recognition or non recognition leads to discrimination on the grounds of identity or even the ignoring of some fundamental rights of non-recognized minorities, it should be prohibited, as it leads to the violation of the basic principles of human rights. This issue will be discussed in more detail in the next section.

---

140 *Ibid.*
141 General Comment 23, *supra* note 49, para. 6.2.

CHAPTER SIX

Current Application of Public Aspects of *Dhimmah*

6.1. Recognition of Non-Muslim Religious Minorities by Muslim States

Among Muslim states, only a few have named in their Constitutions a specific religion or religious group. According to the Constitution of Pakistan representatives of Buddhists, Sikhs, Hindus, Zoroastrians (Parsis) and Christians along with Ahmadies, are allocated special seats in parliament.[142] Also in Algeria Articles 3 and 4 of Act 63–278 of 26 July 1963 concerning holidays recognize the right of Algerian nationals and aliens of the Jewish or Christian faiths to have rest days to celebrate religious feasts.[143]

Similarly, Article 2 of the Constitution of Iraq names three religious groups: "This Constitution guarantees the Islamic identity of the majority of the Iraqi people and guarantees the full religious rights of all individuals to freedom of religious belief and practice such as Christians, Yazedis, and Mandi Sabeans."[144] Yet, the scope of Article 18 and 27 of the ICCPR is not distinguished by the provision. While a reference to the identity of the majority is made, only the religious rights of minorities and not their identity rights are referred to.

On the other hand, Iran is the only Muslim country whose Constitution lists three religious groups as recognized religious minorities. According to Article 13 of the Constitution of Iran, "Zoroastrian, Jewish, and Christian Iranians are the only recognized religious minorities, who, within the limits of the law, are free to perform their religious rites and ceremonies, and to act

142 On declaring Ahmadies as non-Muslim in Pakistan Section 4.2.1 of this book. Also see Abdelfattah Amor, Special Rapporteur of the Commission on Human Rights, Implementation of the Declaration on the Elimination of All Forms of Intolerance and Discrimination Based on Religion or Belief, Report Relating to Visit to Pakistan, para. 9, U.N.Doc.E/CN.4/1996/95/Add.1 (2 Jan. 1996) (hereinafter Abdelfattah Amor, Visit to Pakistan).

143 See Human Rights Committee: Consideration of Reports Submitted by States Parties, Second periodic report (Algeria), para. 75, U.N.Doc.CCPR.C.101.Add.1 (11 March 1998). Also see section 4.2.1 of this book.

144 Law of Administration for the State of Iraq for the Transitional Period (Constitution of Iraq), approved by a referendum on 15 Oct. 2005.

according to their own canon in matters of personal affairs and religious education."[145] Finally Saudi Arabia is the only Muslim country which, in contrast to the Muslim legal traditions, does not recognize any religious community other than Muslims.

Recognition of religious minorities in Turkey and Pakistan is partly rooted in the treaties concluded between these two countries and their neighbouring countries. Turkey has recognized Armenians Orthodox Christians, Jews, and Greek Orthodox Christians as the three religious minorities under the 1923 Lausanne Treaty.[146] With regard to a similar treaty which was concluded in 1950 between Pakistan and India Capotorti states:

> Under the agreement between Pakistan and India, signed at New Delhi on 8 April 1950, the governments of India and Pakistan solemnly agreed that each should ensure to the 'minorities' throughout its territory, complete equality of citizenship, irrespective of religion, a full sense of security in respect of life, culture, property and personal honour, freedom of movement within each country and freedom of occupation, speech and worship, subject to law and morality. Members of the minorities were to have equal opportunity with members of the majority community to participate in the public life of their country, to hold political or other office, and to serve in their country's civil and armed forces. Both governments declared these rights to be fundamental and undertook to enforce them effectively. The two governments emphasized that minorities owe allegiance and loyalty to the state whose citizenship they possess and that to obtain compensation they must apply to the governments of that state. It was planned to set up minority commissions with a view to the effective implementation of the agreement.[147]

Not all Muslim states have explicitly recognized particular religions or religious groups. In Oman Christians and Hindus have been recognized as minorities. Yet, with a great number of Christians, Syria doesn't explicitly recognize any religious group. Similarly in Bangladesh and Malaysia, Christians, Buddhists

---

145 Constitution of Islamic Republic of Iran, 1979, amended on 28 July 1989.

146 According to a report, there are an estimate 65000 Armenians Orthodox Christians, 25000 Jews, and 3000 to 5000 Greek Orthodox Christians in Turkey. According to the same report there are also other non-recognized religious minorities, including approximately 10000 Baha'is, an estimated 15000 Syrian Orthodox (Syrian) Christians, and 3000 Protestants. See U.S. Department of State, International Religious Freedom Report on Turkey, 2003.

147 Capotorti Study, *supra* note 41, p. 30.

and Hindus have not been recognized as minorities or as a religion. However, the same religions have been recognized as a minority in Indonesia and followers of these religions have to officially register with the government."[148]

Finally, recognition of religious family law of specific religious groups in Muslim countries, as will be discussed in more detail in the next chapter, can imply their recognition as a religious minority. In this sense, with their inherited long history of recognition as People of the Book, Jews, Christians and Zoroastrians are considered as recognized religious minorities in all Muslim countries, with the exception of Saudi Arabia, whether these minorities exist in a country or not. In other Muslim countries with more diverse religions this recognition has been extended at least to those of longer established religions.

Due to religious sensitivities, like non-Muslim states, Muslim states are hesitant in the recognition of new minorities. For example according to a report on Sudan, "the government generally is less restrictive to Christian groups that historically have had a presence in the country, such as Coptic Christians and Greek Orthodox, and is more restrictive of newer arrivals."[149] According to another report on Syria, "in 1964 the government banned Jehovah's Witnesses as a politically motivated Zionist organization. However, members of Jehovah's Witnesses have continued to practice their faith privately despite the official ban."[150] In the same sense, recognition of Baha'is, as will be discussed in more detail in the next section, has been refused in almost all Muslim countries. Yet, among the major new religious groups, the Ahmadies, due to some specific conditions, is the only new group which has been officially recognized in Pakistan.

Being affected by the *Dhimmah* traditions, the instances provided by Capotorti in a list under the title of "juridical status to a religion professed by a minority" are more or less applied in all Muslim countries as far as recognized religions are concerned. As already mentioned two elements in the list which are related to identity rights of religious minorities are: the question of the recognition and the question of the validity of the laws and customs of the religion professed by a minority.[151] Other instances in the list, related

148 Arzt, The Role of Compulsion, *supra* note 9. Also see U.S. Department of State, International Religious Freedom Reports.

149 U.S. Department of State, International Religious Freedom Report on the Sudan, 2003.

150 U.S. Department of State, International Religious Freedom Report on Syria, 2003.

151 Capotorti Study, *supra* note 41, pp. 66–72.

to religious rights of minorities, which are similar to the instances included in Article 6 of the Religion Declaration, are as follows:

- Freedom of persons belonging to religious minorities to worship and practice the rites of their religion;
- The right of persons belonging to religious minorities not to be compelled to participate in the activities of other religions;
- The right of persons belonging to religious minorities to administer the affairs of their own religious communities;
- The right of persons belonging to religious minorities to establish educational institutions.[152]

Allocation of Special Seats to Representatives of Religious Minorities in the Parliament

Along with the issue of the recognition of religious minorities, in the parliament of some Muslim countries special seats have been allocated to the representatives of religious minorities. In Iran the minority religious groups recognized by the Constitution are represented in the parliament by five members who are elected by the minority groups themselves. According to Article 64 of the Constitution of Iran:

> There are to be 270 members of the National Consultative Assembly. After every ten years, in case of an increase in the country's population, representatives will be added to each constituency at the rate of one per 150,000 additional persons. The Zoroastrians and Jews will each elect one representative; Assyrian and Chaldean Christians will jointly elect one representative; and Armenian Christians in the north and those in the south of the country will each elect one representative. If the population of these minorities increases, after every ten years, they will be given additional representation at the rate of one per 150,000. Regulations concerning elections will be determined by law.[153]

Also in Egypt "traditionally two Copts [are appointed] as ministers to [the] cabinet and [the president] is authorized to appoint up to ten members of the parliament, typically consisting of Copts and women."[154] In Lebanon there is special arrangement for representatives of different religious groups in parlia-

152 *Ibid.*

153 Constitution of Iran, *supra* note 145.

154 Scott Kent Brown II, 'The Coptic Church in Egypt: A Comment on Protecting Religious Minorities from Non-state Discrimination' *Brigham Young University Law Review* 1049 (2000).

ment. In Pakistan the following seats within the National Assembly have been assigned to religious minorities: Christians, four seats; Hindus and persons belonging to scheduled Castes, four seats; Sikhs, Buddhist, Parsis and other non-Muslims, one seat; Ahmadies, one seat.[155]

Furthermore, in Pakistan, unlike Iran and Egypt, such an assignment for religious minorities is applied to local assemblies as well. Apart from this, in Pakistan religious minorities along with their special representatives, from 2002 can participate in national elections as general candidates and voters.[156] Before that date, the issue of the separate electoral system was a controversial issue in Pakistan for a period of approximately seventeen years.

In Pakistan, in 1985 an amendment to the Constitution established a separate electoral system, according to which elections to the National Assembly, provincial assemblies and local authorities were conducted with separate electoral rolls for Muslims and non-Muslims. Muslims were authorized to vote only for Muslim candidates, and non-Muslims could only vote for non-Muslims.[157]

There were two extremely different views on this system. According to the authorities, this split electoral system guaranteed political representation to minorities despite their small number. Yet, according to non-governmental sources, the system affected the political rights of non-Muslim communities and based citizenship on religion, going against the notion of citizenship free of any distinction, including religion.[158]

Finally, in January 2002, the government eliminated the country's system of separate electorates. While minorities welcomed the opportunity to be able to elect local representatives to the national and provincial assemblies, it was unlikely that any of the future elected officials would come from minority groups; but by having reserved seats for the minorities, they believed they could achieve more to increase their presence in law-making bodies. Consequently, in a positive response to this demand, the government announced in August

---

155 Article 51(2A) of the Constitution of Pakistan. Similar reservation of seats is made in provincial legislative under Article 106(3) of the Constitution. Constitution of Pakistan, 1973.

156 In Iran also religious minorities are free to elect candidates from outside their own groups. See Human Rights Committee: 1251st meeting (Iran), para. 42, U.N.Doc.CCPR/C/SR.1251 (29 July 1993).

157 The 1985 amendments, Articles 51, 2A and 106.3. See Abdelfattah Amor, Visit to Pakistan, *supra* note 142, paras. 8, 19, 20, 57, 58. Also see Javid Rehman, 'Minority Rights and the Constitutional Dilemmas of Pakistan' 19 *Netherlands Quarterly of Human Rights* 4 (2001), p. 429.

158 See Abdelfattah Amor, Visit to Pakistan, *supra* note 142.

2002 that the reserved seats for religious minorities would be restored in the October 2002 elections. Now, non-Muslims vote twice: once for the general candidate, and once for the seats set aside for their particular group.[159]

The authorities in Pakistan and Iran have always insisted on the advantages of the allocation of special seats to representatives of religious minorities. In Pakistan "the authorities have indicated that this system 'ensures that all minorities are represented, even if numerically small'."[160] Similarly in Iran "the authorities often used the term 'privilege' in referring to minorities, particularly their representation in parliament even though they are fewer in number than required by the Constitution."[161] The representative of Iran provided more reasoning on the advantages of this system:

> Although some representatives of minority groups might be elected by as many as two million or more voters, the Zoroastrian minority population had amounted to only about 30,000 persons at the last count. Zoroastrian candidates were required to obtain at least 5,000 votes to be elected to the Islamic Consultative Assembly. Representatives elected by minority groups enjoyed the same rights as other members of the Islamic Consultative Assembly. They were entitled to participate in the making of decisions, the submission of proposals, voting on legislation, the adoption of recommendations, etc., which affected not only their own minority groups but also the population as a whole.[162]

6.2. THE RIGHTS OF NON-RECOGNIZED RELIGIOUS MINORITIES

6.2.1. *'Krishnaswami Study' and Different Practices of Muslim States in Recognition of Religions*

On the status of religion in relation to the state Krishnaswami broadly classifies states into three different categories: "Those which have an established

---

159 See *Ibid.* Also see U.S. Department of State, International Religious Freedom Report on Pakistan, 2003.

160 Abdelfattah Amor, Visit to Pakistan, *supra* note 142, para. 58.

161 Abdelfattah Amor, Special Rapporteur of the Commission on Human Rights, Implementation of the Declaration on the Elimination of All Forms of Intolerance and Discrimination Based on Religion or Belief, Report Relating to Visit to Iran, para. 16, U.N.Doc. E/CN.4/1996/95/Add.2 (9 Feb. 1996). (hereinafter Abdelfattah Amor, Visit to Iran).

162 Summary record, 1993 (Iran), *supra* note 156, para. 42.

church or state religion, those in which several religions are recognized by the state, and those in which state and religion are separate."[163] Then, while setting Muslim countries under the second category he adds: "There is no strict dividing line between countries having an established church or a state religion and those where several religions are recognized; in many Muslim countries, for example, Islam is the state religion, but recognition is accorded to a number of other religious communities as well."[164]

Yet, unlike Capotorti who focuses on identity rights in his study, Krishnaswami doesn't have a positive approach towards the issue of recognition; the focus of his attention is non-discrimination and religious rights. However according to him such recognition does not necessarily affect the religious rights and equality of members of different religious groups:

> In the countries of this group a considerable variety of arrangements may be found. In some of them only two or a few religions have a status in law. In others, any religion may be granted recognition upon application and the completion of certain formalities. But even in countries where only a limited number of religions are recognized, this fact does not necessarily imply that there is discrimination against the unrecognized religion or their followers, since in many cases such religions can avail themselves of the general law of association and since, in addition, their followers, as citizens, are equal under the law.[165]

Krishnaswami further adds: "Of course if the state has discretionary power to grant or to refuse recognition, and if the privileges accorded to recognized religions, or to their followers, are very different from those accorded to unrecognized ones, this may lead to discrimination."[166] Then, to provide one example of such discrimination, he refers to a specific concern with regard to almost all Muslim countries, which is the possible effect of personal autonomy regimes on the right to change one's religion:

> Where the cumulative impact of such arrangements is severe, as in countries where to a large extent the personal status of each individual is regulated by the religious law of his community, even the basic right of an individual to change his religion or belief may be seriously impaired.

163 Krishnaswami Study, *supra* note 134, p. 46.
164 *Ibid.*
165 *Ibid.*, p. 47.
166 *Ibid.*

> This right may also be curtailed more directly or even nullified, where religious leaders are entitled to prevent, or to refuse to recognize, the withdrawal of a member from his religion.[167]

6.2.2. *The Rights of Non-recognized Religious Minorities in the Constitution of Iran*

While there are no clear provisions in the Constitution of Iran on non-recognized religions, Article 14 addresses 'non-Muslims' in general. The Article apparently is not a matter related to citizens of states but about the way Muslims had to treat non-Muslims in general. Furthermore the Koran verse quoted is referring specifically to time of war in early Muslim history and the way Muslims had to treat non-believers who did not belong to the camp of enemy. It reads as follows:

> In accordance with the sacred verse, 'God does not forbid you to deal kindly and justly with those who have not fought against you because of your religion and who have not expelled you from your home,' (60:81) the government of the Islamic Republic of Iran and all Muslims are duty-bound to treat non-Muslims in conformity with ethical norms and the principles of Islamic justice and equity, and to respect their human rights. This principle applies to all who refrain from engaging in conspiracy or activity against Islam and the Islamic Republic of Iran.[168]

Apart from its ambiguity, the second part of the article on conspiracy implies that such criminal acts deprive the perpetrators of their human rights. The wording of the article, therefore, has been widely criticized by different observers. For example Ghanea states:

> Presumably 'conspiracy or activity against' the Islamic Republic of Iran refers to espionage and treason, but its conjunction with such activity against 'Islam' makes it less determinate and more ideologically subjective. In any case, respect for human rights is made dependent on this somewhat vague conditionality, and is therefore very problematic according to international human rights standards.[169]

---

167 *Ibid.*

168 Abdelfattah Amor, Visit to Iran, *supra* note 161, para. 11.

169 Nazila Ghanea, *Ethnic and Religious Groups in the Islamic Republic of Iran*, U.N.Doc. E/CN.4/Sub.2/AC.5/2003/WP.8 (5 May 2003).

In response to the concerns of one Human Rights Committee member on the ambiguity of the article, the representative of Iran states:

> The expression 'conspiracy or activities against Islam and the Islamic Republic of Iran' had been clearly defined in the relevant legal rules and regulations as the action of individuals who resorted to conflict or endangered the security or independence of the country or of the Islamic system. Punishment was imposed so as to fit the particular crime; it might consist of imprisonment or, in some cases, capital punishment.[170]

Such a justification is against both human rights norms and the Koranic principles. As mentioned before the focus of the Koranic verse quoted in the article is on the earlier times of Muslims, when they were in a state of war and under significant pressure by non-Muslim enemies. According to this verse enmity and hatred of a group must not be an obstacle for implementing justice and it should not lead to violating human rights. Koranic ethical norms and the principles of justice and equity embodied in the quoted verse and in the following verses apply even to those who are fighting against Muslims:

- "Whoever does evil, he is requited only with the like of it."[171]
- "And if you take your turn, then punish with the like of that with which you were afflicted. But if you show patience, it is best for the patient."[172]
- "And the recompense of evil is punishment like it; but whoever forgives and amends, his reward is with *Allah*."[173]
- "O you who believe, be upright to *Allah*, bearers of witness with justice; and let not hatred of a people incite you not to act equitably. Be just; that is nearer to observance of duty."[174]

The verse quoted in Article 14 is linked with the relationship of a Muslim government with non-Muslim citizens and is obviously irrelevant. Such usage in fact implies a dividing line between Muslim citizens and non-Muslim citizens of a country. Furthermore, the article in itself does not provide a free-standing protection for non-recognized religious groups. In contrast, it suggests further

170 Summary record, 1993 (Iran), *supra* note 156, para. 37.
171 The Koran, 40:40.
172 *Ibid.*, 16:126.
173 *Ibid.*, 42:40.
174 *Ibid.*, 5:8.

grounds for restrictions against non-Muslims. Therefore the omission of the article is much more favourable for religious minorities than its existence.

Considering the ambiguities and shortcomings in the legislation of Iran, Abdelfattah Amor in his report reiterates the necessity of a more clear and efficient legislation on the recognition of the religious rights of followers of non-recognized religions:

> Although the situation of the other non-recognized minorities or communities, such as the Baha'is, is covered by Articles 14, 22 and 23 of the Constitution in which the concepts of citizen, individuals and persons are used, the Special Rapporteur recommends that a legislative enactment should give clearer recognition to these rights for every citizen, individual or person, regardless, *inter alia*, of his beliefs or the community to which he belongs.[175]

Article 20 of the Constitution of Pakistan can be considered as an excellent example of progressive legislation on the religious rights of all citizens:

> Subject to law, public order and morality:
>
> (a) Every citizen shall have the right to profess, practice and propagate his religion; and
>
> (b) Every religious denomination and every sect thereof shall have the right to establish, maintain and manage its religious institutions

6.2.3. *The Legal Status of Baha'is in Muslim Countries*

The Baha'is are among those religious groups whose legal status in Iran, the country of its origin, and in other Muslim countries has been under debate. In fact, in the Middle East only Israel has recognized the Baha'is as a religious minority.[176]

While the number of Baha'is in Iran has been reported as approximately 300,000,[177] their existence has clearly been ignored in the legal system of this

---

175 Abdelfattah Amor, Visit to Iran, *supra* note 161, para. 90.

176 See Steiner & Alston, Comments on State, Religion, and Personal Law in Israel, *supra* note 33.

177 Abdelfattah Amor, Visit to Iran, *supra* note 161, para. 55. The Special Rapporteur has not offered official figures concerning the size of the Baha'i community in Iran. Yet, according to him, Baha'i representatives and other non-governmental bodies estimate the number at 300,000, which, numerically, makes them the largest religious minority in Iran.

country and their rights have been subject to restrictions.[178] Similarly, while Abdelfattah Amor in his report has declared the situation of recognized minorities in Iran as being "generally satisfactory",[179] the situation of unrecognized minorities, especially the Baha'is, has been subject to criticism by him.[180] In response to these critics Iranian authorities have indicated that "the fact of belonging to the Baha'i community did not entail loss of the rights to which every Iranian citizen was entitled."[181]

Baha'is believe that their nineteenth century religious leaders, Bab and Baha-ullah, are the latest in a series of God's messengers. To Muslims, however, any prophet after Muhammad is not acceptable, as they consider their prophet to be the 'Seal of the Prophets', God's final messenger. Along with this aspect of the Baha'i faith being contradictory to Muslim beliefs, their proselytizing practices are not accepted by Muslim governments. For example, with regard to Iran it is not only the Baha'is, but even recognized religious minorities, that become active in proselytizing, face difficulties. Along with the issue of proselytizing, Abdelfattah Amor in his report has made a distinction between restricted and unrestricted religious groups in Iran based on their ethnicity in terms of their similarity to the Iranian majority:

> Those without any ethnic distinction, combining Armenians, Assyro-Chaldeans, Jews, Baha'is and Muslim converts, sometimes face difficulties in obtaining legal recognition of their existence. For example, the Universal Church has not been recognized since the revolution. These obstacles seem to be linked to the fact that those churches are of an international nature and, in general, are not restricted to a specific ethnic group seeking to preserve its identity. On the contrary, those Protestant associations go beyond the ethnic framework in order to attract all components of society, including Muslims who might convert and join those associations.[182]

On the other hand, because the Baha'i World Centre is located in Israel, the extraterritorial relations of Baha'is have been abused by some Muslim

178 See for example Human Rights Committee: Consideration of Reports Submitted by States Parties, Concluding Observations of the Committee (Iran), U.N.Doc.CCPR/C/79/Add.25 (3 Aug. 1993).

179 Abdelfattah Amor, Visit to Iran, *supra* note 161, para. 94. Also see para. 103.

180 *Ibid.*, paras. 8, 106, 107, 109, 111, 112. In this report he also provides some interesting recommendations on the improvement of the situation of Baha'is in Iran.

181 *Ibid.*, para. 70 also see para. 74.

182 *Ibid.*, paras. 71, 79–85.

governments in the region as a pretext against their legal activities. With regards to the accusations of Iranian officials against Baha'i organizations, Abdelfattah Amor in his report stated: "The Baha'i organization [in Iran] has been...characterized by its espionage activities for the benefit of foreign entities, particularly Israel."[183] The Baha'is' representatives in Iran, however, have refuted these accusations:

> They pointed out that, according to the fundamental principles of their religion, Baha'is should show loyalty and obedience to their government and should refrain from any political involvement. The Baha'is indicated that the accusations of espionage in favour of Zionism were based solely on the fact that the Baha'i World Centre was in Israel. They pointed out that this centre was established on Mount Carmel in the last century, before the establishment of the state of Israel, in accordance with the explicit instructions of Baha-ullah, the founder of the Baha'i faith, who had lived there in exile after being banished from Persia.[184]

It is interesting to note that Jews have similar extraterritorial links with Israel. Yet, while travelling to Israel with an Iranian passport is not allowed according to Iranian law, Iranian Jews have been exempted from this law.

The legal status of Baha'is in some other Muslim countries is also not satisfactory. For example "in Egypt in 1960 president Abdel Nasser issued a decree (Law 263 for 1960) banning Baha'i institutions and community activities. All Baha'i community property, including Baha'i centres, libraries and cemeteries were confiscated."[185] According to Egypt's report to Human Rights Committee, the constitutionality of this decree has been challenged in case law. Consequently the court ruled that Baha'is ceremonies are forbidden only when they intend to preach their beliefs in a manner inconsistent with public order:

> ...concerning legal proceedings against members of the Baha'i community, it has been argued that Decree Law No. 264 of 1960, concerning the dissolution of Baha'i forums, is unconstitutional. The argument was put forward during a criminal case in which a number of individuals were charged with propagating pro-Baha'i propaganda by carrying out activities

183 *Ibid.*, para. 56.
184 *Ibid.*, para. 8.
185 U.S. Department of State, International Religious Freedom Report on Egypt, 2003.

> designed to encourage individuals to embrace this faith in contravention of the said Decree Law. The plea was argued before the Supreme Court (later replaced by the Supreme Constitutional Court), which rejected it on the ground that the contested Decree Law did not contest the freedom of the Baha'i faith or detract from it in any way, but merely challenged the Baha'i forums in which members gathered and engaged in activities and performed ceremonies intended to preach their beliefs in a manner inconsistent with public order.[186]

On the legal status of the Baha'is the report continues: "From a strictly legal point of view, Baha'i forums are private associations that are subject to the law. The Constitution prohibits the establishment of associations whose activities are inimical to social security and public order."[187]

In a further development, on April 4, 2006, the Administrative Court of Egypt recognized the right of Egyptian Baha'is to have their religion acknowledged on official documents. The ruling was the result of a lawsuit filed by a married Baha'i couple against interior minister Habib al-Adly in June 2004. According to the reports officials from the Civil Status Department (CSD) confiscated the couple's official documentation because it cited their religious affiliation as Baha'i. Yet, as shown in the following report, despite this improvement, the question of the full recognition of Baha'is as a religion in Egypt is not easy to predict:

> For a religious denomination to be officially recognized by the state, a request must be submitted to the Religious Affairs Department at the ministry of interior, which assesses whether the proposed religion would pose a threat or upset national unity or social peace. The department also consults the leading religious figures recognized in the country, particularly the Pope of the Coptic Orthodox Church and the Sheik of Al-Azhar. The registration is then referred to the president, who issues a decree recognizing the new religion according to Law 15 of 1927.[188]

Also, with regard to the recognition of Baha'is in Iran and other Muslim countries, it seems that such an approach is not feasible in near future. For

---

186 Human Rights Committee: Consideration of Reports Submitted by States Parties, The combined third and fourth periodic reports (Egypt), para. 677, U.N.Doc.CCPR/C/EGY/2001/3 (15 April 2002).

187 *Ibid.*

188 U.S. Department of State, International Religious Freedom Report on Egypt, 2003.

example Abdelfattah Amor in his report on Iran states: "The authorities indicated that only the religious dignitaries could decide on the possibility of granting religious minority status to the Baha'is."[189] Yet, such complexity cannot be used as a pretext for the non-recognition of religious rights and identity rights of Baha'is. Furthermore, similar to the recognition of religious groups in some European Countries like Germany, Baha'is may also simply be registered in Iran as a corporation which at least can help in the recognition of its properties.

In 1981 Falk noted that, "[m]aintaining respect for the Baha'i religion and people will be one severe test of human rights in an Islamic republic."[190] It seems that such a respect has been afforded by the public in Iran as over the last two decades, not one case of arbitrary action by ordinary people against Baha'is has been reported from Iran.[191] This fact shows that the ordinary religious practices of Baha'is in Iran cannot be restricted on grounds of consideration of general public concerns.

On the other hand, Baha'is could also resort to some measures in addressing the security sensitivities in Muslim countries with regard to their proselytizing activities and especially their extraterritorial relations with Israel. As sated by Maoz: "In Israel, there are some 300 Baha'is, most of them foreign citizens who serve in the community's institutions."[192] Therefore, Baha'i communities could suggest the transfer of their headquarters temporarily from Israel to another country. This could also be considered as a symbolic sign of sympathy by Baha'is toward Palestinians in the occupied territories and be greeted positively in other Muslim countries in the area.

---

189 Abdelfattah Amor, Visit to Iran, *supra* note 161, para. 57.

190 Richard Falk, *Human Rights and State Sovereignty* (New York & London: Holmes & Meier, 1981), p. 212.

191 For more information on situation of Baha'is in Iran see Abdelfattah Amor, Visit to Iran, *supra* note 161, paras. 55–70; Nazila Ghanea, *Human Rights, the UN and the Baha'is in Iran* (Oxford: George Ronald; the Hague: Kluwer, 2003); Sanasarian, *supra* note 20. Also see the related reports on freedom of religion in Iran during this period, for example, reports by UN Special Rapporteur on freedom of religion or belief; U.S. Department of State, International Religious Freedom Reports on Iran; and reports by Amnesty International and Human Rights Watch.

192 Asher Maoz, 'Religious Human Rights in the State of Israel' in Van der Vyver & Witte, *supra* note 107, p. 354.

6.3. DISCRIMINATION ON GROUNDS OF RELIGION IN LEGISLATION

6.3.1. *Provisions of the Constitutions*

The Constitution or the legislation of the majority of Muslim states explicitly prohibits discrimination against individuals on grounds of religion. For example, according to Article 40 of the Constitution of Egypt: "All citizens are equal before the law. They have equal public rights and duties without discrimination between them due to race, ethnic origin, language, religion or creed."[193] Similarly Article 14 of the Constitution of Iraq refers to an explicit prohibition of discrimination, among others, based on religion: "Iraqis are equal before the law without discrimination based on gender, race, ethnicity, origin, colour religion, creed, belief or opinion, or economic and social status."[194]

Yet, Article 22 of the Constitution of Afghanistan does not mention the grounds of discrimination but simply points out: "Any kind of discrimination and privilege between the citizens of Afghanistan is prohibited."[195] A similar wording exists in Article 50 of the Constitution: "The citizens of Afghanistan are employed for state services on the basis of qualification without any kind of discrimination and in accordance with the law."[196]

In the same sense, Article 19 of the Constitution of Iran does not explicitly refer to religion as a ground for discrimination: "The people of Iran, of whatever tribe and clan, shall enjoy equal rights, and colour, race, language and the like shall not be a privilege."[197] Also Article 20 of the Constitution is not helpful in this regard: "All members of the nation, both men and women, shall receive equal protection of law and enjoy all human, political, economic, social and cultural rights, with due observance of the principle of Islam."[198]

In the Constitution of Pakistan the issue of non-discrimination on grounds of religion, is addressed with regard to special rights, in the following articles:

---

193 The Constitution of the Arab Republic of Egypt, amendment ratified on 22 May 1980.

194 Constitution of Iraq, *supra* note 144.

195 Constitution of the Islamic Republic of Afghanistan, ratified 26 Jan. 2004.

196 *Ibid.*

197 Constitution of Iran, *supra* note 145.

198 *Ibid.*

- Article 22(3)(b): No citizen shall be denied admission to any educational institution receiving aid from public revenues on the ground only of race, religion, caste or place of birth.
- Article 26(1): In respect of access to places of public entertainment or resort not intended for religious purposes only, there shall be no discrimination against any citizen, on the ground only of race, religion, caste, sex, residence or place of birth.
- Article 27(1): No citizen otherwise qualified for appointment in the service of Pakistan shall be discriminated against in respect of any such appointment on the ground only of race, religion, caste, sex, residence or place of birth.[199]

6.3.2. *Discrimination in Legislation Concerning the Head of State and Other Official Positions*

In the Constitutions of several Muslim countries only Muslims are qualified to be the president or the head of state. In Pakistan, Algeria and Egypt, for example, the president must be Muslim[200] and in Iran, the leader and the president, both must be Shiite Muslims.[201]

In Iran, because of the religious character of the state, apart from those of the leader and the president, some other senior positions are reserved for *mujtahids*. These are clerical members of the Guardian Council and members of the Council of Experts. On the other hand, unlike other Muslim countries[202] Iran is the only country, where according to legislation judges at any level have to be Muslims. The Constitution states in Article 163 that "[t]he qualifications and conditions of judges shall be laid down by law in accordance with the criteria of *fiqh*."[203] According to the Law on the Selection of Judges of 1983, the judge must be a Muslim.[204]

---

199 Constitution of Pakistan, *supra* note 155.

200 See Article 41.2 of Constitution of Pakistan, Article 73 of the Constitution of Algeria and Article 15 of the Constitution of Egypt.

201 Articles 5, 109 and 115 of Constitution of Iran. Constitution of Iran, *supra* note 145.

202 For example in Jordan four of the ten judges in the Court of Cassation are Christians. See Human Rights Committee: Summary record of the 1323rd meeting (Jordan), para. 43, U.N.Doc.CCPR/C/SR.1323 (12 July 1994).

203 Constitution of Iran, *supra* note 145.

204 See Human Rights Watch, 'Iran, Religious and Ethnic Minorities: Discrimination in Law and Practice' Vol. 9, No. 7 (E) (Sept. 1997). On this law also see Jamshid Sharifiyaan,

In Pakistan as well, in specific courts or for certain trials, only Muslim judges are considered as qualified:

> The judicial system encompasses several different court systems with overlapping and sometimes competing jurisdictions, which reflect differences in civil, criminal, and Islamic jurisprudence. The Federal *Shariah* Court and the *Shariah* bench of the Supreme Court serve as appellate courts for certain convictions in criminal court under the *Hudood* Ordinances, and judges and attorneys in these courts must be Muslims.[205]

With regard to the military there is no explicit legislation in Iran prohibiting the participation of members of religious minorities in the army or their access to senior positions there. However, the language of Article 144 of the Constitution which insists on the Islamic characteristics of the army is ambiguous: "The Army of the Islamic Republic of Iran shall be an Islamic army, which is an ideological and people's army, and must recruit into its service individuals who have faith in the objectives of the Islamic revolution and are devoted to the cause of achieving its goals."[206]

In response to a question by Abdelfattah Amor with regard to the possibility of access by members of recognized minorities to the army and the judiciary, the Iranian minister of foreign affairs said that "for political and national reasons and in order to be sure of the loyalty of their officials, all countries had special requirements for access to posts in the army and intelligence services."[207] However, other government officials said that "there was no discrimination against minorities in respect of access to the civil service."[208]

Concerning the ambiguity of legislation of Iran with regard to discrimination on grounds of religion and especially professional access by members of minorities to the army and the judiciary (Articles 104 and 163 of the Constitution), Abdelfattah Amor in his report recommends that "a legislative enactment regulating the administration in general should prohibit discrimination against any Iranian citizen regardless of, *inter alia*, his or her beliefs or the community to which he belongs."[209]

The Strategy of Islamic Republic of Iran in Respect to Human Rights in the United Nations (The Institute for Political and International Studies, Tehran, 2001) in Persian, p. 456.

205 U.S. Department of State, International Religious Freedom Report on Pakistan, 2003.

206 Constitution of Iran, *supra* note 145.

207 Abdelfattah Amor, Visit to Iran, *supra* note 161, para. 17.

208 *Ibid.*

209 Abdelfattah Amor, Visit to Iran, *supra* note 161, para. 89.

6.3.3. *Discrimination Concerning Issues of Evidence and Punishment: Mixed* Dhimmah–Hudood *Related Muslim Legal Traditions*

Discrimination on the Value of Evidence

In Pakistan, for the application of the *Hudood* Ordinance, special rules of evidence apply in *hadd* cases, which might discriminate against non-Muslims. According to Abdelfattah Amor in his report:

> Under *Hudood* Ordinances (for the offences of drinking, adultery, *qazaf* [False accusation of adultery or other forms of unlawful intercourse], gambling and theft), a non-Muslim's evidence would not be admissible in cases liable to *hadd*. . . . and would carry less weight than the evidence of a Muslim in cases liable to 'secular punishments'. Indeed, in these latter cases, the law of evidence does not accept a non-Muslim as a full witness (there have to be two non-Muslim witnesses where one Muslim is sufficient).[210]

Similar rules of evidence are embodied in the Penal Code of Iran, mainly with regard to *hudood* offences. Yet, the discriminatory rule of evidence in Iran, unlike Pakistan, is not just for litigation involving Muslims, but is even for cases where both sides are non-Muslims. In Articles 74–76, 117–119, 128, 137, 153, 170, 189(b), 199(1), 237, and other related articles on testimony, when a reference is made to the testimony of a 'just man', in fact it means the testimony of 'a Muslim just man'. For example according to Article 117 of the Penal Code: "The penance for sodomy, if it should have been sodomy alone, will be proven by the testimony of four just men, who have witnessed the committing of the sodomy."[211]

Discrimination in Punishment and Blood Money

While in Pakistan only the legislation on evidence is discriminatory against non-Muslims, in Iran, where sets of rules of traditional *hudood* code are literally incorporated into the legislation, other discriminatory provisions against non-Muslims exist in the Penal Code with regard to punishment. In Iran the Penal Code provides for a more severe punishment for non-Muslims in Muslim-non-Muslim mixed litigation with regard to sexual offences. For example, Article 88 of the Penal Code states that if a Muslim man commits adultery with

210 Abdelfattah Amor, Visit to Pakistan, *supra* note 142, para. 28.

211 Iran Penal Code (Islamic Punishment Act), approved on 30 July 1991, amended on 11 May 1996.

a Muslim woman, the penalty is 100 lashes for the man. However, according to Article 82(C) if a non-Muslim man commits adultery with a Muslim woman, his penalty is death. No penalty is specified in the Penal Code for a Muslim man who commits adultery with a non-Muslim woman.[212]

Similar discrimination against non-Muslims exists in Articles 121, 139 and 147 of the Penal Code.[213] However in terms of the possibility of the actual practice of this legislation, as mentioned in the concluding remarks of part A of this book, it should be noted that the *hadd* punishments require a high standard of evidence. In this sense according to a report about Pakistan: "In the 20 years since the *Hudood* Ordinances were adopted, not a single *hadd* punishment has been carried out."[214]

Under Muslim legal traditions, the family or relative of a murder victim can claim '*diah*' (blood money), pardon the murder, or allow '*qisas*' (retaliation) to be carried out. *Qisas* is the right of revenge belonging to the victim's heir. It implies that the punishment be equivalent in nature and severity to the offence. In the case of a murder, such punishment is the death penalty. '*Diah*' or 'blood money' compensation is the possibility offered to the victim's heir to forgo their right to '*qisas*' by accepting monetary compensation in exchange.

Articles 207, 209, 210 and 212 of the Penal Code of Iran provide different sets of rules for murder of a Muslim by a Muslim on the one hand and a person of People of the Book by another person of People of the Book on the other, when in both cases *qisas* applies. Article 207 on Muslims reads as follows: "If a Muslim is murdered, the murderer will be retaliated and the accessory to the murder will be sentenced to between three and fifteen years imprisonment."[215] Article 210 on litigation involving non-Muslims reads as follows: "If an infidel [a person of People of the Book] premeditatedly murders another infidel the murderer will be retaliated, even if they are followers of two different religions."[216]

The law is completely silent about the murder of, for example, an atheist or a Buddhist (who is a non-People of the Book) by a Muslim or non-Muslim. The law is also silent about the mixed litigation of a Muslim and a

212 *Ibid.*
213 *Ibid.*
214 U.S. Department of State, International Religious Freedom Report on Pakistan, 2003.
215 Penal Code of Iran, *supra* note 211.
216 *Ibid.*

non-Muslim. Yet, according to the majority of traditional Muslim jurists the murder of a Muslim by non-Muslims leads to *qisas*, but if a Muslim kills a person of People of the Book, the law does not require *qisas*, but merely half of the blood money of a Muslim.

Ayatollah Khomeini had earlier a specific penalty in such cases: If the Muslim was a habitual killer of non-Muslims, then he had to be killed; if he was not a habitual killer, then he had to pay financial compensation (blood money) to the non-Muslim family.[217] However after coming to power in 1979 his view progressively changed in favour of non-Muslims. According to his new opinion the punishment of non-Muslims, whether among recognized minorities (People of the Book) or others, is the same as Muslims.[218]

Articles 297–300 of the Penal Code of Iran set forth the rules for the calculation of the amount of blood money to be paid to the family when the victim is a Muslim man. The Penal Code is silent about non-Muslims. Yet, the exact value is set each year by the judiciary according to which the blood money for a person of People of the Book victim remained half of the *diah* of a Muslim. This procedure later was amended by parliament in January 2002 in a bill intended as an addition to Article 297, so that the same blood money can be applied to Muslims and non-Muslims.[219] And finally, Article 494 of

217 Shirin Ebadi, *History and Documentation of Human Rights in Iran* (trans. Nazila Fathi, Bibliotheca Persica Press, New York, NY, 2000), p. 88.

218 In 1983 the Higher Judicial Council of Iran raised a question that if a non-Muslim, whether a member of People of the Book or not, commits a crime which is subject to *hadd* or *tazir*, such as robbery or *zena* (adultery), does he or she have to be punished similar to Muslim or not. Ayatollah Khomeini replied, "...the mentioned non-believers are under the protection of Islam and the rules of Islam is applied to them the same as other Muslims. They are protected by the law and their property is also respected." Cited in Hosein Mehrpour, 'Minorities in the Constitution of the Islamic Republic of Iran' in Hosein Mehrpour (ed.) *The President and the Responsibility of Implementation of the Constitution, A Collection of the Issues Discussed in the Seminars of the Committee, Responsible for the Follow up and Supervise the Implementation of the Constitution* (Tehran, Ettela'at Publisher, 2001), in Persian, p. 171.

219 The Guardian Council of the Constitution rejected the bill twice, in Jan. 2003 and April 2003, citing certain discrepancies with the Constitution and *Shariah*. Finally in Dec. 2003 the Expediency Council (EC) approved the parliament bill. EC Secretary Mohsen Rezaei told Iranian News Agency (IRNA) that the decision of the EC was based on a state verdict by the Supreme Leader Ayatollah Khamenehei. For further information see for example 'Iran's Minorities Hail Approval of Law on Equal Blood-money', available at the website of Payvand at: <http://www.payvand.com/news/03/dec/1211.html> visited Dec. 2003.

the Penal Code provides penalties for violating the corpse of a Muslim;[220] no penalties are stipulated for violating the corpse of a non-Muslim.

There is rarely reporting on the practical effects of the silence of the law with regard to non-recognized minorities. According to one case reported by Sanasarian, "a Baha'i was killed in a car accident; although the driver was found guilty, the relatives of the victim were not entitled to financial compensation. The driver paid some financial retribution to the government."[221]

6.3.4. *Discrimination in Legislation against the Employment of Non-recognized Religious Minorities*

Iran is a party to the Discrimination (Employment and Occupation) Convention (ILO No. 111).[222] According to Article 1(a), for the purpose of the Convention the term 'discrimination' includes "any distinction, exclusion or preference made on the basis of race, colour, sex, religion, political opinion, national extraction or social origin, which has the effect of nullifying or impairing equality of opportunity or treatment in employment or occupation."[223] However, some of the Iranian legislation on employment is in conflict with the provisions of this Convention.

According to Article 14 (E) of the Law on Governmental Employment, one of the conditions of employment in Iran is "non-conviction of corruption of beliefs." Baha'is or followers of other non-recognized religions when applying for a governmental job might be accused of corruption of belief.[224] Similarly the Law on the Selection of Teachers and the Employees of the Ministry of Education (1995–1996), which subsequently was extended to other governmental employment, provides in Article 2 that belief in Islam or one of the recognized religions is one of the conditions of employment. It further stresses "belief and commitment to the doctrine of *Velaayat-e Faqih*,[225] the

220 Article 494 of the Penal Code stases: "The mulct for crimes against a deceased Muslims are as follows..." Iran Penal Code, *supra* note 211.

221 Sanasarian, *supra* note 20, p. 134.

222 Discrimination (Employment and Occupation) Convention (ILO No. 111), 362 U.N.T.S. 31, entered into force, 15 June 1960.

223 *Ibid.*

224 See Sharifiyaan, *supra* note 204, p. 457.

225 The guardianship of a body of competent Muslim jurists over the people. This was the doctrine explored by Ayatollah Khomeini as the foundation of the political system of Iran after the 1979 Islamic Revolution. See also the related footnote 249 at section 3.2 of this book.

system of the Islamic Republic and the Constitution" as other conditions for employment.[226]

Similarly the legislation on employment in the army (1979–1980) explicitly excludes followers of non-recognized religions from employment in the Iranian army. It states: "Employment of those who are not followers of one of the religions of Islam, Zoroastrianism, Judaism and Christianity, in the army of the Islamic Republic of Iran is absolutely forbidden."[227]

---

226 See Sharifiyaan, *supra* note 204, p. 457.
227 *Ibid.*, p. 458.

CHAPTER SEVEN

Current Application of Personal Aspects of *Dhimmah*

7.1. Recognition of Marriage and Personal Law of Minorities

While marriages performed by recognized religious groups are recognized and registered in all Muslim states, the practices of other states are not the same. In the Federal Republic of Germany, for instance, as in other European states, marriages of Gypsies performed according to their traditional laws are not recognized by the state. In Australia, while official policy is not to interfere with traditional aboriginal laws and customs, it has generally been considered inappropriate to accord formal recognition to them. Thus while the form of aboriginal marriage has not been officially restricted, neither has it been officially recognized.[228]

In this sense, the practices of states with regard to the recognition of personal laws of minorities differ as well:

> In Africa and Asia, particularly in those countries in which customary law is an integral part of the general legal system, various ethnic groups are still governed in matters of personal status and other fields of private law by their own rules. Also Gypsies in Europe and indigenous population in some countries are allowed under certain conditions to apply their own customary laws in the field of private law.[229]

With regard to Canada, according to a report submitted by its government, "religious laws and customs do not receive any recognition except insofar as they are embodied in a statute".[230] The policy in the United Kingdom as Jones-Pauly argues is based on the principle of territoriality:

---

228 The source of information included in this paragraph is Capotorti Study, *supra* note 41, p. 67.

229 *Ibid.*

230 *Ibid.*, pages 70 and 105. Since 1991, in Ontario, the most populous province in Canada, an arbitration law has allowed Catholic and Jewish faith-based tribunals to settle family law matters on a voluntary basis. As these courts have been contributing to the peaceful settlement of civil disputes government of Ontario considered a report which recommended that this law be extended to Muslim religious law arbitration. Yet, this proposal was resulted to a debate

> Today in family law the principle of territoriality means that every person domiciled in Britain is subject to the general family law, regardless of religious belief. Culture is taken into account only when evaluating evidence of consent, such in the case of petition for nullity of marriage on the grounds that the Muslim father under Islamic law must co-sign a marriage contract with his adult daughter.[231]

Similarly in other parts of Europe, minorities and in particular Muslim minorities generally have no authority over their family law; Jones-Pauly continues: "Although Europe proclaims to be a pluralistic society and tolerates pluralistic religious beliefs, it still does not grant the right to one's own legal culture in intimate family areas for Muslims non-citizens or citizens. In other words, it is religiously pluralistic, but not legally... non-European societies are religiously and legally pluralistic."[232]

In addition to the institution of marriage, in Muslim countries the personal law of recognized religious groups is also recognized. In this connection the representative of Iran points out:

> The important point was to know what were the effects of the recognition or non-recognition of a religion for its followers. In the Islamic Republic of Iran no distinction was made between the recognized religions and others, and the rights of all individuals to pray and worship were respected. The consequences of recognition, which some might call 'concessions' or 'privileges', were simply that, in matters of personal status and inheritance, marriage and divorce, the social rules of the religion professed by the individual were applicable; in the event of conflict, Iranian judges referred to the relevant codes or sought the opinion of the leaders of the religion in question.[233]

---

between supporters of the proposal and those who believed that Muslim law would violate women's rights. This debate faced officials in Canada, where multiculturalism is a deeply held value, to decide whether to exclude one religion or whether they should scrap the religious family courts altogether. On this debate see for example, Ayelet Shachar, 'Religion, State, and the Problem of Gender: New Modes of Citizenship and Governance in Diverse Societies' 50 *McGill Law Journal* (2005).

231 Jones-Pauly, *supra* note 117.

232 *Ibid.*

233 Human Rights Committee: Summary record of the 1252nd meeting (Iran), para. 40, U.N.Doc.CCPR/C/SR.1252 (27 June 1994). Also see Abdelfattah Amor, Visit to Iran, *supra* note 161, para. 37.

Religious groups in most Middle Eastern countries include Christians and Jews.[234] Yet, depending on the presence of other minorities, this recognition of personal law is mostly extended to the other main religious groups. For example, the marriage and personal laws of the ancient Iranian religion, Zoroastrianism, have always been recognized in Iran. Based on Article 5 of Civil Code of Iran, the personal status of non-Shiite Iranians is subject to 'Single Article of 1 August 1933', according to which:

> As regards the personal status, inheritance and will of non-Shiite Iranians, whose religion are recognized, the courts should comply with the customs and usages prevalent in their religion, except in those cases where the provision of the law are concerned with public order as follows:
> a) In questions related to marriage, divorce, and the prevalent rules of the religion to which the husband adheres;
> b) In questions related to inheritance, will and the prevalent rules of the religion of the deceased;
> c) In questions related to the adoption, the prevalent and customs of religion to which the godfather (adopted father) or godmother adheres.[235]

In Pakistan, in addition to Christians, the law recognizes Hindus, Sikhs, Buddhists, Zoroastrians (Parsis) and Ahmadies as minorities and consequently recognizes their marriage and personal laws.[236]

Regarding legal plurality in Muslim countries, Jones-Pauly points out that: "One of the fundamentals of the non-European Islamic legal culture is the right to one's own legal culture especially in family and inheritance law. One finds an equivalent in the European continental system, which allows for

---

234 Nowadays that most of Jews have left Muslim Middle Eastern and North African countries as a result of the creation of Israel in 1948, only Christian minorities remain there as the only People of the Book, with a few exceptions. The estimated 75,000 Jews are still living in these Muslim countries: the Jews of Morocco (30,000) and two non-Arab Muslim countries, i.e. Turkey (20,000), and Iran (25,000). Zoroastrians of Iran (450,000) are the other People of the Book who live in the area. See Fargues, *supra* note 30.

235 Single Article of the Law of 1 Aug. 1933, concerning the personal status of non-Shiite Iranians in courts, quoted in Human Rights Committee: Consideration of Reports Submitted by States Parties, Second periodic report (Iran), paras. 201 and 258, U.N.Doc.CCPR/C/28/Add.15. (1992).

236 Ahamdies consider themselves as Muslim and apparently have similar personal law with other Muslim groups.

the application of the law of the guest, for non-citizens residing in foreign territory."[237]

On the origin of this phenomenon in Muslim countries, Mayer says: "In most Muslim countries today, remnants of [the *Dhimmah*] system persist, since personal – status matters remain for the most part governed by the religious law of the parties involved."[238]

The recognition of marriage and family law of minorities is not just for non-Muslims. In some Muslim countries which are inhabited by followers of minor branches of Islam, the personal law of those branches is recognized as well. For example, while in Iran the Shiite Ja'fari is the predominant religion, with regard to the recognition by the law of minor schools in the country, Article 12 of the Iranian Constitution states that:

> Other Islamic schools, including the Hanafi, Shafi'i, Maliki, Hanbali, and Zaydi, are to be accorded full respect, and their followers are free to act in accordance with their own jurisprudence in performing their religious rites. These schools enjoy official status in matters pertaining to religious education, affairs of personal status (marriage, divorce, inheritance and wills) and related litigation in courts of law. In regions of the country where Muslims following any one of these schools of jurisprudence constitute the majority, local regulations, within the bounds of the jurisdiction of local councils, are to be in accordance with the respective school of jurisprudence, without infringing upon the rights of the followers of other schools.[239]

It also should be added that sometimes public law of religious minorities replaces the state's public law. For example Articles 165 and 174 of the Iran Penal Code on prohibition of drinking alcohol does not include non-Muslims.[240]

Similar to Muslim countries, in some countries neighbouring Muslim countries the marriage and personal law of minorities, particularly of Muslims, are afforded recognition. In Ethiopia a law was adopted in 1942 which was intended to allow Muslims to apply their religious law in civil and religious matters. In Greece, members of the Muslim community are governed by their religious laws in all matters relating to family law. In Singapore and Thailand,

---

237 Jones-Pauly, *supra* note 117.
238 Mayer, *supra* note 8, p. 140.
239 Constitution of Iran, *supra* note 145.
240 Iran Penal Code, *supra* note 211.

religious courts are empowered to hear cases relating to the personal status of the members of the Muslim religious groups. Similarly in Ghana, Sri Lanka and India marriage and personal laws of Muslims and other religious minorities are recognized. Yet, in the Philippines, only marriages of minorities in non-Christian provinces may be recognized.[241] The situation in Israel, succeeding the Ottoman *Millet* system, is as follows:

> [The legal system] recognizes the ten previously recognized religious communities, including [the] Jewish, Muslims, and a number of Christian sects, each with its own court system and judges and religiously based personal law, along with two more communities added later by [the] Israeli government (the Druz and the Baha'i). The Israeli government deleted from the list of personal law[s], adoption, inheritance, wills and legacies. These matters are now handled in civil courts, unless both parties to a dispute consent to the jurisdiction of the relevant religious court.[242]

Finally, once again referring to the scope of Articles 18 and 27 of the ICCPR, a survey of the periodic reports presented by Muslim states to the Human Rights Committee on the implementation of the ICCPR shows that Iran and Egypt are the only Muslim state that correctly make a link between the recognition of personal law of religious minorities with the requirements of both Articles of 18 and 27.[243]

Other states consider the issue only for the purposes of Article 18. For example Lebanon, despite its multi-religious population and a long history of applying a personal law autonomy regime, with respect to Article 18 makes a short reference to the issue of personal religious law of minorities but finds nothing to include under Article 27. Its report under this article is limited to the following: "There is nothing to report in connection with these articles [26 and 27] apart from what was stated in the initial report and in connection with other articles in this report."[244]

---

241 The sources of information included in this paragraph is Capotorti Study, *supra* note 41, pages 67 and 71.

242 Steiner & Alston, Comments on State, Religion, and Personal Law in Israel, *supra* note 33.

243 *For Egypt* see para. 482 under Article 18 and para. 634 under Article 27, at: Consideration of Reports, 2002 (Egypt), *supra* note 281. For Iran see para. 201 under Article 18 and paras. 255 and 258 under Article 27 at: Consideration of Reports, 1992 (Iran), *supra* note 235.

244 See para. 81 under Article 26 and 27 at: Human Rights Committee: Consideration of Reports Submitted by States Parties, Second periodic report (Lebanon), U.N.Doc.CCPR/C/42/Add.14 (22 Nov. 1996).

7.2. Areas of Discrimination

As already mentioned in section 5.2.4, one of the most common forms of *de-facto* religious based discrimination against minorities is imposed by those apparently neutral governmental laws that are in fact rooted in the religious law of the majority. However, *de-jure* religious based discrimination might take place when Muslim legal traditions prevails in mixed cases of religious family laws between a Muslim and a non-Muslim, for example in cases of marriage or inheritance.

With respect to marriage, Article 16 of the UDHR clearly states that the right to enter into marriage is without any limitation due to race, nationality or religion.[245] However, nearly all religious traditions contain impediments for a mixed marriage. "All major religions have developed precepts which are contrary to one or more of the [human rights'] provisions relating to the right to enter into marriage. Catholicism, Hinduism, and Judaism all have difficulty in fully accepting all of the implications of this right."[246]

With regard to Muslim legal traditions, rules restricting inter-religious marriage, such as the prohibition of marriage between a Muslim woman and a non-Muslim man, are maintained either in personal codes or in the legal practices of the majority of Muslim states. For example according to the report of Abdelfattah Amor on Pakistan, "the Muslim personal law recognizes this right only for Muslim men marrying non-Muslims, but not for Muslim women."[247] Also, as mentioned in section 2.3.1 of this book, according to Article 881(bis) of the Civil Code of Iran which is an identical incorporation of the legal traditions in legislation, a non-Muslim does not inherit from a Muslim.[248]

Among other reports which consider the issue under Article 18, see para. 219 at: Human Rights Committee: Consideration of Reports Submitted by States Parties, Fifth periodic report (Morocco), U.N.Doc.CCPR/C/MAR/2004/5 (11 May 2004); and also for the Sudan see para. 125 at: Human Rights Committee: Consideration of Reports Submitted by States Parties, Second periodic report (Sudan), U.N.Doc.CCPR/C/75/Add.2 (13 March 1997).

245 Article 16(1) of the UDHR reads as follows: "Men and women of full age, without any limitation due to race, nationality or religion, have the right to marry and to found a family. They are entitled to equal rights as to marriage, during marriage and at its dissolution." UDHR, *supra* note 63.

246 De Jong, *supra* note 111, p. 527.

247 Abdelfattah Amor, Visit to Pakistan, *supra* note 142, para. 30.

248 Civil Code of Iran, (trans. M.A.R. Taleghany, Fred B. Rothman & Co., U.S., 1995). For further information on inheritance of non-Muslim from Muslim in legislation of Iran see Ebadi, History and Documentation, *supra* note 217.

On the other hand, despite the advantages of the application of religious law for recognized religious minorities, non-recognition of personal laws of unrecognized minorities and the non-existence of a separate civil law for followers of other beliefs and religions is clearly discriminatory against them; these citizens either have to categorize themselves among one of the recognized religions or be deprived of their rights entirely. Abdallah Zakhia a member of Human Rights Committee concerns about this situation in Morocco:

> It would seem that, in terms of personal status, Moroccans were obliged to follow Muslim law or Judaic law, which meant that they had no freedom of choice. Thus, if a person was a Christian or had no religion, he was nevertheless required, against his will, to conform to a law which was not his. Those problems could be resolved by the adoption of a civil and optional personal status.[249]

Also, according to another report from Jordan:

> The Protestant denominations registered as 'societies' come under the jurisdiction of one of the recognized Protestant church tribunals. There are no tribunals assigned for atheists or adherents of unrecognized religions. Such individuals must request one of the recognized courts to hear their personal status cases.[250]

Similar concern has been raised by the Committee with regard to Lebanon:

> The Committee notes with concern that every Lebanese citizen must belong to one of the religious denominations officially recognized by the government, and that this is a requirement in order to be eligible to run for public office. This practice does not, in the Committee's opinion, comply with the requirements of Article 25 of the Covenant.[251]

The same problem exists in Israel:

> All religious courts exercise an exclusive jurisdiction over members of the respective communities, no matter what the personal religious

---

249 Human Rights Committee: Summary record of the 1788th meeting (Morocco), para. 25, U.N.Doc.CCPR/C/SR.1788 (24 Jan. 2000).

250 U.S. Department of State, International Religious Freedom Report on Jordan, 2003.

251 Human Rights Committee: Consideration of Reports Submitted by States Parties, Concluding Observations of the Committee (Lebanon), para. 23, U.N.Doc.CCPR/C/79/Add.78 (01 April 1997).

> convictions (believer, agnostic, or atheist) or ritual or other observance may be. Thus, two Jews or two Muslims who view themselves as secular and non-believers and who wish to marry in Israel must do so within the religious court system.[252]

Chad has addressed this problem by application of either the Civil Code or customary family law to individuals on voluntary bases. In Chad "the Civil Code applies only to individuals who have voluntarily expressed their willingness to be governed by it, but the majority of the population observes local customary practices."[253]

With regard to Iraq, though its new Constitution has insisted on freedom of religious groups when applying their religious family law, it has left the details to further related legislation. Article 39 of the Constitution reads as follows: "Iraqis are free in their commitment to their personal status according to their religions, sects, beliefs, or choices. This shall be regulated by law."[254]

According to the representative of Iran: "Individuals belonging to other religions not recognized by the Constitution were subject to the ordinary law of the land."[255] However, it should be remembered that in Iran and almost in all other Muslim or non-Muslim countries, the ordinary law of the land in family matters is influenced by the predominant religion. Finally, as discussed in part A, the discriminatory aspects of Muslim legal traditions are more clearly demonstrated by the case of conversion from Islam. Such an act automatically leads to some family law consequences, such as dissolving the marriage of the convert.

To facilitate inter-faith marriage in Lebanon, those marriages that take place outside the country are considered legal, though the prevailing law in mixed cases is not clear:

> The Lebanese must belong to one of the religious denominations Lebanon officially recognizes. Since civil marriage does not exist, a Lebanese couple that wishes to marry has to follow the procedure and the ceremony of

252 Steiner & Alston, Comments on State, Religion, and Personal Law in Israel, *supra* note 33, p. 495.

253 U.N.Doc.CRC/C/3/Add. 50, para. 62, quoted in Syed Safir, 'The Impact of Islamic Law on the Implementation of the Convention on the Right of the Child: The Plight of Non-marital Children under *Shariah*' 6 *The International Journal of Children's Rights* (1998), p. 388.

254 Constitution of Iraq, *supra* note 144.

255 Summary record, 1993 (Iran), *supra* note 162, para. 36.

> one of the recognized religious communities. However, a valid civil marriage celebrated abroad is recognized in Lebanon even if both spouses are Lebanese.[256]

As a solution to the problems of interfaith marriages, General Comment 19 of the Human Rights Committee reaffirms the importance of providing civil marriage along with religious marriage, "the legislation of each state should provide for the possibility of both religious and civil marriages".[257]

In response to this requirement, Iran has recognized civil marriage.[258] On the other hand while recognition of civil marriage seems to be a sufficient solution so that any couple can register legally, some states, as already mentioned, refuse to recognise this marriage. The reason for this apparently is the legal consequences of these marriages in countries with a greater number of minority populations such as Egypt, Lebanon, Jordan and Malaysia. In these countries, allowing interfaith marriage might cause a rapid increase of related mixed cases such as divorce, inheritance, and custody before the courts. Yet, these cases have already been problematic enough with regard to situations of conversion of religion.

To resolve these problems, along with the recognition of civil marriage, another requirement for these states is the adoption of a neutral governmental law to be applied for mixed cases and for any individual who wishes to be exempt from his or her own group's personal law. As mentioned above Abdallah Zakhia has considered this requirement with respect to the situation in Morocco.[259]

Also the Third Committee of the General Assembly reiterated that application of religious law on members of religious minorities should be on a voluntary base:

---

256 Consideration of Reports, 1996 (Lebanon), *supra* note 244.

257 Human Rights Committee, General Comment 19, Article 23 (Thirty-ninth session, 1990), Compilation of General Comments and General Recommendations Adopted by Human Rights Treaty Bodies, U.N.Doc.HRI/GEN/1/Rev.6 at 149 (2003), para. 4.

258 In February 2000, following the approval of a bill by the Expediency Council of Iran, the head of the Judiciary issued a circular letter to all registry offices throughout the country allowing couples to be registered as husband and wife without being required to state their religious affiliation. By providing the possibility of civil marriage the raising problems with regard to marriage of Baha'is and legitimacy of their children are expected to be over in this country.

259 Summary record, 2000 (Morocco), *supra* note 249.

> The question was raised whether protection should be accorded to individual members of a minority group or to the group as such. It was emphasized in this connection that any assimilation which might take place must be clearly voluntary, and that members of minority groups should not be deprived of the rights enjoyed by other citizens of the same state, so that they may be able to integrate should they so desire.[260]

Finally, it should be added that, providing such a governmental law to address the principle of non-discrimination among all religious groups is not an easy task. Further, to keep a balance between the application of religious laws and governmental law is always complicated; the case of India below is a good example:

> The relation between different religious laws and the application of civil law is somehow complicated; to simplify: (1) Any two persons, irrespective of religion can marry under the Special Marriage Act of 1954. This is a civil secular marriage by registration before a state official. Secular law governs family matters like divorce. (2) But the legal effects of such a marriage on matters like succession differ for individuals depending on whether one party or both of the married couple are Hindus. For example, if both are Hindus, they are governed by the Hindu Succession Act, 1955, whereas if one or both are non-Hindus, they are governed by Indian Succession Act, 1955. But relatively few marriages are performed under the Special Marriage Act of 1954.[261]

Application of Personal Autonomy Regimes by Muslim States According to 'The Krishnaswami Study'

Krishnaswami in his study admires *Millet* and finds that it was necessary for the protection of minorities in Muslim countries in the past but prefers secularization of the law over group autonomy in the present day. Unlike Capotorti, whose main concern in his study is the identity rights of minorities, Krishnaswami's main concern is freedom of religion. In this connection, as mentioned in the previous chapter, the application of religious law by Muslim

260 The third Committee of General Assembly, at its 1103rd and 1104th meetings (1961–1962), Official Records of the General Assembly, Sixteenth Session, Annexes, agenda item 35, document A/5000, paras. 116–126, quoted in Capotorti Study, *supra* note 41, pp. 33–34.

261 Henry J. Steiner & Phillip Alston, 'Comments on Personal-Religious Law in India', in Steiner & Alston, *supra* note 33, pp. 502–503.

countries may negatively affect the freedom of individuals to change their religion. The Krishnaswami study reads as follows:

> In Islamic countries, where there are recognized religions, the '*Millets*' enjoyed in the past a large measure of autonomy in their religious and civil affairs; this concession was necessary because the state law was based upon Islamic religious law and members of non-Islamic communities were otherwise left outside the pale of the dominant society. Today, however, most Islamic states have secularized their legal system, and the trend is to consider all communities as part and parcel of society and to grant them a position similar to that enjoyed by members of the state religion. This has naturally resulted in a reduction of group autonomy and a greater emphasis upon the liberty of the individual.[262]

262 Krishnaswami study, *supra* note 134, p. 59.

Concluding Remarks

The *Dhimmah* system, though parts of its conditions with the standards of today have been discriminatory against non-Muslims, provides a clear example of protection of minorities. Mayer points out that "[i]n particular, the treatment of the Jewish minority in Muslim societies stands out as fair and enlightened when compared with the dismal record of Christian European persecution of Jews over the centuries."[263] She also states: "The annals of history point out to the fact that the same degree of religious freedom as granted by *Shariah* to the non-Muslims living in Islamic state were non-existent in the history of other religions."[264]

Bielefeldt has a similar comparison as follows: "Historic evidence shows that some Christian minorities and dissidents preferred living under Islamic rule to being persecuted by their fellow Christians in the Byzantine and Habsburg empires. Thus, with regard to religious tolerance, Islam seems to have a better historical record than Christianity."[265]

In fact, Muslims by applying the *Dhimmah* system have established the widest and oldest system for recognition and regulating the status of religious minorities within majority Muslims and their protection; the system has survived for about fourteen centuries in an extended area from Spain in Western Europe to Pacific Ocean in East Asia. In recent centuries the *Dhimmah* system, by the name of *Millet*, governed the status of minorities in multi-religious areas under the Ottoman reign in parts of Eastern Europe and most areas of the Middle East and North Africa.

Furthermore, it seems that recognition of the personal law of religious minorities which is applied in non-Muslim countries such as India, Ethiopia and Greece, similar to Israel, is the effect of *Dhimmah* system; as these countries have had a longer history of including Muslim minorities in their inhabitants, the recognition of Muslims' personal law by them might have been a historical

263 Mayer, *supra* note 8, p. 136.

264 Doi, *supra* note 24.

265 Heiner Bielefeldt, 'Muslim Voice in the Human Rights Debate', 17 *Human Rights Quarterly* 4 (1995), pp. 597–8.

reciprocal response toward recognition of religious law of their co-religions by their neighbouring Muslim rulers.

Comparing the scope of Articles 18 and 27 of the ICCPR and examining the related UN documents and state practices with regard to the protection of religious or ethno-religious minorities in their right to identity, one might conclude that in the absence of any clear binding provision for states, the application of personal legal autonomy regimes could be considered as a clear instance of protecting this right.

Once again referring to the scope of Articles 18 and 27 of the ICCPR, a short survey of the periodic reports presented by Muslim states to the Human Rights Committee on the implementation of the ICCPR shows that Iran and Egypt are the only Muslim states that correctly make a link between the recognition of personal law of religious minorities with the requirements of both articles 18 and 27. That means even Muslim countries, have not considered the importance of the issue with regard to identity rights of religious minorities under the Article 27.

Interestingly enough, none of the positive aspects of Muslim legal traditions of *Dhimmah*, such as recognition of religious minorities, application of personal law autonomy regimes and allocation of special seats for representatives of religious minorities in parliaments and local councils has been considered favourably by the Special Rapporteur of Sub-commission on Minorities and the relevant UN bodies. In fact, such allocation of special seats and even allocation of special governmental positions for representatives of minorities is a praiseworthy policy of which other countries with similar religious or ethnic demography should be persuaded. Such allocation unfortunately has been ignored in the new legislation of Iraq and Afghanistan. Similar measures can be suggested for representatives of indigenous peoples or ethnic minorities in countries with ethnic sensitivities.

Despite the advantages of the Muslim legal traditions of *Dhimmah* for minorities, their discriminatory aspects stand sharply in contrast with the main principle of human rights law, i.e. the principle of non-discrimination. Among different types of discrimination mentioned in this part, incorporation of mixed *hudood-Dhimmah* traditions in matters of evidence and punishment into the legislation of Iran and Pakistan was found to be the most noticeable examples of *de-jure* discrimination.

At the present time, while independent Muslim countries have adopted concepts of citizenship designed for application in modern nation-states, simultaneous application of an old model of categorization of citizens according to their belief is not justifiable. It is worth mentioning that the contemporary application of *Dhimmah* rules by Muslim states, whether in its positive aspects or in its discriminatory features, has been rarely linked to the requirements of Islam, *Shariah* or similar terms in official positions of the related states.

Considering the divine Koranic principle of the recognition of diversity, and considering the Muslims' clear historical record in the treatment of religious minorities, Muslim states, apart from their commitments under international law, are under a moral and historical obligation to be purified from the insidious instances of discrimination and must maintain the progressive features of their traditions.

As a practical approach for states to overcome these discriminatory aspects in the cases of marriage, recognition of civil marriage seems to be a sufficient solution, so that after any civil or religious rites the couple could register legally. This approach must be further accompanied by providing a neutral governmental personal law that can be applied to:

- any individual member of the recognized minority groups who intends to be excluded from the application of his or her own religious/ethnic legal tradition;
- any mixed ethnic/religious law cases before the courts;
- all followers of non-recognized minority groups and any citizen asking for application of this law.

Preparation of a model code for this neutral governmental personal law has to be considered as the first legal priority in achieving non-discrimination with regard to minorities. The experience of Iran in adopting the civil marriage bill, along with the experiences of India, and also some non-Middle Eastern Muslim countries such as Pakistan and Bangladesh which apparently have improved arrangements in the field of personal law, would be helpful.

Another issue of concern is the disadvantage of recognition of some minority groups for non-recognized minorities which has been evident, especially with regard to Baha'is in Iran. According to Abdelfattah Amor in his report, "recognition of some religions by legislation of some Muslim countries should not be exploited at the expense of the rights of other minorities and the rights associated with other citizenship."[266] In this sense, legislation of related states, particularly Iran should contain clear provisions on the protection of all rights

266 Abdelfattah Amor, Visit to Iran, *supra* note 161, para. 8.

of members of minority groups including their religious and identity rights, whether these groups are recognized as minority or not. Here Article 20 of the Constitution of Pakistan can be considered as an excellent example of progressive legislation.

Finally, considering the long-distance consistency and the wide geographical extension of their application, the system of recognition of religious minorities and their personal law in Muslim territories deserves to be recognized under international law as a regional customary system for protecting minorities. Further, considering its invaluable historical contribution to the protection of minorities and its capacity for further contribution, it might also be held as a model for protection of the right to identity of minorities by other multi-cultural, multi-religious communities.

Part C

Rights of the Child

Introductory Remarks

This part will undertake a comparative study, based on the relevant UN documentation, on the ways that Muslim legal traditions impact the implementation of the Convention on the Rights of the Child (the CRC or the Convention)[1] by Muslim states. This study also draws a dividing line between effects of personal (family) Muslim legal traditions and public Muslim legal traditions on rights of the child.

The CRC, which came into force more than seventeen years ago, is the most universally accepted human rights treaty. It is "the first legally binding international instrument to incorporate the full range of human rights- civil, cultural, economic, political and social rights."[2] Also as Van Bueren states, the Convention "offers greater opportunities than most human rights instruments for balancing traditional values and international rights because it was not primary the product of the industrial West.[3] Notably, this convention is the only international treaty that includes an explicit reference to 'Islamic law'.

In the meantime, along with the Convention on the Elimination of Discrimination Against Women (CEDAW)[4] the CRC has received the most religious based reservations of Muslim states on different articles and/or on the treaty as a whole. This study will also examine the relevance of these reservations to the practice of Muslim legal traditions. A secondary issue of this part is to what extent the commitment of Muslim states to the CRC has encouraged them to abandon or modify the problematic aspects of their traditions (problematic traditions).

There are two possible areas of relations between Muslim legal traditions and the CRC. First, there are matters which are specific to children, such as the issues of adoption, child marriage and children born out of wedlock.

---

1 Convention on the Rights of the Child (CRC), G.A. res. 44/25, annex, 44 U.N. GAOR Supp. (No. 49) at 167, U.N.Doc.A/44/49 (1989), entered into force, 2 Sept. 1990.

2 See UNICEF website at: <http://www.unicef.org/crc/crc.htm>.

3 Geraldine Van Bueren, 'Children's Rights: Balancing Traditional Values and Cultural Plurality' in Gillian Douglas & Leslie Sebba (eds.) *Children Rights and Traditional Values* (Artmund & Ashgate, England, 1998), p. 19.

4 Convention on the Elimination of All Forms of Discrimination Against Women (CEDAW), G.A. res. 34/180, 34 U.N. GAOR Supp. (No. 46) at 193, U.N.Doc.A/34/46, entered into force 3 Sept. 1981.

Second, there are issues which are common between children and adults, such as freedom of religion and discrimination on the grounds of sex. To limit the scope of the discussion, this study will mainly focus on those areas of relations that are specific to children.

The reports of Muslim states to the Committee on the Rights of the Child (the Committee), documentation on consequent discussions of the reports in the Committee, and Concluding Observations of the Committee on state reports comprise the main sources of this part. Other relevant sources, especially with regard to other non-Muslim legal systems or practices of non-Muslim states, are mostly cited in the footnotes.

The Committee on the Rights of the Child is the body of independent experts that monitors implementation of the CRC by its states parties. It also monitors implementation of two optional protocols to the Convention, on involvement of children in armed conflict and on the sale of children, child prostitution and child pornography.[5] The Committee is comprised of ten members from different states and legal systems who are of high moral standing and experts in the field of human rights.[6] States parties are obliged to submit regular reports to the Committee on how the rights are being implemented. States must report initially two years after acceding to the Convention and then every five years. The Committee examines each report and addresses its concerns and recommendations to the state party in the form of 'Concluding Observations'.[7]

This part is comprised of one chapter which is divided into seven sections. The first section is devoted to an introduction to Muslim religious principles regarding children, Muslim legal traditions, and reservations of Muslim states to the CRC. The concept of maturity in Muslim legal traditions with regard to Articles 1 and 37 of the Convention will be studied in the second section. Article 1 defines 'child' and Article 37, among other things, prohibits capital

5 Optional Protocol to the Convention on the Rights of the Child on the Involvement of Children in Armed Conflict, 25 May 2000, A/RES/54/263, entred into force, 12 Feb. 2002 & Optional Protocol to the Convention on the Rights of the Child on the Sale of Children, Child Prostitution and Child Pornography, 25 May 2000, A/RES/54/263, entered into force, 18 Jan. 2002.

6 See United Nations Committee on the Rights of the Child website, *at:* <http://www.ohchr.org/english/bodies/crc/>.

7 See United Nations Treaty Body Database, *at*: <http://www.unhchr.ch/tbs/doc.nsf/RepStatfrset?OpenFrameSet.>.

punishment and life imprisonment without the possibility of parole for children under the age of eighteen.

In the third section different areas of distinction and discrimination will be examined with regard to Article 2 of the Convention. Then, with regard to Article 14 of the Convention, the fourth section is devoted to the issues relevant to children's freedom of religion. The fifth section is on Articles 20 and 21 of the Convention and the issue of adoption.

As Articles 2, 14, 20, and 21 have been the subject of major specific reservations of Muslim states, the issue of reservations to these articles will be discussed as well. The sixth section of this part is on approaches of the Committee towards the problematic traditions and reservations of Muslim states. Finally, the concluding section will be a summary of the discussions along with some realistic suggestions.

CHAPTER EIGHT

Implementation of the Convention on the Rights of the Child by Muslim States*

8.1. Related Muslim Legal Traditions and Reservations of Muslim States to the Convention

None of the four great Abrahamic prophets had a normal childhood situation. Abraham was adopted by his uncle. Moses, an abandoned child, was adopted by the wife of Freon. Jesus was raised by Mary in a very difficult situation, under the suspicion of conceiving a child outside of wedlock. Mohammad himself was an orphan and grew up under the guardianship of his grandfather and then his uncle.

Based on the principle of mercy, Islam, similar to all other great religions, is very much concerned about vulnerable people such as the poor, the old, the disabled, children and especially children deprived of family.[8] Iran reiterates this in its report to the Committee:

> It is well known that the lofty Islamic *Shariah*, the unique heavenly Book which has recommended pardon and forgiveness even in the heaviest and harshest of crimes, such as those calling for retribution, and the great and kind Prophet of the religion has recommended the giving of love to children and showing kindness to them. They cannot but look at children and their rights with kindness and generosity.[9]

Based on this principle and customs of the time, early Muslims established special arrangements and legal institutions for the care of children. Regarding rights of the child and the duties of parents and guardians of children, these

---

* Kashemi, Kamran. Religious Legal Traditions, Muslim States and the Convention on the Rights of the Child: An essay on the Relevant UN Documentations. Human Rights Quarterly 29:1 (2007), 194–227.

8 For example on Orphans see the Koran, 2:83, 177, 215, 220; 4:2, 3, 6, 8, 10, 36, 127; 6:152; 8:41; 17:34; 59:7; 76:8; 89:17–20; 90:14, 15; 93:6, 9, 10; 107:1–3.

9 Committee on the Rights of the Child: Consideration of Reports Submitted by States Parties, Second periodic report (Iran), para. 204, U.N.Doc.CRC/C/104/Add.3 (1 Dec. 2003).

rules covered such matters as maintenance, kinship, breastfeeding, care, and custody.[10] As will be discussed later, the majority of these traditions are still considered as contributing to the rights of the child, and few of them are inconsistent with modern standards of human rights.

Based on Muslim legal traditions, or so called *Shariah* or Islamic law, some Muslim states have entered reservations to the Convention. These reservations are either to the whole Convention (general religious based reservation) or to its specific articles (specific religious based reservation).[11] Qatar, Iran, Saudi Arabia, Brunei Darussalam, Syria, and Oman are states with general religious based reservations,[12] among which Brunei Darussalam, Syria, and Oman have also specified in their reservations some articles of the Convention, including Articles 14 and 21, as the focus of their general reservations. As an example of general religious based reservation, the reservation of Qatar states that it "enter(s) a general reservation by the state of Qatar concerning provisions incompatible with Islamic Law."

All 57 Muslim states are states parties to the Convention, including the 22 states who entered reservations or declarations. Algeria, Djibouti, and Kuwait have declarations on the CRC. Bangladesh, Bosnia and Herzegovina, Brunei Darussalam, Egypt, Indonesia, Iran, Iraq, Jordan, Maldives, Mali, Morocco, Oman, Qatar, Saudi Arabia, Syria, Turkey and the United Arab Emirates entered reservations to the convention. Finally, Malaysia and Tunisia have

---

10 On Muslim family law regarding children, see for example, Jamal J. Nasir, *The Islamic Law of Personal Status*, Third Edition (Kluwer Law International, the Hague, 1990), pp. 189–190.

11 For the reservations and declarations to the CRC see Office of the United Nations High Commissioner for Human Rights, Ratifications and Reservations: Convention on the Rights of the Child, at <http://www.ohchr.org/english/countries/ratification/11.htm>, last updated May 8, 2006. It is not the purpose of this research to examine the legality of these reservations. For an analysis of issues concerning legality of such reservations, the role of the Committee with respect to reservations, and the consequences of a determination that a reservation is illegal see William A Schabas, 'Reservations to the Convention on the Rights of Child' 18 *Human Rights Quarterly* 2 (1996).

12 Mauritania and Afghanistan had similar reservations upon signature but their reservations were not confirmed on ratification. Pakistan also had a similar general religious based reservation upon ratification but withdrew from it later. Among non-Muslim states part of the reservation of the Holy See is similar to the general religious based reservations of Muslim states. It reads as follows: "The Holy See declares that the application of the Convention be compatible in practice with the particular nature of the Vatican City state and of the sources of its objective law (Art. 1, Law of 7 June 1929, n. 11) and, in consideration of its limited extent, with its legislation in the matters of citizenship, access and residence." See reservations and declarations to the CRC, *supra* note 11.

entered both declarations and reservations. Yet, as will be discussed further, not all of these reservations are necessarily ones based on religion.

8.2. THE CONCEPT OF MATURITY IN MUSLIM LEGAL TRADITIONS AND ISSUES CONCERNING 'AGE': ARTICLES 1 AND 37

Apart from those articles of the CRC to which Muslim states have reservations, implementation of some other articles of the Convention may also be affected by Muslim legal traditions. Article 1 of the Convention on definition of 'Child' and Article 37(a), among other issues, on capital punishment and life imprisonment of juveniles, are among these provisions.

According to Article 1 of the CRC: "For the purposes of the present Convention, a child means every human being below the age of eighteen years unless under the law applicable to the child, majority is attained earlier."[13] Capital punishment of children under the age of eighteen is also in conflict with the provisions of Article 6(5) of the International Covenant on Civil and Political Rights (the ICCPR)[14] and Article 37(a) of the CRC that requires states parties to ensure that, "no child shall be subjected to torture or other cruel, inhuman or degrading treatment or punishment. Neither capital punishment nor life imprisonment without possibility of release shall be imposed for offences committed by persons below eighteen years of age."[15]

Legislation in some Muslim states on the age of adulthood is influenced by the concept of maturity in religious legal traditions. According to this concept, the criterion for adulthood is not merely a child's age, but a child's maturity (*Boulough*). The Sudan observed that maturity is marked in two ways:

---

13 CRC, *supra* note 1.

14 International Covenant on Civil and Political Rights (ICCPR), adopted, 16 Dec. 1966, G.A. res. 2200A (XXI), U.N. GAOR, 21st Sess., Supp. No. 16, U.N.Doc.A/6316 (1966), 999 U.N.T.S. 171, entered into force, 23 March 1976. Article 6(5) of the ICCPR reads as follows: "Sentence of death shall not be imposed for crimes committed by persons below eighteen years of age and shall not be carried out on pregnant women." Among fifty-seven Muslim member states of the CRC, forty-four are signatories to the ICCPR and therefore committed to the provisions of this treaty as well. Thirteen states that are not signatories to the ICCPR are including Bahrain, Brunei, Comoros, Guinea-Bissau, Kazakhstan, Indonesia, Malaysia, Maldives, Oman, Pakistan, Qatar, Saudi Arabia, and United Arab Emirates.

15 CRC, *supra* note 1, Art. 37(a). See William A Schabas & Helmut Sax, 'Article 37, Prohibition of Torture, Prohibition of Death Penalty and Life Imprisonment and the Deprivation of Liberty', in André Alen, Johan Vande Lanotte, Eugeen Verhellen, Fiona Ang, Eva Berghmans & Mieke Verheyde (eds.) *A Commentary on the United Nations Convention on the Rights of the Child* (Leiden/Boston: Martinus Nijhoff Publishers, 2006).

> The first is the appearance of the usual outward 'signs of maturity', such as puberty, the growth of pubic hair and, in the case of young girls, menstruation and the ability to conceive. The second is the attainment of full legal age, a subject on which jurists hold differing views and on which other positive laws are also at variance.[16]

According to Muslim legal traditions " when a minor matures mentally and attains puberty he becomes an adult and all his dispositions become enforceable."[17] Upon reaching the stage of maturity a child is subject to all the rights, duties and responsibilities of an adult. These responsibilities and rights include criminal responsibility, the right to dispose of and possess his or her property as well as the right to make decisions regarding his or her marriage. Among these issues, child marriage has been of special concern to the Committee.

As far as the criteria for determining the age of maturity is concerned, Muslim legal traditions provide age limits for girls that are lower than for boys. As a result, girls are eligible for marriage earlier than boys. This is mainly because the relevant Muslim legal traditions are influenced by traditions of the place of their emergence, i.e. Saudi Arabia, where girls reach physical maturity earlier than boys. The different ages of marriage for boys and for girls will be discussed in the next section and is another concern of the Committee with regard to Article 2 (non-discrimination) of the Convention.

As mentioned earlier, according to Muslim legal traditions, having reached the age of maturity a child is entitled to make decisions about his or her marriage. However, before this age his or her father or guardian can marry him or her to somebody.[18] These rules, which are the reflection of tribal traditions at the time of the emergence of traditional Muslim law, are incorporated in the legislation of some Muslim states. Yet, according to a provision of tradi-

---

16 Committee on the Rights of the Child: Consideration of Reports Submitted by States Parties, Second periodic report (Sudan), para. 30, U.N.Doc.CRC/C/65/Add.17 (6 Dec. 2001).

17 Mohammad Javad Maghniyyah, *The Five School of Islamic Law* (Ansarian Publications, Qom, Iran, 1995), p. 584. See also Nasir, *supra* note 10.

18 Concerning marriage of child by his guardians under Muslim legal traditions see Mostafa Mohaghegh Damad, *The Fiqhi Study of Family Law, Marriage and Its Dissolve (Articles 1034–1157 of the Civil Code)*, Eleventh Edition (Markaz-e Nashr-e Olum-e Eslami Publisher, Tehran, 2005), in Persian, pp. 48–50. In comparison with other legal traditions unlike Hindu traditions, in Muslim legal traditions practices of giving bride as a gift, which is current in India and other parts of Indian sub-continent, are not legitimized. See Savitri Goonesekere, 'The Best Interest of the Child: A South Asian Perspective', in Philip Alston (ed.) *The Best Interests of the Child, Reconciling Culture and Human Rights* (Clarendon Press, Oxford, 1994).

tional Muslim law, called 'option of puberty', "where the marriage of a young girl [or boy] is arranged by her [or his] guardian, she [or he] can repudiate the marriage upon the attainment of puberty"[19] if "contract by a guardian [is found] contrary to the interest of the child";[20] otherwise, the contract is considered valid.

Consistent with Article 1 of the Convention, many Muslim states have adopted the age of eighteen as the age of maturity.[21] However, the age of maturity for boys in Muslim legal traditions, i.e., fifteen years, has been considered by some Muslim states such as Syria, Sudan, Iran, and Pakistan as the age of criminal responsibility.[22]

In comparison with other legal systems, for example, In English common law, the minimum age at which a person could be convicted of a crime was seven. The current minimum age is ten. The position in a range of other European jurisdictions is currently as follows: seven in Cyprus, Ireland, Liechtenstein, and Switzerland; eight in Scotland and North Ireland; nine in Malta; twelve in Greece, Netherlands, San Marino, Turkey; thirteen in France; fourteen in Austria, Bulgaria, Germany, Hungary, Italy, Latvia, Lithuania, Romania, Slovenia; fifteen in Czech Republic, Denmark, Estonia, Finland, Iceland, Norway, Slovakia, Sweden; sixteen in Andorra, Poland, Portugal and Spain; eighteen in Belgium and Luxembourg.[23]

Interestingly, Saudi Arabia and Oman, both with general religious based reservation, find Article 1 of the Convention to conform to Muslim legal traditions. In its report, Saudi Arabia states that "Article 1 of the Convention

19 Committee on the Rights of the Child: Consideration of Reports Submitted by States Parties, Second periodic report (Pakistan), para. 108, U.N.Doc.CRC/C/65/Add.21 (11 April 2003).

20 Goonesekere, *supra* note 18, pp. 120–121.

21 See e.g., Committee on the Rights of the Child: Consideration of Reports Submitted by States Parties, Initial report (Pakistan), para. 20, U.N.Doc.CRC/C/3/Add.13 (28 May 1993); Committee on the Rights of the Child: Consideration of Reports Submitted by States Parties, Second periodic report (Indonesia), para. 50, U.N.Doc.CRC/C/65/Add.23 (7 July 2003); Committee on the Rights of the Child: Summary record of the 361st meeting (Syria), para. 13, U.N.Doc.CRC/C/SR.361 (21 Mar. 1997).

22 See Summary record, 1997 (Syria), *supra* note 21; Committee on the Rights of the Child: Summary record of the 817th meeting (Sudan), U.N.Doc.CRC/C/SR.817 (27 Sept. 2002); Committee on the Rights of the Child: Summary record of the 1016th meeting (Iran), para. 68, U.N.Doc.CRC/C/SR.1016 (28 Jan. 2005); Committee on the Rights of the Child: Summary record of the 134th meeting, (Pakistan), para. 5, U.N.Doc.CRC/C/SR.134 (11 Apr. 1994).

23 See Gillian Douglas, 'The Child's Right to Make Mistakes: Criminal Responsibility and the Immature Minor', in Douglas & Sebba, *supra* note 3, p. 265.

on the Rights of the Child is totally in harmony with Islamic law with regard to the definition of the child."[24] Oman also declares that "[t]he Decree [No. 32/97 on the Personal Law] is in accordance with the principles of Islamic *Shariah*." This law established eighteen years as the majority age (legal adulthood).[25] Yet, in practice, especially regarding the age of marriage, Muslim states have different policies.

8.2.1. *Child Marriage*

There is no provision in the CRC relevant to child marriage,[26] but Article 16(2) of the CEDAW bans the practice of child marriage. This article reads as follows: "The betrothal and the marriage of a child shall have no legal effect, and all necessary action, including legislation, shall be taken to specify a minimum age for marriage and to make the registration of marriages in an official registry compulsory."[27] Though this article does not specify a minimum age of marriage, a UN General Assembly Recommendation set fifteen for this age.[28]

Among the state reports, the case of Sudan is a clear example of the legality of child marriage at a very young age: ten for both Muslim boys and girls. The age for non-Muslims is fifteen years for boys and thirteen for girls.[29] In Saudi Arabia there is no age limit for marriage:

> The regulations do not define a specific age for marriage, as Islamic law regulates this matter in a manner that ensures happiness for both spouses and prevents the countless social dangers inherent in delaying the age of marriage. In this context, it stipulates that a person wishing to marry

24 Committee on the Rights of the Child: Consideration of Reports Submitted by States Parties, Initial report (Saudi Arabia) U.N.Doc.CRC/C/61/Add.2. para. 30 (29 Mar. 2000).

25 Committee on the Rights of the Child: Consideration of Reports Submitted by States Parties, Initial report (Oman), paras. 12–14, U.N.Doc.CRC/C/78/Add.1 (18 July 2000).

26 On child marriage and relevance of provisions of the CRC to the issue see Ladan Askari, 'The Convention on the Right of the Child: The Necessity of Adding A Provision To Ban Child Marriages' 5 *ILSA Journal of International & Comparative Law* 1 (1998).

27 CEDAW, *supra* note 4.

28 Principle 11 of this Declaration reads as follows: "Member states shall take legislative action to specify a minimum age for marriage, which in any case shall not be less than fifteen years of age; no marriage shall be legally entered into by any person under this age, except where a competent authority has granted a dispensation as to age, for serious reasons, in the interest of the intending spouses.", General Assembly Recommendation on Consent to Marriage, Minimum Age for Marriage and Registration of Marriages, G.A. Res. 2018 (XX), 20 U.N. GAOR Supp. (No. 14) at 36, U.N.Doc.A/60141 (1 Nov. 1965).

29 Consideration of Reports, 1997 (Sudan), *supra* note 15, paras. 37, 54.

> must have the capacity therefore. This flexibility in Islamic law helps to close loopholes and safeguard the interests of both parties.[30]

Also, in Pakistan guardians can marry their wards from the time of birth. As mentioned earlier, if the marriage is not rejected by the children at the time of maturity, it will be considered legal.[31] Yet, in Oman, a state with general religious based reservation, the minimum age of marriage for both boys and girls is eighteen. The report affirms that this age "is in accordance with the principles of Islamic *Shariah*."[32]

In Iran, another state with general religious based reservation, fifteen is the age of marriage for boys and thirteen for girls.[33] Yet, despite its reservation, Iran is reviewing its legislation to withdraw from problematic traditions. A member of the Iranian delegation states that, "the relevant *Shariah* provisions were currently being reconsidered in the light of the need for children to have attained a certain level of maturity before entering into marriage. The government was considering the preparation of legal provisions to formalize the reforms."[34]

8.2.2. *Penalizing of Premarital Sexual Intercourse*

One important matter which is linked to the issue of child marriage is the penalizing of premarital or extramarital sexual intercourse in the legislation of some Muslim states. Apparently in the legislation of Indonesia this issue is left as a private matter and the age for sexual consent is twelve.[35] In contrast, in Syria and Sudan sexual intercourse is permitted only within marriage.[36] Likewise, in Pakistan, by reviving part of traditional penal code called *hudood*, laws penalize sexual relations out of marriage.[37]

This code, when extended to children under the age of eighteen, is in conflict with the provisions of both Articles 37(a) and 37(b) of the Convention. In conflict with Article 37(a), a child might be faced with "cruel, inhuman

---

30 Consideration of Reports, 2000 (Saudi Arabia), *supra* note 23, para. 33.
31 Consideration of Reports, 1997 (Pakistan), *supra* note 19, para. 108.
32 Consideration of Reports, 2000 (Oman), *supra* note 24, paras. 12–14.
33 See Summary record, 2005 (Iran); *supra* note 22, para. 73.
34 *Ibid.*
35 See Consideration of Reports, 2003 (Indonesia), *supra* note 21, para. 50.
36 Summary record, 1997 (Syria), *supra* note 21, para. 38.
37 See Summary record, 1994 (Pakistan), *supra* note 22, para. 6; Consideration of Reports, 1997 (Sudan), *supra* note 15, para. 38.

or degrading treatment or punishment" such as flogging for engaging in premarital sex. Article 37 (b) of the convention also states that "deprivation of liberty should only be used as a measure of last resort and for the shortest period of time."

The *hudood* code severely affected female children in Pakistan. The statement by Marta Santos Pais, a member of the Committee on the Rights of the Child, elaborates on the result of application of this code in Pakistan as follows:

> The statement in paragraph 20 of the report (CRC/C/3/Add.13) that premarital/extramarital sex was prohibited and therefore the question of sexual consent did not arise was particularly difficult to comprehend, since the difference between adultery and rape was determined by the question of consent [both are considered as offence]. UNICEF, reporting on the situation of women and children in Pakistan, had found that girls of twelve and thirteen years of age had been punished for adultery because rape could not be proved. Had the question of consent been used, deprivation of liberty might have been prevented in those cases. Depriving a child awaiting trial of his liberty was in any case contrary to the principle of presumption of innocence established in Article 40 of the Convention.[38]

Thomas Hammarberg, a member of the Committee, offers the following recommendation for a major overhaul of the legislation of Pakistan: "(1)[E]liminate the apparent inconsistencies in the ages of criminal responsibility; (2)[eliminate] the conflict between *hudood* and other criminal legislation; (3)[eliminate] the imprisonment of rape victims as a result of that conflict, and the many other violations of internationally recognized children's rights."[39]

In contrast to Pakistan, Iran with its similar punishment system based on *hudood* has not been criticized by the Committee for penalizing premarital sexual intercourse of children.[40] One of the reasons for the better situation in

38 Summary record, 1994 (Pakistan), *supra* note 22, para. 6. According to Article 40(2) (b) of the CRC states parties shall, in particular, ensure that: "Every child alleged as or accused of having infringed the penal law has at least the following guarantees: (i) To be presumed innocent until proven guilty according to law;..."

39 *Ibid.*, para. 9.

40 See Summary record, 2005 (Iran), *supra* note 22; Committee on the Rights of the Child: Summary record of the 617th meeting (Iran), U.N.Doc.CRC/C/SR.617 (14 July 2000);

Iran, along with other social and economical factors, is the legality of temporary marriage (*mut-eh*) in legislation of Iran. This Shiite legal tradition provides the possibility of legal sexual relations before and outside (permanent) marriage. Though not applied widely, this law prevents unmarried children, especially pregnant girls, from being suspected of having committed a sexual offence and mitigates the severe consequences such as those existing in Pakistan.

Moreover, Shiites, unlike Sunnis, do not require the presence of two witnesses for the validity of a marriage contract. Therefore, even pregnant girls who are under suspicion of illegal sexual relations can claim that they are married, because they do not need to provide witnesses for their unofficial marriages.[41]

Despite the above mentioned advantages of *mut-eh*, it has been an issue of concern with the chairperson of the Committee "that such arrangements might facilitate the exploitation of girls."[42] In response, the member of the Iranian delegation reiterates that, "temporary marriage agreements were concluded in full recognition of children's and women's rights, and women and girls were protected against all forms of exploitation. Temporary marriage contracts could be concluded only with the woman's consent."[43]

Despite the advantages of prohibition of child marriage, some disadvantages of this prohibition in traditional societies should be considered. First, even in those states where premarital sexual relations are not penalized, these kinds of relations are not tolerated by the communities because it is considered severely immoral. Considering this situation, the only legal and moral way for sexual intercourse after reaching the age of maturity (twelve to fifteen years of age) is marriage.

Second, in communities where marriage is restricted by many different thorny traditions, it is very important for parents, especially in poor families, not to miss any chance of suitors marrying their daughter even if this marriage

---

Committee on the Rights of the Child: Consideration of Reports Submitted by States Parties, Concluding Observations of the Committee (Iran), U.N.Doc.CRC/C/15/Add.123 (28 June 2000); Committee on the Rights of the Child: Summary record of the 618th meeting (Iran), U.N.Doc.CRC/C/SR.618. (23 May 2000).

41 On differences between Shiite and Sunni views on temporary marriage and the issue of witness see Nasir, *supra* note 10, pp. 69–71.

42 See Summary record, 2005 (Iran) *supra* note 21, para. 70.

43 *Ibid.*, para. 74.

should happen before age eighteen. Without such marriages their daughter may be unable to marry or to have legal sexual relations for the rest of her life.

Regarding child marriage, in some Muslim countries one may suggest that legislation penalizing premarital sexual intercourse should be eliminated. Also, an earlier age of marriage than eighteen can be applied, subject to the decision of the courts and with a focus on the best interests of the child.[44] In any case, the issue of 'full consent for marriage' and 'possibility of child-abuse' should remain under special consideration by the courts, particularly in poor and underdeveloped areas.

With regard to Shiite societies, *mut-eh* or temporary marriage has been criticized widely. This is particularly true among women's rights advocates, because this institution might give cause to child abuse and polygamy. Yet it seems that if applied properly this tradition, because it is based on the consent of both partners, can enhance the possibility of a legal male- female relation before permanent marriage.

8.2.3. *Capital Punishment of Juveniles*

As mentioned earlier, the concept of maturity in Muslim legal traditions regarding the age of liability for punishments is in conflict with Article 37 of the Convention. Yet, not a single Muslim state has had a specific reservation to Article 37. Furthermore, the majority of Muslim states, even those with general religious based reservations, have explicitly reiterated in their reports their commitment to the provisions in Article 37. For example, Oman declares that, "no sentence of death or life imprisonment shall be pronounced on a person who has not reached eighteen years."[45]

---

44 On the principle of "best interest of the child" Article 3(1) of the CRC reads as follows: "In all actions concerning children, whether undertaken by public or private social welfare institutions, courts of law, administrative authorities or legislative bodies, the best interests of the child shall be a primary consideration."

It should also be noted that along with Article 3(1), the principle is referred to in several other places within the convention itself as well as in a number of other important international human rights instruments. Within the Convention the phrase 'the best interest of the child' appears in relation to the separation of the child from the family setting (Art. 9); with reference to parental responsibility for the uprising and development of the child (Art. 18); in relation to the adoption and comparable practices (Arts. 20, 21); in the context of the child's involvement with the police and the justice system (Arts. 37, 40). See Goonesekere, *supra* note 18, p. 3.

45 Consideration of Reports, 2000 (Oman), *supra* note 24, para. 56; Also see Summary Record, 2000 (Iran), *supra* note 39, para. 37.

Unlike the majority of Muslim states, especially those with general religious based reservation, Sudan is a non-reserving state that in its reports explicitly refers to the possibility of child execution in its legislation. Sudan, in its initial report, considers an exception to the application of Article 37 of the Convention as:

> Article 27 (2) of the Criminal Law Act of 1991 provides that, with the exception of offences punishable by penalties and sanctions, the death penalty may not be imposed on a person under the age of eighteen or over the age of seventy. A juvenile delinquent may be sentenced to death only for an offence punishable by penalties and sanctions, in accordance with provisions of Islamic law. Nor may he be sentenced to life imprisonment.[46]

In its second periodic report, Sudan refers to murder as one example of an offence that is punishable by death even for children younger than eighteen.[47] Also, according to Article 33 paragraph 3 of the Sudan Penal Code, life imprisonment might be handed down to persons under eighteen years of age for the crime of brigandry.[48] Furthermore, considering that the age of maturity for girls might be even earlier than fifteen years old it is unclear whether in Sudan the minimum age for the application of the death penalty and life imprisonment for girls could likewise be earlier than fifteen.

The same problem exists in legislation of other states, such as Iran and Pakistan, that penalize murder and sexual offences under traditional *hudood* code. In these states, though no specific instances are reported, in theory the application of *hudood* might cause the execution of children even under the age of fifteen, a possibility refers to by Pakistan in its initial report:

> According to section 45(1) of the Punjab Youthful Offenders Ordinance, 1983 (and in similar laws in other provinces) no offender below the age of fifteen years shall be sentenced to death or transportation or any imprisonment. However, a young person even below the age of fifteen years who has reached puberty can be given the punishment prescribed by the *hudood* laws.[49]

---

46 Committee on the Rights of the Child: Consideration of Reports Submitted by States Parties, Initial report (Sudan), para. 166, U.N.Doc.CRC/C/3/Add.3 (16 Dec. 1992).

47 Consideration of Reports, 1997 (Sudan) *supra* note 15, para. 41.

48 *Ibid.*, para. 42.

49 Consideration of Reports, 1993 (Pakistan), *supra* note 21, para. 158.

But in 2000, in a withdrawal from part of the *hudood* tradition, Pakistan approved new legislation on the prohibition of capital punishment for juveniles under the age of eighteen.[50]

Other issues that have not been greatly considered by the Committee are those cases where executions of offenders fewer than eighteen years of age are postponed until such time as they reach the age of eighteen. This is one issue of concern with Judith Karp, a member of the Committee, when discussing the report of Saudi Arabia: "With regard to the juvenile justice system, it was unclear whether the prohibition of the death penalty referred to children who were under eighteen years of age, or to those who had committed the respective offence when they were under eighteen years of age."[51] The response by the member of the Saudi delegation to this concern is still unclear. He says: "It was prohibited to use the death sentence for juveniles. If, however, the accused had reached the age of majority by the time of the trial, the judge was responsible for deciding to what extent criminal responsibility should be applied."[52] First, the response doesn't refer to the age of majority, whether it is before or after eighteen years of age. It also refers to the "time of trial" and not the time of crime; that means it is possible that the crime took place before the child has reached the age of majority, but the trial would be postponed until the age of majority has been reached.

8.3. POSSIBLE AREAS OF DISTINCTION AND DISCRIMINATION: ARTICLE 2 OF THE CONVENTION

Article 2 of the Convention, on prohibition of discrimination, reads as follows:

> 1. States parties shall respect and ensure the rights set forth in the present Convention to each child within their jurisdiction without dis-

50 Committee on the Rights of the Child: Summary Record of the 901st Meeting, 34th Sess(Pakistan). paras. 70, 73, U.N.Doc.CRC/C/SR.901 (30 Sept. 2003); On relevant cases and legislation in Iran see article written in Persian by Shirin Ebadi, the Iranian winner of 2004 Nobel Peace Prize, entitled 'On the Occasion of Cancellation of Leyla Mafi's Death Sentence –2: Isn't Now the Time for Reviewing the Related Legislation' (30.6.2005), available Roozonline Electronic Daily at: <www.roozonline.com/02article/008238.shtml>; Also, on other aspects of legislation of Iran regarding children see Shirin Ebadi, *The Rights of the Child: A Study on Legal Aspects of Children's Rights in Iran* (trans. M. Zaimaran, UNICEF, Tehran, 1994).

51 Committee on the Rights of the Child: Summary record of the 688th meeting, 26th Sess. (Saudi Arabia), para. 42, U.N.Doc.CRC/C/SR.688 (24 Jan. 2001).

52 *Ibid.*, para. 83.

> crimination of any kind, irrespective of the child's or his or her parent's or legal guardian's race, colour, sex, language, religion, political or other opinion, national, ethnic or social origin, property, disability, birth or other status.
> 2. States parties shall take all appropriate measures to ensure that the child is protected against all forms of discrimination or punishment on the basis of the status, activities, expressed opinions, or beliefs of the child's parents, legal guardians, or family members.[53]

In the preparatory discussions of the Convention the only matter of concern for some Muslim states with regard to this article was the issue of children born out of wedlock.[54] Yet, under Muslim legal traditions there are two other areas of distinction on the grounds of sex affecting implementation of Article 2. First, linked to issues concerning age, discussed in the previous section of this chapter, is the different ages of maturity and marriage between boys and girls. Second is the differences in rights (duties) of custody and guardianship of children between men and women.

Malaysia has included Article 2 in the list of articles in its reservation.[55] Tunisia is another reserving state that has entered a specific reservation to this article only. Tunisia's reservation reads as follows: "The government of the Republic of Tunisia enters a reservation with regard to the provisions of Article 2 of the Convention, which may not impede implementation of the provisions of its national legislation concerning personal status, particularly in relation to marriage and inheritance rights."[56] Malaysia has not submitted

---

53 The wording of Article 2(1) of the CRC is taken from Articles 2 and 24 of the ICCPR. Article 2(1) of the ICCPR reads as follows: "Each state party to the present covenant undertakes to respect and to ensure to all individuals within its territory and subject to its jurisdiction the rights recognized in the present Covenant, without distinction of any kind, such as race, colour, sex, language, religion, political or other opinion, national or social origin, property, birth or other status." ICCPR, *supra* note 14.

Article 24 (1) of the ICCPR reads as follows: "Every child shall have, without any discrimination as to race, colour, sex, language, religion, national or social origin, property or birth, the right to such measures of protection as are required by his status as a minor, on the part of his family, society and the state." *Ibid.*

54 For more information on the preparatory discussions see Sharon Detrick, *The United Nations Convention on the Rights of the Child: A Guide to the Travaux Preparatoires* (Dordrecht, London: M. Nijhoff Publishers, 1992), pp. 148–50.

55 Reservations and declarations to the CRC, *supra* note 11.

56 *Ibid.* Interestingly, those states parties who objected in preparatory discussion to the inclusion of provisions for non-marital children in the article, such as Algeria, Morocco, and

any report to the Committee. Therefore, the report of Tunisia as a state with specific religious based reservation along with the reports of some other Muslim states, in particular those with general religious based reservation, will be examined in this section.

8.3.1. *Children Born out of Wedlock*

In theory according to Muslim legal traditions, where a child is born outside of lawful wedlock, "[n]o paternity can be established."[57] Consequently, the non-marital child has no claim of maintenance, custody, guardianship or inheritance rights whatsoever as regards his father.[58] In a comparison with Western legal systems Meeusen argues that:

> By historical comparison with Western society, even as recent as the first half of this century, Islam was revolutionary as a force in reforming and elevating the status of the non-marital child. Constrained by the Christian doctrine of the sanctity of marriage, the non-marital child in common law jurisprudence, in contrast, was deemed *filius nullius* – a child of no one.[59]

As another comparison with other legal systems, according to Jewish legal traditions a child born as a result of sexual relations between parents who are in the category of *isurey orayot* (forbidden relations) – such as relations between mother and son, brother and sister, other first-degree relatives, and a married woman with a man who is not her husband is considered a *mamzer*. The personal status of a *mamzer* is highly problematic, since he or she cannot marry most Jews.[60]

Iraq, didn't enter reservations with respect to Article 2. On the preparatory discussions of the Convention see Detrick, *supra* note 53.

57 Nasir, *supra* note 10, p. 157.

58 Asef A.A. Fyzee, *Outlines of Muhammadan Law*, Third Edition (London: Oxford University Press, 1964), p. 215; I. Fganem, 'Islamic Medical Jurisprudence' 21 *Medicine, Science and the Law* (1981), p. 280; Joseph Schacht, *An Introduction to Islamic Law* (Oxford At the Clarendon Press, 1964), p. 168, quoted in Syed Safir, 'The Impact of Islamic Law on the Implementation of the Convention on the Right of the Child: The Plight of Non-marital Children under *Shariah*' 6 *The International Journal of Children's Rights* (1998), pp. 376–377.

59 John Meeusen, 'Judicial Disapproval of Discrimination against Illegitimate Children: A Comparative Study of Development in Europe and the United States' 43 *American Journal of Comparative Law* pp. 119–20 (1995). Also see Safir, *ibid.*, p. 377; Goonesekere, *supra* note 18.

60 See Yehiel S Kaplan, 'The Interpretation of the Concept of the Best Interest of the Child in Israel', in Douglas & Sebba, *supra* note 23, p. 57. Yet, according to Kaplan "[in practice] for

In practice, as will be discussed further, from the above mentioned list of restrictions against children born out of wedlock in Muslim legal traditions, only the right of the child to inherit from his or her unmarried father is ignored in the legislation of some Muslim states. General Comment 17 of the Human Rights Committee on Article 24 of the ICCPR addresses this issue of discrimination in inheritance: "Reports by states parties should indicate how legislation and practice ensure that measures of protection are aimed at removing all discrimination in every field, including inheritance, particularly as between children who are nationals and children who are aliens or as between legitimate children and children born out of wedlock."[61]

Most Muslim states, for example Egypt, Indonesia, Syria, Iran and Tunisia have satisfactory provisions in recognition of children born out of wedlock.[62] Also some of these states have passed legislation on the recognition of the father of these children, such as a search for paternity through genetic imprinting tests, taking the father's name for the child and sharing the responsibility of the child.[63] For example Tunisia as a state with a specific reservation to Article 2 points out that:

> Proceeding from the same desire to remove obstacles concerning this category of child and any discrimination, Act No. 98–75 of 28 October 1998 relating to granting a patronymic family name to children of unknown parentage or abandoned children, grants children born outside marriage the right to a complete identity; to seek their paternity and the right to maintenance. Indeed this law goes further. It facilitates the search

---

many generations rabbinical courts were extremely cautions and only on rare occasions did they rule that a child was a mamzer." *Ibid.*

61 Human Rights Committee, Committee on Economic, Social and Cultural Rights, Committee on the Elimination of Racial Discrimination, Committee on the Elimination of Discrimination Against Women: Compilation of General Comments and General Recommendations Adopted by Human Rights Treaty Bodies, Note by the Secretariat, para. 5, U.N.Doc. HRI/GEN/1/Rev.1 (29 July 1994).

62 Committee on the Rights of the Child: Summary record of the 68th meeting (Egypt), para. 7, U.N.Doc.CRC/C/SR.68 (20 Dec. 1993); Committee on the Rights of the Child: Consideration of Reports Submitted by States Parties, Second periodic report (Syria), para. 59, U.N.Doc.CRC/C/93/Add.2 (18 Oct. 2002); Summary record, 2005 (Iran), *supra* note 22, para. 20. On legislation of Egypt concerning children born out of wedlock also see Breger, *supra* note 25, pp. 577–578.

63 Summary record,1993 (Egypt), *ibid.*, para. 7; Consideration of Reports, 2003 (Indonesia), *supra* note 21, para. 147; Consideration of Reports, 2002 (Syria), *ibid.*, para. 59; Consideration of Reports, 2003 (Iran), *supra* note 9, para. 20.

> for paternity through genetic imprinting tests and confers on the child whose paternity is thus established the right to maintenance.[64]

Syria is an example of Muslim states that has explicitly recognized the right of inheritance of the child born out of wedlock in its legislation. In this country "[w]here a child is born of a marriage that is not valid under religious law or is the fruit of an unlawful relationship, its interests are safeguarded by recognizing its descent from its parents, even though the marriage is not valid."[65] The rules of parentage are regulated under the articles of the Personal Status Code as follows:

> – If, after the consummation of an invalid marriage, a child is born 180 or more days after the date of consummation, its family name shall be established as that of the husband (Art. 132, para. 1).
> – If it is born after a desertion or separation (Art. 132, para. 2).
> – If, between the minimum and maximum periods for the duration of a pregnancy, a child is born to a woman who has had carnal relations, the child's family name shall be established as that of the man with whom the woman had relations (Art. 133, para. 1).
> – When the family name is established even from an invalid or improper marriage, all the consequences of kinship shall apply. The child will be prohibited from marrying relatives in the prohibited degrees of kinship and shall be entitled to receive support from its parents and an inheritance (Art. 133, para. 2).[66]

Yet, unlike the majority of Muslim states in Oman according to the 1999 Civil Status Law a child born out of wedlock is indicated in the birth register.[67] Furthermore an unmarried mother in this country might become subject to persecution by the court. As discussed earlier, in those Muslim states that penalize extramarital sexual intercourse under the traditional *hudood* code, an unmarried mother is under suspicion of having committed a sexual offence. This situation is explained by a member of the Omani delegation:

---

64 Committee on the Rights of the Child: Consideration of Reports Submitted by States Parties, Second periodic report (Tunisia), para. 36, U.N.Doc.CRC/C/83/Add.1 (30 Oct. 2001).

65 Consideration of Reports, 2002 (Syria), *supra* note 62, para. 59.

66 *Ibid.*

67 See Committee on the Rights of the Child: Consideration of Reports Submitted by States Parties, Concluding Observations of the Committee (Oman), para. 24, U.N.Doc.CRC/C/15/Add.161 (6 Nov. 2001).

> In Oman, the Constitution was based on Islamic law, which did not tolerate adultery or fornication. Requiring the father of an illegitimate child to provide financial support, would thus run counter to the law. There were criminal provisions against both men and women who committed adultery or fornication. A woman who delivered an illegitimate child thus risked prosecution if she tried to prove paternity, because she would in effect be admitting that she had committed a crime.[68]

Of those states parties which have enacted legislation to deal with children born out of wedlock, almost all have provided for supporting measures for these children. Therefore, supporting measures with regards to children born out of wedlock have not been considered an issue of concern by the Committee and most of these arrangements apparently are satisfactory.[69]

Normally Muslim states in their reports make no reference to the right of inheritance of the child from his or her unmarried father. Nigeria is among the few states that had a reference to this discriminatory aspect of Muslim legal traditions in its initial report. It further refers to the "good foster laws" as a remedy for this discriminatory aspect:

> The Constitution of the Federal Republic of Nigeria (S.39 (2)) of 1979 stipulates that no child shall be discriminated against due to the circumstances of his birth. Traditional and religious values, however, infringe on the full implementation of this part of the Constitution. For example, in the Muslim tradition, a child born out of wedlock has no right to inheritance.... There exist, however, very good foster laws in those states with such traditions.[70]

In its second periodic report Nigeria does not refer to Muslim legal traditions but merely mentions some "subtle social discrimination."[71] Also a member

---

68 Committee on the Rights of the Child: Summary record of the 728th meeting (Oman), para. 44, U.N.Doc.CRC/C/SR.728 (5 Oct. 2001).

69 See Consideration of Reports, 2001 (Tunisia), *supra* note 64, para. 166; Summary record, 2001 (Saudi Arabia), *supra* note 50, para. 65; Committee on the Rights of the Child: Consideration of Reports Submitted by States Parties, Initial report (Kuwait), para. 255, U.N.Doc. CRC/C/8/Add.35 (9 Dec. 1996).

70 Committee on the Rights of the Child: Consideration of Reports Submitted by States Parties, Initial report (Nigeria), para. 38, U.N.Doc.CRC/C/8/Add.26 (21 Aug. 1995).

71 See Committee on the Rights of the Child: Consideration of Reports Submitted by States Parties, Second periodic report (Nigeria), para. 96, U.N.Doc.CRC/C/70/Add.24 (17 Sept. 2004).

of the Morocco delegation refers to the issue of inheritance of children born out of wedlock in traditional Muslim law and suggests a remedy for it on a voluntary basis:

> The Islamic principle that a natural child or a child born out of wedlock could not inherit was precise and absolute; no possibility of derogation existed. Remedies would have to be sought by other means. A father was, for example, not precluded from leaving a legacy to a natural child. Although Islamic principles could not be modified, efforts were being made to introduce changes in a number of areas by making certain options available on a voluntary basis. That was the way in which conformity to the Convention could be achieved and equal opportunities in the social sphere ensured. A number of such measures had already been taken to soften the impact of classical Islamic law; others would follow.[72]

For Tunisia, as a state with specific religious based reservation to Article 2, it seems that there is a trend of withdrawing from problematic Muslim legal traditions. In the Concluding Observation of the second periodic report of Tunisia, the Committee notes its satisfaction with "the adoption of a series of new laws regarding children born out of wedlock and with regard to the joint responsibility of the spouses..."[73] Furthermore, the Committee "welcomes the information on the measures taken to address discrimination against children born out of wedlock, in line with the Committee's previous recommendations..."[74] Yet, the Committee remains concerned about "the implementation of the legislation in practice."[75]

On the other hand, in referring to instances of discrimination under Article 2, the Committee no longer refers to children born out of wedlock. Rather, it refers to many other discriminatory aspects such as "discrimination based on the political and human rights activities, expressed opinions or beliefs of children or their parents, legal guardians or family members; disability; national, ethnic, or social origin..."[76]

Generally, discrimination against children born out of wedlock is one of the main concerns of the Committee with regard to some Muslim states

---

72 Committee on the Rights of the Child: Summary record of the 319th meeting, 13th Sess. (Morocco), para. 22, U.N.Doc.CRC/C/SR.319 (30 Sept. 1996).

73 Consideration of Reports, 2001 (Tunisia), *supra* note 64, para. 5.

74 *Ibid.*, para. 22.

75 *Ibid.*

76 *Ibid.*

such as Djibouti, Oman, and Tunisia.[77] Yet, while discrimination in the field of inheritance from the father is the only aspect that can directly be linked to Muslim legal traditions, the Committee has referred to the right to inherit as an instance of discrimination only in few cases. For example, in Concluding Observations of Qatar and Brunei a reference is made to inheritance: "In particular, the Committee is concerned about discrimination against females and children born out of wedlock under existing personal status law (e.g. in inheritance, custody and guardianship)."[78]

It seems that more problematic than Muslim legal traditions on the right of inheritance are other discriminatory aspects and factors against children born out of wedlock. These include violations of rights due to social and economic shortcomings in providing efficient support for children. In traditional societies bearing a child out of marriage is considered a great sin against the moral values of the community and results in the isolation of the mother and her child. This fact increases the responsibility of the state in these societies for providing affirmative measures supporting this vulnerable and handicapped unmarried mother and her child. In those states where such a mother is subject to the threat of being penalized or the child is subject to discriminatory treatment, both child and mother are discriminated against twice over. They are subject to punishment, legal disability in matters of personal status and, in addition, social stigmatization.

8.3.2. *Different Ages of Marriage for Boys and Girls*

As discussed in the previous section, influenced by the traditional concept of maturity and by other factors, the majority of Muslim states consider the legitimate age of marriage to be younger for girls than for boys. Along with other discriminatory aspects, the Committee has voiced its concern about

---

77 See Committee on the Rights of the Child: Consideration of Reports Submitted by States Parties, Concluding Observations of the Committee (Djibouti), para. 9, U.N.Doc. CRC/C/15/Add.131 (28 June 2000). See also Consideration of Reports, 2001 (Oman), *supra* note 67, para. 24; Committee on the Rights of the Child: Consideration of Reports Submitted by States Parties, Concluding Observations of the Committee (Tunisia), para. 7, U.N.Doc. CRC/C/15/Add.39 (21 June 1995).

78 See Committee on the Rights of the Child: Consideration of Reports Submitted by States Parties, Concluding Observations of the Committee (Qatar), para. 30, U.N.Doc.CRC/C/15/Add.163 (6 Nov. 2001); Committee on the Rights of the Child: Consideration of Reports Submitted by States Parties, Concluding Observations of the Committee (Brunei Darussalam) para. 24, U.N Doc. CRC/C/SR.907 (3 Oct. 2003).

the lower marriageable age for girls than for boys in many Muslim states. For example, in Indonesia and Pakistan the age of marriage for girls is sixteen. In Syria it is the age of seventeen. In these three countries the marriageable age of boys is eighteen or older.[79] Apparently the legislation on the age of marriage in none of these three states is consistent with Muslim legal traditions; the legislation in Iran, a state with general religious based reservation, is in more conformity with traditional Muslim law. In Iran, as mentioned earlier, the marriageable age for girls is thirteen and fifteen for boys.[80] On the other hand, Oman, another state with general religious based reservation, has the minimum age of eighteen for marriage for boys and girls.[81] Interestingly, Oman finds that this provision "is in accordance with the principles of Islamic *Shariah*."[82]

Although applying a consistent age of marriage for boys and girls seems like the best policy to further equality, this could exacerbate discrimination against girls because of the illegality or immorality of premarital sex. As girls normally mature physically earlier than boys and thus are ready for sexual relations earlier, imposing a similar age barrier for boys and girls to enter into marriage as the only legal and moral possibility for sexual intercourse is discrimination against girls' right to moral and legal sexual relations. They should have access to this right earlier than boys to further true equality. This policy is consistent with Article 3 of the Convention, which prioritizes the best interests of the child.[83]

8.3.3. *Difference between the Mother and the Father in Their Rights (Duties) of Custody and Guardianship of Children*

The issue of guardianship and custody of children under traditional Muslim law is controlled through two legal institutions: *hizanat* (custody) and *wilayat* (guardianship). While custody of the child is the duty (right) of both parents, guardianship, where the issue of payment of the maintenance for the child is concerned, is only the duty (right) of the father or in his absence

---

79 Consideration of Reports, 2003 (Indonesia), *supra* note 21, para. 50; Committee on the Rights of the Child: Consideration of Reports Submitted by States Parties, Initial report (Syria), para. 37, U.N.Doc.CRC/C/28/Add.2 (14 Feb. 1996).

80 Summary record, 2005 (Iran), *supra* note 22, para. 73.

81 Consideration of Reports, 2000 (Oman), *supra* note 24, paras. 12–14.

82 *Ibid.*

83 On the principle of 'best interest of the child' see *supra* note 44.

the male relatives of the child. In a comparison with other old legal systems, for example, old English common law did not create a forcible legal duty of maintenance for parents.[84]

The right to guardianship in Muslim legal traditions gives the father, but not the mother, the authority to interfere in various aspects of his children's lives, especially those of his daughters, even after their age of maturity. For example, according to the majority of Muslim jurists a father must give permission for the marriage of his daughter for her first marriage, and to his son if he is under the age of maturity.[85]

In a comparison with other old legal systems, for example the English law of 1980s concedes the superiors parental right of the father which will prevail unless he is 'unfit' to be guardian. According to this system, the father's legal right of custody over a marital child was so absolute that he could claim the physical custody of a child who was being nursed at the mother's breast. Also Roman–Dutch law, which combined Roman law with Germanic custom, recognized the husband's marital power over his wife and his natural guardianship over minor children. This protective authority of husband over the wife and marital children was deeply entrenched in the system.[86]

Another distinction is that Muslim legal traditions recognize specific rules in regard to the custodial rights of either the father or the mother. In the case of divorce, deciding custody issues in Muslim legal traditions was primarily based on the child's age, rather than the child's best interests, the principle proclaimed in Article 3 of the Convention.[87] For example according to the previous provision of Civil Code of Iran:

> In the event of separation of parents, if the child is male, he will remain under the custody of the mother for two years and afterwards the custody

---

84 See Goonesekere; *supra* note 18, p. 121.

85 For more information on *hizanat* and *wilayat* see Summary record, 2001 (Oman), *supra* note 68, para. 43; Consideration of Reports, 2000 (Saudi Arabia), *supra* note 23, para. 143; Committee on the Rights of the Child: Consideration of Reports Submitted by States Parties, Initial report (Iran), para. 255, U.N.Doc.CRC/C/41/Add.5 (23 July 1998).

86 See Goonesekere, *supra* note 18, pp. 125–127. Such distinction between the role of father and mother is not necessarily the result of religious traditions but mainly the consequence of social underdevelopment. For example, irrespective of the different religions and other considerations, and similar to other underdeveloped societies, the father's right to control religion appears to be given special significance in Indian Subcontinent, so as to determine the issue of guardianship and custody. See *ibid.* p. 129.

87 On the principle of 'best interest of the child, see *supra* note 44.

> of the child will pass to the father. In the case of a female child, she will remain under the protection and custody of the mother until she is seven years old. Guardianship rests with the father and paternal grandfather; the mother has less responsibility in this regard.[88]

Similarly in Jewish legal traditions it is mostly believed that until the child is six years old he needs his mother, especially emotionally. Therefore, when the mother is fit to meet her child's needs the right of custody of a child up to the age of six will be granted to her. Above the age of six a son should be in the custody of his father, who is obliged to teach him the religious principles of Jewish law and a profession.[89]

According to the consequent discussions of the Committee after the second periodic report of Iran, legislation with regard to custody of children has been changed but still remained partly on the basis of age: "[I]n most cases, mothers were granted custody of children up to the age of seven, and fathers were granted custody of children over that age. If custody of a child was awarded to the father, the mother could appeal the decision in court."[90]

Pakistan has a similar provision to the one stated in the initial report of Iran. But in the case of divorce the related age for a boy is seven years; for a girl the time of puberty is the deciding factor and not the age. However, granting custody can be decided by the courts too:

> The courts have always given importance to the best interests and welfare of the child while deciding questions of custody in divorce and separation cases. Under the provisions of Islamic law, as applied in Pakistan, the general rule is that custody of a boy who has not attained the age of seven and that of a girl who has not attained puberty is to remain with the mother. The male child up to this age, and the female child during most of her young age, is considered to be better off in the custody of the mother.[91]

Indonesia has another understanding of "Islamic law" with regard to custody of children. Indonesia does not differentiate between boys and girls, but refers to another concept of Muslim legal traditions, i.e., the age of *mumayiz* (discerner, children who though not mature but may distinguish between good and evil

88 Consideration of Reports, 1998 (Iran), *supra* note 85, para. 71.
89 See Kaplan, *supra* note 60, pp. 50–51.
90 See Summary record, 2005 (Iran), *supra* note 22, para. 46.
91 Consideration of Reports, 2003 (Pakistan), *supra* note 19, para. 89.

auditor). "According to Islamic law, which applies to Muslims in Indonesia, in the event of a divorce, the child, if he or she is under the age of twelve (not yet *mumayiz*) will be brought up by the mother (*hadhanah*), while the father remains responsible for providing for day-to-day expenses and the cost of the child's education. But if the child is twelve or over (*mumayiz*), the child is free to choose whether he or she wishes to be brought up by the mother or the father."[92] Oman, despite its general religious based reservation, makes no reference to Muslim legal traditions. It considers the best interest of the child warrants giving custody to the mother for children of all ages.[93]

In the Concluding Observations concerning the reports of Pakistan, Egypt and Saudi Arabia, the Committee has announced its concern with regard to matters relating to custody upon separation in family law. These laws, under which custody is determined by the child's age rather than the child's best interests, have been considered by the Committee as discrimination against mothers.[94]

8.4. FREEDOM OF RELIGION: ARTICLE 14 OF THE CONVENTION

Freedom of religion is a broad issue that was discussed partly under the scope of Article 18 of the ICCPR in part A of this study. This section addresses only those aspects of the issue that under Article 14 of the CRC are of particular relevance to children.

As discussed earlier, according to the concept of maturity in Muslim legal traditions, a boy at fifteen years and a girl at nine to thirteen years of age are considered adults. From this age on, boys and girls have the same duties, responsibilities and rights as an adult of older age, including the right (duty) to choose their religion.

---

92 Consideration of Reports, 2003 (Indonesia), *supra* note 21, para. 146.

93 Consideration of Reports, 2001 (Oman), *supra* note 67, para. 41.

94 For example, see Committee on the Rights of the Child: Consideration of Reports, Concluding Observations, 2003 (Pakistan), para. 44, U.N.Doc.CRC/C/15/Add.217 (27 Oct. 2003); Committee on the Rights of the Child: Consideration of Reports, Concluding Observations of the Committee, 2001 (Egypt), para. 33, U.N.Doc.CRC/C/15/Add.145 (21 Feb. 2001); Concluding Observations of the Committee (Saudi Arabia), para. 25 U.N.Doc.CRC/C/15/Add.148 (22 Feb. 2001).

According to Islamic principles of freedom of belief, every human being is free to choose his or her religion or belief.[95] In fact, the Koran rejects non-believers justifying their following of the religion because of their parents.[96] In the same sense, according to Shiites jurists every Muslim from the age of maturity (a boy at fifteen years and a girl at nine to thirteen years of age) should stand for his or her own beliefs. According to all the grand Shiite jurists (*mujtahids*), as proclaimed in the first article of their main jurisprudential treatise called '*al-risalatul-amaliyah*' or '*resalah tawdhih-al-masael*', that, "*taqlid* (following others) in principles of religion is not permissible, and a Muslim should be certain about principles of the religion [by his or her own findings]."[97] But in contrast to this progressive rule, according to other Muslim legal traditions, a Muslim child or adult is not allowed to choose a religion other than his father's, i.e. Islam.[98]

Despite the restrictions against conversion in Muslim legal traditions, in practice there has never been a single case where a child changed his or her religion or where a child was punished for such a conversion. In this sense, the effect of Muslim legal traditions on freedom of religion of children has never been a serious one. Yet, during the preparatory discussion of the Convention, the matter was an issue of concern for some Muslim states.[99] This concern was introduced by Bangladesh in the preparatory discussions of the Convention: "Article 7(bis) [Article 14]...appears to run counter to the traditions of the major religious systems of the world and in particular to Islam...It appears to infringe upon the sanctioned practice of a child being reached in the religion of his parents."[100]

---

95 According to the Koran every human being is free to choose his or her religion or belief on his or her own will: "Duress is not permissible in religion, as the path has become clear from falsehood." Koran, 2:256.

96 See Koran, 2:170; 5:104; 7:28; 10:78; 21:53, 54; 26:74–76; 31:21; 43:22, 23.

97 See for example the view of Ayatollah Fazel Lankarani in English, available at his website: <http://www.lankarani.org>.

98 To briefly elaborate on the reasoning for this contradiction, see section 1.1.1 of this book.

99 For more information see Detrick, *supra* note 53, p. 238; David Johnson, 'Cultural and Regional Pluralism in the Drafting of the UN Convention on the Rights of the Child', in Michael Freman & Philip Veerman (eds.) *The Ideologies of Children's Rights* (Martinus Nijhoff Publishers, 1992), pp. 99–103.

100 Paper Submitted by the Permanent Representative of Bangladesh, U.N.Doc.E/CN.4/1986/39, Annex IV, at 2, quoted in Detrick, *supra* note 53, p. 244.

Eventually, no explicit reference to the right of children to choose religion was added to the final version of the article. Furthermore, a paragraph respecting the rights and duties of parents in providing direction for their children's religion was included in it. However, similar to Article 18(3) of the ICCPR, according to Article 14(3) of the CRC, not freedom to have or choose a religion, but freedom to manifest a religion can be subject to limitations by states.[101] The final version of Article 14 reads as follows:

> 1. States parties shall respect the right of the child to freedom of thought, conscience and religion.
> 2. States parties shall respect the rights and duties of the parents and, when applicable, legal guardians, to provide direction to the child in the exercise of his or her right in a manner consistent with the evolving capacities of the child.
> 3. Freedom to manifest one's religion or beliefs may be subject only to such limitations as are prescribed by law and are necessary to protect public safety, order, health or morals, or the fundamental rights and freedoms of others.[102]

Despite the modified version of Article 14 as explained above, ten Muslim states – Bangladesh, Maldives, Morocco, United Arab Emirates, Brunei, Syria, Malaysia, Oman, Jordan, and Iraq – entered specific religious based reservation to this article. Algeria also entered a declaration on the article.[103] The other three states with general religious based reservations, Qatar, Iran, and Saudi Arabia can be considered as reserving states to this article as well.[104] However, among the fifty-seven Muslim states that are parties to the CRC, forty-four of them are signatories to the ICCPR and none of them have entered reservations to its Article 18 on freedom of religion.[105]

---

101 Article 18(3) of the ICCPR reads as follows: "Freedom to manifest one's religion or beliefs may be subject only to such limitations as are prescribed by law and are necessary to protect public safety, order, health, or morals or the fundamental rights and freedoms of others." ICCPR, *supra* note 14.

102 CRC, *supra* note 3, Art. 14.

103 Similarly some non-Muslim states such as Poland and the Holy Sea have entered declarations to the effect that a child's right to freedom of religion, as defined in Article 14, shall be exercised with respect for parental authority.

104 Reservations and declarations to the CRC, *supra* note 11.

105 See *supra* note 14 for the name of Muslim states that are not signatories of the ICCPR. Among reserving states to Article 14 of the CRC seven states: Maldives, United Arab Emirates, Brunei, Malaysia, Oman, Qatar, and Saudi Arabia are not member of the ICCPR. The six other

Unlike other reserving states that have no reference in their reservations to the conflicting area of Muslim legal traditions and the provisions of the article, Jordan and Iraq insist in their reservation that the freedom of religion in Article 14 conflicts with Muslim legal traditions. The reservation of Iraq to this article reads as follows: "The government of Iraq has seen fit to accept [the Convention]...subject to a reservation in respect to Article 14, paragraph 1, concerning the child's freedom of religion, as allowing a child to change his or her religion runs counter to the provisions of the Islamic *Shariah*." Jordan, in its reservation, announces that Article 14 which "grant[s] the child the right to freedom of choice of religion" along with Articles 20 and 21 "are at variance with the precepts of the tolerant Islamic *Shariah*" and excluded itself from commitment to these three articles.

Part of a report by a nongovernmental organization that is attached to the second periodic report of Jordan, finds "freedom to choose a religion" not only in conflict with Islam, but also with Christianity. The report reads as follows: "The freedom of individuals to choose or abandon their religion is incompatible with the provisions of the divinely revealed laws. In Jordan there are two divinely revealed religions, Islam and Christianity, neither of which permit an individual to abandon his religion or choose another religion."[106]

However, the same report correctly refers further to a real reason for ignoring this right, i.e. the family system of the country. The report states that, "moreover, the individual's family links and the religious and ideological upbringing that individuals receive within their families in Jordan do not permit the renunciation of religion."[107] Syria, when explaining its reservation, has a reference to the same family law concerns and does not refer to Muslim legal traditions.[108] The report reads as follows:

> The prevailing principle in Syria is that children are brought up in the religion of their fathers. This principle is dictated by the nature of the

---

reserving states i.e., Bangladesh, Morocco, Syria, Jordan, Iraq, and Iran, despite their reservations to the CRC, are members of the ICCPR and therefore committed to Article 18.

106 Committee on the Rights of the Child: Consideration of Reports Submitted by States Parties, Second periodic report (Jordan), Appendix, National Task Force for Children, Periodic report by the non-governmental organizations in Jordan on the implementation of the Convention on the Rights of the Child during the period 1993–1998, para. 9(33), U.N.Doc. CRC/C/70/Add.4 (17 Sept. 1999).

107 *Ibid.*, Jordan.

108 On the issue of conflicts of religious family laws in Muslim countries see sections 1.1.5, 2.3, 5.1.1 and 7.2 of this book.

> Syrian family, which is based on the patriarchal system, i.e. the father is the head of the family and the harmony and spiritual cohesion of the family make it necessary to avoid any discord in religious belief between the head of the family and his children as long as the latter are below the age of maturity. However, it should be noted that freedom of religious belief is based on the concept of volition, the criterion of which is legal capacity. Since children are lacking in legal capacity, expression of their volition would be vitiated by the element of consent. Hence, the principle of religious freedom should not be adopted in the absolute sense since it would lead to disintegration of the family and, consequently, of society of which the family forms the basic unit.[109]

As was expected from the beginning, in practice Muslim legal traditions have not been in any conflict with the provisions of Article 14. That is the reason why none of the reserving Muslim states have a reference in their reports to the practical aspects of their reservations. By the same token, the Committee has never raised any concern on the issue of changing or choosing religion by children with regard to the reports of Muslim states.

8.5. *KAFALAH* OF MUSLIM LEGAL TRADITIONS AND ADOPTION: ARTICLES 20 AND 21 OF THE CONVENTION

While "Roman – Dutch law, like English law, did not have the institution of adoption",[110] traditional Muslim law recognized a similar institution to adoption, called *kafalah*. Yet, according to *kafalah* "if a child is adopted, the links between the child and his biological parents must not be broken."[111] On the essential differences between *kafalah* and adoption Duncan states:

> [T]he latter does not have the effect of integrating the child into the new family. The child remains in name a member of the birth family, and there are no inheritance rights in respect of the new family. However, *kafalah* may if necessary involve delegation of guardianship in respect of

109 Consideration of Reports, 1996 (Syria), *supra* note 79, para. 82.
110 Goonesekere, *supra* note 18, p. 120.
111 Consideration of Reports, 2003 (Indonesia), *supra* note 21, para. 207.

> the person and property of the child, and in an inter-country situation it mat result in a change in the child nationality.[112]

In a comparison with other traditional legal systems, for example according to Hindu religious traditions "men who have attained the age of discretion (15 years) may adopt boys only. A Hindu woman may adopt a boy only with the consent of her husband. There is no provision for the adoption of girls."[113]

In the preparatory discussions of the Convention on adoption a paper was submitted by Bangladesh showing its concern and those of some other Muslim states on the acceptance of adoption:

> Article 11 [article 20] is liable to give difficulties in Muslim countries since the understanding of Bangladesh is that adoption is not a recognized institution under Muslim law. In cases of such adoption the question of inheritance rights will rise to complex problems in Islamic jurisdictions. A form of words may be found to protect Islamic conceptions on the subject.[114]

In response to this concern of Muslim states, two provisions were considered in the draft Convention. First, in Article 20, a reference to "*kafalah* of Islamic law" was included as follows:

> A child temporarily or permanently deprived of his or her family environment, or in whose own best interests cannot be allowed to remain in that environment, shall be entitled to special protection and assistance provided by the state. Such care could include, *inter alia*, foster placement, *kafalah* of Islamic law, adoption or if necessary placement in suitable institutions for the care of children....

Second, those sates that do not recognize adoption were excluded from the scope of Article 21. This article starts with, "[s]tates parties that recognize and/or permit the system of adoption shall ensure that...."

Yet, even these provisions did not prevent some Muslim states entering reservations to relevant articles of the CRC on adoption. Seven states, Bang-

---

112 William Duncan, 'Children's Rights, Cultural Diversity and Private International Law', in Douglas & Sebba, *supra* note 3, p. 32, p. 265.

113 Committee on the Rights of the Child: Consideration of Reports Submitted by States Parties, Second periodic report (Bangladesh), para. 137, U.N.Doc.CRC/C/65/Add.22 (14 Mar. 2003).

114 Paper Submitted by the Permanent Representative of Bangladesh, *Supra* note 100.

ladesh, Maldives, United Arab Emirates, Kuwait, Oman, Syria, and Indonesia made a reservation to Article 21 and three others, Brunei Darussalam, Jordan, and Egypt on both Articles 20 and 21.[115] As Qatar, Iran, and Saudi Arabia are states with general religious based reservations, they also can be considered as reserving states to Articles 20 and 21. Among those specific reservations to Articles 20 and 21, the reservation of Egypt reads as follows:

> Since the Islamic *Shariah* is one of the fundamental sources of legislation in Egyptian positive law and because the *Shariah*, in enjoining the provision of every means of protection and care for children by numerous ways and means, does not include among those ways and means the system of adoption existing in certain other bodies of positive law, the government of the Arab Republic of Egypt expresses its reservation with respect to all the clauses and provisions relating to adoption in the said Convention, and in particular with respect to the provisions governing adoption in Articles 20 and 21 of the Convention.[116]

Along with Egypt, Qatar, Syria, and Jordan refer to Muslim legal traditions in order to justify their reservation.[117] Jordan is the only Muslim state that refers to the Koran and the teachings of the Prophet in its report to prove the prohibition of adoption. The report reads as follows:

> Adoption is not legally permissible in Islam, being clearly prohibited in the fourth and fifth verses of the chapter of the holy Koran entitled 'The Confederate Tribes' which read as follows: '...and He does not regard your adopted sons as your own sons. These are mere words which you utter with your mouths, but God declares the truth and guides to the right path. Name your adopted sons after their fathers; that is more just in the sight of God.' With these words, God abolished the system of adoption and prohibited the use of such false patronymics, it being more just and proper for people to be known by their true lineages. This was confirmed by the words of the Prophet: 'Paradise shall be closed to

115 Reservations and declarations to the CRC, *supra* note 11.

116 *Ibid.*

117 Committee on the Rights of the Child: Consideration of Reports Submitted by States Parties, Initial report (Qatar), para. 76, U.N.Doc.CRC/C/51/Add.5 (11 Jan. 2001); Consideration of Reports, 1996 (Syrian Arab Republic), *supra* note 107, para. 124; Committee on the Rights of the Child: Summary record of the 67th meeting, 3d sess. (Egypt), para. 16, U.N.Doc.CRC/C/SR.67 (17 Aug. 1993); Consideration of Reports, 1999 (Jordan), *supra* note 106, para. 63.

> anyone who claims to be the son of a person other than his true father' and 'Anyone who knowingly claims to be the son of a person other than his true father commits an act of unbelief'.[118]

Muslim states have introduced different alternatives for adoption in their reports. For example, adoption is accepted in Iran under the title of guardianship, under which children may be put under the tutorship and supervision of a competent family by a judicial decree.[119] Similarly, Bangladesh and Pakistan introduce guardianship as an alternative for adoption in their reports, noting that, "Guardianship ensures that the child knows his or her paternity."[120]

Despite its earlier statement, Pakistan finds little difference between adoption and what exists in Muslim traditions regarding the issue of inheritance: "The court-appointed guardian is similar in some cases to adoption and the recommendation in this article of the Convention is not totally alien to the law in Pakistan."[121] Syria introduces a new concept of filiation that is similar to the concept of adoption. The report of Syria reads as follows:

> Although adoption is not recognized, Syrian legislation permits filiation. The concept of filiation is similar to the system of adoption, the difference between them lying in the fact that, under the adoption system, one or both of the parents must be known whereas, under the filiation system, the filiated child must be of unknown parentage or the offspring of an unlawful marriage.[122]

To minimize the differences between adoption and *kafalah*, some states suggest solutions that a child under *kafalah* can inherit from his or her adopted parents. A member of the Jordanian delegation says: "Such a [n adopted] child had no legal right to inherit from that family but, in practice, part of the inheritance was reserved for him or her."[123] Sudan considers a possibility of the abandoned child inheriting from its guardians through testamentary succession. The report of Sudan reads as follows:

---

118 Consideration of Reports, 1998 (Jordan), *supra* note 113, para. 63.

119 See Consideration of Reports, 1998 (Iran), *supra* note 85, para. 90–91.

120 Consideration of Reports, 2003 (Pakistan), *supra* note 19, paras. 203–204; Committee on the Rights of the Child: Consideration of Reports of States Parties, initial report (Bangladesh), para. 101, U.N.Doc.CRC/C/3/Add.38 (7 Dec. 1995).

121 Consideration of Reports, 2003 (Pakistan), *supra* note 19, para. 205.

122 Consideration of Reports, 1996 (Syria), *supra* note 107, para. 124.

123 Committee on the Rights of the Child: Summary record of the 621st meeting (Jordan), para. 29, U.N.Doc.CRC/C/SR.621 (11 July 2000).

> Islam prohibits adoption and, in accordance with the provisions of the Islamic *Shariah*, foster children cannot inherit. They may, however, be saved from destitution on the death of their foster carer by means of such bequests (*miras-e tarakeh*), a subject which is covered under Articles 315 and 316 of the Personal Status for Muslims Act. This type of bequest is defined in Article 315 as 'a bequest enabling a person who is not entitled to inherit to acquire a specific share of the estate of the testator', which is unquestionably in the interests of the foster child.[124]

On the other hand, in Indonesia there is a trend of withdraw from problematic aspects of religious traditions:

> According to Islam, if a child is adopted, the links between the child and his biological parents must not be broken. However, it is not uncommon that when a child is adopted, his adoptive parents keep the identity of the parents a secret from the child in order to make him believe that his adoptive parents are his biological parents.[125]

Another issue concerning adoption in Muslim states is that non-recognition of adoption is different from its illegality. "Adoption is practiced by some Islamic communities in South Asia, and has been described as a practice which is not prohibited, but an act that is *mubah* 'towards which religion is indifferent.'"[126] Marta Santos Pais, a member of the Committee states, in regard to Pakistan, states, "it had been indicated that,...adoption was not expressly recognized but that it was not illegal. That meant that it was authorized and, consequently, that all the guarantees provided for in Article 21 of the Convention should apply."[127]

Apparently the Committee is satisfied with the different alternative systems of adoption in practice in Muslim states, which are mostly based on Muslim legal traditions. Yet, shortcomings in legislation and the non-existence of an efficient adoption law in states such as Bangladesh and Maldives have been the subject of concern.[128] On the other hand, the Committee has always found

124 Consideration of Reports, 1997 (Sudan) *supra* note 15, para. 71.

125 Consideration of Reports, 2003 (Indonesia), *supra* note 21, para. 207.

126 Goonesekere, *supra* note 18, p. 121.

127 Committee on the Rights of the Child: Summary Record of the 133d Meeting, 6th Sess. (Pakistan), para. 31, U.N.Doc.CRC/C/SR.133 (21 Nov. 1995).

128 See Committee on the Rights of the Child: Summary record of the 380th meeting (Bangladesh), para. 21, U.N.Doc.CRC/C/SR.380 (29 May 1997); Committee on the Rights of the Child: Consideration of Reports Submitted by States Parties, Concluding Observations of

reservations to Articles 20 and 21 unnecessary. For example with regard to Egypt the Committee observes that:

> The state party's reservation to Articles 20 and 21 of the Convention is unnecessary. It points out that Article 20 (3) of the Convention expressly recognizes *kafalah* of Islamic law as a form of alternative care. Article 21 expressly refers to those states that 'recognize and/or permit' the system of adoption, which does not apply to the state party because it does not recognize the system of adoption.[129]

Yet, some states parties still insist on their reservations, though their justification does not seem logical. For example the member of Egyptian delegation states:

> The reservation filed by Egypt related exclusively to the use of the word 'adoption'. Adoption was not permitted under Islamic law, for reasons relating inter alia to inheritance practices. However, the government of Egypt had no objection to the content of Articles 21 and 22 of the Convention.[130]

Some others are reviewing their reservations. For example, according to the Committee, Oman is re-examining its reservation to Article 21 and some other articles.[131] Also in consequent discussions of the initial report of Bangladesh, a member of the Bangladesh delegation shares with the Committee his view on

---

the Committee (Bangladesh), para. 47, U.N.Doc.CRC/C/15/Add.221 (27 Oct. 2003); Committee on the Rights of the Child: Consideration of Reports Submitted by States Parties, Initial report (Maldives), para. 59, U.N.Doc.CRC/C/8/Add.33 (5 Aug. 1996). Interestingly both states despite their reservations have been urged by the Committee to become a party to 'the Hague Convention on Protection of Children and Cooperation in Respect of Inter-country Adoptions'. See Committee on the Rights of the Child: Summary record of the 382nd meeting (Bangladesh), para. 36, U.N.Doc.30 CRC/C/SR.382 (30 May 1997); Committee on the Rights of the Child: Consideration of Reports Submitted by States Parties, Concluding Observations of the Committee (Bangladesh), para. 40, U.N.Doc.CRC/C/15/Add.74 (18 June 1997); Committee on the Rights of the Child: Summary record of the 468th meeting (Maldives), para. 31, U.N.Doc. CRC/C/SR.468 (4 June 1998).

129 Considerations of Reports, 2001 (Egypt), *supra* note 94, para. 33. On the issue of adoption in legislation of Egypt also see Maurits S. Berger, 'Conflicts Law and Public Policy in Egyptian Family Law: Islamic Law through the Backdoor' 50 *American Journal of Comparative Law, Summer* 3(2002), p. 578.

130 Committee on the Rights of the Child: Summary record of the 680th meeting, 26th sess. (Egypt), para. 60, U.N.Doc.CRC/C/SR.680 (22 Jan. 2001).

131 Consideration of Reports, 2001 (Oman), *supra* note 67, paras. 8–9.

the necessity of its state withdrawing the reservation to Article 21.[132] Similarly Indonesia in its report declares its willingness to review its declaration.[133]

8.6. THE COMMITTEE ON THE RIGHTS OF THE CHILD, RESERVATIONS AND MUSLIM LEGAL TRADITIONS

It is the policy of all UN treaty bodies to ask reserving member states to withdraw from their reservations.[134] In following this policy, the Committee has continually encouraged Muslim states to review and withdraw all their reservations.

According to Article 51 of the CRC: "a reservation incompatible with the object and purpose of the present Convention shall not be permitted."[135] Two kinds of reservations of Muslim states have been found by the Committee as possibly having an effect on the object and purpose of the Convention. First, on the reservation of Tunisia to Article 2 of the Convention, the Committee stated that, "the reservation relating to the application of Article 2 raises concern as to its compatibility with the object and purpose of the Convention."[136] The Committee makes a similar statement with regard to Tunisia's second periodic report.[137]

Second, regarding general religious based reservations, the committee has voiced its concern that the broad nature of these reservations may affect the implementation of the rights guaranteed in these articles and may raise

---

132 Committee on the Rights of the Child: Summary record of the 380th meeting, 15th Sess. (Bangladesh), para. 47, U.N.Doc.CRC/C/SR.380 (29 May 1997).

133 Consideration of Reports, 2003 (Indonesia), *supra* note 21, para. 16.

134 In this regard the Vienna Declaration and Program of Action states: "The World Conference on Human Rights encourages states to consider limiting the extent of any reservations they lodge to international human rights instruments, formulate any reservations as precisely and narrowly as possible, ensure that none is incompatible with the object and purpose of the relevant treaty and regularly review any reservations with a view to withdrawing them." The Vienna Declaration and Program of Action, part I, para. 5, U.N.Doc.A/CONF.157/24 (12 Jul. 1993).

135 Also Para. 46 of Vienna Declaration and Program of Action (1993) "urges states to withdraw reservations to the Convention on the Rights of the Child contrary to the object and purpose of the Convention or otherwise contrary to international treaty law." *Ibid.*

136 Consideration of Reports, 1995 (Tunisia), *supra* note 77, para. 6.

137 *Ibid.*, para. 10.

questions about the compatibility of the reservations with the object and purpose of the Convention.[138]

When addressing the problematic Muslim legal traditions the Committee takes a multifaceted approach towards the relevant reports. First, it emphasized the areas of consensus among Muslims, such as Islamic principles of tolerance and equality. Second, it stated its preference for a wider interpretation of religious texts. For example, with regard to Egypt and Qatar the Committee has stated, in a similar wording, "Noting the universal values of equality and tolerance inherent in Islam, the Committee observes that narrow interpretations of Islamic texts by authorities, particularly in areas relating to family law, are impeding the enjoyment of some human rights protected under the Convention."[139]

The Committee has also welcomed those interpretations of the *Shariah* that are consistent with human rights standards. For example with regard to Egypt, Thomas Hammarberg, a member of the Committee, "noted with satisfaction that there were different interpretations of some aspects of the application of *Shariah* (Islamic law) and that Egypt had adopted an attitude consistent with the spirit of human rights in that regard."[140]

Third, the Committee has recommended related states consider either the practice of other Muslim states that have been successful in reconciling fundamental rights with Islamic texts or their own previous successful experiences. Yet, the name of these states has not been noted in the relevant documents. For example, by the same wording with regards to Egypt and Saudi Arabia the Committee encouraged the states parties "to consider the practice of other states that have been successful in reconciling fundamental rights with Islamic texts."[141] By the same token, Judith Karp, a member of the Committee, recalled that previous successes of Morocco in modifying problematic religious tradi-

138 See Committee on the Rights of the Child: Consideration of Reports Submitted by States Parties, Initial report (Jordan), para. 1. U.N.Doc.CRC/C/8/Add.4 (26 Nov. 1993); Consideration of Reports, 2003 (Brunei Darussalam), *supra* note 78, para. 73–76; Consideration of Reports, 2001 (Saudi Arabia) *supra* note 94, para. 7–8; Consideration of Reports, 2000 (Djibouti) *supra* note 76, paras. 9–10.

139 Consideration of Reports, 2001 (Egypt), *supra* note 94, para. 6; Consideration of Reports, 2001 (Qatar), *supra* note 78, para. 9. Also there is a similar wording with regard to Saudi Arabia, see Consideration of Reports, 2001 (Saudi Arabia), *supra* note 94, para. 6.

140 Summary record, 2001 (Egypt), *supra* note 130, para. 56.

141 Consideration of the Reports 2001 (Egypt), *supra* note 94, para. 30; Consideration of Reports, 2001 (Saudi Arabia), *supra* note 94, para. 24.

tions, reaffirms a similar treatment for the conflict of these traditions with the right of child born out of wedlock:

> The law relating to children born out of wedlock appeared to be in conflict with many principles of the Convention. The Islamic principle involved was apparently clear and not open to a different interpretation, but, provided that no categorical prohibition was involved, some legislative means could perhaps be found to allow it to be waived and so permit the gap between the Code on Personal Status and the Convention to be closed. Moroccan lawmakers had, for example, managed to find a way to avoid confrontation with the religious principle that permitted a man summarily to divorce his wife.[142]

Fourth, to encourage states to exchange information on reconciliation of problematic religious traditions and human rights, the Committee has recommended Muslim states hold meetings.[143] In response to the Committee a member of the Iranian delegation has made a reference to these meetings:

> Iranian representatives held meetings with those of other Muslim countries periodically to discuss such matters. In 1998 a conference of Islamic scholars and the United Nations High Commissioner for Human Rights had been held at the United Nations Office at Geneva to discuss Islamic commentary on the Universal Declaration of Human Rights."[144]

Fifth, in reconciling problematic religious traditions with human rights, especially regarding gender issues, the Committee has recommended states mobilize religious leaders to be gender sensitive. For example, under the scope of Article 2 the Committee recommended Oman and Qatar, "train members of the legal profession, especially the judiciary, to be gender-sensitive. Religious leaders should be mobilized to support such efforts."[145]

Considering that in most Muslim states religious leaders are government employees, the government has greater responsibility regarding them and their religious schools and institutions. In this sense, the Committee has also suggested the training of religious leaders. For example, the Committee asked

142 Summary record, 1996 (Morocco), *supra* note 72, para. 15.

143 Summary record, May 2003 (Iran), *supra* note 40, para. 25.

144 *Ibid.*, para. 26.

145 Consideration of Reports, 2001 (Qatar), *supra* note 78, para. 31; Consideration of Reports, 2000(Oman), *supra* note 24, para. 25; Also there is similar advice for Egypt; see Consideration of Reports, 2001 (Egypt), *supra* note 94, para. 30.

the government of Tunisia to "develop skills-training programs in community settings for teachers, social workers, local officials and religious leaders to enable them to assist children to express their informed views and opinions and to have them taken into consideration..."[146]

Sixth, for those articles to which there are no reservations, the Committee has encouraged Muslim states to avoid justifying their shortcomings by resorting to *Shariah*. For example, Mr. Kolosov, a member of the Committee, said, regarding Egypt, that, "he was aware that the *Shariah* was the fundamental source of legislation for the Arab states. However, Egypt had made no specific references to differences between the sexes in its reservation to the Convention, which it must now strictly uphold."[147]

---

146 Consideration of the Reports 2001 (Tunisia), *supra* note 69, para. 26.

147 Committee on the Rights of the Child: Summary record of the 66th meeting (Egypt), para. 40, U.N.Doc.CRC/C/SR.66 (28 Jan. 1993).

Concluding Remarks

Van Bueren states that "the very concept that children possess rights has a far older tradition in Islamic law than in international law, where the notion did not emerge until the twentieth century."[148] It has even been suggested that child- rearing practices in medieval Islamic societies revealed a greater concern for the child's needs than in recent European societies.[149] Benefiting from their religious principles and the cultural heritage of their nations in respecting and loving children, Muslim states generally joined the CRC.

It seems that even according to today's standards, most of Muslim legal traditions are either consistent with or contribute to rights of the child. Despite this fact, Muslim states, based on their religious traditions, entered six general reservations to the whole Convention, two reservations to Article 2 on non-discrimination, ten reservations to Article 14 on freedom of religion, and ten reservations to Article 20 or/and Article 21 on adoption.

The further implementation of the Convention by Muslim states, however, showed that in practice the provisions on which reservations are made are not necessarily the indicators of the areas of inconsistency between Muslim legal traditions and rights of the child. While the main reservations of Muslim states are on Articles 14, 20, and 21 of the Convention, implementation of these articles by Muslim states has not been a subject of special concern for the Committee. For example, nowhere has the Committee given any concern to the issue of changing religion under Article 14. Other areas of Muslim legal traditions such as the issues relating to age and matters relevant to the principle of non-discrimination, have been the subject of greater concern for the Committee, even though there are few reservations on relevant articles by Muslim states.

It should be noted that entering a religious based reservation doesn't mean that the related reserving state is applying relevant traditions more strictly than other non-reserving states. As was discussed in detail, two non-

148 Geraldine Van Bueren, *The Best Interests of the Child – International Cooperation on Child Abduction, Program on the International Rights of the Child* (QMWC, London, 1993), p. 51.

149 See Anver Giladi, 'Concept of Childhood and Attitudes towards Children in Mediaeval Islam' 32 *Journal of the Social and Economic History of the Orient* (1989).

reserving states, Pakistan and Sudan, have been the subjects of criticism by the Committee for the application of problematic religious traditions, more than many of the reserving states.

Remaining separate from the core negotiations in the early participating stages for the preparation of main international treaties, Muslim states used their reservations as a preventive measure against unexpected consequences of their ratification of the treaty. The statement by a member of the Syrian delegation is an elaboration about this precaution, "the authorities of this country had entered reservations to Article 20 of the Convention as a precaution in order to avoid any misunderstanding."[150]

On the issue of withdrawing from reservations, Pakistan is the only Muslim state with general religious based reservation that withdrew its reservation. Interestingly enough, Pakistan finds nothing in the Convention in direct conflict with "any of the major precepts of Islam." As it states in its report, "[p]ractically no provision of the Convention comes into direct conflict with any of the major precepts of Islam, barring the matter of adoption for which an appropriate provision has already been made in the Convention."[151]

Also Some other general religious based reservations are under reviewing by states parties. Oman has been re-examining its reservations to Articles 7, 9, 21 and 30 of the Convention. Yet, its reservation on Article 14 is not included in this re-examination. Similarly, the Committee has welcomed information that Qatar is re-examining its reservation to the Convention with a view to amending or withdrawing it. On the other hand, while these reserving states have remained optimistic with regard to the issue of withdrawal, some others, like Jordan, argue that they should maintain their reservations.[152]

Some Muslim states are making progress withdrawing from problematic Muslim legal traditions. This fact appears when comparing the initial report of these states with their second periodic report. For example, in traditional Muslim law the dividing line for maturity was fifteen for boys and nine to thirteen for girls. Any step forward in applying Article 1 of the Convention can be considered a withdrawal in the application of problematic religious traditions. Another indicator is the elimination of juvenile executions in several

---

150 Summary record, 1997 (Syria), *supra* note 21, para. 10.

151 See Consideration of Reports, 1993 (Pakistan), *supra* note 21, para. 31.

152 See Consideration of Reports, 2001 (Oman), *supra* note 67, para. 8; Consideration of Reports, 2001 (Qatar), *supra* note 72, para. 10; Consideration of Reports, 1999 (Jordan) *supra* note 106, para. 173.

Muslim states following ratification of the Convention. However, it is difficult to have a detailed assessment of this trend, as yet.

Another important issue is that a distinction should be made between effects of personal (family) Muslim legal traditions and Public Muslim legal traditions on rights of the child. Regarding the scope of this study many aspects of personal Muslim legal traditions even today can be considered as contributing to the rights of the child. Yet, as was elaborated in this study considering modern standards, some rules are in conflict with human rights criterions, such as the right of children born out of wedlock to inherit from their father.

With regard to the relation of public Muslim legal traditions to the provisions of the CRC, two issues, i.e. freedom of children to choose their religion and the punishment of children were studied in this part. The main concern of Muslim states with regard to the issue of freedom of children to choose or change their religion is a family law matter. According to Muslim legal traditions, changing religion entails changing applicable religious family law, especially on inheritance and marriage, for the converted person. On the other hand, the public aspects of these traditional rules of freedom of religion, for example punishment of children for apostasy, have never been an issue of concern by human rights advocates. Yet, the major problematic aspect of public Muslim legal traditions with regard to children is contemporary application of the traditional *hudood* code, part of which is in sharp contrast with Article 37 of the Convention.

CONCLUSION

Considering the areas of inconsistency between Muslim legal traditions and human rights, some legislation related to apostasy, as discussed in part A, was found generally to be in contradiction with the main principles of human rights, or at least restricting freedom of opinion, expression and religion.

Considering the areas of contribution of Muslim legal traditions to human rights, as discussed in part B, the current application of the *Dhimmah* system by states provides a clear example of the protection of minorities' rights to identity, although parts of its conditions have been discriminatory. In part C, most of Muslim legal traditions on rights of the child were evaluated as being consistent or even contributing to the modern standards of human rights.

Also it was concluded that the three areas of Muslim legal traditions discussed in this study shared a common major problematic aspect in the incorporation of traditional *hudood* penal code, in the legislation of some Muslim states. And as this study distinguishes between legislation and legal practices, the unwritten rules on prevailing Muslim law in cases of conflict of religious family laws were found to be the most problematic Muslim legal traditions in practice.

WRITTEN LEGISLATION AND LEGAL PRACTISE

When distinguishing between legislation and legal practices, it was concluded in part A that there are rules of public legal traditions of apostasy which, although incorporated in the legislation of some Muslim states, have never been applied and are in fact impractical. Conversely, parts of the public Muslim legal traditions on recognition of religious minorities, although not included in legislation, have been practiced almost in all Muslim countries. Similarly, as was discussed in parts A and B, there are problematic personal Muslim legal traditions which are applied widely in case law, although again they are mainly not incorporated in legislation.

In the same sense, in other parts of the book it was mentioned that the official position of Muslim states in favour of *Shariah* is not necessarily a reflection of practice of the relevant Muslim legal traditions by those states. In this sense, it was explained in part C that the CRC has received several religious based reservations by Muslim states in respect of different articles and, in some cases, the treaty as a whole. However, by investigating the further implementation of the Convention, it was concluded that the provisions of those articles on which religious based reservations were made are not necessarily the indicators of the areas of overlap or inconsistency between Muslim legal traditions and rights of the child. Also, despite what appears at first sight, entering a religious based reservation by a state does not mean that this particular state is applying relevant Muslim legal traditions more strictly than any other non-reserving states.

INTRODUCING '*SHARIAH*' AS A REFERENCE TO ISLAM

In searching for common approaches by Muslim states facing problematic religious legal traditions, three difference were distinguished between theory and practice: first the differences between statutory law and legal practices influenced by Muslim legal traditions, second between formal positions of Muslim states in favour of *Shariah* and their real commitment and loyalty to Muslim legal traditions, and finally between religious based reservations of Muslim states to international treaties of human rights and the effects of these reservations in practice. Considering these three approaches, it may be concluded that such general references to Islam, *Shariah*, Islamic law or similar terms in the legislative sources of Muslim states and even literally embodying Muslim legal traditions in legislation, are not necessarily a reflection of the application of these traditions by states. These references in fact may have some other purposes such as local policies and consideration of general public concerns.

This argument might be extended to the other general references to *Shariah* and other similar terms such as 'principles of *Shariah*', 'principles of Islam', 'Islamic criteria', in the Constitutions of Muslim states, mentioned in the introduction; as they are not necessarily a law related reference, they can be compared to the mentioning of 'Islam' as the official religion in the Constitutions of Muslim states.

Considering the above, this study does introduce a new conception of *Shariah* in addition to what already has been comprehended as a legal system; this new conception is the one being understood by Muslim public opinion or ordinary Muslims. In the view of ordinary Muslims, *Shariah* constitutes a main part of their identity, is known as the whole religion or way of life, a combination of the Koran, their beliefs, their traditions of worship, their moral values, along with part of their customs concerning their personal status, as of inheritance and the family relations. Vessey-Fitzgerald has a similar reference to this broader conception of *Shariah*:

> Law, then, in any sense in which a Western lawyer would recognize the term, is but a part of the whole Islamic system, or rather, it is not even a part but one of several inextricably combined elements thereof. '*Shariah*', the Islamic term which is commonly rendered in English by 'law', is rather, the 'Whole Duty of Man'. Moral and pastoral theology and ethics; high spiritual aspiration, and the detailed ritualistic and formal observance which to some minds is a vehicle for such aspiration and to others a substitute for it; all aspects of law; public and private hygiene, and even courtesy and good manners are all part and parcel of the *Shariah*, a system which sometimes appears to be rigid and inflexible; at others to be imbued with that dislike of extremes, that spirit of reasonable compromise, which was part of the Prophet's own character.[1]

Likewise Baderin states: "*Shariah* broadly covers the moral, legal, social and spiritual aspects of the Muslims' life."[2] In short, as Muslim public opinion does not make any distinction between the different aspects of the religion, for them '*Shariah*' means 'Islam'.

IN LINE WITH THIS STUDY

The Overlapping Areas of 'Ethnic' and 'Religion' in International Human Rights Law: Exploring the Concept of 'Ethno-religiosity'

In 2000 Abdelfattah Amor, the former UN Special Rapporteur on Religious Intolerance stated that:

> There are borderline cases where racial and religious distinctions are far from clear-cut. Apart from any discrimination, the identity of many minorities, or even large groups of people, is defined by both racial and

1 S.G. Vessey-Fitzgerald, 'Nature and Sources of the *Shariah*' in Majid Khadduri & Herbert J. Liebesny (eds.) *Law in the Middle East, Volume 1, Origin and Development of Islamic Law* (The Middle East Institute, Washington, D.C., 1995), p. 85.

2 Mashood A. Baderin, *International Human Rights and Islamic Law* (Oxford University Press, U.S.A., New York, 2003), p. 34.

> religious aspects. Hence, many instances of discrimination are aggravated by the effects of multiple identities.[3]

The issue of overlapping areas between religion and ethnicity matters was discussed to some extent in part B of this book on distinguishing between religious and ethnic discrimination and identity, under the scope of Articles 18 and 27 of the International Covenant on Civil and Political Rights (ICCPR).[4] Also the issue of hate speech within the scope of Article 20(2) of the ICCPR was examined in part A. On the issue of overlapping, Gordon states:

> Anyone who is considered an 'other' can be the object of racist violence whether this is on grounds of skin colour, ethnic origin, religion or culture. Frequently, of course, such grounds merge, as in the case of Arabs who may be attacked because of their religion, their ethnicity or their skin colour, or Jews who may be seen as both culturally and religiously different. One should not look for pure grounds for such hate, but accept that many groups are in practice vulnerable to the expression of what might loosely be called 'race hate'. In Europe at the present moment such groups include migrant workers and their families, refugees and asylum-seekers, Muslims, Jews and Gypsies.[5]

In this connection a new comprehensive research might examine all possible overlapping areas of ethnicity and religion. Such a study may start with a survey considering the historical co-existence of the two conceptions of race and religion from the late 1940s and the later separation of the two concepts, and up to date to a comparative study on related legislation and legal practices of different states on matters including hate speech, non-discrimination and protection of minorities.

The main argument of the research focuses on the purposes of Articles 18(3) and 19(2) of the ICCPR on one hand, and Articles 20(2) and 27 of the

---

3 Abdelfattah Amor, Special Rapporteur of the Commission on Human Rights, 'Racial Discrimination and Religious Discrimination: Identification and Measures', presented at the World Conference against Racism, Racial Discrimination, Xenophobia and Related Intolerance at Geneva, 1–5 May 2000, U.N.Doc.A/CONF.189/PC.1/7 (13 April 2000).

4 International Covenant on Civil and Political Rights (ICCPR), G.A. res. 2200A (XXI), 21 U.N. GAOR Supp. (No. 16) at 52, U.N.Doc.A/6316 (1966), 999 U.N.T.S. 171, entered into force, 23 March 1976.

5 Paul Gordon, 'Racist Violence: The Expression of Hate in Europe', in Sandra Coliver (ed.) *Striking a Balance: Hate Speech, Freedom of Expression and Non-discrimination* (University of Essex, 1992), pp. 9–10.

ICCPR and Article 4 of the Convention on the Elimination of All Forms of Racial Discrimination (ICERD),[6] on the other hand. While the purpose of the limitation clauses of the former article is addressed to such matters as public order or rights of others, the main purpose of the latter articles is protection of vulnerable 'others', and this is similar to the purpose of all international and regional instruments on protection of vulnerable, for which affirmative measures have to be undertaken.

In this line and for the strengthening of legal bases of protection of minorities and combating xenophobia, and finally to include all 'others' under the umbrella of human rights protection, the study may introduce the new concept of ethno-religiosity to be replaced with terms with merely an ethnic (racial) or religious element.

Muslim Traditional Penal Code and the Issue of Impractical Legislation

The issue of impracticality of legislation that was discussed partly in this study can be further elaborated by a special focus on the traditional Muslim penal code called *hudood*. While few Muslim states have incorporated part of the *hudood* code in their legislation, the code in reality appears mainly impractical and even in conflict with the requirements of daily judicial life.

For example, according to an official report by Iran: "Islamic law provided for the punishment of theft by amputation. However, before such a punishment could be imposed, fourteen separate conditions must first be met, failing which the offender would be imprisoned instead."[7] Another example of this code which is literally incorporated in legislation of some Muslim states is punishment for adultery and other sexual offences. While adultery can only be proved by the simultaneous testimony of four male eyewitnesses, it seems that the law even in the time of its emergence was a moral code for preventing people of accusing others for adultery rather than a criminal code.[8]

6 G.A. res. 2106 (XX), Annex, 20 U.N. GAOR Supp. (No. 14) at 47, U.N.Doc.A/6014 (1966), 660 U.N.T.S. 195, entered into force, 4 Jan. 1969.

7 Human Rights Committee: Summary record of the 1251st meeting (Iran), para. 33, U.N.Doc.CCPR/C/SR.1251 (29 July 1993).

8 With regard to the practice of this penal code in Pakistan as stated in a report: "The maximum punishment for this offence [adultery] is public flogging or stoning; however, there are no recorded instances of either type of punishment since the 1980s." The report adds: "The *hadd* punishments require a high standard of evidence. In the twenty years since the *Hudood* Ordinances were adopted, not a single *hadd* punishment has been carried out. However, on the

In a similar sense, Bielfieldt states: "The *hadd*-punishments, which in theory stand out as the most prominent part of the classical criminal law because they are [said to be] based on the Koran and the *Sunnah*, had only a minor practical importance in the history of Islamic societies."[9] He adds: "Narrow definitions of the crimes in question, short statutes of limitation, and extremely high evidentiary requirements ensured that those punishments would be executed only in exceptional cases."[10] By the same token in his analysis of the classical Muslim law Schacht concludes: "There is a strong tendency to restrict the applicability of *hadd* punishments as much as possible...."

The issue of the death penalty in the legislation and practise of Muslim states is of particular relevance in such a study. The study might also examine the phenomenon of impractical legislation in other legal systems. One example of this are laws against blasphemy. As Krishnaswami states, "in some countries the laws against blasphemy, although still on the statue books, are no longer applied because the times have changed and society is stronger than before."[11]

Application of Principle of Sanctity of Treaties in Muslim Legal Traditions for the Sake of Human Rights

In the introduction and other parts of this study different references have been made to religious principles as the essence of the religion. A complementary study might seek further application of these principles for the sake of human rights. For example a related issue to public Muslim legal traditions which was discussed in part B of this book was *Dhimmah* contracts between Muslim government and non-Muslim citizens, *Aman* contracts between Muslim and non-Muslim individuals and rulers, and finally peace contracts between the rulers. The application of the principle of the sanctity of treaties (*pacta sunt servanda*) in Muslim legal traditions may also be discussed with regard to current application of other public and personal Muslim legal traditions by

basis of lesser evidence, ordinary punishments such as jail terms and fines were imposed." See U.S. Department of State, International Religious Freedom Report on Pakistan, 2003.

9 Heiner Bielefeldt, 'Muslim Voice in the Human Rights Debate', 17 *Human Rights Quarterly* 4 (1995), p. 612.

10 *Ibid.*

11 Arcot Krishnaswami, Special Rapporteur of the Sub-Commission on Prevention of Discrimination and Protection of Minorities, *Study of Discrimination in the Matter of Religious Rights and Practices* (United Nations Publication, Sales No. 60.XIV.2, New York, 1960), p. 41.

states. For example an important practical advantage of this principle already applied by some Muslim states is adding some new articles in the marriage contract, which has modified some discriminatory rules of their religious legal traditions against women.[12]

It seems that when a problematic religious legal traditions exists, in the majority cases there is no restriction to resolve the problem by resorting to similar contractual solutions. Bielfieldt states: "These examples may suggest that, not only in consciously liberal approaches, but also in moderately conservative strains of Islam, a reconciliatory mediation between tradition and modernity seems conceivable."[13]

According to Muslim legal traditions the commitments of Muslims towards their treaties prevail other all religious and legal duties and commitments. Mahmasani states: "Islamic law imposes the respect of covenants and treaties even above the respect of religious solidarity.[14] By extension of the effects of this principle one might conclude that the provisions of all bilateral, regional and international human rights treaties which have been concluded by Muslim states prevail all other local legislation.

---

12 The 1917 Ottoman Law of Family Rights, for instance, tried to curb polygamy by explicitly recognizing stipulations that, on a voluntary basis, can be inserted into the marriage contract to bestow the wife with the right to judicial divorce once the husband takes a second wife. Similarly in 1986 the government of Iran issued a 12-point 'contract' to serve as a model for marriage and divorce, which limits the privileges accorded to men by custom and religious legal traditions.

13 Bielefeldt, *supra* note 10, p. 613.

14 Subhi Mahmasani, 'The Principles of International Law in the Light of Islamic Doctrine', in *Recuell Des Cours 1996 I Tome 117 de la Collection, Academie De Droit International* (A.W. Sijthoff, Leyde [Pays-Bas], 1967), p. 268.

SELECTED BIBLIOGRAPHY

English

Abu Zahra, Muhammad, 'Family Law', in Khadduri, Majid & Liebesny, Herbert J. (eds.) *Law in the Middle East, Volume 1, Origin and Development of Islamic Law* (The Middle East Institute, Washington, D.C., 1995).

Abu Zayd, Nasr Hamed, *Rethinking the Koran: Towards a Humanistic Hermeneutics* (Humanistics University Press, Utrecht, 2004).

Akhavan, Payam, 'Implication of Twelve Shi'i *Mihdism* on Religious Tolerance, The Case of the Baha'i Minority in the Islamic Republic of Iran", in Lindholm, Tore & Vogt, Kari (eds.) *Islamic Law Reform and Human Rights, Challenges and Rejoinders* (Nordic Human Rights Publications, Oslo, 1993).

Al-Azmeh, Aziz, *Islamic Law, Social and Historical Contexts* (Routledge, London, 1988).

Al-Islam Hamad, Ahmed Seif, 'Legal Plurality and Legitimation of Human Rights Abuse: A Case Study of State Council Ruling Concerning the Rights of Apostates' in Berger, Maurits & Al-Zwaini, Laila (eds.) *Legal Pluralism in the Arab World* (Kluwer Law International, the Hague, 1999).

Al-Marzouqi, Ibrahim A., 'Political Rights and Democracy in Islamic Law', in Cotran, Eugene & Omer Sherif, Adel, *Democracy, the Rule of Law and Islam* (Kluwer Law International, the Hague, 1999).

Aly Gibaly, Hanafy, 'The Freedom of Expression', in Cotran, Eugene & Omar Sherif, Adel (eds.) *The Role of the Judiciary in the Protection of Human Rights* (Kluwer Law International, the Hague, 1997).

Amin, Seyed Hassan, *Islamic Law in the Contemporary World* (Royston Limited, Glasgow, 1985).

Anderson, J. Norman D., *Islamic Law in the Modern World* (New York University Press, New York, 1959).

——, *Law Reform in the Muslim World* (Athlone Press, London, 1976).

An-Na'im, Abdullahi Ahmed, *Toward an Islamic Reformation: Civil Liberties, Human Rights and International Law* (Syracuse University Press, Syracuse, NY, 1990).

——, 'Mahmud Muhammad Taha and the Crisis in Islamic Law Reform: Implications for Interreligious Relations' 25 *Journal of Ecumenical Studies* 1 (1988).

——, 'Religious Minorities under Islamic Law and the Limits of Cultural Relativism' 9 *Human Rights Quarterly* 1 (1987).

——, 'The Position of Islamic States Regarding the Universal Declaration of Human Rights', in Baehr, Peter & Flinterman, Cees & Senders, Mignon (eds.) *Innovation and Inspiration: Fifty Years of the Universal Declaration of Human Rights* (Royal Netherlands Academy of Arts and Sciences, Amsterdam, 1999).

——, 'Islam and Human Rights: Beyond the Universal Debate', in Asil, *Proceedings of the 94th Annual Meeting*, April 5–8 2000, Washington, D.C.

——, 'State Responsibility under International Human Rights Law to Change Religious and Customary Law', in Steiner, Henry J. & Alston, Phillip (eds.) *International Human Rights in Context, Law, Politics, Morals*, Second Edition (Oxford University Press, Oxford, 2000).

Arabi, Oussama, *Studies in Modern Islamic Law and Jurisprudence* (Kluwer Law International, the Hague, 2001).

Arzt, Donna E., 'The Role of Compulsion in Islamic Conversion: *Jihad, Dhimmi* and *Ridda*' 8 *Buffalo Human Rights Law Review* 15 (2002).
Askari, Ladan, 'The Convention on the Right of the Child: The Necessity of Adding A Provision To Ban Child Marriages' 5 *ILSA Journal of International & Comparative Law* 1 (1998).
Badar, Mohamed Eleva, 'Basic Principles Governing Limitations on Individual Rights and Freedoms in Human Rights Instruments', 7 *The International Journal of Human Rights* (2003).
Baderin, Mashood A., 'Establishing Areas of Common Ground between Islamic Law and International Human Rights' 5 *The International Journal of Human Rights* 2 (2001).
——, *International Human Rights and Islamic Law* (Oxford University Press, New York, 2003).
——, 'Islam And Human Rights in the Muslim World: A Reflection on Approaches', paper presented at the conference: *Reframing Islam: Politics into Law*: 10–11 September 2005 at Irish Centre for Human Rights, National University of Ireland, Galway, available at: <http://www.nuigalway.ie/human_rights/reframing_Islam/Docs/Papers/Baderin.pdf>.
Bassiouni, M. Cherif, 'Sources of Islamic Law, and the Protection of Human Rights in the Islamic Criminal Justice System', in Bassiouini, M. Cherif (ed.) *The Islamic Criminal Justice System* (Oceana Publications, Inc, London, Rome, New York, 1982).
Bazargan, Mehdi, 'Religion and Liberty', in Kurzman, Charles (ed.) *Liberal Islam: A Sourcebook* (Oxford University Press, New York and Oxford, 1998).
Berger, Maurits S., 'Apostasy and Public Policy in Contemporary Egypt: An Evaluation of Recent Cases from Egypt's Highest Courts' 25 *Human Rights Quarterly* 3 (2003).
——, 'Conflicts Law and Public Policy in Egyptian Family Law: Islamic Law through the Backdoor' 50 *American Journal of Comparative Law*, 3 (2002).
Bielefeldt, Heiner, 'Muslim Voice in the Human Rights Debate' 17 *Human Rights Quarterly* 4 (1995).
Boyle, Kevin & Sherif Adel, Omer (eds.), *Human Rights and Democracy, The Role of the Supreme Constitutional Court of Egypt* (Kluwer Law International, the Hague, 1995).
Boyle, Kevin, 'Religious Intolerance and the Incitement of Hatred', in Coliver, Sandra (ed.) *Striking a Balance: Hate Speech, Freedom of Expression and Non-discrimination, Article 19* (London and Human Rights Centre, University of Essex, 1992).
——, *Freedom of Religion and Belief: A World Report* (Routledge, London, 1997).
Brems, Eva, 'Islam and Human Rights Views', in Brems, Eva, *Human Rights: Universality and Diversity* (Kluwer Law International, the Hague, 2001).
——, *Article 14: The Right to Freedom of Thought, Conscience and Religion* (Martinus Nijhoff Publishers, Leiden/Boston, 2006).
Brown, Nathan J., 'Islamic Constitutionalism in Theory and in Practice', in Cotran, Eugene & Omer Sherif, Adel, *Democracy, the Rule of Law and Islam* (Kluwer Law International, the Hague, 1999).
Capotorti, Francesco, Special Rapporteur of the Sub-commission on Prevention of Discriminating and Protection of Minorities, *Study on the Rights of Persons Belonging to Ethnic, Religious and Linguistic Minorities* (Centre for Human Rights Geneva, United Nations, New York, 1991).
Chourci, Cardahi, 'Conflict of Law', in Khadduri, Majid & Liebesny, Herbert J. (eds.) *Law in the Middle East, Volume 1, Origin and Development of Islamic Law* (The Middle East Institute, Washington, D.C., 1995).
Charlesworth, Hilary, 'The Challenges of Human Rights Law for Religious Traditions', in Janis, Mark W. & Evans, Carolyn (eds.) *Religion and International Law* (Kluwer Law International, the Hague, 1999).

Chase, Anthony, 'Legal and Political Context for Questioning the Human Rights and Islam Paradigm', paper presented at the conference: *Reframing Islam: Politics into Law*: 10–11 September 2005 at Irish Centre for Human Rights, National University of Ireland, Galway, available at: <http://www.nuigalway.ie/human_rights/reframing_Islam/Docs/Papers/Chase.pdf>.

——, 'Legal Guardians: Islamic Law, International Law, Human Rights Law, and the Salman Rushdie Affair' 11 *The American University Journal of International Law and Policy* 375 (1996).

Cohn, Haim H., *Human Rights in Jewish Law* (KTAV Publishing House Inc, New York, 1984).

Connors, Jane, 'The Women's Convention in the Muslim World' in *Human rights as General Norms and a State's Right to Opt out: Reservations and Objections to Human Rights Conventions* (The British Institute of International and Comparative Law, 1997).

Cotran, Eugene & Yamani, Mai (eds.) *The Rule of Law in the Middle East and the Islamic World: Human Rights and the Judicial Process* (I.B. Tauris & Co. Ltd., London, 2000).

Coulson, Noel J., *A History of Islamic Law* (Edinburg University Press, Edinburg, 1964).

Cox, Neville, *Blasphemy and the Law in Ireland* (The Edwin Mellen Press, Ltd., 2000).

Cox Cohan, Carolyn, 'International Mavericks: A Comparative Analysis of Selected Human Rights and Foreign Policy Issues in Iran and United States' 23 *The George Washington International Law Review* 2 (2001).

Cumper, Peter, 'Religious Human Rights in the United Kingdom'10 *Emory International Law Review*1 (1996).

De Jong, Cornelis D., *The Freedom of Thought, Conscience and Religion or Belief in the United Nations (1946–1992)* (School of Human Rights Research, Antwerpen: Intersentia; Oxford: Hart, c. 2000).

Derck H., Davis, 'The Evolution of Religious Freedom as a Universal Human Right: Examining the Role of the 1981 United Nations Declaration on the Elimination of All forms of Intolerance and of Discrimination Based on Religion or Belief' 2 *Brigham Young University Law Review* (2002).

Detrick, Sharon, *The United Nations Convention on the Rights of the Child: A Guide to the Travaux Preparatoires* (Martinus Nijhoff Publishers, Dordrecht/London, 1992).

Dinstein, Yoram, 'Freedom of Religion and the Protection of Religious Minorities', in Dinstein, Yoram (ed.) *The Protection of Minorities and Human Rights* (Martinus Nijhoff Publishers, Leiden/Boston, 1992).

Doi, Abdur Rahman I., *Non-Muslims under Shariah (Islamic Law)*, Third Edition (Ta Ha Publishers Ltd., London, 1983).

Douglas, Gillian, 'The Child's Right to Make Mistakes: Criminal Responsibility and the Immature Minor' in Douglas, Gillian & Sebba, Leslie (eds.) *Children Rights and Traditional Values* (Artmund & Ashgate, England, 1998).

Duncan, William, 'Children's Rights, Cultural Diversity and Private International Law' in Douglas, Gillian & Sebba, Leslie (eds.) *Children Rights and Traditional Values* (Artmund & Ashgate, England, 1998).

Ebadi, Shirin, *The Rights of the Child: A Study on Legal Aspects of Children's Rights in Iran* (trans. M. Zaimaran, UNICEF, Tehran, 1994).

——, *History and Documentation of Human Rights in Iran* (trans. Nazila Fathi, Bibliotheca Persica Press, New York, 2000).

El Hassan, Abd El-Wahab Ahmed, 'Freedom of Contract, the Doctrine of Frustration, and Sanctity of Contracts in Sudan law and Islamic Law' 1 *Arab Law Quarterly* 51 (1985).

Elman M.A., Peter, *An Introduction to Jewish Law* (Lincolns-Prager Publishers Ltd., London, 1958).

Eltayeb, Mohammed S.M., 'A Human Rights Framework for Defining and Understanding Intra-religious Persecutions in Muslim Countries', in Ghanea, Nazila (ed.) *The Challenge of*

Religious Discrimination at the Dawn of the New Millennium (Martinus Nijhoff Publishers, Leiden/Boston, 2003).

Evans, Carolyn, 'Religious Freedom in European Human Rights Law, the Search for a Guiding Conception', in Janis, Mark W. & Evans, Carolyn (eds.) *Religion and International Law* (Kluwer Law International, the Hague, 1999).

——, *Freedom of Religion under the European Convention* (Oxford University Press, New York, 2001).

Fargues, Philippe, 'Demographic Islamization: Non-Muslims in Muslim Countries' 21 *SAIS Review* 2 (2001).

Ferrari, Silvio & Bradney, Anthony, *Islam and European Legal Systems* (Ashgate & Dartmouth, Aldershot, Hants, England; Burlington, Vt. 2000).

Fetzer Joel S. & Soper J. Christopher, *Muslims and the State in Britain, France, and Germany* (Cambridge University Press, Cambridge, 2005).

Fyzee, Asef A.A., 'Shi'i Legal Theories', in Khadduri, Majid & Liebesny, Herbert J. (eds.) *Law in the Middle East, Volume 1, Origin and Development of Islamic Law* (The Middle East Institute, Washington, D.C., 1995).

Ghanea, Nazila, 'The Right to Freedom of Religion or Belief in International Human Rights Law and Inter-faith Dialogue', in Mofid University, *Collected Papers of the International Conference on Human Rights and Dialogue of Civilization, May 2001* (Mofid University Publication Institute, Qom-Iran, 2001).

——, 'The 1981 UN Declaration on the Elimination of All Forms of Intolerance and of Discrimination Based on Religion or Belief: Some Observation', in Ghanea, Nazila (ed.) *The Challenge of Religious Discrimination at the Dawn of the New Millennium* (Martinus Nijhoff Publishers, Leiden/Boston, 2003).

——, '*Human Rights of Religious Minorities and of Women in the Middle East*' 26 *Human Rights Quarterly* 3 (2004).

——, *Human Rights, the UN and the Baha'is in Iran* (Kluwer, Oxford: George Ronald; the Hague, 2003).

—— & Xanthaki, Alexandra & Thornberry, Patrick (eds.) *Minorities, Peoples, and Self-determination: Essays in Honour of Patrick Thornberry* (Martinus Nijhoff Publishers, Leiden/Boston, 2005).

Ghari Seyed Fatemi, Seyed Mohammad, 'Nationality or Citizenship? A Normative Appraisal of International Law, Shi'i *Fiqh* and the Iranian Legal System', in Mofid University, *Collected Papers of the International Conference on Human Rights and Dialogue of Civilization, May 2001* (Mofid University Publication Institute, Qom-Iran, 2001).

Gibb, H.A.R., 'Constitutional Organization', in Khadduri, Majid & Liebesny, Herbert J. (eds.) *Law in the Middle East, Volume 1, Origin and Development of Islamic Law* (The Middle East Institute, Washington, D.C., 1995).

Giladi, Anver, 'Concept of Childhood and Attitudes towards Children in Mediaeval Islam' 32 *Journal of the Social and Economic History of the Orient* (1989).

Gildenhusy, Jannet, 'The Freedom to Change One's Religion or Belief in International Human Rights Law' 15 *SA Public Law* 1 (2000).

Glenn H., Patrick, *Legal Traditions of the World, Sustainable Diversity in Law* (Oxford University Press, Oxford, 2000).

Goonesekere, Savitri, 'The Best Interest of the Child: A South Asian Perspective', in Alston, Philip (ed.) *The Best Interests of the Child, Reconciling Culture and Human Rights* (Clarendon Press, Oxford, 1994).

Gordon, Paul, 'Racist Violence: The Expression of Hate in Europe', in Coliver, Sandra (ed.) *Striking a Balance: Hate Speech, Freedom of Expression and Non-discrimination* (University of Essex, 1992).

Great Britain, Law Commission, *Offences against Religion and Public Worship* (H.M.S.O., London, 1981).
Hamilton, Carolyn, *Family, Law, and Religion* (London: Sweet & Maxwell, 1995).
Hashemi, Kamran, 'The Right of Minorities to Identity and the Challenge of Non-discrimination: Study on the Effects of Traditional Muslims' *Dhimmah* on Current States Practices' 13 *Journal of Minorities and Group Rights* 1 (2006).
——, 'Religious Legal Traditions, Muslim States and the Convention on the Rights of the Child: An Essay on the Relevant UN Documentation', 29 *Human Rights Quarterly* 1 (2007).
Heckel, Martin, 'Religious Human Rights in Germany, 10 *Emory International Law Review* 1 (1996).
International Committee for the Defence of Salman Rushdie and his Publishers, *The Crime of Blasphemy: Why It Should Be Abolished* (London: [s.n.], 1989).
Ipgrave, Michael, 'Religious Freedom: A Christian Perspective from Britain', in Mofid University, *Collected Papers of the International Conference on Human Rights and Dialogue of Civilization, May 2001* (Mofid University Publication Institute, Qom-Iran, 2001).
Jahanbakhsh, Forough, *Islam, Democracy and Religious Modernism in Iran (1953–2000), From Bazargan to Soroush* (Brill, Leiden/Boston, 2001).
Johnson, David, 'Cultural and Regional Pluralism in the Drafting of the UN Convention on the Rights of the Child', in Freman, Michael & Veerman, Philip (eds.) *The Ideologies of Children's Rights* (Martinus Nijhoff Publishers, Leiden/Boston, 1992).
Kadivar, Mohsen, 'Freedom of Thought and Religion in Islam', in Mofid University, *Collected Papers of the International Conference on Human Rights and Dialogue of Civilization*, May 2001 (Mofid University Publication Institute, Qom-Iran, 2001).
——, 'The Rights of Non-Moslems in Contemporary Islam', paper presented at the conference: *Reframing Islam: Politics into Law*: 10–11 September 2005 at Irish Centre for Human Rights, National University of Ireland, Galway, available at: <http://www.nuigalway.ie/human_rights/reframing_Islam/Docs/Papers/Kadivar.pdf>.
Kamali, Mohammad Hashim, 'Islamic Law: A Critique of the *Hudood* Bill of Kelantan, Malaysia' 13 *Arab Law Quarterly* 3 (1998).
Kaplan, Yehiel S., 'The Interpretation of the Concept of the Best Interest of the Child in Israel', in Douglas, Gillian & Sebba, Leslie (eds.) *Children Rights and Traditional Values* (Artmund & Ashgate, England, 1998).
Kent Brown II, Scott, 'The Coptic Church in Egypt: A Comment on Protecting Religious Minorities from Non-state Discrimination' *Brigham Young University Law Review* 1049 (2000).
Khadduri, Majid, *War and Peace in the Law of Islam* (Johns Hopkins Press, 1955).
——, 'International Law', in Khadduri, Majid & Liebesny, Herbert J. (eds.) *Law in the Middle East, Volume 1, Origin and Development of Islamic Law* (The Middle East Institute, Washington, D.C., 1995).
——, *The Islamic Conception of Justice* (Johns Hopkins University Press, U.S.A., 1984).
——, *The Islamic Law of Nations* (The Johns Hopkings Press, U.S.A., 1966).
Khan, Maimul Ahsan, *Human Rights in the Muslim World: Fundamentalism, Constitutionalism, and International Politics* (Carolina Academic Press, Durham, N.C., 2003).
Kilian, Bälz, 'The Secular Reconstruction of Islamic Law: The Egyptian Supreme Constitutional Court and the Battle over the Veil in State-Run Schools', in Berger, Maurits & al-Zwaini, Laila (eds.) *Legal Pluralism in the Arab World* (Kluwer Law International, the Hague, 1999).
Krishnaswami, Arcot, Special Rapporteur of the Sub-commission on Prevention of Discrimination and Protection of Minorities, *Study of Discrimination in the Matter of Religious Rights and Practices* (United Nations Publication, Sales No. 60.XIV.2, New York, 1960).
Labib Gabr, Hatem Aly, 'Recent Judgments of the Supreme Constitutional Court of the Arab Republic of Egypt Upholding Human Rights' in Cotran, Eugene & Omar Sherif, Adel (eds.)

The Role of the Judiciary in the Protection of Human Rights (Kluwer Law International, the Hague, 1997).
Lerner, Natan, *Religion, Secular Beliefs and Human Rights: 25 Years after the 1981 Declaration* (Martinus Nijhoff Publishers, Leiden/Boston, 2006).
Lindholm, Tore, 'Human Rights in Christianity and in Islam', in Suvikki, Silvennoinen & Suksi, Markku (eds.) *Human Rights and Religion: The Case of the Sudan* (Institute for Human Rights, Abo Akademi University, Turku/Abo, Finland, 1997).
—— & Durham, W. Cole & Tahzib, Bahia G. (eds.), *Facilitating Freedom of Religion or Belief: A Deskbook* (Martinus Nijhoff Publishers, Leiden, 2004).
Maghniyyah, Mohammad Javad, *The Five School of Islamic Law* (Ansarian Publications, Qom, Iran, 1995).
Mahmasani, Subhi, 'Transactions in the *Sariah*', in Khadduri, Majid & Liebesny, Herbert J. (eds.) *Law in the Middle East, Volume 1, Origin and Development of Islamic Law* (The Middle East Institute, Washington, D.C., 1995).
——, 'The Principles of International Law in the Light of Islamic Doctrine', in *Recuell Des Cours 1996 I Tome 117 de la Collection, Academie De Droit International* (A.W. Sijthoff, Leyde [Pays-Bas], 1967).
——, *Falsafat Al-Tashri fi Al-Islam, the Philosophy of Jurisprudence in Islam* (trans. Ziadeh, Farhat, Brill, Leiden, 1961).
Mallat, Ghibli, *The Renewal of Islamic Law, Muhammad Baqer As-Sadr, Najaf and the Shi'i International* (Cambridge University Press, Cambridge, 1993).
—— & Connors, Jane (eds.), *Islam and Public Law, Classical and Contemporary Studies* (Graham & Trotman, 1993).
—— (eds.), *Islamic Family Law* (Graham & Trotman, 1993).
Marmur, Dow, 'Secular Justice and Religious Law' 26 *Justice* (2000).
Martinez, Patricia A., 'The Politics of Power over the *Shariah* in Malaysia', paper presented at the conference: *Reframing Islam: Politics into Law*: 10–11 September 2005 at Irish Centre for Human Rights, National University of Ireland, Galway, available at: <http://www.nuigalway.ie/human_rights/reframing_Islam/Docs/Papers/Martinez.pdf>.
Marty, Martin E., 'Religious Dimensions of Human Rights' 10 *Emory International law Review* 1 (1996).
Masters, Bruce, *Christians and Jews in the Ottoman Arab world* (Cambridge University Press, New York, 2001).
Maydani, Riyad, '*Uqubat*: Penal law', in Khadduri, Majid & Liebesny, Herbert J. (eds.) *Law in the Middle East, Volume 1, Origin and Development of Islamic Law* (The Middle East Institute, Washington, D.C., 1995).
Mayer, Anne Elizabeth, 'A Critique of An-Na'im Assessment of Islamic Criminal Justice', in Lindholm, Tore & Vogt, Kari (eds.) *Islamic Law Reform and Human Rights, Challenges and Rejoinders* (Nordic Human Rights Publications, Oslo, 1993).
——, *Islam and Human Rights, Tradition and Politics*, Third Edition (Westview Press, London, 1999).
——, 'Islam and Human Rights, Different Issues, Different Contexts, Lessons From Comparison', in Lindholm, Tore & Vogt, Kari (eds.) *Islamic Law Reform and Human Rights, Challenges and Rejoinders* (Nordic Human Rights Publications, Oslo, 1993).
——, 'The Islam and Human Rights Nexus: Shifting Dimensions', paper presented at the conference: *Reframing Islam: Politics into Law*: 10–11 September 2005 at Irish Centre for Human Rights, National University of Ireland, Galway, available at: <http://www.nuigalway.ie/human_rights/reframing_Islam/Docs/Papers/Martinez.pdf>.
McCoubrey, Hilaire, 'Natural Law, Religion and the Development of International Law', in Janis,

Mark W. & Evans, Carolyn (eds.) *Religion and International Law* (Kluwer Law International, the Hague, 1999).
Mehdi, Rubya, *The Islamization of the Law in Pakistan* (Curzon Press, Richmond, Surrey, 1994).
Meeusen, John, 'Judicial Disapproval of Discrimination Against Illegitimate Children: A Comparative Study of Development in Europe and the United States' 43 *American Journal of Comparative Law* 119–20 (1995).
Moreen, Vera B., 'The Status of Religious Minorities in Safavid Iran, 1617–1661' 40 *Journal of New Eastern Studies* (1981).
Mottahedeh, Roy P., 'Toward an Islamic Theology of Toleration', in Lindholm, Tore & Vogt, Kari (eds.) *Islamic Law Reform and Human Rights, Challenges and Rejoinders* (Nordic Human Rights Publications, Oslo, 1993).
Motala, Ziyad & Ramaphosa, Cyril, *Freedom of Religion, in Constitutional Law* (Oxford University Press, Oxford, 2002).
Murray, John & El-Molla, Mohamed, 'Islamic *Shariah* and Constitutional Interpretation in Egypt', in Cotran, Eugene & Omer Sherif, Adel, *Democracy, the Rule of Law and Islam* (Kluwer Law International, the Hague, 1999).
Murphy, Theresa, 'Incitement to Hatred; Lessons from Northern Ireland' in Coliver, Sandra (ed.) *Striking a Balance, Hate Speech, Freedom of Expression and Non-discrimination, Article 19* (London and Human Rights Centre, University of Essex, 1992).
Muta, Makau, 'Limitations on Religious Rights: Problematizing Religious Freedom in the African Context', in Steiner, Henry J. & Alston, Phillip (eds.) *International Human Rights in Context, Law, Politics, Morals*, Second Edition (Oxford University Press, Oxford, 2000).
Nasir, Jamal J., The *Islamic Law of Personal Status*, Third Edition (Kluwer Law International, the Hague, 1990).
Nielsen, Jorgen S., 'Contemporary Discussions on Religious Minorities in Islam' *Brigham Young University Law Review* 2 (2002).
Noonan Jr, John T., 'Religious Human Rights in the United States' 10 *Emory International law Review* 1 (1996).
Nosseir, Abdel-Rahman, 'The Supreme Constitutional Court of Egypt and the Protection of Human Rights', in Cotran, Eugene & Omar Sherif, Adel (eds.) *The Role of the Judiciary in the Protection of Human Rights* (Kluwer Law International, the Hague, 1997).
Novak, David, 'Religious Human Rights in Judaic Tradition' 10 *Emory International law Review* 1 (1996).
O'Connor, Caroline, *Direct Discrimination? An Analysis of the Scheme of Direct Provision in Ireland* (Dublin Free Legal Advice Centres, 2003).
Okin, Susan Moller (ed.), *Is Multiculturalism Bad for Women?* (Princeton, N.J.: Princeton University Press, 1999).
Oslo Conference on Freedom of Religion and Belief (1998), *Facilitating Freedom of Religion or Belief: A Deskbook* (Martinus Nijhoff Publishers, Leiden/Boston, 2004).
O'Sulivan, Declan, 'The Death Sentence for Mahmud Muhammad Taha: Misuse of the Sudanese Legal System and Islamic *Shariah*' 15 *The International Journal of Human Rights* 3 (2001).
Owsia, Parviz, 'Sources of Law under English, French, Islamic and Iranian Law – A Comparative Review of Legal Techniques' 6 *Arab law Quarterly* 1 (1991).
Oyediran, Jonna, 'Article 13(5) of the American Convention on Human Rights', in Coliver, Sandra (ed.) *Striking a Balance: Hate Speech, Freedom of Expression and Non-discrimination, Article 19* (London and Human Rights Centre, University of Essex, 1992).
Packer, Corinne, *Using Human Rights to Change Tradition: Traditional Practices Harmful to Women's Reproductive Health in Sub-Saharan Africa* (Antwerp: Intersentia, 2002).

Paradelle, Murielle, 'Legal Pluralism and Public International Law: An Analysis Based on the International Convention on the Right of the Child' in Berger, Maurits & Al-Zwaini, Laila (eds.) *Legal Pluralism in the Arab World* (Kluwer Law International, the Hague, 1999).

Rehman, Javid, 'Minority Rights and the Constitutional Dilemmas of Pakistan' 19 *Netherlands Quarterly of Human Rights* 4 (2001).

——, 'Accommodating Religious Identities in An Islamic State: International Law, Freedom of Religion and the Rights of Religious Minorities' 7 *International Journal on Minority and Group Rights* 2 (2000).

Renucci, Jean-François, *Article 9 of the European Convention on Human Rights: Freedom of Thought, Conscience and Religion* (Council of Europe Publishing, Strasbourg, 2005).

Riffat, Hassan, 'On Human Rights and the Koranic Perspective', in Swidler, Arlene (ed.) *Human Rights in Religious Traditions* (The Pilgrim Press, New York, 1982).

——, 'Religious Human Rights in Koran' 10 *Emory International law Review* 1 (1996).

Rizvi, Sayyid Muhammad, 'Apostasy (*Irtidad*) in Islam', available at: <http://www.al-islam.org/short/apostacy.htm>.

Saeed, Abdullah & Saeed Hassan, *Freedom of Religion, Apostasy, and Islam* (Ashgatee, Aldershot, Hants, England; Burlington, VT, 2004).

Safir, Syed, 'The Impact of Islamic Law on the Implementation of the Convention on the Right of the Child: The Plight of Non-marital Children under *Shariah*' 6 *The International Journal of Children's Rights* (1998).

Saidzadeh, Sayyid Mohsen, '*Fiqh* and *Fiqahat*' 1 *UCLA Journal of Islamic and Eastern Law* 2 (2002).

Saleh, Nabil, 'Origins of the Sanctity of Contracts in Islamic Law' 13 *Arab law Quarterly* 3 (1998).

Sanasarian, Eliz, *Religious Minorities in Iran* (Cambridge University Press, Cambridge, 2000).

Sardar Ali, Shaheen, *Gender and Human Rights in Islam and International Law, Equal before Allah (Unequal before Man?)* (Kluwer Law International, the Hague, 2000).

——, 'The Conceptual Foundation of Human Rights: A Comparative Perspective' 3 *European Public Law* 1 (1997).

——, 'The Rights of Ethnic Minorities in Pakistan: A Legal Analysis' 6 *International Journal on Minority and Group Rights* 1 (1998/99).

Schabas, William A., 'Reservations to the Convention on the Rights of Child' 18 *Human Rights Quarterly* 2 (1996).

——, 'Islam and the Death Penalty' 9 *William and Mary Bill of Rights Journal* 1 (2000).

——. & Sax, Helmut, 'Article 37, Prohibition of Torture, Prohibition of Death Penalty and Life Imprisonment and the Deprivation of Liberty', in Alen, André & Vande Lanotte, Johan & Verhellen, Eugeen & Ang, Fiona & Berghmans, Eva & Verheyde, Mieke (eds.) *A Commentary on the United Nations Convention on the Rights of the Child* (Martinus Nijhoff Publishers, Leiden/Boston, 2006).

Schacht, Joseph, 'The Schools of Law and Later Developments of Jurisprudence' in Khadduri, Majid & Liebesny, Herbert J. (eds.) *Law in the Middle East, Vol. 1, Origin and Development of Islamic Law* (The Middle East Institute, Washington, D.C., 1995).

——, *An Introduction to Islamic Law* (Clarendon Press, Oxford, 1964).

——, 'Pre-Islamic Background and Early Development of Jurisprudence' in Khadduri, Majid & Liebesny, Herbert J. (eds.) *Law in the Middle East, Vol. 1, Origin and Development of Islamic Law* (The Middle East Institute, Washington, D.C., 1995).

Schmemann, Serge, 'Israel Learns Some Are More Israeli Than Others', in Steiner, Henry J. & Alston, Phillip (eds.) *International Human Rights in Context, Law, Politics, Morals*, Second Edition (Oxford University Press, Oxford, 2000).

Seif al-Islam, Hamad, 'Legal Plurality and Legislation of Human Rights Abuses: A Case Study of State Council Ruling Concerning the Right of Apostates', in Berger, Maurits & al-Zwaini, Laila (eds.) *Legal Pluralism in the Arab World* (Kluwer Law International, the Hague, 1999).
Shah, Niaz A., *Women, the Koran and International Human Rights Law: The Case of Pakistan* (Martinus Nijhoff Publishers, Leiden, 2006).
Shari'ati, Ali, 'Humanity and Islam', in Kurzman, Charles (ed.) *Liberal Islam: A Sourcebook* (Oxford University Press, New York and Oxford, 1998).
Shelton, Dina & Kiss, Alexander, 'A Draft Model Law on Freedom of Religion', in Steiner, Henry J. & Alston, Phillip (eds.) *International Human Rights in Context, Law, Politics, Morals*, Second Edition (Oxford University Press, Oxford, 2000).
Shestack, Jerome J., 'The Philosophic Foundations of Human Rights' 20 *Human Rights Quarterly* 2 (1998).
Skutsch, Carl, *Encyclopaedia of the World's Minorities* (Vol. 1, Routledge, New York, 2005).
Soroush, Abdolkarim, 'Text in Context', in Kurzman, Charles (ed.) *Liberal Islam, A Sourcebook* (Oxford University Press, New York and Oxford, 1998).
——, 'Contraction and Expansion of Women's Rights, An Interview with Dr. Abdolkarim Soroush' available at: <http://www.seraj.org/zanan.htm> (2000).
——, 'Reason and Revelation, Reason Defines Truth, Public Interest, and Humanity', in Soroush, Abdolkarim, *Reason, Freedom and Democracy in Islam: Essential Writings of Abdolkarim Soroush* (Oxford University Press, Oxford, 2000), available at: <http://www.iranian.com/Opinion/2001/February/Soroush/>.
Stahnke, Tad, 'Proselytism and the Freedom to Change Religion in International Human Rights Law', *Brigham Young University Law Review* 251 (1999).
Stanley, Alessandra, 'Pope Tells India His Church Has Right to Evangelize', in Steiner, Henry J. & Alston, Phillip (eds.) *International Human Rights in Context, Law, Politics, Morals*, Second Edition (Oxford University Press, Oxford, 2000).
Steiner, Henry J. & Alston, Phillip, 'General Comments No. 22 of the Human Rights Committee', in Steiner, Henry J. & Alston, Phillip (eds.) *International Human Rights in Context, Law, Politics, Morals*, Second Edition (Oxford University Press, Oxford, 2000).
——, 'Declaration on the Elimination of All Forms of Intolerance and of Discrimination Based on Religion or Belief', in Steiner, Henry J. & Alston, Phillip (eds.) *International Human Rights in Context, Law, Politics, Morals*, Second Edition (Oxford University Press, Oxford, 2000).
——, 'Provisions in Religious Texts on Charitable Giving', in Steiner, Henry J. & Alston, Phillip (eds.) *International Human Rights in Context, Law, Politics, Morals*, Second Edition (Oxford University Press, Oxford, 2000).
——, 'Comment on Saudi Arabia under the 1503 Procedure', in Steiner, Henry J. & Alston, Phillip (eds.) *International Human Rights in Context, Law, Politics, Morals*, Second Edition (Oxford University Press, Oxford, 2000).
——, 'Case Study Iran: Report of the Special Representatives on Iran in 1991, Report of the Special Representative on Iran 1999', in Steiner, Henry J. & Alston, Phillip (eds.) *International Human Rights in Context, Law, Politics, Morals*, Second Edition (Oxford University Press, Oxford, 2000).
——, 'Comment on Autonomy Regimes, in International Human Rights', in Steiner, Henry J. & Alston, Phillip (eds.) *International Human Rights in Context, Law, Politics, Morals*, Second Edition (Oxford University Press, Oxford, 2000).
——, 'Autonomy Regimes: Religion-based Personal Law, Comments on Autonomy Regimes', in Steiner, Henry J. & Alston, Phillip (eds.) *International Human Rights in Context, Law, Politics, Morals*, Second Edition (Oxford University Press, Oxford, 2000).

——, 'Comments on State, Religion, and Personal Law in Israel', in Steiner, Henry J. & Alston, Phillip (eds.) *International Human Rights in Context, Law, Politics, Morals*, Second Edition (Oxford University Press, Oxford, 2000).

——, 'Comments on Personal-Religious Law in India', in Steiner, Henry J. & Alston, Phillip (eds.) *International Human Rights in Context, Law, Politics, Morals*, Second Edition (Oxford University Press, Oxford, 2000).

Strong, S.I., 'Law and Religion in Israel and Iran: How the Integration of Secular and Spiritual Laws Affects Human Rights and the Potential for Violence' 19 *Michigan Journal of International Law* 1 (1997).

Sulivan, Donna, 'Advancing the Freedom of Religion or Belief through the UN Declaration', in Steiner, Henry J. & Alston, Phillip (eds.) *International Human Rights in Context, Law, Politics, Morals*, Second Edition (Oxford University Press, Oxford, 2000).

Taha, Mahmud Muhammad, *Second Message of Islam* (trans. An-Na'im, Abdullahi Ahmed, Syracuse University Press, Syracuse, 1987).

Tahzib, Bahiyyih G., *Freedom of Religion or Belief: Ensuring Effective International Legal Protection* (Martinus Nijhoff Publishers, the Hague/London, 1996).

Talbi, Mohammed, 'Religious Liberty: A Muslim Perspective', in Swidler, Leonard (ed.) *Religious Liberty and Human Rights in Nations and Religions* (Hippocrene Books and Ecumenical Press, New York and Philadelphia, 1986).

Thornberry, Patrick, *International Law and the Rights of Minorities* (Clarendon Press, Oxford, 2001).

Tutu, Desmond M., 'Religious Human Rights in Bible' 10 *Emory International law Review* 1 (1996).

Van Bueren, Geraldine, *The Best Interests of the Child – International Cooperation on Child Abduction, Program on the International Rights of the Child* (QMWC, London, 1993).

——, 'Children's Rights: Balancing Traditional Values and Cultural Plurality' in Douglas, Gillian & Sebba, Leslie (eds.) *Children Rights and Traditional Values (*Artmund & Ashgate, England, 1998).

Van der Vyver, John D. & Witte Jr, John (eds.) *Religious Human Rights in Global Perspective: Legal Perspective* (Kluwer Law International, the Hague, 1996).

—— (eds.), *Religious Human Rights in Global Perspective: Religious Perspective* (Kluwer Law International, the Hague, 1996).

Vesey-Fitzgerald, S.G., 'Nature and Sources of the *Shariah*' in Khadduri, Majid & Liebesny, Herbert J., *Law in the Middle East, Vol. 1, Origin and Development of Islamic Law* (The Middle East Institute, Washington, D.C., 1995).

Vikor, Knut S., 'The Development of *Ijtihad* and Islamic Reform, 1750–1850', in *The Third Nordic Conference on Middle Eastern Studies: Ethnic Encounter and Culture Change*, Joensun, Finland, 19–22 June 1992 available at: <www.hf-fak.uib.no/institutter/smi/paj/Vikor.html>.

Vogel, Frank E., 'The Trial of Terrorists under Classical Islamic Law' 43 *Harvard International Law Journal* 1 (2000).

Waltz, Susan, 'Universal Human Rights: The Contribution of Muslim States' 26 *Human Rights Quarterly* 4 (2004).

Welchman, Lynn, *Beyond the Code: Muslim Family Law and the Shariah Judiciary in the Palestinian West Bank* (Kluwer Law International, the Hague, 2000).

——, *Islamic Family Law: Women's Rights and Perspectives on Reform* (Zed Books, New York, 2003).

Weller, Paul, 'The Dimensions and Dynamics of Religious Discrimination: Findings and Analysis from the UK', in Ghanea, Nazila (ed.) *The Challenge of Religious Discrimination at the Dawn of the New Millennium* (Martinus Nijhoff Publishers, Leiden/Boston, 2003).

Woodman, Gordon R., 'The Idea of Legal Pluralism', in Berger, Maurits & Al-Zwaini, Laila (eds.) *Legal Pluralism in the Arab World* (Kluwer Law International, the Hague, 1999).
Wright, Robin, 'An Iranian Luther Shake the Foundation of Islam' *The Guardian* (1 February 1995, quoted from the Los Angeles Times – January 1995) available at: <http://www.seraj.org/guard.htm>.
——, 'Abdulkarim Soroush, in Islam and Liberal Democracy, Two Visions of Reformation' *Journal of democracy*, (April 1996) available at: <http://www.seraj.org/democ.htm>.
Yilmaz, Ihsan, 'Secular Law and the Emergence of Unofficial Turkish Islamic Law' 56 *The Middle East Journal* 1 (2002).
——, *Muslim Laws, Politics, and Society in Modern Nation States: Dynamic Legal Pluralisms in England, Turkey, and Pakistan* (Ashgate Pub., Aldershot, Hants, England; Burlington, VT, 2005).
Zaharaa, Mahdi & Malek, Norm 'The Concept of Custody in Islamic Law' 13 *Arab Law Quarterly* (1998).
Zarif, M. Javad, 'Islamic Contribution to Enriching the Universal Declaration of Human Rights' A paper presented at: *The Seminar on Islamic Perspective on Enriching the Universal Declaration of Human Rights*, Geneva, October 1998.
Zisser, Eyal, 'The Alavies, Lords of Syria: From Ethnic Minority to Ruling Sect', in Bengio, Orfa & Ben-Dor, Gabriel (eds.) *Minorities and the State in the Arab World* (Lynne Rienner Publishers, USA, UK, 1999).

Persian

Azimi Shushtari, Abbasali, *Hoquq-e Qaradadha-ye Beynolmeleli dar Eslam*, [*The Law of International Treaties in Islam* (The Centre of Publication of the Office of Islamic Propagations of the Islamic Seminary of Qom-Qom, Iran, 1999).
Baghi, Emadeddin, *Eedam va Qesas: Chaleshha-ye Fekr-e Dini dar Iran-e Emruz* [Execution and Retaliation: The Challenges of Religious Thought in Today Iran] (Sarabi Publisher, Tehran, Iran, 2005).
Bastehnegar, Mohamamd (ed.), *Hoquq-e Bashar az Manzar-e Andishmandan* [*Human Rights in the Eyes of Intellectuals*] (Enticer Publication, Tehran, 2001).
Bazargan, Abdolali, *Moqaddameh-ei dar Zamine-ye Azadi dar Koran* [*An Introduction to Freedom in the Koran*] (Qalam Publisher, Tehran, 1994).
——, *Azadi dar Nahjolbalaqeh* [*Freedom in Nahjolbalaqeh*] Second Edition (Rasa Cultural Services Institute, Tehran, 1998).
Ebadi, Shirin, *Hoquq-e Zan dar Qavanin-e Jomhuri-ye Eslami-ye Iran* [*Women's Rights in the Laws of Islamic Republic of Iran*] (Ganjedanesh Publication, Tehran, 2002).
Fazel Meybodi, Mohammad, '*Andishe-ye Dini va Hoquq-e Tabi'i*' [*Religious Thought and Natural Rights*], *Aftab Monthly* 29 (September 2004).
Ghari Seyedfatemi, Seyed Mohammad, *Hoquq-e Bashar dar Jahan-e Moaser-1: Daramadi bar mabahes-e Nazari, Mafahim, Mabani, Qalamro va Manabe* [*Human Rights in the Contemporary World-1: An Introduction to Theoretical Issues, Concept, Foundations, Scope and Sources*] (UNESCO Chair for Human Rights, Peace and Democracy, Faculty of Law, Shahid Beheshti University, Tehran, 2004).
Hosseinin, Seyed Mohammad, *Seyasat-e Jenaei dar Eslam va Jomhuri-ye Eslami-ye Iran* [*Criminal Policy in Islam and Islamic Republic of Iran*] (Tehran University, Tehran, 2004).
Jannaati, Mohammad Ebrahim, *Advar-e Feqh va Keyfeyyat-e Bayan-e an* [*Periods of Jurisprudence and Its Manner of Explanation*] (Kayhan Publisher, Tehran, 1995).

Kadivar, Mohsen, '*Hoquq-e Bashar va Roshanfekri-ye Dini*' [*Human Rights and Religious Intellectuality*], *Aftab Monthly* 27 (June 2004).

Kashani, S. Mahmoud, *Estandardha-ye Jahani-ye Dadgostari: Naqd va Barrasi-ye Qanun-e Dadgah-ha-ye Omumi va Enqelab* [*Universal Standards on the Administration of Justice: A Critical Study on the Law of General and Revolutionary Courts*] (Mizan Publication, Tehran, 2005].

Mehrpour, Hossein, *Hoquq-e Bashar va Rahkarha-ye Ejra-ye An* [*Human Rights and Its Implementation Instruments*] (Ettela'at Publisher, Tehran, 1999).

——, *Hoquq-e Bashar dar Asnaad-e Beynolmelali va Moze-e Jomhuri-ye Eslami-ye Iran* [*Human Rights in International Instruments and the Position of Islamic Republic of Iran*] (Ettela'at Publisher, Tehran, 1995).

——, *Mabahesi az Hoquq-e Zan, az Manzar-e Hoquq-e Dakheli, Mabani-ye Feqhi, va Mavazin-e Beynolmelali* [*Certain Issues on Women's Rights from the Viewpoint of Domestic Law, Islamic Jurisprudence Principles and International Criteria*] (Tehran, Ettela'at Publisher, 2000).

——, *Nezam-e Beynolmelal-e Hoquq-e Bashar* [*International Human Rights Law*] Second Edition (Ettela'at Publisher,Tehran, 2004).

—— (ed.) *Reis-e Jomhur va Masuleyat-e Ejraay-e Qanun-e Asaasi, Majmueh Mabahes-e Hamayesh-ha-ye Heyat-e Peygiri va Nezaarat bar Ejray-e Qanun-e Asaasi* [*The President and the Responsibility of Implementation of the Constitution, A Collection of the Issues Discussed in the Seminars of the Committee, Responsible for the Follow up and Supervise the Implementation of the Constitution*] (Ettela'at Publisher, Tehran, 2001).

Mohaghegh Damad, Mostafa, *Qavaed-e Fiqh: Bakhsh-e Madani-1, Malekeyyat, Masuleyat* [*The Rules of Islamic Jurisprudence, Civil Section-1*] Fifth Edition (SAMT, Tehran, 2002).

——, *Qavaed-e Fiqh: Bakhsh-e Madani-2, Malekeyyat, Masuleyat* [*The Rules of Islamic Jurisprudence, Civil Section-2*], Eleventh Edition (Markaz-e Nashr-e Olum-e Eslami Publisher, Tehran, 2003).

——, *Qavaed-e Fiqh: Bakhsh-e Qaza-ei* [*The Rules of Islamic Jurisprudence, Judicial Section*] Second Edition (Markaz-e Nashr-e Olum-e Eslami Publisher, Tehran, 2002).

——, *Mabahesi az Osul-e Fiqh, Daftar-e Avval* [*The Principles of Islamic Jurisprudence*] Vol. 1, Eleventh Edition (Markaz-e Nashr-e Olum-e Eslami Publisher, Tehran, 2002).

——, *Mabahesi az Osul-e Fiqh, Daftar-e Dovvom* [*The Principles of Islamic Jurisprudence*] Vol. 2, Tenth Edition (Markaz-e Nashr-e Olum-e Eslami Publisher, Tehran, 2002).

——, *Mabahesi az Osul-e Fiqh, Daftar-e sevvom* [*The Principles of Islamic Jurisprudence*] Vol. 3, Second Edition (Markaz-e Nashr-e Olum-e Eslami Publisher, Tehran, 2002).

——, *Qavaed-e Feqhi, Bakhsh-e Jaza-ei* [*The Rules of Islamic Jurisprudence, Penal Section*] Forth Edition (Markaz-e Nashr-e Olum-e Eslami Publisher, Tehran, 2004).

——, *Barrasi-ye Fiqhi-ye Hoquq-e Khanevadeh: Nekah va Enhelal-e an (Mavadd-e 1034–1157-e Qanun-e Madani)* [*The Fiqhi Study of Family Law, Marriage and Its Dissolve (Articles 1034–1157 of the Civil Code)*] Eleventh Edition (Markaz-e Nashr-e Olum-e Eslami Publisher, Tehran, 2005).

——, '*Khataa-paziri dar Ijtihad*' [*Mistakenness in Ijtihad*], *Bokhara Quarterly* 23 (March 2002).

Mojtahed Shabestari, Mohamamd, *Naqdi bar Qara'at-e Rasmi az Din (Bohran-ha, Chalesh-ha, Rah-e Hal-ha)* [*A Critique of the Official Reading of Religion (Crises, Challenges and Solutions)*] Second Edition (Tarh-e No Publisher, Tehran, 2002).

——, *Hermeneutic-e Ketab va Sonnat* [*Hermeneutic, the Scripture and the Tradition*] Fifth Edition (Tarh-e No Publisher, Tehran, 2000).

——, *Iman va Azadi* [*Faith and Freedom*] Third Edition (Tarh-e No Publisher, Tehran, 2000)].

Mirmohammadsadeghi, Hosein, *Jara-em Elay-he Amneyyat va Asayesh-e Omumi* [*Offences against Security of the State and Public Tranquillity*] Fourth Edition (Mizaan Publisher, Tehran, 2004).

Mohammad, Abolhasan, *Mabani-ye Estenbat-e Hoquq-e Eslami* [*Principles for Inference of Islamic Law*] Fourteenth Edition (Tehran University, Tehran, 2001).

Sharifiyaan, Jamshid, *Rahbord-e Jomhuri-ye Eslami-ye Iran dar Zamine-ye Hoquq-e Bashar dar Sazman-e Melal-e Mottahed* [*The Strategy of Islamic Republic of Iran in Respect to Human Rights in the United Nations*] (The Institute for Political and International Studies, Tehran, 2001).

Soroush, Abdolkarin, *Qabz va Bast-e Teoric-e Shariat* [*Theoretical Contraction and Expansion of Shariah*] Fourth Edition (Serat Cultural Institution, Tehran, 1995).

Zamiran, Mohammad & Ebadi, Shirin, *Sonnat va Tajaddod dar Hoquq-e Iran* [*Modernity and Tradition in the Iranian Legal System*] (Ganjedanesh Publication, Tehran, 1996).

INDEX